INSIDE GORBACHEV'S KREMLIN

INSIDE GORBACHEV'S KREMLIN

The Memoirs of

YEGOR LIGACHEV

Introduction by Stephen F. Cohen

Translated from the Russian by
Catherine A. Fitzpatrick, Michele A. Berdy,
Dobrochna Dyrcz-Freeman, and Marian Schwartz

WestviewPress

A Division of HarperCollinsPublishers

Grateful acknowledgment is made to Simon & Schuster, Inc., for permission to reprint from *Against the Grain* by Boris Yeltsin.
English translation copyright © 1990 by Summit Books. Reprinted by permission.

Originally published in Russia as *The Gorbachev Enigma* by "Interbook" of Novosibirsk.
Copyright © 1992 by Siberian Center "Interbook."
English translation copyright © 1993 by Random House, Inc.
Introduction copyright © 1993 by Stephen F. Cohen.
New material copyright © 1996 by Westview Press, Inc., A Division of HarperCollins Publishers, Inc.
Published by arrangement with Pantheon Books, a division of Random House, Inc.

Augmented new edition published in 1996 in the United States of America by Westview Press, Inc., 5500 Central Avenue, Boulder, Colorado 80301-2877, and in the United Kingdom by Westview Press, 12 Hid's Copse Road, Cumnor Hill, Oxford OX2 9JJ

A CIP catalog record for this book is available from the Library of Congress.
ISBN 0-8133-2887-X

The paper used in this publication meets the requirements of the American National Standard for Permanence of Paper for Printed Library Materials Z39.48-1984.

10   9   8   7   6   5   4   3   2   1

CONTENTS

Introduction
LIGACHEV AND THE TRAGEDY OF SOVIET CONSERVATISM

by Stephen F. Cohen

The credibility of memoirs, unlike fiction, depends on the biography and character of the author. Yegor Ligachev has written the first real political memoirs of the fateful Gorbachev years, which may have brought Soviet history to an end and changed world politics forever. Indeed, for general readers and specialists alike, there is for now no comparable insider's account of Soviet politics at the highest levels during any period in Soviet history. But who is Yegor Kuzmich Ligachev?

In the conventional story told by most Western observers since the 1980s, Ligachev was the arch-villain of Soviet politics under Mikhail Gorbachev and his reforms—the chief "enemy of perestroika," a "diehard conservative," even a reactionary "neo-Stalinist."[1]

---

[1] After Gorbachev, Ligachev probably was the most written-about political figure of the perestroika years. The standard version of his role appears in almost all of the journalistic accounts. For scholarly studies of Ligachev, see Jonathan Harris, *Ligachev on Glasnost and Perestroika* (University of Pittsburgh Center for Russian and East European Studies, No. 706, 1989); Baruch A. Hazan, *Gorbachev and His Enemies* (Boulder, Colo., 1990); and Jeffrey Surovell, "Ligachev and Soviet Politics," *Soviet Studies,* No.

Empowered by his position as the No. 2 leader, he opposed and obstructed Gorbachev's political and economic changes with the connivance of the Communist Party's apparatus, particularly its powerful provincial bosses throughout the country, and in the name of a dogmatic Marxism-Leninism. Ligachev's intrigues, in this telling, were behind many of the worst deeds in the bitter struggle over perestroika, from protection of corrupt officials and attempts to conceal Stalin's murderous crimes to bloodshed in the streets of Tbilisi in April 1989. In short, Ligachev is said to have represented almost everything bad and unrepentant in the Soviet system that collapsed at the end of 1991.

Some aspects of this standard account have a partial basis in actual events, but much of it continues the long Western tradition of imposing gray stereotypes on complex Soviet realities—and now post-Soviet ones. Insisting that he was made the "fall guy" for the Gorbachev leadership's failures and the victim of a "witch hunt" by his opponents, Ligachev's memoirs are intended to refute "scandalous" and "blasphemous" accusations that originated in the Soviet media and spread to the West. (Blaming the press for political misfortunes turned out to be something latter-day Soviet politicians shared with their American counterparts.) Readers should judge for themselves whether Ligachev defends himself convincingly. But consider briefly a few complexities, documented in other sources, that do not conform to the stereotypical version of his political role.

Without Ligachev's full backing, Gorbachev probably could not have come to power in March 1985 against the wishes of a pro-status quo majority in the top Party and state councils. In that case, no reform leadership would have been possible. Nor could Gorbachev have initiated liberalizing and even democratizing policies during the next two or three years without Ligachev's collaboration, or at least acquiescence. Take three bitterly disputed examples, two

---

2 (1991), pp. 335–74. The latter goes to the other extreme, presenting a Ligachev without any real political or ideological differences with Gorbachev.

of special interest to Americans. Ligachev actively supported the decisions to release a previously banned film, *Repentance,* that dramatically reopened public discussion of Stalin's mass terror in the 1930s; to ease Soviet controls over Eastern Europe; and to end the seven-year Soviet war in Afghanistan.[2] And even though his policy disagreements with Gorbachev were acute by 1989, along with his feeling of having been betrayed, there is no evidence that Ligachev joined any of the intrigues under way in the apparatus to remove Gorbachev as Communist Party leader or the failed tank coup in August 1991 that stripped him of his presidential powers.

Ligachev's personal qualities may be a more subjective question, but they, too, are hard to squeeze into the stereotype. Even political figures loyal to Gorbachev and generally admired in Western accounts characterize Ligachev as being deeply sincere, proudly incorruptible, and habitually straightforward in his political relations.[3] Indeed, such was his reputation in virtually all Soviet political quarters before 1985, and for some time thereafter. Even later, when the leadership was angrily divided, no reliable insider seems to have believed the corruption charges leveled against him in 1989 by two politically motivated, and subsequently discredited, prosecutors—a ramifying scandal that inflames an entire chapter of these memoirs. And while suspicions about Ligachev's political role behind the

---

[2]For some testimony on *Repentance* and Afghanistan, see Eduard Shevardnadze, *The Future Belongs to Freedom* (New York, 1991), p. 173; and the interview with Shevardnadze in *Nezavisimaia gazeta,* 21 November 1991. For Eastern Europe, see the account of Ligachev's trip to Hungary in the *Washington Post,* 26 April 1987.

[3]See, for example, Nursultan Nazarbaev, *Bez pravykh i levykh* (Moscow, 1991), pp. 165–66; Vadim Bakatin, "Nedopisannaia kniga," *Sovershenno sekretno,* No. 10 (1991); Shevardnadze in *Nezavisimaia gazeta,* 21 November 1991; and the interview with Abel Aganbegyan in *New Perspectives Quarterly,* Winter 1988–89, p. 28. On the other hand, for two leaders with nothing good to say about Ligachev, see Boris Yeltsin, *Against the Grain* (New York, 1990); and Anatoly Sobchak, *For a New Russia* (New York, 1992), though Sobchak says Ligachev "was sincerely convinced that he was in the right" (p. 47). For a highly critical but in some ways empathetic portrait by a Soviet liberal journalist, see Vitalii Tretiakov, *Gorbachev, Ligachev, Yeltsin* (Moscow, 1990), pp. 31–41.

scenes were understandable, there is little in the documentary record or personal testimonies to suggest an intriguer, at least not more so than is customary among professional politicians.[4] With the rough-hewn and blunt Ligachev, what friends and foes alike saw seems to have been about what they got.

That was my own impression when I first met him in 1990, as he was exiting the political stage, unwillingly and defiantly, at age seventy. A stocky, still strongly built figure of medium height, with thin but impressive white hair atop a ruddy Siberian complexion and riveting blue eyes, Ligachev's emphatic way of speaking and gesturing reminded another American of the "hard-knuckle stage presence of James Cagney in old age,"[5] though Spencer Tracy's anachronistic politician in *The Last Hurrah* also comes to mind. As I got to know him better, Ligachev always seemed old-fashioned— in his down-home traditional values, political outlook, and courtly manners—and like another American type: the native of the provincial heartland who after many urban years still felt and looked out of place in the big city. Unknowingly, Ligachev once even uttered the Russian version of our cliché: "I prefer Siberia, where people tell you what they think to your face. In Moscow they stab you in the back."

Old-fashioned did not, however, mean "dogmatic," though the word was attached to Ligachev like a hereditary title in the radical politics of perestroika. In our conversations about history and politics, he always had strong views, but also a willingness, even an eagerness, to consider different opinions. On the few occasions his aides joined us, they seemed more ideologically "dogmatic" than their considerably older boss. In fact, as Ligachev maintains below and as the public record indicates, he "rethought many things"

---

[4]See the accounts cited in footnote 3, p. ix above. Ligachev discusses at length the two cases in which he was accused of serious intrigue—the Andreyeva affair and the bloodshed in Tbilisi—in the memoirs.

[5]David Remnick, "A Soviet Conservative Looks Back in Despair," *Washington Post,* 15 October 1990. For a different, negative impression, see Svetlana Allilueva, "Kniga dlia vnuchek," *Dialog,* No. 8 (1991), pp. 109–10.

about the political and economic system in which he had lived his entire life and risen to the top. Not so many things as Gorbachev and others rethought, but more than we expect from successful politicians and after middle age.

Even Ligachev's decision to write and publish these unusually detailed and candid memoirs was unorthodox in the Soviet context. Like almost all memoirs of former political leaders everywhere, our own included, they are not, of course, objective, thoroughly trustworthy, or the whole story. Retired powerholders issue such books for self-serving purposes, even leaving aside financial motives: to settle old political scores, embellish their careers, and influence future historians, who therefore need versions from other participants to sort out the truth. But until now, there have been no Soviet leadership memoirs worthy of the name—a lack that has made even the best histories of Soviet politics, most of them written in the West, elliptical and speculative. (The most informed kind of speculation, which relied on reading between the lines and seeing through the cracks, was called Kremlinology.)

Political memoirs suffered the same fate as history writing, historians, and millions of other people in the Soviet Union: they were repressed, forbidden, and heavily censored, beginning with the revolutionary founding fathers and continuing into the early Gorbachev years. Lenin's co-leaders were murdered by Stalin; Stalin's, terrorized by his despotic personality cult; Khrushchev's, allowed to tell only fragments of the truth; and Brezhnev's, blended into his own "cult without a personality," as a popular quip put it. Only two former Soviet leaders produced books even approximating real memoirs as we understand that genre: Trotsky's *My Life,* published in exile in 1930, which said little about actual leadership politics; and Khrushchev's reminiscences, dictated to family members after his ouster in 1964, which were of great historical interest but virtually silent about contemporary matters.[6]

---

[6]Khrushchev's memoirs, prepared by his family from oral reminiscences, appeared in three volumes as *Khrushchev Remembers* (Boston, 1970, 1974, and 1990). Something

Gorbachev's reforms, particularly the gradual abolition of censorship known as glasnost, brought personality back into Soviet public politics, and with it, a spate of alleged political memoirs and autobiographies. None of them was the real thing or otherwise comparable to Ligachev's book about the rise and fall of perestroika. After decades in office, Andrei Gromyko, the longtime foreign minister and Politburo member, published a thick volume of "memoirs" that continued his tradition of tight-lipped diplomacy. Gorbachev's foreign minister and close ally in the leadership, Eduard Shevardnadze, wrote a semi-autobiographical book that was frankly "not a political memoir" and thus almost entirely reticent about leadership politics. And Boris Yeltsin, briefly a junior member of the Gorbachev team, issued in 1990, on the eve of becoming Russia's president, a "confessional" autobiography that was surprisingly uninformative and, not surprisingly, more akin to a campaign biography.[7] Other members of the last Soviet leadership, including Gorbachev, will no doubt publish authentic and important memoirs, but Ligachev is the first in Soviet history to have done so.[8]

---

akin to fragmentary oral memoirs by Vliacheslav Molotov appeared in a book by the Soviet poet Feliks Chuev, *Sto sorok besed s Molotovym* (Moscow, 1991). Fragments from memoirs by other secondary Soviet leaders have appeared in the press, and others may still reside in state or family archives.

[7]Andrei Gromyko, *Memoirs* (New York, 1990); Shevardnadze, *The Future Belongs to Freedom;* Yeltsin, *Against the Grain*. The Russian-language edition of Shevardnadze's book was titled *My Choice* (Moscow, 1991), and that of Yeltsin's book, *Confessions on an Assigned Subject* (Moscow, 1990).

[8]This generalization is chronologically correct. Ligachev completed his memoirs prior to December 1991, and indeed sections began to appear in the Soviet press in 1990. The full Russian edition was published later as E. K. Ligachev, *Zagadka Gorbacheva* (Novosibirsk, 1992). A fragmentary memoir by a lower-ranking member of the Gorbachev administration, Vadim Bakatin, also appeared at about the same time: *Osvobozhdenie ot illiuzii* (Kemerov, 1992). And a thick volume of memoirs by Gorbachev's premier, Nikolai Ryzhkov, was published in Moscow later in 1992 as *Perestroika: istoriia predatelstv*. I omit from this discussion the memoirs of Gorbachev's wife, Raisa Gorbachev, *I Hope* (New York, 1991), as well as semimemoir books by aides to former Soviet leaders. See, for example, Aleksei Adzhubei, *Te desiat let* (Moscow, 1989); Fedor Burlatskii, *Vozhdi i sovetniki* (Moscow, 1990); Georgii Arbatov, *Zatianuvsheesia vysdo-*

Admire him or not, we, and his fellow citizens, should be grateful for the tradition-breaking precedent.

None of this is meant to transform Ligachev into a political hero. Many Russians who share his angry view that a hijacking of perestroika led to the tragic collapse of the Soviet system still think of him in that way, but like the great majority of American readers, I cannot. As Ligachev says below about our encounters, "I did not share Cohen's views on the processes taking place in the USSR, and . . . he was not among those who shared my position." But if we persist in judging Soviet and post-Soviet leaders by the extent to which they embrace our ideas, try to replicate our system, or otherwise resemble us, we will never understand what happened there or what lies ahead. Ligachev's book challenges us to understand more by judging less. Or, as another prominent Russian, considerably more Westernized than Ligachev, likes to advise foreigners about the future of his country: "You can't expect people to leap out of their biographies or society out of its history any more than you expect a man to leap out of his skin."[9]

Yegor Ligachev's biography spans almost the entire history of the Soviet Union, reflecting many of its contradictions and complexities, as well as catastrophes we can hardly imagine. Ten years older than Gorbachev, his personal experiences help explain his ambivalent attitudes toward the past, which later caused conflicts with other members of the leadership.

Ligachev was born into a Siberian peasant family in November

rovlenie (Moscow, 1991); Leonid Abalkin, *Neispolzovannyi shans* (Moscow, 1991); and Evgenii Chazov, *Zdorove i vlast* (Moscow, 1992); Vadim Pechenev, *Gorbachev: k vershinam vlasti* (Moscow, 1991). The books by Nazarbaev and Sobchak cited in footnote 3, p. ix above, are semimemoir accounts by lesser leaders. The memoirs of Andrei Sakharov fall into a separate category. See his *Memoirs* (New York, 1990) and *Moscow and Beyond* (New York, 1991).

[9]Aleksandr Bovin, who commented similarly in an interview in Stephen F. Cohen and Katrina vanden Heuvel, *Voices of Glasnost: Interviews with Gorbachev's Reformers* (New York, 1989), p. 225.

1920, when Lenin's Communist Party was consolidating its rule by winning the three-year Russian civil war. As often happened in the 1920s, the family left its village for a city, Novosibirsk, where his father found work in a factory. Unlike Gorbachev and many other leading *perestroishchiki,* Ligachev grew to full manhood and began his career in the Stalin era, when the modern-day Soviet system was actually created. Even today, many Russians have profoundly conflicting feelings about the Stalinist 1930s and 1940s, a traumatic epoch of towering achievements and monstrous crimes that are hard to reconcile. Millions of people fell victim to the despot's brutal collectivization of the peasantry and capricious mass terror—killed or flung into the Gulag of forced labor camps—but millions of others labored heroically and rose in the campaigns to forge a mighty industrial nation and defeat the Nazi German invaders.

Both experiences were part of Ligachev's life. Presumably a good student and from a politically correct family,[10] he was admitted at college age in the late 1930s to a prestigious institute of aviation engineering in Moscow, and thus began a not untypical Soviet version of our Horatio Alger saga. Immediately after graduation, he returned to Novosibirsk to work in a plant building fighter planes for the Soviet victory in World War II. That war cost the nation at least twenty-seven to thirty million lives, among them Ligachev's older brother, who was killed and buried in Germany. The war might be remembered triumphantly, but not a darker episode in Ligachev's life. His wife's father, an army general, had been executed in 1937 after a ten-minute "trial" by a Stalinist terror tribunal. As Ligachev explains in the interesting chapter on his encounters with Stalin's crimes, he, too, was therefore stigmatized as "family of an enemy of the people," as were relatives of millions of victims.[11] Not

---

[10]There is some uncertainty about this. Ligachev says that his father was expelled from the Communist Party during the terror years but soon was readmitted.

[11]On the other hand, not too much should be read into this. The Gorbachev leadership included several other people whose families had suffered similarly during the terror, among them Shevardnadze, Vadim Bakatin, and Gorbachev himself.

surprisingly, he speaks harshly of Stalin and warmly of Nikita Khrushchev, who in the 1950s began exonerating Stalin's victims, including Ligachev's father-in-law.

Little is known about the beginning of Ligachev's political career. Having joined the Communist Party in 1944, he soon left his original profession to become a full-time Party functionary in the local Young Communist League (Komsomol). In a private communication, Ligachev says he was told to do so and had no choice. "Things were simple in those days: Either you agreed or you were expelled from the Party, which meant being fired from the plant." Possibly it happened that way, though Ligachev never seems to have looked back with regret. In the memoirs, he recounts seven unemployed and perilous months in 1949 when he was under Moscow's suspicion of being a Trotskyist "enemy of the people" and fired as chief of the Novosibirsk Komsomol organization. But apart from that brush with Stalin's terror machine, he moved gradually up the Party's nomenklatura ladder—the far-flung pyramid of appointed officials who oversaw the vast Soviet political and economic system.

After a number of secondary positions in Novosibirsk, Ligachev's political career leaped forward under Khrushchev, whose pioneering reforms inspired a still younger generation of would-be Party officials typified by Gorbachev. For Ligachev, the turning point was his appointment in 1958 as Party chief of a district where a large Academy of Sciences town was to be built, and in 1959 of the whole Novosibirsk area. Evidently he oversaw the important project admirably and got along well with freer-minded scientific intellectuals flooding into Academic City, including Abel Aganbegyan, a maverick economist and eventually Gorbachev's adviser. Thirty years later, Aganbegyan recalled Ligachev as having been an innovative, "unorthodox" Party boss, and doubted his current anti-perestroika reputation.[12] Ligachev's work took him occasionally to Moscow, where he began to meet with top leaders, even Khrushchev. In 1961 Ligachev was promoted to the headquarters of the

---

[12]See Aganbegyan, footnote 3, p. ix above.

Central Committee apparatus in Moscow—a "big honor," as he says privately—where he served until 1965 as deputy chief of propaganda, and then of Party personnel, for the whole Russian Republic.

Why Ligachev returned to Siberia in 1965, and did not resume a Moscow position for seventeen years, isn't fully clear. Few Party bureaucrats, or anyone else, would willingly give up the capital's special powers and privileges for life in the provinces. Ligachev says he requested the transfer himself because he yearned to work with "real people." Did he feel uneasy with the new Brezhnev leadership that had overthrown Khrushchev in October 1964 and already was staffing Party headquarters on Old Square with antireformist officials, some of them highly corruptible? Certainly Ligachev was not on a fast track during Leonid Brezhnev's long reign. Ligachev describes the seventeen years as head of the Tomsk Province Party organization as the best of his life, but admits that the appointment was both remote and relatively "insignificant." Thus, while the younger Gorbachev, who held the same job in the central province of Stavropol, became a full member of the Central Committee in 1971, Ligachev achieved that exalted standing only in 1976. If nothing else, Ligachev's flinty rectitude evidently irritated the Moscow power mafia around Brezhnev, as illustrated by its attempt in the early 1980s to send him into ambassadorial exile, and his stubborn refusal to go.[13]

On the other hand, Ligachev hardly fell out of the power elite during his years in Tomsk. As Communist Party first secretary for an entire province, he was one of about seventy-five such bosses who directly ruled Soviet Russia, where the great majority of citizens lived. Many observers have portrayed provincial Party bosses as congenitally conservative tyrants running roughshod over their region's populace and resources. But some scholars have viewed them as increasingly qualified—though never elected—governors

---

[13]Ligachev may relate this story to remind readers that his archrival in the leadership, Alexander Yakovlev, accepted diplomatic banishment to Canada in 1973.

or prefects trying to cope with an impossible array of technical problems and everyday responsibilities, from economic production and distribution to educational and cultural life, in an often irrational system. Suffice it to say that they were exceedingly powerful rulers in their provinces, unilaterally capable of benevolent or evil deeds but frequently at the mercy of higher authorities in Moscow. Nor were all provincial Party bosses alike. Among them in the 1970s, for example, were Ligachev, Gorbachev, Shevardnadze, Yeltsin, and a host of others who later enthusiastically supported or opposed the reforms of the 1980s.

What little we know about Ligachev's role in Tomsk generally corresponds to the sparse account he gives in this book. Teetotaling, self-confident, hard-working, a little self-righteous, and a scandal-free family man, he modernized the province's industry and agriculture, developed new enterprises, preserved Tomsk's historic wooden buildings, patronized the arts, and minded the Party's monopolistic interests wherever necessary. It is easy to understand why Ligachev was proud of his tenure in Tomsk and did not like Gorbachev's post-1985 practice of indiscriminately branding the Brezhnev years an "era of stagnation." By 1988 Ligachev had become a lightning rod for unleashed resentments against powerholders under Brezhnev, even though others in the Gorbachev leadership had been more high-ranking. Rising to defend himself at a nationally televised Party conference, and also to condemn the Brezhnev regime for what it had done to the country, Ligachev made a statement that was widely mocked but no doubt came from the heart:

In the years of stagnation, I lived and worked in Siberia—a harsh but truly wonderful land. I am often asked what I was doing during that time. I answer with pride: I was building socialism. And there were millions like me. It would be an act of betrayal if I did not mention those with whom I linked my fate and shared joys and sorrow. Many of them have left this life. Not everything turned out as we wanted. . . . But we worked without looking over our shoulders, perhaps because we knew they couldn't send us any farther away than Siberia.

> We worked in order to give the people a better life, to give the state more, and to protect the interests of the province.[14]

There he remained until 1983, when Yuri Andropov, Brezhnev's successor as Party general secretary, recalled him to Moscow. Readers will note Ligachev's admiration, bordering on nostalgia, for Andropov, who died fifteen months after becoming leader. By the end of the 1980s, that sentiment was widespread among Party officials disenchanted with Gorbachev's reforms. Andropov was neither the radical reformer portrayed by some Soviet writers nor the "strongman" Western observers mistook him to be when he took office, at sixty-eight and already gravely ill, in November 1982. Not unlike the conflicted political figures that appear so often in Russian literature, he had been an enthusiastic anti-Stalinist under Khrushchev, but fifteen years as head of the KGB under Brezhnev had deeply implicated him in many "stagnant" policies, from the cover-up of the country's grave economic condition and the repression of dissidents to the 1979 invasion of Afghanistan. So contradictory was Andropov's role—privately he wrote poetry and shunned the rampant corruption around Brezhnev—that even the great dissenter Andrei Sakharov, one of his victims, later commented sympathetically on this "duality."[15]

Nonetheless, Andropov was the godfather of Gorbachev's original perestroika. Determined to use his brief time in office to address the country's growing problems, Andropov infused political life with expectations of change for the first time since the 1960s, initiated a series of economic "experiments" that promised to be more than half-measures, and behind the scenes encouraged far-reaching reconsiderations of Brezhnev's domestic and foreign policies. Apart from disciplinarian and anticorruption campaigns directed mainly against the old-guard Brezhnev establishment, few new policies

---

[14]*XIX vsesoiuznaia konferentsiia Kommunisticheskoi Partii Sovetskogo Soiuza: stenograficheskii otchet,* Vol. 2 (Moscow, 1988), pp. 84–85.

[15]In Iurii Afanasev, ed., *Inogo ne dano* (Moscow, 1988), p. 125.

were actually adopted by Andropov. Opposition was great, time short, and his own outlook no doubt deeply ambivalent.

In another respect, however, Andropov mattered greatly. Using the appointment powers of the general secretary, he gathered a team of younger reform-minded officials on behalf of his preferred successor, Mikhail Gorbachev, and put it in a position to contend for power. Ligachev, at sixty-three, was one of its oldest but also most important members. They were unable to make Gorbachev leader when Andropov died in February 1984; the septuagenarian old guard, unnerved by prospects of major reforms and retirement, preferred an ailing seventy-two-year-old Brezhnev surrogate, Konstantin Chernenko. But when Chernenko died thirteen months later, Andropov's protégés succeeded, as Ligachev explains below more fully than has anyone else.

The Gorbachev leadership that launched the most fateful reforms of the twentieth century therefore was actually assembled by Andropov. Even the original inner Politburo group—in addition to Gorbachev and Ligachev, it included the new head of the state ministries, Nikolai Ryzhkov, and the KGB chief, Viktor Chebrikov—numbered men of varying political outlooks and loyalties. Later, as Gorbachev began to rely on his more radical Politburo allies, notably Shevardnadze and Alexander Yakovlev, protests could be heard in the apparatus that he had betrayed Andropov's legacy and that Ligachev was its real representative.[16] Like most political nostalgia, much of this was mythical; but not all of it. Just as the Party elite had always been full of conflicting views and interests, so was the Gorbachev leadership that governed the Soviet Union from 1985 to its collapse in 1991.

*   *   *

---

[16]I heard such murmurings in Moscow in 1988. They were in print regularly by 1990. A former Ligachev aide later extended the argument back to 1985, though Ligachev never publicly embraced it. See the series of articles by Valerii Legostaev in *Den,* Nos. 13–16 (1991).

Contrary to images in the West, neither the Soviet Communist Party nor its elite had ever been politically monolithic. How could they have been in a one-party system with twenty million members by the 1980s, where anyone who wanted to engage in big-time politics had to enter the Communist establishment, and in a country with such a traumatic history? Ideological and policy disputes raged openly in the Party elite from 1917 until Stalin settled those issues by firing squad and frightened survivors into silence. When terror ended in the 1950s, conflicting policy and ideological views reappeared in the Party-controlled press, sometimes rather candidly but usually in muted and Aesopian ways, depending on the degree of censorship at the time.

In modern times, the fundamental conflict was between Party conservatives and Party reformers.[17] American conservatives dislike the idea that they had Soviet Communist counterparts, but this is another example of refusing to understand foreign politics in its own context. (Ligachev doesn't help by maintaining that extremists were the "real conservatives.") Every political society has a status quo; and thus conservatives who wish to preserve it, usually in the name of historical practices and values, and reformers who insist on improving it, usually arguing that existing practices are obsolete and national values unfulfilled. In the Soviet Union, the status quo was the system called socialism inherited from Stalin.

Khrushchev's reforms undermined Stalinist dogmas and liberalized the system in important ways in the 1950s and early 1960s, but they did not dismantle its essential institutional nature: the Party-state's monopolistic bureaucratic controls over society, including the vast economy run by Moscow ministries. Nonetheless, his reforms were so divisive that something akin to subterranean crypto-parties formed inside the Communist Party system. Officially concealed and denied in the name of "Party unity," those rival political movements finally burst into the open thirty years later in response to Gorbachev's more radical reforms. In the late 1980s,

---

[17]For a fuller analysis, see Stephen F. Cohen, *Rethinking the Soviet Experience: Politics and History Since 1917* (New York, 1985; exp. ed., 1993), chap. 5.

even the official Communist Party newspaper acknowledged the "secret rivalry that always existed," and wondered: "How many parties are there in our Party?"[18]

At least three intra-Party movements had taken shape by the time Khrushchev was overthrown in 1964: anti-Stalinist reformers who called for a substantial reduction of controls over society, including more political liberalization and some marketization of the state economy; neo-Stalinist reactionaries who charged that Khrushchev's reforms had gravely weakened Party-government controls and orthodoxies, and who demanded that they be strengthened; and Party conservatives who objected to the "excesses" of Khrushchev's reforms but mainly sought to preserve the new post-Stalin status quo by opposing any further changes, whether forward or backward. The conservative majority headed by Brezhnev ruled the Soviet Union for the next two decades, with concessions mostly to the neo-Stalinists. The Party's reform movement barely survived, but it came to power in 1985 with Gorbachev.

Ligachev's political evolution prior to 1985 illustrates and helps explain that dramatic turnabout. Several large factors lay behind the reemergence of reform-minded officials in the Communist Party on the eve of Brezhnev's death—the country's development into a more urban and educated society, the aging of the old guard that had risen to high office under Stalin, the ascent of the Gorbachev generation that had entered politics under Khrushchev, the Soviet elite's greater exposure to the West—but the approaching economic crisis was the most important. Hypercentralized, bureaucratic management had made the economy increasingly irrational and inefficient, thwarting even minor changes and isolating it from the technological revolution in capitalist countries. By the late 1970s, economic growth had virtually stopped, while enormous state expenditures for the military and for the cradle-to-grave welfare provisions of Soviet socialism, including large subsidies for most essential goods and services, continued to grow.

The Brezhnev leadership did nothing about the "precrisis," as

---

[18]*Pravda*, 14 February 1988; 18 May 1989; and 31 December 1989.

Gorbachev later termed it, but Ligachev and other provincial Party officials could not ignore it. They had long been the political mainstay of Brezhnev-era conservatism—maliciously called the "golden era of the nomenklatura"—but now had to cope daily with economic decay and a plethora of related social ills. Even regional Party bosses with no interest in real political reform believed that Brezhnev's status quo policies "had led the country into a dead end."[19] Enlightened bureaucrats in the Moscow state ministries, represented by Ryzhkov, had reached the same conclusion. Two decades of conservative consensus in the Communist Party elite had ended; longtime conservatives were ready for an "antistagnation" coalition with their erstwhile reformist foes. Anti-Stalinist intellectuals were already gathered around Gorbachev, who had earlier put himself at the head of the resurgent reform movement. And there is no reason to doubt Ligachev's account of why and how an influential group of provincial Party bosses also backed Gorbachev in March 1985.

That Ligachev and other conservatives-turned-reformers soon clashed with Gorbachev, and eventually accused him of betraying his mandate, is not surprising. They wanted to save the system by improving it, not by reinventing it, as Gorbachev set out to do. But this should not obscure their crucial role in Soviet history. Again, without their participation, there could not have been a reform leadership in the 1980s, or perhaps even in the 1990s. Like the best conservatives in the history of other countries, they understood that when it was time to change, it was necessary to change. And thus Ligachev and Ryzhkov—Gorbachev's "closest comrades" in the original leadership, according to these memoirs—became progressives, moderate reformers, or, as Ligachev likes to say, "realists." That they supported, or tolerated, Gorbachev's increasingly radical reforms as long as they did was a tribute to his leadership abilities, but also to their own political qualities. Ligachev may have remained a conservative with old-fashioned Soviet values, but he was hardly a diehard or reactionary one.

---

[19]Aleksandr Galkin, "Blizok li kriticheskii chas?" *Poisk,* 28 December 1989.

In fact, both reformers and conservatives in the Communist Party had "rethought many things" since the 1950s, and again after 1985. Gorbachev's reformers evolved far beyond Khrushchev's anti-Stalinist legacy, which called for a return to the more tolerant kind of one-party dictatorship associated with Lenin in the 1920s and for rationalizing the statized economy. Gorbachev's program by the late 1980s called for a mixed economy based on market relations, a multiparty parliamentary democracy based on the rule of law, a real federation of Soviet republics, and "universal human values" instead of Marxist-Leninist ones.[20] Such tenets closely resembled those of European social democratic parties, and not at all those long practiced by the Soviet Communist Party. For some Communist officials like Boris Yeltsin, Gorbachev's "humane democratic socialism" was too little or too late. But for a great many Party functionaries, his heresy was too much. They fought against every plank of Gorbachev's program, clinging to Brezhnev-era fundamentalism or even lurching back to neo-Stalinism.

Ligachev's reaction, like that of a number of other influential antiradicals, was significantly different. As deputy Party leader, and even after losing the post in 1988 but remaining in the leadership, he supported Gorbachev's general reforms while trying to guide them in "healthy" directions and guard them against "excesses." Ultraradicals later accused Gorbachev of being a centrist, but that probably best describes the position Ligachev thought he occupied between Gorbachev and the Party's real diehards. Having abandoned many Communist dogmas of the past, Ligachev accepted the need for a significant degree of economic marketization and demonopolization, glasnost, political liberalization, and reforms in the ersatz union, but always while protesting their "extremes," as he saw them—"anti-Communism" in politics, "slander" in history-

---

[20]For English translations of Gorbachev's increasingly explicit "humane democratic socialism," see Mikhail Gorbachev, *The Socialist Idea and Revolutionary Perestroika* (Moscow, 1990), which first appeared in 1989; *Towards a Humane and Democratic Socialist Society: Report by Mikhail Gorbachev* (Moscow, 1990); and the materials published in *The Current Digest of the Soviet Press*, Nos. 30–31 (1991).

writing, "capitalism" in economics, "anti-Sovietism" in the republics. Eventually he was willing to relinquish the Communist Party's dictatorship in politics, the state's monopoly in economics, and the central government's dominance over the republics, but not the primacy of those institutions in a reformed Soviet system. To yield any more, he said elsewhere, "I'd have to cross out my whole life."[21]

In the end, Ligachev became a tragic figure—a moderate reformer in radical times, a progressive conservative when everything sacred fell under attack. Not surprisingly, he occasionally retreated into fundamentalist postures, but only briefly and not often. In some respects, he shared the tortuous fate of most Communist Party conservatives who until the Gorbachev years were trapped in a pseudorevolutionary ideology. Despite their authentic conservatism—a cultlike belief in the past, deep attachment to the present, and abiding fear of change—they could not even acknowledge their real political identity: officially, "conservatives" were all those anti-Communists in the West.

Liberated by Gorbachev's political reforms, they finally came out of the closet to protest the radicalization of perestroika. In 1990, younger, tougher-minded conservatives formed their own, predominantly anti-Gorbachev Russian Communist Party. Its leader responded candidly to Communist reformers "who call us conservatives, investing that word with exclusively negative meaning. But the real content of conservatism, if we take its scholarly definition, is the preservation and maintenance of the basic foundations of state and social life. . . . In this sense, we are conservatives, and let us not be ashamed of the word."[22]

As readers will discover, Ligachev remains, if not ashamed, a little ambivalent about the word. Often the "real conservatives" are forces that wanted to abolish the Soviet socialist system for a capitalist one, and to destroy the union on behalf of nationalist separation.

---

[21]Quoted in Angus Roxburgh, *The Second Russian Revolution* (London, 1991), p. 80.

[22]Ivan Polozkov in *Sovetskaia Rossiia*, 7 March 1991; and similarly in *Literaturnaia Rossiia*, 29 June 1990, where he remarks that "no civilized country can manage without conservatives."

But ultimately he counts himself among the proponents of "healthy conservatism"—the "true supporters of perestroika who were trying to prevent it from falling into the pernicious trap of radicalism." And yet the new generation of Communist conservatives had little use for Ligachev by the 1990s. In their eyes, he had supported Gorbachev too much and too long, was insufficiently militant, or perhaps too old. When Ligachev rose to commit another unorthodox act by running for election as deputy Party leader against Gorbachev's hand-chosen candidate at the national congress in 1990—the first ranking Communist to act so boldly in sixty years—they gave him a rousing ovation and then voted against him.[23]

The Soviet Communist Party Congress that retired Ligachev turned out to be its last. In the aftermath of the failed coup in August 1991, the Party was banned by Russian president Yeltsin and, after his release from house arrest, by Soviet president Gorbachev; it largely disintegrated. Four months later, a Yeltsin-led group of former Communist officials, now acting as presidents of republics, declared their respective independence and dissolved the Soviet Union. For Gorbachev, it was the end of his six-year struggle to carry out a full-scale Soviet reformation, and of his power. For Ligachev, it was the collapse of everything he held "most sacred."

Russian political culture has always been leader-dominated, so it is not surprising that Ligachev puts much of the blame on Gorbachev. If he often does so more indirectly and gingerly than we might expect, surely it is because he stood alongside Gorbachev, sharing "full responsibility," as he ruefully acknowledges, for much of the time. Indeed, his relationship—perhaps even obsession—with Gorbachev is a central theme of this book. (Ligachev's original title was *The Gorbachev Enigma*, which he changed for this edition

---

[23]Only 776 of the 4,035 delegates voted for him. Talking with delegates during the Congress, and later reading their speeches, I had a strong sense that the majority preferred Ligachev's views to Gorbachev's. Why they nonetheless supported Gorbachev's candidate is a separate and complicated story.

only when persuaded that it was inappropriate for his own memoirs.) As he tells the story of perestroika, and thus the last chapter in Soviet history, the country came to ruin partly, even largely, due to his own inability to win the "battle for Gorbachev" against ever-destructive forces around the leader. Here, of course, we must understand that Ligachev is writing primarily for his fellow citizens, and remember the self-serving nature of all political memoirs.

According to his account, the golden years of perestroika—and in his relations with Gorbachev—were from 1985 to 1987, or perhaps to early 1988. It is easy to understand why Ligachev eulogizes this period. He was at the height of his power and contentment as the No. 2 Party leader, and Gorbachev was still in the initial stage of his emergence as a radical reform leader. The new leadership removed a large number of corrupt and flatly anti-reformist officials, began to end the decades-long cover-up of historical crimes and current problems by reducing censorship in the media, introduced limited innovations to "accelerate" the state economy, took consequential steps in foreign policy to defuse the Cold War, and cajoled the Party's Central Committee into endorsing several more ambitious aspects of Gorbachev's domestic program. Apart from a disastrous anti-alcohol campaign, and a lack of glasnost during the first days of the Chernobyl nuclear disaster, those years were for Ligachev a model of moderate, gradual reform.

Even though Gorbachev's own radical intentions were evident earlier, the first unmistakable harbinger of fundamental change did not come until the 19th Communist Party Conference in mid-1988. The conference had great ramifications for two reasons. The public spectacle of the Communist ruling elite deeply divided over policy and ideology, for the first time since the 1920s, quickly incited—or inadvertently legitimized—more boundless kinds of "pluralism" in society. For example, a direct confrontation between Ligachev and Yeltsin, still a ranking Party official, was electrifying.[24] Secondly,

---

[24]A popular documentary film about the conference, titled *Pluralism,* clearly conveyed the point. Soon after the conference, Moscow's flea markets began featuring political buttons that proclaimed, "Tell Them—Boris!" and "Yegor—You're Wrong!"

after a major struggle and with considerable guile, Gorbachev manipulated the national conference into voting for the "democratization" of the Soviet system. Most Party functionaries no doubt thought the resolution would be merely ceremonial, as others had been in the past, but that was not the case.

Readers will recall the dramatic events that followed. In March 1989, Gorbachev's democratizing policies produced the country's first relatively free, multicandidate national elections since 1917, and its first real parliament ever. (Some of the 2,250 deputies were given uncontested seats, including Ligachev, Gorbachev, and 98 other representatives of the Communist Party establishment.) Sitting as a constitutional congress, the legislature elected Gorbachev president of the Soviet Union, thereby partially freeing him from constraints imposed by the Party Central Committee, which had made him its general secretary in 1985. In 1990, similar elections took place in Russia and other republics that further changed the Soviet political landscape. An embryonic multiparty system began to emerge, along with political leaders unbeholden to the Communist Party nomenklatura, among them two who figure prominently, and negatively, in Ligachev's memoirs—Yeltsin and Anatoly Sobchak, a parlimentary leader and later mayor of St. Petersburg.

The election of a parliament and the creation of Gorbachev's executive presidency in 1989 were turning points in Soviet history. They broke the Communist Party's seven-decade monopoly on political life and thus fundamentally eroded the Leninist political system. Much that now ensued, and is so greatly lamented by Ligachev, was aftermath. The democratization process greatly outran Gorbachev's still modest economic reforms while generating popular protests against growing consumer shortages, rising inflation, and longstanding elite privileges. Even more destabilizing, it allowed nationalist discontent in several of the fifteen republics to develop into anti-Soviet movements for independence, first and most assertively in the Baltics. By 1990, powerful counterreform forces had regrouped and begun to strike back, finding many allies among unnerved Andropov-style reformers in the state, Party, and security bureaucracies. Their self-appointed leaders, most of them members of Gorbachev's own government, staged the abortive coup in August 1991 that promised "national salvation" and "order" but triggered the collapse of everything they had sent the tanks to save.

In his memoirs, Ligachev insists unconvincingly that his own serious concerns about the direction of Gorbachev's reforms surfaced only in the fall of 1987, when he clashed with Alexander Yakovlev over the media's "slanderous" portrayal of Soviet history. It was an important confrontation that sharpened divisions in the Gorbachev leadership. Opinions about the Stalinist past were inherently related to opinions about the amount of reform needed in the existing Stalinist system; Ligachev wanted a "balanced" approach to both questions. And though Yakovlev may not have been the *éminence grise* behind Gorbachev's stunning radicalization, as Ligachev presents him, he had been Gorbachev's confidant for several years and now was a member of the top Party leadership, the Politburo. It is also true that Yakovlev had considerable influence among liberal Communist intellectuals and journalists—"foremen of perestroika," as Ligachev pejoratively calls them—many of whom he appointed to important editorial positions.

But it is not true that this was the first serious conflict inside the Gorbachev leadership; earlier ones, about which Ligachev's memoirs are silent or highly elliptical, were equally portentous. At the first Party Congress held under Gorbachev, in February 1986, for example, Ligachev strongly protested attacks on the Party apparatus's power and privileges; only Gorbachev could have stood behind such attacks at the time. That issue continued to fester and contributed to the infamous Yeltsin affair in October 1987, when Gorbachev, in effect taking Ligachev's side in a bitter controversy, moved to expel Yeltsin from the leadership. Ligachev portrays himself as a relatively minor participant in this prolonged and ramifying affair; his only regret is having recommended Yeltsin for a leadership position in the first place. Similarly, though Ligachev criticizes at length a "fateful" economic decision made in late 1987, he is silent about earlier disputes over proposals to marketize sections of the Soviet economy. That controversy, about which Ligachev could tell us much, probably delayed such decisions considerably and thus made them harder to implement.

Above all, Ligachev is virtually silent about behind-the-scenes struggles over political reform beginning in mid-1986, or perhaps even earlier, and leading up to a watershed meeting of the Central Committee in January 1987. It was there that Gorbachev first persuaded the recalcitrant assembly of Communist oligarchs to adopt at least a faint version of his calls for the democratization of the Soviet system and of the Communist Party itself. The latter proposal, if actually carried out, would have destroyed Ligachev's base of power in the central Party Secretariat, as Gorbachev did by other means only in September 1988. (At the January 1987 meeting, Gorbachev also signaled his own readiness to open candid discussion of the Stalin era.) Nor does Ligachev explain where he stood on a related and highly symbolic issue: the decision made in December 1986 to free Andrei Sakharov from seven years of internal exile, which was a major step toward legitimizing liberal democratic dissent, past and present.

In short, most of the great disputes that later disenchanted Ligachev, and plunged the Communist Party into its fateful schism, were latent in the Gorbachev leadership from the beginning and divided its members almost as soon as they began to exercise power. Ligachev's memory of his original relationship with the No. 1 leader therefore needs revision. It was a political coalition, with all the need for bargaining and potential for conflict inherent in such arrangements everywhere, not a perfect marriage that fell apart due to the envious competitors, unwise decisions, and inexplicable behavior recounted in Ligachev's memoirs.

Several factors eventually estranged Ligachev and Gorbachev, but what was the crucial one? The answer can be found in Ligachev's book, I think, though he never states it clearly and may not even fully understand it. Gorbachev remained devoted to the "socialist idea." But for whatever reasons, at some moment in his own biography he crossed the rubicon from Communist Party liberalizer to authentic democratizer. This interpretation is not generally accepted in the United States or in Russia today, but there is considerable evidence to support it, as a few Western scholars have already indicated.[25] Hence Gorbachev's dramatic evolution after 1985, which Ligachev is at pains to explain, from proponent of "socialist pluralism" to proponent simply of "pluralism," from advocate of "socialist democracy" to advocate of "democracy," from defender of the Communist Party's "leading role" to defender of the need for a multiparty system.

Both Gorbachev and Ligachev had spent their entire political lives rising through a ruling Communist Party apparatus created under Lenin, transformed into a vast, castelike system by Stalin, and largely preserved by Khrushchev and Brezhnev. Gorbachev—like his closest Politburo colleagues, Yakovlev and Shevardnadze—somehow broke with that world and its characteristic ideology. Like the great majority of Party officials, Ligachev, for all his notable evolution in other respects, did not—or at least not until he put the finishing touches on these memoirs and it no longer mattered.

Ligachev is partly right, therefore, about a Gorbachev enigma: How did he evolve from provincial Soviet Party apparatchik into a seminal leader of Russian and twentieth-century democracy? Though many books have already been written about Gorbachev, he still awaits his real biographers. Like all students of modern Soviet history, they will be indebted to Ligachev's memoirs for valuable information and firsthand insights. Few of them, however, are likely to accept his interpretations of major political developments or his answer to the large "mystery of Gorbachev."

Some of Ligachev's explanations of Gorbachev's behavior, while not implausible, are contradictory and lack context. He is right, for example, that Gorbachev often was captive rather than master of events. But was this due primarily to the "personal qualities" of an indecisive and evasive leader, or to another factor discussed by

---

[25]See, for example, John Gooding, "Gorbachev and Democracy," *Soviet Studies,* No. 2 (1990), pp. 195–231; and, on a related issue, Gregory Freidin, "How Communist Is Gorbachev's Communism?" in George W. Breslauer, ed., *Dilemmas of Transition in the Soviet Union and Eastern Europe* (Berkeley, 1991), chap. 3.

Ligachev, which he calls "the Khrushchev syndrome"—Gorbachev's fear of being deposed behind closed doors by the Central Committee as was his reformist predecessor? (It helps us understand, by the way, his puzzling failure to take seriously the possibility of a tank coup.) On the one hand, Ligachev insists that Gorbachev had no reason to fear such a fate because provincial Party bosses, who formed the most powerful bloc on the Central Committee, always "supported Gorbachev and only him." In fact, by 1989 many of them feared and loathed Gorbachev and wanted to be rid of him. On the other hand, Ligachev inadvertently confirms Gorbachev's anxiety about a vengeful Party apparatus by pointing out that Gorbachev did not try to oust him from the leadership until 1990 because the Central Committee "would not have supported it."

Above all, Ligachev cannot explain why Gorbachev ultimately remained "loyal to the radicals," by which he means the democrats. When told that Gorbachev "wants to go down in history as a clean man, whom no one can accuse of dictatorship," Ligachev does not ask if this might reflect a decisive resolve to break with centuries of Russian and Soviet leadership practices. Instead, he essentially argues that a rudderless, impressionable Gorbachev was captured and remade politically by the *éminence grise* Yakovlev and his band of "pseudodemocrats." Yakovlev and many other people probably did influence Gorbachev's thinking over the years, but no leader determined enough to initiate and sustain a radical reformation in such dangerously hostile circumstances, as Gorbachev did in the 1980s, could have been as weak-willed, indecisive, or susceptible to far lesser figures as Ligachev suggests. Indeed, it is not even certain that Gorbachev's conversion began only after 1985. We simply do not yet know, and for an answer we must await more testimony, including Gorbachev's own memoirs.

It is Ligachev's book, however, that now commands our attention, and from it emerges not only a political figure more complex than his reputation but also a Ligachev enigma. Some questions about his conduct will be of interest only to scholars, but general readers may wonder why this purposeful, self-confident man, who had "much influence" in the Party's power structure, did not oppose

Gorbachev's policies more forcefully or, when disillusionment set
in after 1987, try to remove him as leader. Even the latter course
might have been possible in the Central Committee prior to the
1989 elections, which gave Gorbachev a new power base in the
parliament and presidency, and millions of aroused citizens a stake
in the political process.

Ligachev's portrayal of himself as always having been the victim
of intrigue and never the victimizer is not, of course, fully believable.
And yet, he does seem to have been curiously acquiescent in the
face of policies he did not like. There are only two substantive cases
in which Ligachev was even accused of playing an aggressively anti-
Gorbachev role—the Andreyeva affair of March 1988, which fea-
tured the mysterious appearance of an antiperestroika manifesto in
a leading Party newspaper, and the Soviet army's attack on street
demonstrators in Tbilisi in April 1989. Ligachev discusses both
cases at length, denying having instigated either, and in fact the
evidence in both is highly inconclusive.[26]

Indeed, his memoirs are in part actually an apologia for having
borne "full responsibility" for Gorbachev's policies, and at one point
he condemns his own "unprincipled" passivity. At most, Ligachev
began to function as unproclaimed leader of a kind of loyal Communist opposition at the 1988 Party conference, but his loyalty—
or old-fashioned adherence to the idea of "Party unity"—still
seemed to exceed his opposition. He wrote long (sometimes prophetic) letters of protest to Gorbachev and the Central Committee,
but appears never to have acted on them. Under previous leaders,
such behavior would have been risky, but no longer, as Ligachev
admits in an oddly revealing lament: "Under Stalin, you would
have lost your head for a letter like that. Under Khrushchev, you
would have been fired. Under Brezhnev, you would be made an
ambassador to Africa. And under Gorbachev, you were simply ignored." In the end, when Gorbachev finally moved to retire him,

---

[26]Anatoly Sobchak, head of the parliamentary commission that investigated the Tbilisi
Affair, presents evidence against Ligachev in his book *For a New Russia,* chap. 5.

Ligachev's most defiant protest was to try to become his deputy again.

These memoirs provide some clues as to why Ligachev was unwilling or unable to break decisively with Gorbachev. (Perhaps the promised second volume will be more introspective and candid.) In his role as the Party's No. 2 leader and overseer of its nationwide apparatus, Ligachev represented the powers and resentments of provincial officials, but probably not so fully as he suggests or as Western observers have thought. By 1987, some of their resentments were directed at him for having fired, on behalf of Andropov and Gorbachev, a large number of their colleagues. And others who remained in place could not have been happy with Ligachev's contempt for the "former style of the ruling Party apparatchik," who "groveled before the strong and lorded it over the weak." Still more, by 1988 and certainly after the March 1989 elections, many provincial bosses could hardly forgive him for complicity in political reforms that were already destroying their traditional power and privileges. No wonder they began looking for a younger, less tainted, more reliable representative.

As for Ligachev, his policy stance between Gorbachev's radical reforms and the Party's reactionary wing put him in an inherently ambivalent position. Unlike the majority of Party functionaries, in 1985 he had "cast his fate"—as Russians say—with the small group of leaders who began perestroika, and even when Gorbachev's version grew too radical for his taste, Ligachev had no wish to turn the clock back to 1985, only to 1987. Nor is it clear, despite his angry charges that Gorbachev and Yakovlev let democratization and nationalist movements run out of control, that he was ready to use the kind of force necessary by then to restore "discipline and order." To these larger factors that may have bound Ligachev to Gorbachev, we might add the apparent lack of any personal animus in relations between the two men, as well as any evidence that Ligachev ever saw himself as an alternative leader.

Whatever the full explanation, when push finally came to shove, Ligachev was not among the coup plotters in August 1991, though some of his old comrades from the apparatus were. Amid wild rumors that he, Gorbachev, and even Yeltsin were secretly involved, he again cast his lot with the embattled Gorbachev: "I know one thing for sure. Two people from the Party knew nothing about the plans . . . Gorbachev and Ligachev."[27]

Finishing this book, readers may feel that they have encountered a relic from a bygone age. The Soviet Union no longer exists; its fifteen republics now are self-proclaimed independent states. The Communist Party has been driven from power across much of Russia and the other republics—its organization in shambles, membership dispersed, and ideology condemned by the new authorities. Ligachev and Gorbachev are on pension. And yet, Ligachev still insists that the anti-Communist "pseudodemocrats" who came to power under Boris Yeltsin cannot bring wellbeing or stability to Russia, and that the "era of changes is not over." He remains certain that Russia's future will bear a strong resemblance to the Soviet past, though it will be reformed and more humane.

We would be foolish to assume that Ligachev is entirely wrong, at least about Russia itself. The old Communist Party is unlikely to return to power, and economic change toward market relations will almost certainly continue. But it would be a mistake to think that the Soviet system over seven decades, or what we might call Sovietism, was nothing more than the Communist Party. It was also a distinct political culture, collectivist economic attitudes, and bureaucratic state dominance over society, all of which had deep roots in Russian history long before the Communists came to power. If we believe that Communism, or Sovietism, was something alien to and imposed upon Russia, as many Western and Russian commentators now say, we might assume that the country will quickly escape its Soviet past. But if Russian Communism grew out of and perpetuated older native traditions, as many scholars believe, then Ligachev may be right about the future.

---

[27]*Izvestiia,* 23 October 1991.

This perspective does not mean that Russia has not changed and will not change still more in the post-Communist era. Already the nation is far more urban, educated, and Westernized than it was only one or two generations ago, and more democratized than when Gorbachev took office. But many old problems, attitudes, and practices remain. The Communist Party no longer controls the state, but the state, still staffed overwhelmingly by former Communists, retains control over almost all essential economic production. None of the various political movements today believes any longer in a wholly state-owned economy, but even many democrats want a "mixed economy" with substantial "public ownership" of the kind advocated by Ligachev. Many citizens are ready to venture into a competitive marketplace, but many others still demand the cradle-to-grave entitlements that were a large part of latter-day Soviet socialism. Communist Party secretaries no longer rule the provinces, but President Yeltsin appointed provincial prefects to perform a similar function, trying to administer the vastness of Russia from Moscow as did tsars and Communists.

Ligachev therefore also may be right that while Russia can and must borrow from the West, it cannot transplant a Western system into its native soil. Even many anti-Communists now believe that a stable Russia must find its destiny both within and beyond its own historical experiences. If so, perhaps we should not dismiss the importance of what Ligachev calls "healthy conservatism." In fact, the concept was endorsed even by a liberal opponent of Ligachev with good credentials in the West, Eduard Shevardnadze, to distinguish Communist reactionaries whom he feared from Communist conservatives whose legitimate views he acknowledged. Ligachev clings to some kind of Communist faith, but as he remarked plaintively elsewhere: "In the West, they respect people with conservative views."[28]

---

[28]Quoted in Remnick, "A Soviet Conservative Looks Back in Despair." For Shevardnadze's remarks, which came during his famous speech resigning from Gorbachev's government, see *Izvestiia*, 21 December 1990. He said, "I respect the conservatives, because they have their own views which are acceptable to society."

In Russia, however, "healthy" conservatives of all stripes have fared very badly in recent years, driven to reactionary positions or scorned by the country's increasingly polarized politics. If every society needs conservatives, as Ligachev now professes to believe, Russia's twentieth-century tragedy may not be over.

New York–Moscow
APRIL 1992

A NOTE TO AMERICAN READERS

In 1985, when I began perestroika along with Gorbachev, I scarcely could have foreseen that it would lead to the collapse of the USSR six years later, or that Gorbachev himself would be forced to step down from the leadership in a welter of complex and contradictory circumstances. Sadly, it came to pass as in an old Russian proverb: "Man proposes, but God disposes."

The outcome of the turbulent political events known as Russian perestroika is well known. But let me begin this note by assuring Western readers that the era of change is not yet over. The USSR played a major role in the crushing defeat of fascism, decolonization, a half century without war in Europe, the social achievements of the working people of the West, humankind's leap into space, and much more. As a consequence of the enormous influence on the course of world development and its position as a factor for international stability, the upheavals in the USSR—one-sixth of the earth's surface—and before that, in Eastern Europe, undubitably will have far-reaching effects.

In fact, at the finish line of the twentieth century—or, viewed in a broader historical context, at the twilight of the second millennium since the birth of Christ—a new stage has begun in the development of the international community. The world can no longer be what it was in the twentieth century. Relations among world powers will change, and new centers will arise. Let us hope that these will be economic and cultural centers and not military and political ones. I believe that a single Union government will be restored in our country, of course on a new foundation. The entire world is following the path of integration, and in their historical ties our peoples have a sound basis for the process of integration.

Nevertheless, there are many political obstacles to the coming economic harmony of the twenty-first century. The collapse of the USSR into independent states has created a new and very explosive situation entailing a new perestroika of international relations, or as it has been put, a remaking of the world. How will this process proceed? What can and should be done to guide it along a peaceful course?

Today, neither politicians nor prophets are in a position to offer thoroughly reliable answers to these difficult questions. But it is clear that the future always springs from the past. The so-called gift of prophecy is largely the ability to make sense out of the lessons of history. To understand these lessons we must have before us both the facts and various viewpoints. That is why I feel it is extremely important to outline for Western readers my understanding of the events that have occurred in the Soviet Union.

In the initial years of perestroika, I held the No. 2 post in the country's Party hierarchy, essentially serving as Gorbachev's deputy. But the unanimity of purpose with which he and I began the changes in 1985 gave way to a period of disagreement. We began to look differently at many political and economic processes. By 1988 I had become convinced that the original course of perestroika was being very dangerously distorted and, above all, that this was threatening to cause separatism and nationalism to erupt. I warned Gorbachev repeatedly of this danger—evidence in this regard is documented here—but, unfortunately, my warnings were not heeded.

The bitter truth is I turned out to be right. But let me repeat that the era of change is not yet over; the fall of the USSR will have continuing international repercussions. It will be up to politicians and international public opinion to make them less turbulent and dangerous. I therefore regard it as my sacred duty to acquaint the international public with the real causes behind the political struggle waged in recent years in the Kremlin.

For a number of reasons discussed in the book, my position on vital issues of the country's renewal have frequently been distorted and have generally remained little known or even completely unknown to the world public. American readers will find in this book many facts previously unfamiliar to them, and I think they will be able to form their own conclusions. One of my purposes has been to fill in the gaps in foreign coverage of the events of Soviet perestroika stemming from frequently one-sided treatment in the Soviet and world press. In sum, much in the Kremlin was not quite the way it seemed, and some things were not at all as Gorbachev and those close to him at times portrayed them.

With these parting words, I entrust this book to American readers.

Yegor Ligachev
MARCH 1992

INSIDE
GORBACHEV'S
KREMLIN

One
INSIDE THE KREMLIN AND OLD SQUARE

For decades, the foreign press has written about the "secrets of the Kremlin," including under this rubric the process of decisionmaking at the highest level of the Soviet political leadership as well as the battle among advocates of different views of development and among top politicians aspiring to leadership. It is not at all surprising that such secrets exist. Political leaders in all countries must guard their activities from the excessive curiosity of the press and the assiduous attention of foreign political intelligence services. A natural effort to protect state interests dictates this. For example, we learned about the dramatic events that occurred in the White House during the Caribbean Crisis[1] only years later, from the memoirs of Kennedy family members.

But it is also quite natural that events occurring at the top level of every government have their own unique qualities rooted in that country's historic, political, and national traditions. These help us

---

[1]The Soviet term for the Cuban Missile Crisis.—TRANS.

understand better how new courses of action are developed; why an apparently direct and clear path may be interrupted by zigzags; and why the danger of an impasse may loom.

My book is now more or less complete. I printed out several copies and gave them to my close friends to read, in order to recheck my analyses. Then I decided to publish the beginning of one of the chapters about events inside the Kremlin (the highest political body of the country, the Politburo of the Central Committee of the Communist Party of the Soviet Union [hereafter simply Central Committee], held its meetings right in the Kremlin and, of course, in the Central Committee building on Old Square).[2] But the reader should not expect any sensational exposés, startling details, or disparaging characterizations of political figures in the style of the "confessions on a theme" that have appeared not too long ago.[3] This book is something else. It attempts a serious political analysis based on new facts, in addition to those already known to some extent to the reader.

A Late-Night Call

In April 1983, after seventeen years of work in the Siberian city of Tomsk, I was transferred to Moscow and appointed director of the Party Organization Department at the Central Committee, or to put it another way, the Department of Personnel and Party Committees. Under the system of Party-government rule that existed in those years, my position entailed dealing with the "cadres"[4] in the

---

[2]Literally *Staraya* (Old) Square, the former site of the Party's Central Committee. —TRANS.

[3]A reference to Boris Yeltsin's book *Against the Grain*, which was titled in the Russian original *Confession on an Assigned Theme*.—TRANS.

[4]Cadres were the skilled personnel indoctrinated in Communist ideology and methods, and in the broader sense, administrators of the planned economy.—TRANS.

broadest sense of that term, including those in the soviets[5] and economic management.

During this period, the general secretary of the Central Committee[6] was Yuri Andropov. I first became acquainted with him in February 1983. Our second meeting came in April of that year, when I was confirmed in my new post. Andropov categorically rejected his predecessors' practice of selecting the leading cadres on the basis of personal loyalty, choosing only people with whom they had previously worked.

A list of the people Andropov relied on is enough to prove this point. Gorbachev was from the North Caucasus; Nikolai Ryzhkov,[7] from the Ural Mountains; Vitaly Vorotnikov, from Central Russia; Victor Chebrikov,[8] from Ukraine; and Ligachev, from Siberia. Not that Andropov's selections were made randomly. Nor was it by chance that I came to his attention when it was time to find a director for one of the key departments in the Central Committee.

It was a member of the Politburo who proposed me as a candidate to Andropov and actively promoted my transfer to Moscow. Events in those memorable days of April 1983 unfolded unexpectedly and rapidly. I flew to the capital for a meeting on agriculture chaired personally by Andropov. In the Sverdlovsk Hall of the Kremlin, the members of the Politburo gathered along with the secretaries of the Central Committee and the provinces[9] as well as many agricultural planners. These were the people involved with carrying out the food program adopted the previous year. Since Gorbachev

---

[5]The soviet, or council, is the basic unit of government in the Soviet Union, both at the local level in villages, towns, and cities, and at the national level, where it is called the Supreme Soviet, or national legislature.—TRANS.

[6]Effectively, the head of government.—TRANS.

[7]Nikolai Ryzhkov became Soviet prime minister under Gorbachev but was forced to resign under public pressure in 1991.—TRANS.

[8]Viktor Chebrikov was chief of the KGB but was forced to resign in 1990.—TRANS.

[9]Literally *oblast,* an administrative division of territory in the USSR, equivalent to a province or county.—TRANS.

occasionally dealt with agricultural problems during this period, he gave a report at the meeting. He was brusque and pointed, criticizing both local administrators and the center.

I recall that I sent a note up to the presidium[10] of the meeting requesting the floor, although I didn't really expect to be allowed to speak. During the entire Brezhnev period, for the seventeen years that I had worked as first secretary of the Tomsk Province Party Committee, I had not managed to speak a single time at the Central Committee plenums. In the early years I regularly signed up on the speakers' list, but in time my hopes waned. I soon realized that only selected speakers were always allowed at the microphone, probably because they knew perfectly well what they ought to say, and how. I did not perceive any particular intrigues against me personally—many provincial Party secretaries were in the same position and had long and faithfully borne their heavy burden.

But with the advent of Andropov, the provincial Party secretaries immediately began to sense that changes had begun at the Central Committee. There were new hopes, and that was what moved me to send up that note.

Within the hour I was given the floor. As always, I had prepared some remarks beforehand—just in case. But I hardly glanced at the paper; I was speaking about everything I had lived through, how in seven or eight years Tomsk Province had gone from being a consumer of produce to a producer. I spoke of how the population of western Siberia was growing because oil and gas workers were coming into the region, and how they had to be fed primarily from local farming. And finally I recalled the harsh conditions of northwestern Siberia, and Narym Territory, once notorious for its slave labor, and the saying "God created heaven, but the devil made Narym." I mentioned Narym with a purpose: with Suslov,[11] I had

---

[10]The presidium is the collective chair of a meeting, seated at a table at the head of the hall. In Soviet practice, handwritten notes were sent up to the chair to request the floor.—TRANS.

[11]Mikhail Suslov (1902–82) was the chief Kremlin ideologist during the Brezhnev era.—TRANS.

long had in mind the idea of memorializing the victims of Stalinist persecution (more about this later).[12]

The Kremlin meeting finished at about 6:00 P.M., and I hurried to the Central Committee to settle some specific problems regarding Tomsk. As I recall, it wasn't until late in the evening that I finally made it back to my son's apartment to spend some time with him before flying back to Tomsk.

My flight was booked for the morning, and my ticket was already in my pocket. I intended to go to bed early. By Tomsk time, four hours ahead of Moscow, it was already early morning.

But at 10:00 P.M., the phone suddenly rang. The call was for me.

I took the receiver, not suspecting that this late-night phone call would change my whole life drastically and that the same kind of sudden late-night phone calls would sound, like the siren call of destiny, in February 1984, on the day Andropov died, and in March 1985, on the day Chernenko died. I took the receiver and heard:

"Yegor, this is Mikhail. . . . I need to see you in my office tomorrow."

Gorbachev and I had met in the early 1970s, when we happened to be in the same delegation traveling to Czechoslovakia. After that, at the Central Committee plenums and at Party congresses when all the provincial Party secretaries gathered in Moscow, we would always have a friendly conversation, exchanging opinions on both particular and general matters. When Gorbachev became a secretary of the Central Committee, and then a member of the Politburo, and then worked on agricultural problems, I began to visit him frequently. Moreover, given the habits of the top political leadership under Brezhnev, Gorbachev in those years was the only member of the Politburo who could be found in his office until late at night. This practice was of no little importance to a Siberian Party secretary who on his trips to Moscow spent from morning until night making the rounds of the ministries, trying to deal with matters of

---

[12]See Chapter 6.—TRANS.

petrochemical development and the food industry, extracting permits for building modern construction depots, science and cultural centers, and working on a multitude of individual problems involving the life and work of the people of Tomsk.

It was not hard to guess that Gorbachev himself had seen to it that I was allowed to speak at the Kremlin agricultural meeting. And when that phone rang late at night, my first thought was that he wanted to tell me his reaction. In the opinion of those who had approached me after the meeting, my speech had been on target. Yet now he was telling me to be in his office tomorrow.

"But Mikhail Sergeyevich, I already have my ticket in my pocket; I'm flying out early tomorrow," I replied.

It had long been our practice for Gorbachev to call me Yegor, while I spoke to him more formally, using his first name and patronymic.[13]

"You'll have to delay your departure, Yegor," Gorbachev said calmly. His tone made it clear that this phone call had nothing to do with the meeting earlier in the day. "You'll have to turn in your ticket."

"I understand; I'll be in your office tomorrow morning," I conceded without further debate, although in fact I didn't understand a thing.

It was not uncommon for a provincial Party secretary on business in the capital to have to change his flight and return his airplane ticket. In those years, I had to return my ticket and delay my departure back to Tomsk at least a dozen times for various mundane reasons. A meeting with a minister or director at the State Planning Committee would have to be rescheduled; a previously unplanned meeting would suddenly come up—all kinds of unexpected affairs could detain a provincial secretary in the capital, especially if he had come from more than three thousand miles away. Better to stay an extra day than have to fly to the capital again.

---

[13]Patronymics have been dropped throughout this book except for reported direct address and citations.—TRANS.

I could have shown up early, before 9:00 A.M., but I was completely puzzled about the purpose of the meeting. I knew from my own experience that each director started his workday with a briefing, reading emergency reports, and revising the planned schedule if unforeseen circumstances had arisen. Moreover, it was Thursday, and I knew that a Politburo meeting was always held on Thursdays at precisely 11:00 A.M. This custom had been established back in Lenin's day, and was preserved almost up until the 28th Party Congress.

I decided that the most convenient time for Gorbachev would be at 10:00 A.M., and on the stroke of the hour, I opened the door to the waiting room outside his office.

From that moment on, I began to calculate time differently. My life proceeded at a new tempo that made even my stormy Tomsk period pale in comparison.

Gorbachev received me right away, and after exchanging greetings, I was in for an immediate surprise.

"Yegor, people are of the opinion that you should be transferred to work in the Central Committee and assigned to direct the Party Organization Department. That's all I can tell you now. No more. Everything depends on how events develop. Andropov will be inviting you in for a talk. He asked me to go over this with you first, which I'm doing. This is an assignment from him."

Frankly, this troubled me. The matter was not as simple as it seemed at first glance. The problem was that the director of the Party Organization Department at that time was Ivan Kapitonov, a Central Committee secretary, and only the Central Committee plenum was authorized to make such an appointment. Moreover, Chernenko, second secretary of the Central Committee, was on vacation at the time. If he had been there, Gorbachev would hardly have interfered so decisively in personnel matters, especially concerning the post of the director of the Party Organization Department. Among members of the Politburo, there was an unwritten but inviolable pecking order, and you were not to interfere in personnel assignments if they were not part of your duties. I myself later observed this rule strictly; it went a long way to preventing

direct influence on the selection of cadres by any individual Politburo member, and left that right to the general secretary, the second
secretary, and, of course, the Politburo as a whole, since the final
decision was made collegially.

But since events were taking an unusual course, it was clear to
me that Gorbachev had Andropov's trust. And there were other
considerations. I was first asked to work on the Central Committee
in 1961, in the postcult period,[14] when Stalin-era accusations of
Trotskyism[15] were no longer a "blot on my record" barring me from
working in the central government. To give my background briefly,
in the 1950s I had been secretary of a district Party committee in
the city of Novosibirsk, the same district where the famous
Akademgorodok[16] was built. During the whole start-up period of
Akademgorodok, I worked side by side with Mikhail Lavrentyev,
Khristianovich, Guri Marchuk, Gersh Budker, and other prominent
Soviet scientists, from whom I learned a great deal. Subsequently,
I was appointed ideology secretary of the Novosibirsk Province
Party Committee. It was from that position that I was invited to
work in the Central Committee as deputy director of the Depart-
ment of Agitation and Propaganda of the Central Committee Bureau for the RSFSR.[17] Later, after the reorganization that shook
up the Party apparat[18] in those years, I was appointed deputy director of the bureau's Party Organization Department.

For the first two or three years, I found work in the Central
Committee interesting. I was involved in many different matters,
and I came to have a deeper understanding of many social issues.
I went through a period of great intellectual growth. But gradually

[14]The Stalin era was designated the "cult of personality" period in 1956 by then general
secretary Nikita Khrushchev (1894–1971). The term continues to be used.—TRANS.

[15]See Chapter 6 for a discussion of these accusations.—TRANS.

[16]Academic City, an elite community of scholars and scientists in the Siberian city of
Novosibirsk.—TRANS.

[17]Russian Soviet Federal Socialist Republic—i.e., the Republic of Russia.—TRANS.

[18]The apparat was the appointed staff, or Secretariat, of the Party and functioned as
the machinery of state.—TRANS.

I came to yearn for real work with people. I began to lose interest in my job, became depressed and tense, would come home in the evenings in a foul mood. In 1965, after consulting with my wife, I wrote a letter to Brezhnev asking him to send me to do Party work somewhere far away from Moscow, preferably Siberia. (The phrase "somewhere far away from Moscow" wasn't actually in the letter, but I'd had a frank talk beforehand with my immediate supervisor, Kapitonov, the director of the Party Organization Department, and he supported me.)

In the post-Stalin period, the "rotation" of leading Party cadres—that is, their transfer from the center to the provinces and back—was done for a purpose: I would say it was like the movement of the tides. When Khrushchev was finally established in power, he sent his opponents, Vyacheslav Molotov, Georgy Malenkov, Nikolai Bulganin, and Lazar Kaganovich into political oblivion. Then, in 1959, he began a new cycle of replacement of Moscow cadres. Many Party workers were sent away from Moscow under various pretexts. Kapitonov, first secretary of the Moscow Province Party Committee, was sent to work in Ivanovo; Marchenko, the second secretary of that committee, was moved to Tomsk; and so forth.

Under Brezhnev, the process moved in reverse. By 1964, Kapitonov was back in Moscow and had been made director of the Party Organization Department. Marchenko was recalled from Tomsk to the capital. In general, Brezhnev brought together the people who had been dispersed by Khrushchev, and, in turn, dispersed those whom Khrushchev had gathered.

This "tidal" tendency did not affect me. My connections with the Khrushchev team were limited to riding to work in the government car along with Burlatsky[19] and Arbatov.[20] Burlatsky, as people joked

---

[19]Fyodor Burlatsky, a speechwriter for Khrushchev, was a prominent essayist and parliamentary figure in the years of perestroika. He resigned as editor of *Literaturnaya gazeta* after the coup.—TRANS.

[20]Georgy Arbatov has remained the head of the Institute for U.S.A. and Canada since the Brezhnev era.—TRANS.

then behind his back, was the baggage handler on that team—and he didn't even carry Khrushchev's suitcases, only those of his son-in-law, Alexei Adzhubei. (With the passing of years, everything seems to look different. One gets the idea that Burlatsky was Khrushchev's chief adviser, while for some reason hardly anything is heard of Adzhubei.)

A brief digression: In June 1985, I was brought a letter from Adzhubei addressed to the Central Committee in which he expressed support for the new course and requested that ideology chief Suslov's restrictions on publishing under his own name be removed. I hadn't known that such untacit bans existed, and I was shocked: could people really be treated this way? Could a journalist really be prohibited from publishing under his own name? Of course, I showed this letter to Gorbachev, and we resolved the matter favorably. Adzhubei began to publish again in newspapers and journals under his own name. But for some reasons unclear to me, he never really did return to public life. It's possible that some of the very secondary members of the old Khrushchev team stood in his way. After all, Adzhubei's political "resurrection" would have lowered their own status as their roles were downgraded in the public eye from those of Khrushchev's main advisers to something more in keeping with reality.

Getting back to the events of 1965, I had no doubt that my letter to Brezhnev concerning my transfer would be reviewed rapidly. At that time, few people wanted to leave Moscow and move to the provinces, let alone Siberia. But for me it would be the third move from Moscow to Siberia.

Even so, a week went by, then two, then three; and still no news from the top. A month later I received a summons to the general secretary's[21] office. Kapitonov was present as well. I understood that my case must have been resolved favorably in advance; the

---

[21]Strictly speaking, in those years Leonid Brezhnev was first secretary of the Central Committee, although for the sake of simplification I am calling his position by the title later customary.—AUTHOR

gensek[22] did not invite people into his office to turn them down. But I still didn't know where they would be sending me.

Brezhnev, who in those years was energetic and businesslike, said: "Sit down. . . . You were probably worried that we took so long to invite you here. But you weren't the problem; everything's clear about you, we know you. . . . There was a holdup with Marchenko; it took us a long time to find him a spot. So you're asking to go to Siberia? We've been thinking about it here and we've decided to send you to Tomsk. How would you like that?"

The fact that they were sending me to Siberia was good news. But I wasn't particularly happy about Tomsk. I knew that Tomsk Province was a remote area far from the major highways. Its secretary spent his time dozing, dreaming of when he would be returned to the capital, and affairs in his province reflected it.

Naturally, I kept all these concerns to myself and immediately gave my consent. When I left the *gensek*'s office, I thought that it wasn't such a bad alternative. At least you could work to your heart's content in this Siberian province and learn what you were really capable of doing.

Now, with the distance of time, I can say that the Tomsk period was the most interesting and wonderful in my life, and spiritually uplifting. If I had never worked anywhere else, I would still have reason to consider my life a success and myself a fortunate man. There were many difficult days, of course, and it was sometimes impossible to find a free hour for myself, but not a single one was depressing. Perhaps most important, I was fortunate to meet some remarkable people in those years. And without real comrades by your side, a person's life is empty. I remember in 1983, when I was flying to Moscow and members of the local Party bureau came to see me off, I bade them farewell, saying: "Oh, yes . . . seventeen years isn't seventeen seconds. . . ."

But I'm getting ahead of myself again. That morning's unexpected news from Gorbachev reminded me immediately of the events of

---

[22]Familiar Russian abbreviation of *generalny sekretar,* or general secretary.—TRANS.

1964–65, when Kapitonov came to the Central Committee. I could see that a new stage was at last beginning in the Party; the replacement of the director of the Party Organization Department was patent proof. It was strange to think that fate had ordained it so—seventeen years earlier, as I "rotated from below" Kapitonov to Siberia, I never could have imagined that I was destined to replace him. Kapitonov actually wasn't a bad fellow, but objectively speaking, regardless of his personal qualities, the person who had managed personnel under Brezhnev and Andropov obviously had to go.

Meanwhile, Gorbachev was picking up the *kukushka*,[23] the direct telephone connecting the general secretary with members of the Politburo.

"Yuri Vladimirovich, I have Ligachev in my office. When can you receive him? . . . All right, I'll tell him."

Gorbachev hung up the receiver and said to me cheerfully: "Andropov will see you right now. Go on. Well, what can I say but good luck, Yegor."

I went up to the fifth floor and to office No. 6, traditionally occupied by the general secretary. I was sixty-two years old; I had a difficult life behind me, with its full share of drama. I'd accumulated a good bit of political experience through the decades. At various times I'd found myself speaking with the top Soviet leaders as well as—twice—with Mao Zedong. Tomsk Province had confidently "taken off." On the whole, I had confidence in my own worth. But my chief strength was that I wasn't personally ambitious. What kind of career could I have, anyway, at age sixty-two? Although because of my healthy lifestyle I was in great physical shape and ready to shoulder any load, because of my age, I was no longer preoccupied with my future, and I had no wild-eyed notions regarding a possible new appointment to Moscow.

Every age has its strengths and weaknesses. When a man is over sixty, fussiness and preoccupation with daily cares give way to an

---

[23]Literally "the cuckoo," so called because of the noise the telephone makes.—TRANS.

understanding of what his life has been all about. True, not every person is fated to experience these internal, spiritual transformations, but I am very attracted to the thoughts of Lev Tolstoy, who wrote that when a person reaches the peak of his years, he leaves behind personal ambition and has the opportunity to concentrate completely on his sense of civil responsibility toward the Fatherland. (Tolstoy associated this spiritual transformation with the fifties, but this was in the last century, and today life expectancy has increased.)

The highest echelon of power needs leaders of all ages; the healthy arrogance of younger people is just as necessary an element as the experience and good judgment that come with age. I don't agree completely with the dubbing of the Brezhnev period, "the years of stagnation." True, the Party leadership clearly was topheavy with politicians of advanced age who no longer had any future and whose only concern was to hold on to power. For this, "stagnation" is the right word. But across our vast country as a whole, the picture was far more varied.

In those years, in our East, enormous national economic projects were launched, including the world-class Western Siberian Petroleum and Gas Works and Petrochemical Plant. In the European part of the country, the Volga and Kama automobile plants and other manufacturing centers were built. In the 1960s and 1970s, the gross national product increased fourfold, housing more than threefold. Military and strategic parity with the United States was achieved. The efforts of many people kept the country moving forward, although in later years the Brezhnev administration noticeably reduced the rate of economic growth. Abuse of power spread, discipline faltered, and entire regions of the country were immune from criticism.

I would sum it up this way: The stagnation was not in the workplace, but in the leading political body of the country—and in Marxist-Leninist theory as well. As a result, the country remained poised at the threshold of the next stage of the scientific and technological revolution. The developed countries of the world completed this transition in the 1970s, but we kept marking time. This missed opportunity had a dire effect on our country's development.

Our leaders bear a large part of the blame for this, as do the leading social scientists who focused their attention on demonstrating the merits of so-called developed socialism while overlooking the central problem of the last third of the twentieth century, the next stage of the scientific and technological revolution. More to the point, these social scientists included a number of academics who would later talk loudly about stagnation and proclaim themselves champions of perestroika.

In the 1950s I had the fortune to work with a number of the most prominent Soviet scientists in Akademgorodok. In Tomsk, we also devoted much attention to establishing academic centers. The reputation of Tomsk University, the first in Siberia, continues to grow, and Tomsk is today a major science and higher education center. Many famous Soviet scientists came to Tomsk to help set up a network of scientific and medical institutions. I have always had a good number of acquaintances in the world of science, and they kept me informed of what was going on in and around the academic Olympus. They shared with me their concern that insufficient attention was being paid to issues of scientific and technological progress.

Obviously, stagnation must be discussed in the same way as any other sociopolitical phenomenon. In some places and spheres it flourished; elsewhere, life continued to move forward. To be honest, I resist universal political labels—they are part of the legacy of the Stalin era, and many have remained lodged in our public consciousness. Truth is specific. Any attempt to explain everything in life, past and present, with a single word or symbol is no more than a propaganda trick. We've all been through the "cosmopolitanism" and "voluntarism" of the past. "Stagnation" is a term out of the same prosecutor's lexicon, if softened by the circumstances of the time.

I stress this point because in 1983, when Andropov became general secretary, I, like many other provincial Party secretaries, was impatient for change, uncomfortably aware that the country was headed for social and economic disaster. We really had to harness ourselves to a new cause and drag the nation back on course. I took it as a good sign that under Andropov (a wise man whose health unfortunately was very poor), the political importance of the young and energetic Gorbachev began to increase rapidly. And since some role for me was a part of their plans—extremely important, I have to say, but still a supporting player, not a leading role or a career— I was prepared to accept it without hesitation.

It was time to get down to work! The change in personnel planned by Andropov and Gorbachev was historically inevitable. I was sent to accomplish a very practical task, albeit often a thankless one. But it had to be done.

I had no ulterior motives. I figured that the job I was being offered would be my last one, and I was internally prepared to put my shoulder to the wheel and make things pleasant for good people and hot for evil ones.

That was the mood with which I entered Andropov's office. He received me immediately, asking: "Did Gorbachev speak with you?"

"Yes."

"I will be making a recommendation to the Politburo that you be made director of the Party Organization Department. How does that sound to you? We've looked you over pretty well. . . ."

There was no reason to ask superfluous questions. I answered briefly:

"I accept. Thank you for your confidence."

"Then we'll confirm you today at eleven o'clock at the Politburo."

"Today? Like that?" I blurted out involuntarily. I had expected almost anything, but not such a rapid turn of events.

"Why wait? We have to get down to work. . . ."

The entire conversation took about ten minutes. Leaving Andropov's office, I glanced at my watch and saw that I might not make it to the Kremlin in time for the Politburo meeting. The *gensek* would be traveling in a car, but I would have to rely on my own two feet. I could hardly be late for such a Politburo meeting; as a rule they opened with discussion of these very types of personnel assignments. There simply wasn't any time left to look back in on Gorbachev and tell him about the conversation with Andropov. Besides, Gorbachev had probably already left for the Kremlin, since members of the Politburo usually gathered in the Walnut Room before the *gensek* arrived.

I went straight downstairs, came out on Old Square, and strode quickly along Kuibyshev Street toward the Kremlin.

Andropov

Members of the Politburo gathered for meetings in the Kremlin on the third floor of an old building with high ceilings and high windows overlooking the Kremlin wall. Red Square and Lenin's mausoleum were nearby. Of course, the internal layout of this part of the Government Building has undergone substantial changes. The rooms have been remodeled, and all types of communication lines have been installed. This building contained the Politburo conference hall, the Kremlin office of the general secretary, and his waiting room, as well as the Walnut Room, which had a large, round table at which members of the top political leadership exchanged opinions before the meetings. Here, preliminary discussions, unofficial, without minutes or a transcript, would go on about the most important and most complicated issues on the agenda. At times the actual session would not begin at eleven on the dot, but fifteen or twenty minutes later. Candidate members of the Politburo and Central Committee secretaries also took part in the meetings, but they would go directly to an oblong hall and take their regular (unofficial) places at a long table. Guests were seated at small tables along the wall.

In addition to the Kremlin conference hall, as in many other countries, there was the so-called command post, where, in the event of extraordinary circumstances, members of the top political leadership could also meet. The hope was that this reserve command post would never have to be used.

In the last years of the Brezhnev era, Politburo meetings were short and rapid-moving—within an hour, sometimes forty minutes, previously prepared decisions were passed, and everyone would go home. Under Andropov, however, the top political leadership began to work at full strength. The discussions lasted for hours. There were no breaks, and they usually got by with just sandwiches and tea. Under Gorbachev, a lunch break was instituted, and everyone went down to the second floor and dined together at a long table. Lively informal discussion of various questions, including those on the agenda, would continue, and opinions would also be shared on articles in the press, new plays, television broadcasts, and trips around the country.

As a provincial first secretary, I'd had occasion to attend meetings of the Politburo. Hurrying along Kuibyshev Street to the Kremlin, I ran over how the conversation might go, what questions I would be asked, and how I would answer them. I was completely calm. I was confident that the general secretary would be able to push through his plan. Most important, I had no personal stake in moving to Moscow. I was happy with my work in Tomsk, Gorbachev's proposal was unanticipated and sudden, and my feelings in those moments boiled down to: whatever will be, will be.

True, I was still interested in how the question of Kapitonov would be resolved. But, of course, such issues are well thought through in advance. When it came time for the review of personnel questions, Andropov spoke:

"There is a proposal to appoint Yegor Kuzmich Ligachev as director of the Party Organization Department, and Comrade Kapitonov will be assigned to the area of consumer goods production and sale. You know how much significance we assign to this most important area of work. Comrade Ligachev has experience working in a factory, in the Young Communist League, and in the soviets. He has also worked in the Central Committee. [Andropov placed particular emphasis on this point.] That means he knows the work of the Central Committee apparat. How will we proceed, comrades?"

"How many years did he work in Tomsk?" someone asked.

"Seventeen," someone replied.

I corrected them lightly: "Seventeen and a half. . . ."

Andropov smiled. They confirmed me and gave me their blessing, but suddenly Nikolai Tikhonov asked me with feigned seriousness:

"Now, what am I going to do?" Seeing that I didn't understand the question, he went on: "You gave me some assignments, didn't you? So now what am I supposed to do?"

Then, turning to Andropov, he explained. "Ligachev was in my office two days ago to discuss building a concert hall in Tomsk and opening a fourth academic institute, for materials science. I promised to help him out. But now he's leaving Tomsk. . . ."

Andropov understood the joke perfectly, and answered in the same vein: "Well, now, the chairman of the Council of Ministers will have to fulfill the assignments and we will leave the new department director, Comrade Ligachev, to check up on it."

On that light note, my case was finished. By the way, both the concert hall and the academic institute are now operating in Tomsk.

When I left the Politburo meeting hall, it was approximately 11:30 A.M. Only about an hour and a half had passed since the conversation with Gorbachev, but my life had changed course drastically.

Frankly, I don't remember how I spent the rest of that day. But the next morning, yet another surprise awaited me. I stopped in Gorbachev's office to compare notes briefly with him, and he commented: "You know, Gromyko supported you strongly. It happened like this: Andropov, Gromyko, and I were discussing the candidate for the post of Organization Department director, and I said we needed someone like Ligachev. I was pleasantly surprised when Gromyko immediately supported the idea. 'I know about him,' he said. 'He's a worthy candidate.' This was maybe about two months ago. Well, you know how it is; time was needed to clarify things, and so on. You know that Andropov studies the cadres thoroughly."

The support from Gromyko really was unexpected. It surprised me; we weren't personally acquainted, and we'd never met or talked. In fact, I would have supposed that Gromyko knew nothing about me and had only heard my name mentioned. And now it turned out that the dean of the Politburo was backing me. Why? How had he learned about me?

I mulled it over and remembered how at the very beginning of the 1980s, I'd been proposed as a candidate for ambassador to one of the prestigious European countries. Suslov and Rusakov made a motion at the Politburo to this effect. Zimyanin told me about this at one point, emphasizing that the motion had been heartily supported. He then said in praise: "You see, they appointed you ambassador to a good country and didn't even ask you. That means they know and respect you. . . ."

But I didn't let the joke go on.

"Well, it's too bad they didn't ask me, since I don't intend to leave Siberia."

"Well, what can you do now? The decision's already been made in principle."

"Just wait and see. They can't send me any farther away than Siberia, and they can't assign me to a post any lower than secretary of a local Party organization. And that suits me just fine."

Soon after that conversation I was summoned to Suslov. Kapitonov was also in the office, and they both spoke about my appointment to the ambassadorship as a *fait accompli*. Moreover, they spoke about it as a promotion, a sign of great confidence and reward for good work in the difficult conditions of Siberia. But I refused categorically, which irritated Suslov. He didn't pay any attention to my arguments, and when we said good-bye, he left no hope that the decision would be changed.

On the plane to Tomsk the next day, I thought it all over thoroughly and decided not to waste any time in sending a personal appeal to Brezhnev. I immediately set about drafting a petition to him. I wrote that I didn't want to go abroad, and wanted to work in Siberia. I loved that land, and it was there that I felt at home.

My letter was finished by the time the plane landed in Tomsk. I handed it directly to the director of the Party Committee General Department[24] to be typed. It was sent the same day by courier to Moscow.

---

[24]At both the local and national levels, the General Department of the Party was responsible for communications and correspondence within the Politburo and Central

Two days later, Chernenko called me. "Leonid Ilyich has read the letter. The question has been decided in your favor. You can go on working in peace."

This closed the case of my transfer to the diplomatic service. I hadn't seen anyone in the Foreign Affairs Ministry, and no one from their staff had held any discussions with me about my possible assignment. But Gromyko apparently remembered the whole story very well and understood my refusal in his own way. He preferred to send abroad as ambassadors professional diplomats who had passed through elementary schooling in his department. But the Central Committee apparat occasionally imposed other candidates on him. My categorical refusal to work abroad—and in a prestigious European country to boot!—must have been a unique case. And it was firmly lodged in Gromyko's memory.

Later, when I became more closely acquainted with Gromyko, I learned that I'd guessed correctly. But even then, in 1984, I had no idea what trust he vested in me. For at the dramatic moment of Chernenko's death, when the selection of a new general secretary became urgent, I was the one with whom Gromyko decided to consult.

I will describe this in detail later. But getting back to the sequence of events, after my confirmation as Organization Department head, I was forced to remain in Moscow to start work. A few days later, we marked the anniversary of the birth of Lenin, and when we met in the Kremlin Palace of Congresses for a celebration, I unexpectedly ended up in the presidium. People in Tomsk had not yet heard of my new appointment, and they later told me how surprised they had been to see me on television.

Soon afterward, I asked Andropov's permission to travel to Tomsk to wind up my affairs as secretary. Andropov replied: "You'll go there only when you've named the person you recommend to take your place as first secretary."

"Yuri Vladimirovich," I said to Andropov, "there is the second

---

Committee, the processing of citizens' complaints, the issuing of Party cards, and the maintenance of Party archives.—Trans.

secretary, Melnikov, and other comrades who are completely prepared to take up the direction of the provincial Party organization."

"Do you have so many people ready to take your place?"

"I have a few."

And that was the truth, I'll say it right here, and I'm proud of it. The Tomsk Party organization had developed an atmosphere of healthy competition in which people could prove themselves in their work and rise rapidly. Everyone knew that I did not tolerate bootlicking or play favorites. The cadres were promoted exclusively on their professional and personal qualifications.

A rapid renewal of Party and economic cadres had indeed been under way since spring 1983. Unfortunately, toward the end of his career, Brezhnev and those close to him were preoccupied with the problem of cadre stability, which made certain useful people to all intents and purposes "untouchable." Some people held on to their posts for fifteen or twenty years and concentrated on looking out for their own wellbeing. These people often were kept on not because of their competence but because they had good connections with top government officials in Moscow. They had a whole system worked out for reporting to the higher-ups, and knew how to cover up each other's failings and extol individual successes. They knew how to invite members of the Politburo or Central Committee secretaries to their districts at the right time to obtain their favor.

When we met during the plenums, Party congresses, and Moscow conferences, the provincial secretaries would, of course, compare notes. Each of us had struck up ties and friendships. We knew how to size each other up and it was natural that the "workhorses," the true professionals, grouped together, while those who attained honors and posts through personal connections, favors, and homage to higher-ups clung to one another. In seventeen years in the Secretariat of Tomsk Province I got to know many other provincial secretaries well. Among our Party ranks, we knew the personal proclivities of each person: who had a weakness for alcohol, who was particularly notable for bootlicking, and so on. This knowledge of people came in very handy later when I had to decide personnel matters.

And it was precisely with the renewal of Party cadres that

Andropov began. This policy, which slowed down somewhat under Chernenko, picked up new energy under Gorbachev.

I ended up with the unpleasant mission of telling people that they had to submit their resignations. In many cases—officials who were not all that bad but had passed their usefulness owing to age or health—I really suffered, taking ages to prepare myself for the unpleasant conversation. I always conducted it kindly, making certain to recall all the pluses the person had in his record so as to soften somewhat the inevitable blow.

However, in other cases I was forced to have harsh talks with people. It was under Andropov that I was forced to enter into a 1983 battle with Rashidov that I will describe in detail later in this book.

We each had a specific role to play. When someone had to be advised to retire, I would have a talk with him and absorb the psychological blow of his initial reaction. For new assignments and promotions, Gorbachev would invite people in to see him and give them the good news. I took no offense in this division of roles. I thought it completely necessary. Gorbachev was ten years younger and already a member of the Politburo, and I naturally believed it was in the interests of the Party and the country that I help and support him. In 1983, under Andropov, Gorbachev was beginning to be seen as the successor. Under those circumstances, my job was completely clear. I was obliged to shoulder the unpleasant part of the work of renewing cadres. I saw this as an important element of friendly, collegial work. Who could have known then that this work would later grow much more difficult, and then be cut off?

Meanwhile, the process of replacing the leading cadres was proving to be a complicated affair. Its progress was fraught with difficulty. Some provincial secretaries, despite their quite respectable ages, clung to their posts, writing complaints to members of the Politburo, although resolution of their cases was long overdue. In some cases there were material considerations quite understandably significant to the individuals involved.

The problem was that under Brezhnev, Party officials' pensions often depended on their connections with some individual member of the Politburo and Brezhnev himself. This rule, or to be more precise, *mis*rule, obviously reinforced the dependency of local officials on the center and their relations with the Moscow bosses. Everything was decided by the degree of personal favor. Pensions were a subjective matter. The secretaries who worked the most selflessly, who did not pay attention to personal connections with the Central Committee, were left high and dry when they reached pension age.

During those feverish months I often repeated a well-known saying whose author I frankly do not recall: "If you want to have an army fit for battle, don't spare the pensions for the generals."

In early 1984, the USSR Council of Ministers passed a resolution that the pensions of Party and soviet workers should be established on an objective, legal basis. That was the end of "discretionary" pensions.

Rather than go into detail about the difficult personnel matters of that time, which caused me such anguish, let me just cite a chapter on me in a book by the Finnish political scientist I. Iivonen, *Portraits of the New Soviet Leadership,* in which he writes:

> Ligachev's first job was to carry out the "Andropov revolution" among the leaders of provincial Party organizations. By the end of 1983, about 20 percent of the first secretaries of provincial Party committees had been replaced, 22 percent of the members of the Council of Ministers, and also a significant portion of the highest leadership of the Central Committee apparat (directors and deputy directors of departments). These shuffles to a great extent made it possible to consolidate the Andropov innovations. In December 1983, Ligachev became a full-fledged member of the Central Committee apparat. His area of activity was also extended; he now increasingly took positions on both the preparation and review of ideological issues. The election of Yegor Ligachev as a member of the Politburo and chief ideologue of the Party revived the traditional discussion of whether he was a "liberal" or a "conservative." In some Western analyses of spring 1985, it was noted that in Soviet culture, more free opinions began to appear, and

that the well-educated and well-read Ligachev was well disposed to the efforts of cultural figures and the intelligentsia in general. Approximately the same estimations of Andropov had been made in 1982. . . .

As to the percentages of replacements of officials, the Finnish political scientist was close to the truth. But the mention that in December 1983 I was elected as secretary to the Central Committee deserves special comment.

Once again, everything began with Gorbachev. The December Central Committee plenary was approaching, and one day Gorbachev said to me: "Yegor, I'm adamant that you be elected secretary to the Central Committee. The plenum is coming up soon, and I'm putting special effort into this question."

In the past six months, Gorbachev and I had grown even closer. We'd tested each other on the job. Our relationship had reached the point where we could understand each other with a single word, and our conversation was always frank and direct.

So I wasn't surprised when a few days later an aide to Andropov called me: "Yegor Kuzmich, you're to go see Yuri Vladimirovich. He'd like you to come today at 6:00 P.M."

Andropov was severely ill by then and hospitalized, and he no longer chaired the Politburo meetings. I had only the vaguest idea of how and where we were to meet. I said as much to the aide.

"A car will come for you and take you there," he replied.

I remember it was December. Dusk came early, and as we drove through Moscow, the streetlights were already lit. I reflected on the events of the last months. Andropov's political course was already defined: perfecting socialism and maintaining continuity in policy based on the best the people's labor had achieved. We had to rid ourselves determinedly of the aforementioned negative accumulations that subsequently became known as "stagnation phenomena."

I knew that after his election as general secretary, Andropov had received tens of thousands of telegrams and letters with requests to strengthen discipline and order and increase the accountability of officials. And Andropov responded to this cry of the people. "The Andropov Year" remains in the popular memory as a time when order was installed in the interests of simple folk. The central issue was how to make effective use of our country's vast potential. Andropov possessed the rare, true leader's gift of translating general tasks into the language of concrete jobs. He had a handle on such key matters as the relationship between the rates of economic growth and productivity of labor and wages, and the balance between the gross national product and the population's income. For him, these were questions of primary political importance.

As a department director, I often had to report to Andropov about the state of affairs in key aspects of day-to-day government affairs. Andropov would usually start out by saying: "Tell us, now, Yegor Kuzmich, where do we stand?"

Andropov would often begin his work sessions with such phrases as "Give us an analysis of where we stand. Evaluate the current situation." And then he would add: "Let's go after that problem now."

And we would really "go after" some problem, chasing down tea and biscuits at the same time. If it was just the two of us talking, Andropov would very often end our discussion with the following words: "Well, now, I've had a look at you. . . ." This phrase evidently had a meaning known to Andropov alone. I think he ended his meetings with other people with the same words.

I must make the point that no matter how broadly one interprets the notion of "reinstatement of order," to reduce "The Andropov Year" just to this demand alone would be incorrect and one-sided. Andropov had a clear vision of the prospects for the country's development, and he disliked improvisation and a hit-or-miss approach. Rather, on the basis of what had been achieved previously and the creative development of Marxist-Leninist theory, he planned the renewal of socialism, understanding that it needed some deep, qualitative changes. Andropov considered this process an objective necessity. He would often say: "We simply cannot get around this. . . ."

Andropov also paid great attention to the development of our political system. But here, too, he considered it necessary to start by consulting the people. It was Andropov who introduced the practice of holding preliminary discussions of Party and government decisions in work collectives and factories.

Although I cannot enumerate all of Andropov's ideas here, in this book I will have occasion to return frequently to this memorable year, when a great power began to turn toward a new course. Although his health gave Andropov little time, he left a deep imprint on history, and the people remember and honor him. The people accepted his challenge: Aim for deeds, not loud words.

The car taking me to see Andropov turned up Rublyovskoye Avenue. Accompanying me was a comrade from the Ninth Directorate of the KGB in charge of security for the government. He told me we were going to Kuntsevo Hospital. We went through the main gates, turned left, and drove up to a pair of identical small two-story buildings. We went up to the second floor and took off our coats, and I was shown the way to Andropov's hospital room.

The room was very modest—a bed with some sort of medical equipment next to it, and a hanging IV. A man was seated at a little table against the wall.

At first, shaken by his appearance, I wasn't certain that this was Andropov: perhaps this was a comrade who would take me to him?

But no, it was Andropov. Illness had changed his features beyond recognition. A quiet but familiar voice—they say an adult's voice never changes throughout his entire life—invited me in. "Yegor Kuzmich, come in, sit down."

I sat down on the chair that had been made ready for me, but for several minutes I could not collect myself, so startled was I by the drastic change in Andropov's appearance. His face truly bore the imprint of imminent death. Andropov apparently sensed my agitation, but I hoped he attributed it to other reasons, perhaps simply nerves. Surprisingly, he began to reassure me:

"Take it easy, tell me about your work. What are your problems?"

I had known that I would be meeting with a sick man, that it would be harmful to overtire him, and I'd prepared an answer that would not take more than ten minutes. But Andropov interrupted me after seven: "Well, all right, that's enough. . . . I invited you here to tell you that at the next plenum the Politburo will be discussing the question of electing you a secretary of the Central Committee." And here he shifted to the formal form of address and semi-officially added, "You have turned out to be a real find for us."

Tea was brought in, and we talked leisurely for another fifteen minutes about current domestic affairs. Andropov was not dressed in hospital attire, but was informal in a sweatshirt and striped pajama bottoms. Gazing closely at him, I still didn't recognize the Andropov I had been accustomed to seeing at work. Outwardly, he appeared to be a completely different man, and my heart was wrenched with pity for him. I understood that his strength was running out.

We said good-bye calmly, kissing each other on the cheek. I never had another chance to see Andropov alive, and I will always remember that December evening in the hospital room.

The plenum took place several days later, and I was elected a secretary of the Central Committee. The nomination was made by Chernenko, who was chairing the session and who made reference to Andropov's opinion. Chernenko did not talk with me before the plenum, nor did he invite me to the Politburo meeting, where there was a preliminary review of the matter. Later Gorbachev described the meeting to me: "The Politburo members very well received the proposal to elect you as secretary. Gromyko and Ustinov in particular supported you."

When I came back to my office after the plenum, the comrade from the Ninth Directorate of the KGB who had driven me to the hospital was sitting in my waiting room. He had been assigned to me. That evening, Western radio stations broadcast a report of my appointment, accompanying it with the following commentary: "The new Central Committee secretary, Ligachev, is ascetic, modest in his lifestyle, and came to Moscow six months ago with only one suitcase."

Surprisingly, they were absolutely correct. How had they learned that I'd arrived in Moscow with only one suitcase and with a thick sheaf of handwritten speeches and reports accumulated over seventeen years in Tomsk?

Soon afterward preparations began for the elections to the USSR

Supreme Soviet, and I flew to Tomsk for a pre-election speech. I stayed at a familiar place, a dacha at the Blue Cliff. There, another telephone call from Gorbachev found me on the evening of 9 February 1984:

"Yegor, there's been a misfortune. Andropov has died. Fly back here. Be in Moscow by tomorrow morning. You're needed here."

The official coded message about Andropov's death didn't reach the Tomsk Province Party Committee until the next morning. By that time I was already back in Moscow.

We wrote the obituary that morning in Zimyanin's office. There were five or six people; among them I recall Leonid Zamyatin, Arkady Volsky, an aide to Andropov, and someone else. When we wrote that Andropov was "an outstanding Party and government figure," someone expressed doubt: "Aren't we exaggerating Andropov's role? He was *gensek* for a very short time, little more than a year."

But I objected: "It's not a question of time or eras but of progress and results."

Lenin has an interesting idea that "historical merits are judged not by what historical figures *did not give* in comparison with contemporary demands but by what they *gave that was new* in comparison with their predecessors."[25]

Chernenko was chosen general secretary without any problem. Tikhonov, chairman of the Council of Ministers, nominated him as candidate at the plenum, he was supported, and everything proceeded smoothly. There was a hitch somewhat later, when, at an organizational meeting of the Politburo, Chernenko proposed assigning Gorbachev to chair the meetings of the Central Committee Secretariat. Chernenko apparently understood that an energetic, youthful, and physically strong person was needed for this.

However, not all the members of the Politburo held such a sane point of view. Tikhonov immediately reacted to the *gensek*'s proposal: "Gorbachev will turn the Secretariat meetings into a colle-

---

[25]Vladimir I. Lenin, *Polnoye sobraniye sochineniy* [*Complete Works*], Vol. 2, p. 178.— TRANS.

gium of the Ministry of Agriculture and will push only agricultural issues there."

Clearly, this was only a formal pretext to dismiss Gorbachev's candidacy, but someone else immediately took it up and there were several other remarks expressing doubt. But Marshal Ustinov spoke up in favor of the general secretary's proposal.

And then Gromyko took the floor. Making use of his diplomatic experience, he proposed a Solomonic solution to dissipate the tension that had arisen: "Let's give this some thought, let's not be hasty. We'll come back to this question later."

But the rather phlegmatic Chernenko, with his weak health, suddenly displayed some character, and said firmly:

"Nevertheless, I am going to insist that you support my proposal to entrust the chairing of the Secretariat to Comrade Gorbachev."

Yes, that is precisely how it happened. You cannot rewrite the lyrics of a song. Although Chernenko and Gorbachev were never close, it was Chernenko who decided to nominate Gorbachev to the unofficial second-ranking post in the highest Party hierarchy, adamantly insisting on this line and finally getting his way. Chernenko was far from the simple and unambiguous type portrayed by some journalists in the perestroika period. Although ill-wishers whispered all sorts of bad things about Gorbachev in his ear, he managed to distinguish truth from hearsay. And under Chernenko, albeit not without some complications, Gorbachev's role continued to grow.

I want to add that Gorbachev and I conducted ourselves extremely honestly with Chernenko. And as for certain difficulties I will discuss later, I think Chernenko had nothing to do with them.

But the situation was far more serious than I realized at the time. As Gorbachev himself later would note, in 1984 there were people in the Ministry of Internal Affairs whose job apparently was to find compromising material on Gorbachev from the Stavropol period of his career.[26]

---

[26]The first part of this chapter was published in the Soviet weeklies *Veteran* (No. 4) and *Argumenty i fakty* (Nos. 3, 4, 5, 6) in 1991.—AUTHOR

The Leader's Health

The hitch that occurred at the Politburo meeting when Chernenko proposed assigning management of the Central Committee Secretariat to Gorbachev was an indication that new times were beginning after "The Andropov Year." Actually, it would be more precise to say old times, not new. The Brezhnev team of Politburo members had remained almost intact, and much began to revert to the old ways. I don't want to portray this generation of politicians in a uniformly dark light; there were some talented, very professional people among them. But even among those who could have been considered progressive by the notions of that time, Andropov stood out. He looked ahead, beyond the bounds of his own life; and this, in Churchill's well-known words, is what distinguishes the true statesman from the politician who is concerned only about the outcome of the next elections.

After Andropov had passed away and Chernenko had taken his place, it was predictable that intrigues would begin against Andropov's protégés, first and foremost against the Politburo's youngest member, Gorbachev, who was viewed as the successor to Andropov's reformist ideas.

And so it happened. Thus the thirteen months of Chernenko's term proceeded; and thus, when he died, was Gorbachev chosen general secretary against a difficult and at times dramatic background. But before going on to this, I'd like to cite a passage on this subject from Yeltsin's *Against the Grain:*

> Gorbachev's election as general secretary at the March 1985 plenum of the Central Committee has given rise to a large crop of rumors about that election and the origins of *perestroika.* One of these declares that the four Politburo members who supported Gorbachev's candidacy decided the fate of the country. Ligachev said this in so many words at the June 1988 party conference. In my opinion, by doing so he simply insulted Gorbachev and, indeed, everyone who took part in the election of the general secretary. There was, of course, a fight. Grishin's list of the Politburo members who would support him had

been found. He had drawn it up when he was aiming to become the leader of the party. He did not include Gorbachev among his supporters; nor were many other Politburo members included.

In fact, on that occasion it was the plenum of the Central Committee that decided who was to be general secretary. Practically all the participants in that plenum, including many senior, experienced first secretaries, considered that the Grishin platform was unacceptable, that it would have meant the immediate end of both the party and the country. Within a short space of time he would have succeeded in causing the USSR's entire party organization to shrivel into nothing, just as he had done with the party structure in Moscow. This simply could not be allowed to happen. Furthermore, it was impossible to overlook the defects of Grishin's personality: his smugness, his blinkered self-assurance, his sense of his own infallibility, and his thirst for power.

A large number of first secretaries agreed that of all of the Politburo members, the man to be promoted to the post of general secretary had to be Gorbachev. He was the most energetic, the best-educated, and the most suitable from the point of view of age. We decided to put our weight behind him. We conferred with several Politburo members, including Ligachev.[27] Our position coincided with his, because he was as afraid of Grishin as we were. Once it had become clear that this was the majority view, we decided that if any other candidate was put forward—Grishin, Romanov, or anyone else—we would oppose him *en bloc*. And defeat him.

Evidently the discussions within the Politburo itself followed along these lines. Those Politburo members who attended that session were aware of our firm intentions, and Gromyko, too, supported our point of view. It was Gromyko who spoke at the plenum and proposed Gorbachev. . . .[28]

---

[27]Yeltsin here includes me as a member of the Politburo, although at that time I was a secretary of the Central Committee.—AUTHOR

[28]From *Against the Grain*, trans. Michael Glenny (New York, 1990), pp. 137–39.—TRANS.

Yeltsin's words require commentary.

I personally had never heard that "Grishin's list of the Politburo members who would support him had been found." Gorbachev never spoke of this, neither publicly nor in private with those close to him. Common sense says that this claim is at best dubious. Why make up a list when it's easy enough to memorize the names of a Politburo whose members can be counted on your fingertips? Where did they find the list? Who found it? Did they make a search of Grishin's office? After March and April of 1985, Grishin remained in the Politburo, and preceded Yeltsin as first secretary of the Moscow City Party Committee. The list sounds too much like a street rumor. I repeat: at that time I was working in Moscow as a Central Committee secretary, and I never heard a thing about this. Of course, it's possible that in Sverdlovsk, where Boris Yeltsin was working at the time, they knew more than we did about what was happening in the Kremlin.

It is also important to note that Yeltsin speculates about what was going on in the Politburo from the vantage point of "appearances." I will come back to his point about the myth, which deserves special attention.

To understand the "thirteen months of Chernenko" better, I think it is worth describing the person who held the post of general secretary. Very little is known about him in our country or the world at large. Konstantin Chernenko was a classic apparatchik—from head to toe, to his very marrow. He'd spent decades working in offices, at a respectful distance from real life. He was with Brezhnev in Moldavia, then in the Central Committee, after that in the USSR Supreme Soviet; then back in the Central Committee. I would call Chernenko a virtuoso apparatchik, which had its pluses for a career at that time, but drawbacks for a political figure. That is to say, as long as Chernenko remained in Brezhnev's shadow, the art of the apparatchik was his strong suit. But when he began to transform himself into an independent political figure, his removal from real life proved a liability. Nevertheless, even in this period he made a number of sensible, thoughtful, unselfish decisions, chief of which was the promotion of Gorbachev to the Party's second post.

The provincial Party secretaries respected Chernenko when he was director of the Central Committee General Department because he was attentive to their urgent requests from the provinces. If you came to him, told him all about a problem, and then left him a well-reasoned memorandum outlining the essence of the problem, you could rest assured that he would see it through and extract the general secretary's signature. Chernenko was surely in his proper place in this important post in the Central Committee apparat. In addition to his professional qualities, he had to his credit such human traits as responsiveness and a genuine desire to help people.

It is particularly important to note that Chernenko, who was unusually close to Brezhnev and had enormous influence on him at the time, somehow "contrived"—I use that word advisedly— not to sully his own reputation with corruption. Abuse was rife surrounding Brezhnev, and Chernenko had plenty of opportunities to have been up to his neck in corruption. A wink or a nod, and he would have been showered with souvenirs of gratitude. But Chernenko was very modest in his lifestyle and manner. Frankly, I was surprised how he managed under immense pressure from those who loved to give presents not only to resist temptation but also to preserve his influence: a corrupt element usually rejects such foreign bodies. In order not to be drawn into corruption, Chernenko really had to have displayed some spine.

Yes, it would be wrong and untruthful to draw a distorted picture of Chernenko, as some are now trying to do. The fate of this man could be called tragic, for given his health and political and life experience, he was not prepared to take the post of general secretary. His misfortune was to have acceded to the pressure from certain forces to become general secretary in his sunset years, as his strength was waning.

Another trait of Chernenko's seems to me to have been at play here. In a strange, mysterious way, combined with his modesty in life, he loved awards and homages. No sooner was he chosen as general secretary than the same figures who'd become skilled in manufacturing Brezhnev's memoirs were bustling about with similar books by Chernenko. The comrades in Krasnoyarsk came up with memories of his work in their territory; someone spoke up about the border guards where Chernenko had once served—and he did not protest. That was his weakness, perhaps the soft point of a bureaucratic politician who had spent most of his life in the shadows, unknown. But was Chernenko alone in suffering from this weakness? Isn't this the "professional disease" of other bureaucratic figures now in office, who have never directed large organizations or collectives, have never had to bear the burden of a leader, but have made their careers through intrigues in the corridors of power? These bureaucratic politicians have another professional disease in common with Chernenko. Owing to his inclination for office work and papers, and his scant knowledge of real life, he had few direct dealings with workers, peasants, and the scientific and technological intelligentsia.

Here we are talking about disease in the metaphoric sense. But given the events of the Chernenko period, I feel compelled to pay some attention to the question of a leader's physical health. Apropos of this, former French president Valéry Giscard d'Estaing begins his memoirs, recently published in the Soviet Union under the title *Power and Life,* with a chapter titled "The Leader's Health."

In his opinion, the cares of state require enormous effort from a leader, both spiritual and physical strength. Whether a country's politics are active or passive, balanced or impulsive depends on the physical health of the heads of state, government, ministries, and lower-ranking officials. The health of a government figure, particularly of a leader, is not merely a private affair but also a subject of concern and interest for the entire society, since it directly influences the fate of the country and the people.

It is from this standpoint that Giscard, recalling his meetings with Brezhnev at the end of the 1970s, asks: How could a sick person rule such a big country?

The state of health of the general secretary of the Communist Party was long considered a taboo subject. Everyone understood that Chernenko was seriously ill. But it was considered unethical to speak about this in the Central Committee offices, although in private conversations the question interested many people. There were rumors, for example, that medical specialists could make an approximate diagnosis of a disease based on the person's appearance during a live television broadcast, and that their diagnosis was quite unsettling for Chernenko.

In my view, the fact that neither the Party nor the Central Committee members were kept informed about the health of the general secretary was a serious violation of internal Party democracy. In light of the system of Party-government rule that existed in those years, then it was a violation of democratic procedures in general. As I have said, in all developed, civilized countries the state of the leader's health is a subject of public interest. There can be no secrets here, and any rumors in this regard should be refuted immediately and firmly. Rumors that go undenied constitute a problem in themselves.

Such has long been the practice in all civilized democratic countries. But in ours, everything was different.

The results of Chernenko's medical exams were considered ultrasecret. Everything was done to portray his health in a rosy light. On the other hand, the general secretary was kept fully informed about the state of health of each member of the Politburo. Academician Yevgeny Chazov, the head of the Fourth Main Directorate of the USSR Ministry of Health, reported to Chernenko all deviations from the norm that showed up in medical exams of members of the Politburo, Central Committee members, and ministers. The practice at the time was for the Fourth Directorate to provide Politburo members' families with personal physicians who did not so much treat their patients as observe their health and bring in consultants in case of necessity. Thus Chazov knew the medical problems of all members of the highest political leadership and reported on them all the way to the top.

It is incumbent upon me to note that Chazov, a major organizer of the Soviet health system, did achieve a great deal, not so much for the government directorate, as for the development of medical science as a whole. Chazov came to see us in Tomsk many times, and helped set up affiliates of major All-Union medical centers for cardiology, pharmacology, and mental health. Thanks to his energy, Muscovites were able to outfit the Tomsk affiliates handsomely and give them a channel for cooperation with leading foreign medical centers: Chazov is well thought of in Siberia as a man who did things not for the VIPs but for the people. He supported the well-known Tomsk Medical School, which was continued by such organizers of Siberian health care as R. S. Karpov, A. I. Potapov, E. D. Goldberg, and others.

Chazov also accomplished a good deal in the post of USSR minister of health. Unfortunately, an automobile accident left him unable to bear the heavy burden of a ministerial post, and he then returned to the cardiology center he had created.

But as chief of the Fourth Directorate of the USSR Health Ministry, Chazov naturally played by the time-honored rules of the medical game. The health of the country's leader was one of the central Party and state secrets. Of course, we surmised that the *gensek* was getting frequent treatments during the workday right in the Central Committee building. Afterward, he'd look ruddy and more energetic, but it would last for only an hour or so.

Chernenko's severe illness, which left no doubt of a rapid and sorrowful outcome, initiated certain processes in the top echelon of the Party leadership. Another round was imminent in the power struggle surrounding the choice of a new general secretary. Recalling that difficult year, I keep coming back to the thought that the health of a government or Party leader is a vital element in the formation of policy. In developed countries there is a longstanding practice that candidates for the highest government posts must provide medical certificates. In the United States, for example, every operation that Ronald Reagan underwent, even if insignificant or done only in a doctor's office, was covered widely in the press. But in our country, bulletins on the leaders' state of health appeared only when their case was already extremely critical or the outcome was hopeless.

I think it is time for us to learn how to treat the question of leaders' health calmly, like adults. We should not allow it to become ground for unsettling rumors. We must establish compulsory procedures that would enable us to evaluate objectively and dispassionately a leader's physical and mental capabilities. After all, the health of a person at this level, along with his intellectual, political, business ethical, and other qualities, is a guarantor of successful, sane policy.

Even the wisest politician cannot carry out his program if his health is poor—to wit, Andropov. A leader's waning strength hands his political subordinates—individuals and entire political circles—temptation and opportunities to manipulate him. That is what happened under Chernenko.

Favoring Political Ambitions

The replacement of the cadres begun under Andropov slowed but did not stop under Chernenko. The inherent nature of cadre work made purging the Party's leading ranks of those who abused their official posts a priority, and led us to the director of the General Administration Department of the Central Committee, Konstantin Bogolyubov.

Bogolyubov was especially close to Chernenko and enjoyed his complete trust. This strange generosity by the *gensek* gave me a look at Chernenko's ambiguous character. Chernenko was a modest man, while Bogolyubov clearly abused his high position—and yet, Chernenko trusted him. It's hard to fathom.

But whatever the case, I could not simply ignore Bogolyubov, one of the oldest, most powerful pillars of the apparat upon which, so to speak, rested some of the other high-ranking apparatchiks, all of whom personified the old order of Old Square. Gorbachev shared my opinion, and he and I would frequently discuss the "Bogolyubov problem." The man was arrogant, he boasted incessantly that he was not on the level of the other department directors but enjoyed the general secretary's special favor.

Under Andropov, Bogolyubov, who was usually well at his ease, would literally stand at attention when the *gensek* phoned him. I was once in his office when a call came in from Andropov, and I got a good look at the change that instantly came over Bogolyubov's face. After Andropov died, however, Bogolyubov apparently decided to make an unabashed grab for power.

I recall that in 1984, it was Bogolyubov's seventieth birthday, and the question arose concerning his awards. Gorbachev and I, yielding to pressure from Chernenko, our consciences twinging, were forced to give our consent to award Bogolyubov a prize. But even the chief award seemed too small for him, and he actually wangled out of Chernenko the award of Hero of Socialist Labor, which I learned about later only from the newspapers.

That was how it was, those were the ways of that time, and they bear witness to the fact that the "shower of stars" of the Brezhnev era, when the leaders bedecked each other with medals and prizes, was making a comeback.

The Bogolyubov story stretched on until soon after April 1985. Gorbachev somehow lost interest in it after he became general secretary, but to me it was a question of principle. I had no personal contact with Bogolyubov; he'd never crossed my path. But he personified the old-style ruling Party apparatchik, a bureaucrat not by rank, but at heart. He groveled before the strong and lorded it over the weak. Bogolyubov clearly had abused his power, and as long as he headed one of the most important departments of the Central Committee, it was a sign that the old apparat style had not been broken.

I can give an example of the Old Square apparat style of those years. Literally the day after I was appointed in April 1983 to direct the Organization Department, I was presented with a large, very ostentatious Chaika automobile. But I really didn't like the Chaika; for years, we'd had one in the garage of the Tomsk Province Party office, but we reserved it for visits of high-ranking Moscow guests. In my seventeen years in Tomsk, I never once used the Chaika. I rode in a Volga, or often in a Wazik—you won't find yourself dozing off in one of *those* incredibly rattling all-terrain vehicles. (Although I did know one former minister, with whom I used to drive hundreds of miles along the oil pipelines, who claimed to have accomplished that—he told me he'd acquired his ability to nap under any circumstances on roads at the front during the war.)

In short, I was not accustomed to a Chaika, I did not want to ride in one in Moscow, and I immediately appealed to G. S. Pavlov, the director of operations at the Central Committee: "I beg you to allocate me a Volga instead of a Chaika for my trips. I will be very grateful to you."

But his answer was sharp and unexpected. "What, you want to stick out? Everybody asks for a Chaika, and you aren't like everybody else? . . . Don't, Yegor Kuzmich, don't stick out, you'll put the other department directors in an uncomfortable position. Come on, let's do things the way you're supposed to for workers of your rank."

So that's it. Don't stick out. Back then, Pavlov was powerful enough simply to sweep away my objections. He did not allow himself to violate the apparat style of that era, which was jealously guarded by people like Bogolyubov.

Meanwhile, letters started to come into the Central Committee about the abuses tolerated by Bogolyubov. A tip from Kirghizia revealed that Bogolyubov, who was a deputy to the USSR Supreme Soviet from that republic, had flown there four times for meetings with voters in a special airplane. People rightly saw this as an abuse of his official position. An investigation turned up other serious abuses as well. It emerged that Bogolyubov's doctoral dissertation had been written for him by someone else. He had also procured a false certificate stating that he had taken part in military actions at the front in the years of the Great Patriotic War. And there was more.

Using his official position, Bogolyubov had managed to worm his way into a collective of specialists and receive a State Prize for installing pneumatic tube mail between the Central Committee Building on Old Square and the Kremlin. And he had been a Lenin Prize laureate, along with the architects and builders, for the design and construction of a Central Committee plenum conference hall. Did the hall's builders really rate a Lenin Prize?

For high-ranking Party workers, the question of prizes was not always simple. Efforts were often made to include them in a group of collective competitors in the hope that it increase the chances of their getting the prize. In many cases, Party leaders really did take a very active part in works displayed in competitions. I should mention that I, too, came very close to getting a state prize.

We had installed a large automated manufacturing system at one of the defense plants in Tomsk at a time when such projects depended to a large extent on the persistence of the Party Committee. My position on that score was well known—anything I can do to help—and I put a great deal of effort into expediting the supply of robots and electronic computers to the plant.

In 1986, when I was already a member of the Politburo, documents were brought for my signature concerning the award of the USSR State Prize to a group of Tomsk citizens for the installation of this system. My name was on the list. At that time, such documents went through the Central Committee Secretariat and the Politburo, and the draft of the decree had already been signed by almost all the Politburo members.

As soon as I saw my name among the laureates, I called Gorbachev and asked him to remove me from the list. But he categorically refused, justifying his refusal with the statement that the comrades from Tomsk knew better. There was nothing for me to do but cross my name off the list myself. And I did so, a fact that is known to Leonid Zaikov and Oleg Baklanov. The prize was awarded on a classified subject. Zaikov at that time was in charge of defense in the Politburo, and Baklanov was then minister of medium machine-building.[29]

It was not an easy decision, but I often had to review documents about the awarding of prizes and other high honors, and the fact that I'd turned down the state prize helped me to decide these troublesome and sometimes delicate questions impartially and ethically.

In 1986 we agreed in the Politburo not to give medals to members of the top political leadership. At that time we also agreed to refrain

---

[29]Medium Machine-Building was the cover term for the ministry involved in nuclear weapons manufacturing. Baklanov was later arrested as one of the August 1991 coup plotters.—TRANS.

from awarding any prizes. Each time I remember this and a host of other things, I think how right we were, how honestly and sincerely we began. . . .

But I digress. As for Bogolyubov, it turned out that he had received tens of thousands of rubles for a volume of Central Committee plenum resolutions published by Politizdat.[30] But the preparation of such publications was part of his official duties, and he had no right to receive money for these books. In fact, Politburo members of that period turned over the honoraria from their publications to the Party coffers. While I worked at the Central Committee, I never once took an honorarium for books and publications in newspapers and journals, and always turned them over to the Party account.

Bogolyubov had amassed an impressive collection of abuses, and as soon as the investigative commission handed Gorbachev its conclusions, the case was resolved, and Bogolyubov was expelled from the apparat in dishonor. The Party Committee of the Central Committee apparat also investigated Bogolyubov's abuses thoroughly, and expelled him from the Party.

My point in dwelling on this story is that the cleansing process—the self-purging of the Party—began *inside* the Party, right in its central apparat, and with the help of Communists of the apparat. The process was under way when perestroika was just taking its first steps, and when the practices of former years still flourished in other government and ruling structures. The Communist Party provided the example of self-cleansing, which, in my view, its current critics maliciously choose to forget, even as they themselves succumb increasingly to all sorts of abuses.

I recall that during this period I was given a translation of an article by the Moscow correspondent of the Italian newspaper *Corriere della sera,* with the headline "Ligachev Gorbachev's Influential Guardian of Dogma." The article said that "Ligachev has become Gorbachev's bulwark in the policy of renewal," that "Ligachev was

---

[30]A state publishing house.—TRANS.

the initiator of 'great purges' which were designed to bring new leaders into the highest Party offices, leaders who could really analyze the situation and who knew how to act." The correspondent later wrote: "A career that was slow to develop in its first stage made a vigorous leap when in 1983 Andropov 'summoned' Ligachev to Moscow. It was then that the alliance between Ligachev and Gorbachev was born. . . . That gave Ligachev the chance to battle most effectively corruption, inertia, and bureaucracy."

I quote these articles to illustrate the appraisal of the world press during the initial period of perestroika, which for some unfathomable reason was forgotten when psychological harassment was unleashed against me over the so-called Gdlyan Affair, which I will talk about later.[31]

But *I* wasn't the issue. The Italian correspondent was mistaken in ascribing to me the initiation of "great purges"; it was a collective demand of all the healthy forces in the Party that had awakened under Andropov and gained sway in the early period of perestroika, when Gorbachev headed the Communist Party.

The real drama of perestroika was that the process of self-cleansing of our society begun in the depths of the Communist Party, not only slowed down, but was, I would say, distorted. In place of the old corrupt elements that for decades had been festering in the body of the Communist Party and the society at large, suddenly, in the space of a year or two, came even more horrible and more absolutely corrupt forces that stifled the healthy start made in the Party and the country after April 1985. Like the rapidly multiplying Colorado beetles, which in a moment eat up all the green potato shoots in a field, these proliferating parasitic forces quickly gobbled up all the sprouts of perestroika. As a result, the country, which had risen up to renew itself, lost its balance and faltered. And now we see the country already falling into the abyss of crisis.

What are these forces? What is their nature? Who is behind them, and why did they attain such free range at the same time that the

---

[31]See Chapter 5.—TRANS.

Communist Party, which had begun the self-cleansing process, was bound hand and foot like Gulliver, virtually deprived of the opportunity to wage an active political struggle?

To comprehend fully the bitterness of the cup from which our nation has drunk, we must investigate calmly and thoroughly how perestroika was born, how it began, developed, and . . . disintegrated.

As I re-create the sequence of events, I would like to reinsert in history a Central Committee plenum that never took place, one that was supposed to be devoted to the scientific and technological revolution. Planning for this plenum had begun back in Brezhnev's day. Many people in the Party understood that we were on the threshold of a new scientific and technological revolution that would revitalize our concept of productive forces and relations. The developed countries of the West were just beginning to reorganize their industry and agriculture; with our enormous scientific, technological, and intellectual potential, we could have managed to get on the train of the revolution racing toward the third millennium.

But year after year passed, and the plenum was continually postponed. Unfortunately, as I have noted, some of our social scientists played a part in chilling interest in the most acute problems of the scientific and technological revolution. I recall a May 1975 article in the journal *Planovoye khozyaystvo* [*Planned Economy*] by academician Georgy Arbatov about the management of large national economic projects. It was of particular interest to us in Tomsk, as we happened to be hard at work building a petroleum and gas complex, designing automated management systems for the province's economy, and gearing up research and development. Arbatov's article said that in the United States, a vast amount of experience had been accumulated from mistakes, failures, and miscalculation in systems management, and we should learn from them. One of the most serious and common mistakes was "the enormous overestimation of the role of computers in management—'the electronic boom' which pushed into the background the organizational structures of management, decisionmaking methods, 'the human factor' in management, and so on. . . . An analysis of domestic and world experience allows us to conclude that automated systems of management are a subordinate element with regard to the organizational mechanism of management."

I will not try to debate specific, academic problems of management with an academician. But I must note here that by that time, our country had already invested billions of rubles in the development of automated systems. They had appeared as a separate line in the "Fundamental Directive" passed by several Communist Party congresses. Regrettably, attention to automated systems began to wane once they had been declared a "subordinate element" in management structures. This thesis gladdened the hearts of some of our leaders to whom automated systems posed a threat, and left the field wide open for those with the itch to reorganize. As a result, the enormous investments did not pay off. As for the overestimation of the "electronic boom" in the United States, no comment is necessary. The "mistaken" boom led to the rapid computerization of America, and we were left far behind the developed countries.

I am not about to say that a single article by an academician could seriously influence attitudes toward the prospects of developing automated systems. This opinion was shared by those "upstairs," and the priority such judgments awarded traditional administrative command management methods created the background against which the need for a Central Committee plenum on the scientific and technological revolution seemed less urgent. Moreover, the claim that the United States was making a serious mistake in getting carried away with the "electronic boom" set the minds of our leaders at ease.

Was this idea from across the ocean about the overestimation of the role of automated systems perhaps planted deliberately with the purpose of "easing our minds"?

In any case, it was not until 1984, under Chernenko, that the Politburo scheduled a Central Committee plenum on the science and technology revolution.

Gorbachev was assigned to report at the session. This was both an honor and a great responsibility. It was long-established tradition that whoever gave a report at a Central Committee plenum became an influential figure in the Communist Party. Given Chernenko's weak health, and the related overall instability in the highest echelons of power, such an assignment was viewed as an increase in Gorbachev's political weight in the Party and society.

Gorbachev began intensive preparations for the plenum. He unearthed materials that had been accumulating in the Central Committee for years. Assisted by Central Committee secretary Nikolai Ryzhkov, he consulted with scientists and industrialists. The main point of the report emerged very clearly: it was necessary to execute a technological leap to the new achievements of the scientific and technological revolution.

But in December 1984, shortly before the next Central Committee plenary, Gorbachev suddenly said to me: "You know, Yegor, opinion is beginning to take shape that the plenum on the scientific and technological revolution should be postponed. In fact, they are trying to dump the plenum. . . ."

We realized this new tendency meant only one thing: someone feared the strengthening of Gorbachev's position. I remember Gorbachev exclaiming angrily: "Can you believe it? Trying to dump a subject so important for the country? It's a crucial issue."

The explanation was obvious. Gorbachev knew that someone's personal political ambitions were at stake. We both knew all too well what was going on.

Soon afterward, Chernenko announced at a Politburo session: "The thought has been expressed that it would not be worthwhile to convene the plenum on scientific and technological progress at this time. On what rationale? It's obviously not appropriate to discuss such a major issue with a Party Congress imminent; we'll talk about it there." But the Congress was more than a year away.

Gorbachev was silent at that Politburo meeting. But would those who were determined to sink a plenum on the key issue for the country's destiny have listened in any case? It had all been worked out ahead of time, in offices, at dachas, or in conversations on the *vertushka*.[32] Everything had already been agreed upon by a small

---

[32]From the Russian verb *vertet*, to dial: the special direct-line internal government communications system.—TRANS.

group of Politburo members. Only later was it raised at an official session. The people who once again postponed the science and technology plenum were not thinking about the country's future, only about their own political ambitions.

Thus was buried yet another attempt to mobilize the country's greatest intellectual reserves to discuss the problems of the revolution knocking at the country's doors. Not until the middle of 1985 did an all-Party conference take place in the Kremlin on the problems of science, technology, and manufacturing. Gorbachev, now Party general secretary, gave a report. New times and approaches had been ushered in at last. It was decided that it would be appropriate to convene not a Central Committee plenum, but a conference with a long list of invitees.

That was the first real major action of the new Party leadership in practical implemention of perestroika. The overall direction was chosen very precisely. Moreover, the linchpin of this enormous effort was designated: exhaustive development of the machine-building industry, tool- and instrument-building, electronics, and automation. Priorities for investment were changed drastically; Machine-Building was allocated 200 billion rubles, more than the total for two previous five-year plans.

We needed to replenish funds for capital goods and reconstruct factories. This would assure accelerated economic growth and a resolution of social problems based on new technology. Here was a realistic path, undertaken in the 1970s by many developed Western countries who retreaded their industries to integrate them with new technological systems. This was the proper strategy of socioeconomic acceleration; to my mind the only correct one at this stage of the scientific and technological revolution.

If only we had taken that route; unfortunately, improvisations soon began to be made in policy. We made a serious mistake when we chose tactical alternatives for developing the economy. With prompting from some of the academic economists, the infamous political slogan *uskoreniye*, "acceleration," was coined: Go after immediate results. But things don't work that way. Chasing after instant performance to satisfy political directives is incompatible with renewing capital investments, in which the opposite occurs with growth rates temporarily decelerating as the impetus for a new technological base is established.

In other words, although we defined a correct strategy, we chose a mistaken, unrealistic tactic. As a result, a great deal of work on development of machine-building launched after the Kremlin conference gradually came to naught. The most important task was abandoned halfway. Instead of focusing attention on the technological revolution, as we had agreed to in 1985, we did little to stimulate introduction of the latest production technologies. On the contrary, we slowed the process to the danger point.

The call for acceleration was soon revealed to have been a mistake, and it disappeared from the agenda. We now plunged into the political problems of property ownership and then the market, hoping this would stimulate the economy. But the reality turned out to be quite different. Designing a means of introducing technological achievements into life remained a peripheral concern for both the public and top government officials. As in 1984—although of course for other reasons—the urgent problems of the technological revolution, and vital national interests, fell victim to shifting political whims and ambitions.

What knocked us from the true path we had chosen in April 1985?

This question is one of a series of fateful issues for perestroika that I will try to answer in this book.

Making the Connection

I have related how, when Andropov and Gorbachev assigned me the complex job of replacing the leading cadres in 1983, it was my thankless mission to be the first to inform people of their impending dismissal. This was the unpleasant part of my personnel work. But it was more than compensated for by the satisfaction I got from promoting capable, intelligent people. Konstantin Stanislavsky had the idea that a theater director should "die" into the actor, as it were disappear into him, completely expressing himself in the actor's work.

By analogy, I believe that a real Party worker should also "remain" in those people whom he helped to mature and temper in civic spirit. It really gives me joy to meet managers in whom I once incorporated a particle of my self and who have justified my confidence with honest, selfless work. Fortunately, there are many such occasions.

The official, bureaucratic term for this constant emotional drain is blandly called "cadre work." The corresponding Western term, "management training," has a different sound. But it's essentially the same thing. All over the world, enormous attention is paid to the nurturing of administrative cadres, whether in business schools or university centers preparing future politicians.

It's appropriate here to describe the ideology and practice of preparing administrative cadres during the Brezhnev period. The line at the time was clear: promote local cadres to the provincial offices. At first glance, this principle didn't seem so bad. But if you think about it, you can see it was insidious; it created a situation where it was hard for new major figures to rise—which suited the Moscow leadership just fine.

A major political figure was much more easily formed through work in both the provinces and the center. Being trapped within the bounds of a relatively small district, only rarely coming to the center, was psychologically limiting. It narrowed horizons. I know many provincial-level managers who had intellectual abilities and drive, and a wonderful knowledge of life, who could have become notable figures at the All-Union level. But they never completely unfurled their personal potential, because at some point they had been kept down and not allowed through the political crucible of the center.

The example of Gorbachev proves my point; although his destiny unfolded differently, when in his prime, he was transferred to Moscow following the death of Fyodor Kulakov, who had been in charge of agriculture in the Politburo. Gorbachev, too, could have gotten stuck at the provincial level had he not realized his potential.

In the Stalin era, local management cadres were transferred continually from one province to another, and people were tossed from place to place and never allowed to complete a job they had begun. This was dictated less by concern about their growth than by a fear that the management would grow attached to one area. Hence no area should be "overgrown" with a large number of like-minded comrades.

Both approaches—frequent reshuffling and the "freezing" of cadres in place—had a deleterious influence on the process of developing political leaders. When I was in charge of personnel in the Central Committee, I often criticized the Brezhnev line on this issue, although my own future had turned out successfully. I left Moscow for seventeen years in Siberia, and then returned to Moscow. But that was a rare exception, and besides, I chose my own Siberian destiny in 1965.

Unfortunately, the process of forming a governing team in the Party and the state was largely allowed to run its own course. This will come back to haunt us very painfully. The best thing would have been to combine both lines—to nurture managers in the provinces but not be afraid of inviting them to Moscow, promoting them then from the center to the provinces and republics. The idea would have been to propose and not impose.

I vested great hopes in the people's deputies of the Union and the republics. Unfortunately, with all the ruckus of the widely broadcast and unfulfillable promises and the slander of the Communist Party during the pre-election campaign, quite a few demagogues, loudmouths, and outright careerists appeared among the new deputies. On the whole, however, they include many genuinely intelligent people. Thanks to the rotation system, they will pass through a good school in the supreme soviets and will return to the provinces more politically matured, soon to emerge as real leaders. And for the center, that is good personnel policy.

It would have been good to revive the system of training political leaders in the Party. I say "revive" because, under Andropov, we were moving along that path. In the Central Committee apparat there had long existed the so-called inspectorate, a small subdivision called the "paradise floor," where mediocre workers who had not quite yet reached pension age waited out their terms "with dispensation from the top." Under Andropov, we quickly and decisively got rid of these people, and I proposed selecting as inspectors a group of young, energetic managers with good prospects, who could become political leaders in the future.

When I outlined my plan to the general secretary and asked for nine staff salaries, Andropov supported the idea completely. He added: "Take as many salaries as you need. If you need fifteen, we'll give you fifteen. It's all in a worthy cause."

And it really was a worthy cause. We decided that we would take people forty to fifty years old into the inspectorate for nine to twelve months, and searched all over the country in various republics to find the most promising workers.[33] Now, from the distance of a few years' time, I can say with complete authority that our choice was correct and very successful.

The individuals we selected have performed with distinction in the difficult political circumstances of recent years. Out of a single nest on Old Square came a whole constellation of political figures who went through basic political science training at the inspectorate and who later played a visible role in the public arena. And I am sure we have not heard the last from them, since they are just at the right age.

It is very unfortunate that the significance of the inspectorate for training the reserves of management personnel declined gradually. After the 28th Party Congress, the division was closed. Of course, approaches to promoting people changed. But if we look more closely, it was essentially a return to the "freezing" of cadres in the provinces.

In the years when Gorbachev and I began personnel perestroika on orders from Andropov, the attitude was very, very different.

---

[33]The renewal of the cadres proceeded rapidly, and there were cases when people invited to the inspectorate had to be sent to the territories and provinces within a month or two, since the need for people was so great.—AUTHOR

Yes, in those years, when work was very difficult for us but when we got along well running current affairs, we devoted our main attention to questions of the future. The Gorbachev-Ligachev connection under Andropov was determined fairly rapidly, just as the Italian correspondent said. We made no particular secret of it, since strictly professional considerations were behind it. It was visible to everyone and displayed in specific actions. Gorbachev inevitably supported me at the Politburo sessions, the doors of his office were always open to me, we met often and held many confidential talks. When Chernenko became general secretary, circumstances pushed us closer together; during this period, Andropov's protégés were in what I would call an unstable position.

The postponement of the Central Committee plenum on scientific and technological progress, where Gorbachev was supposed to give a report, was one illustration of this. In addition, a chill of sorts between the general secretary and Gorbachev began to be felt quite keenly. We sensed it from many signs: Chernenko began to hand out various assignments over Gorbachev's head; increasingly, he would go directly to the Central Committees on issues that normally were part of the job of the second in command.

Not only was this worrisome, but a kind of jealousy also began to appear, a desire to put Gorbachev in a different position.

Because of his health, the *gensek* was chairing the Politburo sessions much less frequently. When he attended, he would speak only briefly, from a written text. It was clear that it was very difficult for him and that each session turned into physical torture. But it was never known beforehand whether Chernenko would come to the next Politburo session, or whether the meeting would be chaired by Gorbachev, the second secretary. Suddenly, without notice, a half hour before the meeting, Gorbachev would be informed that the *gensek* was not coming and that he would have to chair the meeting.

These were very difficult moments. I know from my own experience how hard it is to chair a Politburo or Secretariat meeting and how carefully you must prepare. Even for one agenda item that is "yours," you often have to convene working meetings, consult with specialists, and arm yourself with a lot of statistical data. Chairing the meeting meant competence on all the agenda items, subjects that were all varied, but vital; minor problems were not discussed at Politburo meetings. But Chernenko gave Gorbachev only a half hour to prepare to chair the session. Yes, this was really a very severe test for Gorbachev. And if we take into account the fact that in the Politburo at the time there were people waiting for him to fail . . .

We sensed keenly a chill emanating from Chernenko. It became clear that someone was whispering all sorts of things against Gorbachev in his ear.

After thinking all this through, I said to Gorbachev: "Mikhail Sergeyevich, let me call Chernenko and clear things up with him directly. I'll tell him how you work and tell him not to believe the whisperers."

Gorbachev did not object. I began to prepare for the conversation, which seemed far from simple even from a formal point of view. At that time I was only a Central Committee secretary, and I was planning to speak with the general secretary on a very sensitive subject. I could not rule out the worst-case scenario, in which Chernenko would refuse to discuss the matter, and let me know it was over my head.

But there was a chance of success. After I transferred to work at the Central Committee—this happened in Chernenko's absence—my relations with him grew complicated. At first he treated me with caution. But since I had nothing up my sleeve, Chernenko apparently soon understood that he would not have to expect any unpleasantness from me. Our relations gradually improved. I sensed that after he became general secretary, he began to trust me more. When he became very ill and stayed at home, I would sometimes call him at his apartment to discuss important questions. Gorbachev often asked me to do this: "You'd better call Konstantin Ustinovich and check this with him."

Chernenko's wife, Lidiya, always came to the telephone. She impressed me as a modest and kind woman, and, unquestionably, a courageous one. She obviously realized that her husband's days were numbered, but never displayed her alarm, speaking cheerfully, each time replying to my careful question of whether I could speak to Chernenko: "Yegor Kuzmich, hold on a minute, I'll just ask Konstantin Ustinovich to come to the telephone. . . ."

And despite his frailty, Chernenko would take the receiver, and very briefly, so as not to tire him, I would obtain his approval on some matter.

But that memorable telephone conversation was unusually long. The general secretary apparently understood its special importance. He wasn't concerned with sparing his health. I think his aides had reported to him that some Politburo members, taking advantage of the frequent absence of the general secretary, had gone back to the shortened workday of the pre-Andropov era and were not over-exerting themselves. Thus I related how Gorbachev worked very hard, from nine in the morning until nine at night, and spoke about how we would not and could not betray the general secretary.

"Konstantin Ustinovich," I said, "you know that I am from Si-beria and Gorbachev is from the northern Caucasus. Moreover, I just recently came to work at the Central Committee. We have no old connections. Yes, Gorbachev and I work well together, but this work is based on the interests of the job, only on the interests of the job. We have no other motives." And finally, I burst out: "Kon-stantin Ustinovich, if someone is telling you differently, don't be-lieve it! Just don't believe it—Gorbachev is working from morning till night for the sake of the cause, and not for anything else."

I did most of the talking. Chernenko did not ask me any ques-tions. After hearing my heated monologue, he answered simply and briefly: "I believe you, Yegor Kuzmich. We will consider that this conversation took place." And on that note, we said good-bye.

Of course I reported this to Gorbachev, and he was sincerely grateful to me.

As I recall that telephone conversation with Chernenko today, I can with a clean conscience say that I acted with the utmost sincerity. Given the general secretary's illness, the situation in the highest echelon of the Party leadership had become increasingly unstable. Gorbachev and I sensed that there were people inside the Politburo who had begun active preparation for a rapid, inevitable redis-tribution of authority to seize power. The atmosphere around

Gorbachev was such that confidential conversations in his office, especially concerning Chernenko's illness, were made very difficult. We took this into account. There were times when we could not say some things aloud, but wrote to each other on scraps of paper.

My personal relations with such Politburo members as Grigory Romanov, former first secretary of the Leningrad Province Party Committee, and Viktor Grishin, head of the Moscow Party Committee, had become strained. We were different kinds of people, and we had different outlooks on our past positions in society. But on the whole, I felt fairly secure and confident in the Secretariat of the Central Committee. I've already mentioned the attitude Gromyko, dean of the Politburo, had toward me. But I had also established good relations with Nikolai Tikhonov. A fair amount of time has passed since then, and I can say without false modesty that the chairman of the Council of Ministers obviously valued me in a purely professional sense. This had come out in the memorable winter of 1984–85, of which I will speak later. And I've already written about the attitude of General Secretary Chernenko.

In short, I could not help but understand that no particular danger was hanging over me personally. But it was abundantly clear that the growing struggle for power affected the fate of the Party and the country. In my view, only Gorbachev was worthy of occupying the highest post of general secretary of the Central Committee of the Communist Party, and that corresponded with the interests of the Party and the government. That was my sincere, deep conviction, which prevailed over my personal motivations, including considerations of my own safety.

Unfortunately, some of the high-ranking apparatchiks with long tenure were accustomed from time immemorial to checking which way the wind is blowing. For strictly personal motives, they adjusted their relations with higher-ups, including Politburo members, according to their current "rating",[34] whether the general secretary

---

[34]In the perestroika era, *reyting*, a new word in Soviet political parlance, usually meant the ranking assigned to political figures based on public opinion polls and magazine letter campaigns.—TRANS.

was well disposed to a certain official. If he found fault with the person, the reaction among the apparatchiks followed suit. Later, I myself was to suffer the full blast of this attitude characteristic of the entrenched pillars of the apparat. And true to tradition, at the end of 1984, the apparat atmosphere around Gorbachev began to seem like a kind of vacuum. I think Gorbachev himself sensed it, but it was particularly noticeable from the outside. The seasoned old Brezhnev-era officials at first hesitated, not knowing where to place their chips, but then definitely did not take Gorbachev's side.

For reasons of principle, I was relieved of such a choice: I was guided by convictions, not calculations. Many provincial first secretaries also took such a firm position, supporting Gorbachev because they wanted to get the job done. I would put it this way: those who really wanted to work were for Gorbachev; those who wove political and apparat intrigues were against him.

It was this overall situation, not my own personal relations with Gorbachev, that led me to have a candid and frank conversation with Chernenko. To his credit, he not only accepted the conversation but also drew the right conclusions from it. Soon we began to sense the chill between the general secretary and Gorbachev beginning to thaw.

And then an event occurred that tipped the circumstances back in our favor. Chernenko was feeling poorly, and often stayed at home in bed. He announced one day, "The doctors advise me to go to Kislovodsk for treatment. Apparently I will have to obey that advice." But on the sixth or seventh day in Kislovodsk, the general secretary's health declined sharply. He was immediately flown back to Moscow and taken directly to the central clinic hospital in Kuntsevo.

I learned of this later, when the Central Committee received official notice that the general secretary was in the hospital. Grishin had stepped up his activities greatly in this period, beginning to claim almost openly a leading role in the Politburo. We also knew that someone was making attempts to meet with the *gensek* in the hospital, over doctors' objections, and even though Chernenko himself did not want to receive anyone.

I am only writing about facts personally known to me. I cannot rule out the possibility that some members of the Politburo did visit Chernenko in the hospital and speak with him, but I do not know of any such occasion.

I can, however, provide details on the events in which I personally took part. I recall Gorbachev telephoning me and saying briefly, but in a very serious tone, "Yegor, you and I have to go see Konstantin Ustinovich in the hospital. I've made the arrangements. We'll go at six o'clock."

But before describing the details of that singularly important visit to the severely ill Chernenko, in the same hospital cottage where I had last spoken with Andropov (or perhaps a neighboring cottage— they are indistinguishable and it hardly makes any difference), let me mention several other events during that memorable winter.

The winter of 1984–85 was unusually frigid, with snowdrifts in some districts six or eight feet high. Because of the bitter cold and heavy snowfalls, industry and transportation began to break down. It would not be an exaggeration to say that the national economy was on the brink of paralysis. I remember the situation during those months very well. Fifty-four of the largest electric heating plants, our main source of energy, were on the verge of having to shut down their boilers, which were fed by loads of coal coming directly from freight trains. Hundreds of abandoned trains idled in the railyards: 22,000 freight cars had stopped dead on access routes, and it seemed impossible to unload them, since their freight had frozen solid. The government was preparing an emergency option in case of a disaster, and was hoping to shut down and take off-line hundreds of major plants using gas and fuel in order to secure light and heat for residential use and prevent apartments from freezing.

The situation was critical. We were talking about a major disaster that would affect almost three-fourths of the country, not just one region.

The Politburo and the government took desperate measures to prevent a catastrophe and to keep the country's energy system from collapsing. Clearly, the main priority was to maintain uninterrupted operation of the railroads.

Geidar Aliyev, Politburo member and deputy chairman of the Council of Ministers, and Vladimir Dolgikh, Central Committee secretary, were assigned to deal with the daily problems the unusually severe winter was heaping on the national economy. They set up an operations headquarters to coordinate measures to prevent economic paralysis and the stalling of the railroads. By decision of the Politburo, I was assigned to run this operations group. Nikolai Ryzhkov, another Central Committee secretary, also provided assistance.

At that time I was only a secretary of the Central Committee, formally a rank below members and candidate members of the Politburo. But Nikolai Tikhonov, chairman of the USSR Council of Ministers, had insisted on my assignment.

Tikhonov was a unique personality. A man of refined personal demeanor, he conducted himself independently and was able to assert his opinion. He knew the manufacturing industry very well, but in recent years had not traveled to the provinces and was cut off from daily economic problems. Further, his independent style often became an end in itself. At times, he placed his own point of view above the collective opinion and did not listen to intelligent arguments. Perhaps this was a reflection of his advanced years. Tikhonov no longer looked to the future, but narrowed his focus to immediate issues. When I spoke with him, I would often think that if he could just shed twenty years, he would make a good chairman of the Council of Ministers. But he was dangerously past his prime.

In 1989, Tikhonov sent Gorbachev a letter reminding Gorbachev that he had not taken Gorbachev's part at the 1984 Politburo session at which Chernenko had raised the question of assigning Gorbachev to run the Secretariat of the Central Committee. Under the influence of new circumstances, Tikhonov wrote, he had reviewed his previous point of view and decided that he had been wrong.

During the severe winter of 1984–85, the Politburo heard our reports on transportation and industry almost every week. And I remember Tikhonov exclaiming: "Why is this going on? Siberia has the most severe freezing weather, yet breakdowns hardly ever happen there. But we only get heavy frosts here once every ten years, and everything is on the brink of paralysis. Yegor Kuzmich, tell us how you managed to get through the severe winters in Siberia without all this feverish activity."

It was not hard to answer.

"Each time, we prepared very thoroughly for the winter—that's the secret," I said. "If you don't prepare for the frosts, then you won't get through a single winter."

During those difficult winter months, each week—or twice a week, if the situation required—we would conduct All-Union emergency conference-call meetings over the public address system. At the main control room of the Ministry of Transportation, we brought in the officials of that ministry and others, trade union leaders, and national inspectors, to resolve issues efficiently as they came in from the provinces. We invited thirty or forty people, including journalists. As they realized the use of such conference-call emergency meetings, more and more officials were drawn to them, and we soon had to limit the number of those attending.

On the other hand, the size of the audience on the other end of the conference call was unlimited. The Ministry of Transportation has a radio communications system throughout the railroads. In addition, the major coal mines, steel and chemical plants, central committees of republics, provincial Party committees, and provincial executive committees all joined the conference. Without any special order, almost all the leading Party and other officials of the regions threatened with economic paralysis voluntarily gathered at their communications posts. And somehow, also without giving an order, we developed a practice of energetically settling within an hour or so all the main problems requiring involvement from the center. We would then sign off the conference call, and people in the provinces would continue the discussion, coordinating specific tasks.

The persistent battle with the cold and snow lasted a hundred days and nights. The conference calls probably were remembered by tens of thousands of officials of various ranks. Throughout the most severe, freezing winter they constantly sensed the integrity of the national economic organism, and the calm, firm, organizing hand of the center, which enabled resources to be maneuvered and bottlenecks to be cleared. With the help of the operations head-quarters at the center, barriers between or among ministries were broken down. In a critical hour, people from the rail, steel, coal, and petroleum industries did not compete with each other but extended each other a hand. I can say with confidence that during that severe winter, only the political and economic unity of the country saved everyone from great disaster. If the railroads had halted in a snowed-under Russia, then in Ukraine, Kazakhstan, and everywhere else, plants would have shut down and people in the Caucasus, the Baltics, and Central Asia would have been without heat and electricity.

Nikolai Konarev, minister of transportation, always opened up the conference calls and reported carefully and critically on the situation throughout the rail system. That winter convinced me of the respect railroad workers had for Konarev, a selfless person and major organizer. It was no accident the railroads rebelled in 1989, when the USSR Supreme Soviet did not confirm Konarev as minister. Thousands of telegrams poured into Moscow from engineers, traffic controllers, dispatchers, and the stationmasters of local whistle stops. An entire army of railroad workers rose up in a kind of spontaneous collective ultimatum to demand Konarev's confirmation as minister. And he was confirmed.

At our meetings that winter, two or three transportation officials usually would report after Konarev. Some described how they managed to organize work under difficult conditions, others were asked sternly about breakdowns. Then there were questions from local districts. Some were resolved immediately right on the line; others were assigned to very careful follow-up. Then Aliyev would speak, and I usually ended the meeting with a brief summary. Let me say right away that the locals were not trying to undermine the role of the central ministries and economic agencies. It was a question of coordinating action under extreme conditions.

Since I was reporting two or three times a week to Gorbachev on the current situation in industry and transportation, I would

always mention assignments from Gorbachev during each conference call. The audience for these calls, as I said, was really enormous—practically the entire Party and economic management of
the country. I wanted Gorbachev's assignments to be known in the
provincial Party offices and to the Party activists of the soviets and
economic planning units.

As a result, the following picture of the Party leadership emerged
in the provinces. Grishin was on television all the time, emphasizing
his closeness to Chernenko and trying to instill the idea that he was
the successor to the general secretary. Meanwhile, Gorbachev was
quietly, without tooting his own horn, taking care of real business,
stabilizing the economy even in a critical situation.

That's how it really was.

I maintained the same line when I was on business trips that
winter in Novosibirsk, Barnaul, Biysk, Kuibyshev, and Togliatti.
Other Central Committee secretaries also went out to these cold
spots. In that extremely difficult winter, we coped collectively with
a situation on the verge of disaster. We learned lessons from it: how
to build new access routes, freight car heating stations, and mechanisms for snow removal—it was surprising how few of these had
been manufactured per year before that winter, although they were
so necessary in such a large country. But perhaps most important
was the friendly "extraministerial" work in a difficult situation,
which brought people together and imbued them with confidence.
In fact, all the economic losses of that winter were more than made
up that very same year.

Today, when I recall that turbulent epoch, I am bitter about how
unforgivably careless we were with the record harvest of 1990. In
the fall of 1990, weather conditions were poor in the fields. But
instead of putting all their efforts into supplying the country with
large amounts of grain, politicians of all ranks continued a zealous
struggle for power. The city turned away from the country.

How bitter and sad, when what we should have done was to
declare a two- or three-month moratorium on rallies and political
infighting. Since new, economically determined management methods had not yet been created, given the emergency, more effort
should have been spent on organizational work during the harvest

period. I am sure that the people would have understood and accepted this with an eye to results. And from a purely political point of view, it would have been expedient; the intended transition to a market economy would have proceeded more easily in a satisfied country than in a hungry one.

In the end, this did happen. In the face of complete economic collapse, it was decided to increase organizational work and maintain previous trade agreements throughout 1991. If such a decision had been made concerning the 1990 harvest, the people's later mood would have been very different. Alas, in the fall of 1990, the fate of the country was in the hands of bureaucratic politicians and office theoreticians removed from reality. These people do not know or love real life because it constantly interferes with their mental constructs. For decades, they have been sitting in Moscow or abroad. But at a certain stage in perestroika, they gained the upper hand. I really didn't recognize anymore the Gorbachev who had run things in the winter of 1984–85 and who was responsible for getting results.

We all recall how at harvest time the Moscow City Council organized political demonstrations instead of turning out people to bring in the record crops in which Muscovites had a direct interest. The Leningrad City Council gazed serenely at rotting vegetables, waving away the peasants' calls for help. That winter, when ration cards for potatoes were introduced in Leningrad, Mayor Anatoly Sobchak went on television to criticize his deputies for advising irresponsibly that the countryside not be helped to bring in the harvest. So many politicians worrying not about the matter at hand, but only about how to deflect blame from themselves more cleverly and dump it on others. Why should masses of people suffer because of them?

I had spent a lot of time working on agriculture in Siberia and the center. I know how complicated and mutually interdependent matters are in this area. Things can easily go wrong, especially when the weather interferes. No one is so dependent as the peasant on the whims of the heavens. But I know for a fact that in peak agricultural campaigns—and the 1990 harvest was one—everything depends on organization and coordination of actions. Time is of the essence.

The volume of work is enormous and the time pressure incredible. Meanwhile, the so-called democrats simply walked away from the real life of the harvest in the provinces, kicking up a fuss for political reasons, claiming that the collective farms were in no shape to bring in the harvest, and that this was fresh proof of their uselessness. They sat on their hands. In Western countries, when the weather is poor, the army helps farmers with the potato harvest. A day's work truly will feed you for a year—if you don't miss that day. The pathetic result of all these political gambles was the astonishing fact that in a year of record harvest, the country was forced to make enormous food purchases abroad.

The people suffered terribly as a result, and perestroika suffered a blow. The agricultural failure of 1990 impacted political processes negatively and aggravated the food problem and the social and economic crises.

Again, the economy was sacrificed to politics; and worse, to politics of the moment. As an old Russian proverb has it, they could not see the forest for the trees. Blinded by personal political ambitions, they lost sight of the main purpose, the good of the country.

In the fall of 1990, with a huge harvest ripening in the fields, a God-given opportunity to unite the nation with patriotic feeling in a real national cause was lost. Social forces had a common interest in bringing in all the crops, and the battle for the harvest could have become a uniting factor. Success could have dissipated society's pessimistic mood and inspired people with new faith. But no, the chance offered by nature itself was lost, and people talked away the great harvest in fruitless political discussions.

A remarkable opportunity was missed to achieve civic accord and, on that basis, to build a calm, smooth, crisis-free transition to new economic relations. In my view, the leadership of the country and the so-called democrats made a very serious political mistake in not paying sufficient attention to that special situation. It was a mistake that prefigured the country's further drastic plunge into crisis. If everyone had cooperated in bringing in the harvest, they would have been torn away from all those senseless demonstrations and returned to real life. But it didn't happen. . . .

During the memorable winter of 1984–85, with the danger of a crisis and disaster hanging over the country, the Party and government leaders acted completely differently—in concert, and firmly. We understood that such a style was important not only to resolve specific precrisis problems, but also in order to inspire public confidence. In the provinces, in difficult circumstances, it is truly terrible to lose faith in the organizing role of the center. In all countries, in critical situations, people's eyes turn to the central authorities. Central authority must take upon itself the responsibility for difficult decisions. If it makes weak decisions in critical situations and displays inconsistency, serious civic conflicts ensue.

This is a general principle of firm action by any government in an emergency. History confirms that for a country to fall into anarchy, the center must first be destroyed.

In the winter of 1984–85, the harmony of actions among leaders did not extend to the entire higher echelon of power, which at that time consisted of leaders largely incapable of action. A significant portion of the work in the Politburo, which was the highest political body of the country, lay on Gorbachev's shoulders.

Apparently the ailing Chernenko understood this. After our telephone conversation, and perhaps other events, he began to trust Gorbachev, and made his final selection. This is what prompted our meeting in the hospital—under the circumstances, clearly one of great significance.

Gorbachev and I traveled to Kuntsevo Hospital in his Zil. Along the way, we discussed the tactics for our conversation. We decided not to worry the general secretary by bringing up disagreements in the Politburo, but to concentrate on describing our work. In general, we decided to cheer him up and to keep the entire conversation on that note.

Chazov met us and led us to the second floor of the Kuntsevo cottage. Chernenko was waiting for us in a small room, where a table was laden with tea and cookies. He was in faded, old-fashioned striped pajamas. He looked ill, although somewhat better than we had expected. Apparently he had just been through his usual medical routine.

When Gorbachev started talking about our work together, Chernenko broke in: "I know all about that; my aides tell me." Then Chernenko asked how preparations were coming along for the next Central Committee plenum, and where the program and Party charter stood. Intensive work was under way on them at the time. We also discussed several important personnel matters.

I don't remember, but it seems we never even touched the tea, so engrossed were we in the discussion. But within twenty or thirty minutes, we sensed that Chernenko was finding it harder to speak, the ruddiness was disappearing from his cheeks, and he was fading noticeably. No one had come into the room during the meeting, but we understood on our own that it was time to wrap things up. We bade him farewell warmly, hoping against hope that the illness would pass, but unable to bring ourselves to say that. We knew only too well. . . .

A Politburo session took place the next day. Gorbachev opened it, saying: "Yegor Kuzmich and I visited Konstantin Ustinovich in the hospital, and he asked us to tell you—"

But Gorbachev had hardly managed to finish the phrase when someone's surprised voice rang out: "In the hospital? How? When?"

The unexpected news really made an impact. Many people had tried to get into the hospital to see the general secretary, but he had not received them—and suddenly, he himself had invited Gorbachev and Ligachev! It had to mean something.

Our visit to Kuntsevo Hospital was vested with significance. Although Gorbachev's account of our meeting really didn't contain anything except general phrases, greetings, and wishes, we could be certain that our trip to the *gensek* had alarmed some members of the Politburo.

What Will the New Day Bring?

Activity from the other grouping became particularly obvious at the start of the pre-election campaigns for the RSFSR Supreme Soviet. Chernenko was on the ballot in one of the Moscow districts, and Grishin took the election campaign into his own hands.

Meanwhile, the *gensek's* health grew progressively worse. For me, and I think for millions of television viewers as well, it was painful and embarrassing to watch a severely ill man being wheeled out almost forcibly to read torturously a short prepared text. Grishin was always by the general secretary's side. These joint television appearances were designed to instill into the public consciousness the idea that Grishin was the No. 2 man in the Party and that the right to inherit the highest power unquestionably would belong to him. Moreover, with the help of such broadcasts, efforts were being made to show that Chernenko was still functioning and could make decisions, presumably including those concerning his successor.

I felt sorry for Chernenko, who, despite his severe illness, was being exploited unceremoniously for reasons of political ambition. But neither Gorbachev nor I could protect him from that pressure.

Finally, on the eve of the elections, Moscow's Party activists devised a meeting with the general secretary. The event was staged quite pompously in the Central Committee Plenum Hall in the Kremlin, but it turned into a farce. Gorbachev and I sat in the presidium and saw how awkwardly it was all choreographed. Chernenko was in the hospital at the time and obviously could not come to the meeting, but his greetings were read at the meeting by Grishin, who then waxed eloquent with praises of Chernenko.

Another staged event served the same purpose of showing Grishin as the true successor to the *gensek*. That was the handing to Chernenko of his temporary credentials upon election as deputy. On that occasion, Grishin held up the terminally ill Chernenko before the television cameras to gain extra points for himself. But television viewers understood, and were ashamed for him. It was intolerable from both a political and a moral point of view.

But all these political spectacles only testified to the imminence of alarming events. And although we were expecting them from one day to the next, as often happens in these cases, they occurred very suddenly.

On Sunday, 10 March 1985, I was at a dacha in the countryside at Hillside 10. Bogolyubov, then director of the General Department, searched me out.

"Konstantin Ustinovich has passed away. Members and candidate members of the Politburo and Central Committee secretaries are to meet today in the Kremlin. Please come. . . ."

Within about thirty minutes I was in the Politburo conference room, where members and candidate members of the Politburo and Central Committee secretaries had gathered. Soon the Politburo members came out of the Walnut Room, took their seats, and immediately saw with their own eyes the whole complexity and confusion of the emerging situation: Gorbachev, who had been chairing the Politburo sessions in the past months, had seated himself at the table as chairman—not at the center of the table, but a little to the side.

This somehow accentuated the uncertainty surrounding the question of who would be the new general secretary.

We paid tribute to the memory of Chernenko with a minute of silence, and then Gorbachev raised an important issue: when should the Central Committee plenum be convened, and when should the new general secretary be elected? Of course, he put it very simply: "When will we convene the plenum?" And that was it. But what hung in the air was that the plenum must elect the new *gensek*.

After raising the question, Gorbachev himself then answered it: "I think we should hold the plenum tomorrow, and not put it off. . . ."

Someone immediately retorted: "But should it be rushed?"

The objection was not shared, however, and everyone agreed that the plenum should not be delayed. Our enormous country could not function normally without a general secretary of the Communist Party, in whose hands great power was concentrated under the practices of Party-government leadership of the time.

We quickly agreed on the whole range of matters dealing with the funeral, from the publication of the medical statement to ensuring public order. We set about selecting the funeral commission.

And here was the hitch. I would say it was a serious one, in its own way unprecedented. When the funeral commission was approved—and it was very large, since almost all the members of the highest Party leadership and some of the Central Committee secretaries were included—Gorbachev said, as if asking for advice: "Well, now that we have approved the commission, we need to select a chairman. . . ."

Suddenly, silence hung over the Politburo conference room.

It is difficult to remember now how long that obviously nervous and abnormal pause lasted, but it seemed eternal. The question raised by Gorbachev was in a sense crucial. Everyone understood that the selection of the chairman of the funeral commission was like a first, unambiguous step toward selecting a general secretary. In the past, the person chosen as chairman of the funeral commission always had become the *gensek*. When Brezhnev died, this question was decided automatically, almost of itself. Andropov had been selected chairman without any problem. When Andropov died, Chernenko had become chairman of the funeral commission without difficulty. I remember that Politburo session in February 1984 very well: we had no second thoughts. It seemed a matter of course that Chernenko, second secretary of the Central Committee, would head the commission, and he was slated to become *gensek*.

But that was not the way the meeting of the Politburo went on 10 March 1985. The long, difficult pause that arose after Gorbachev's words confirmed the worst suspicions: the question of who would become *gensek* was far from predetermined.

Undoubtedly, members of the Politburo had placed their bets on another political figure. But because of the uncertainty and difficulties, they preferred not to express their point of view openly. As a result, the discussion concerning the chairman of the funeral commission grew vague and finally dissipated. Neither side was willing to engage in a decisive debate at that moment, and the positions of some Politburo members remained unclear. One of them, Vladimir Shcherbitsky,[35] was away at the time on a visit to the United States. Thus, although the question about the new general secretary had been mulled over by all the members of the

---

[35]Vladimir Shcherbitsky was first secretary of the Ukrainian Communist Party Central Committee.—TRANS.

Politburo for several months, Chernenko's death caught each of them to some extent unprepared. Each wanted to reflect anew on events, weigh the balance of forces, and conduct political consultations. Here the interests of various sides coincided.

The session ended at about 11:00 P.M., and everyone went home. Of the top echelon of Kremlin leaders, only Gorbachev, myself, and Chebrikov, who was then head of the KGB, remained. In the final analysis, Gorbachev was the unofficial No. 2 person in the Party and government. He was the one left on behalf of the funeral commission to implement the hefty package of decisions made by the Politburo. I remember Gorbachev saying as much: "Time is very short. Let's get down to work."

We worked intensively in the Politburo conference hall until about 3:00 or even 4:00 A.M. We called everyone at home, summoning to the Kremlin the Central Committee department directors and heads of some agencies. Some of them had to be dragged out of bed; it was the middle of the night. The cars on duty quickly brought people to the Kremlin, we gave them their assignments and efficiently took care of all the problems that arose.

In the tense, inevitable confusion of that night, there was no time to look at our watches. But I vividly recall when Gorbachev, Chebrikov, and I finally went downstairs to get into our cars. We came out onto the wide steps of the Government Building as dawn was breaking over the towers of the Kremlin.

Those famous steps, which led to the building where the highest Soviet political leaders work, overlook the Kremlin Wall and the old Tsar's Armory. In his memoirs, Georgy Zhukov recalls how he was summoned to the Kremlin—"to the steps," in other words, to Stalin. True, Zhukov does not explain which steps he was talking about, but he was likely talking about the same ones. During the day, there is a beautiful view from here of the Nicholas Tower, although at night, with the streetlights, the view is limited to the Kremlin Wall.

As we came out onto the steps just before dawn, my glance fell on this wall—a high, solid wall that cut off the view. Perhaps it was a reflection of the exhaustion and the uncertainty of the situation that pressed on my mind, and I would even say, of the unknown. Perhaps that is why the wall, attracting my gaze involuntarily, seemed to me symbolic. We were really up against a wall blocking the path to tomorrow, against a wall behind which something unknown was hidden. I remember in that hour before dawn, as we stood on the famous Kremlin steps, I expressed our common mood when I recalled the famous words from Lensky's monologue in Pushkin's poem *Eugene Onegin:*

"What will the new day bring?"

Like many other people involved in events at the highest echelons of power, I understood that on that day, the fate of the Party and the country was being decided. It depended directly on who would be chosen as the new general secretary, and the candidates for this post were perhaps too polarized, both purely as individuals and in their political philosophies. I understood this perfectly.

But could I have supposed, in that predawn Kremlin gloominess, in its own way symbolic, that on this day a new period in history, not only for our country but also for the whole world, was destined to be born, a period of great hopes and bitter disappointments, of lofty aims but base intrigues?

Standing in that predawn hour with Gorbachev on the Kremlin steps, could I have predicted what an odd trajectory our relations would take? Could I have thought that the new political period just begun, which would later be dubbed "perestroika," a period conceived as socialist renewal, a deliverance from the Stalinist and post-Stalinist entanglements that bound society, would be used for selfish purposes by some politicians and social forces incredibly removed from the interests of the people and the Fatherland?

No, of course I could not have predicted this. On that early morning, my thoughts could not have run ahead farther than the most acute and most crucial task of the day: who would be chosen as *gensek?*

We said good-bye to each other and went our ways, but agreed to be back at our desks at 8:00 A.M.

Of course, I never got to sleep that night. Frankly, I didn't feel like it. At 8:00 A.M. on the dot I was back at Old Square. I installed myself on the phone, checking on how work was proceeding at the Hall of Columns, where the funeral ceremony would be held, seeing if participants in the Central Committee plenum were coming to Moscow, and so forth.

Sometime between 9:00 and 10:00 A.M., the *vertushka* rang on the first government line. I picked up the phone and heard: "Yegor Kuzmich, this is Gromyko. . . ."

In the two years that I had worked in the Central Committee apparat, I had received only a few phone calls from Andrei Andreyevich Gromyko. The fact was, we had virtually no contact in day-to-day affairs. Gromyko was involved in foreign policy issues, and my main sphere was the domestic. Gromyko and I often chatted after the Politburo sessions, and during the farewells and greetings of the general secretary at Vnukovo-2 Airport. But our telephone communications were few; there was no need.

But suddenly, on such a day, here was a phone call from Gromyko. Of course, I did not doubt for a second that the call was connected to the plenum of the Central Committee that day and the question of choosing a new general secretary. Gromyko, without wasting any time, got right down to business: "Yegor Kuzmich, whom are we going to choose as general secretary?"

I knew that Gromyko knew very well what answer he would get to this direct question. He was not mistaken.

"Yes, Andrei Andreyevich, it's a complicated question," I replied. "I think we have to choose Gorbachev. I know you have your own opinion. But since you've asked me, then I'll tell you I have the following considerations." I added: "I know that many of the provincial first secretaries and Central Committee members are of the same mind."

This was the truth. I knew the thinking of many of the first secretaries, and I thought it necessary to inform Gromyko. He displayed great interest in my information and reacted to it as follows: "I'm also thinking of Gorbachev. I think he is the most suitable figure, and has some prospects." Gromyko seemed to be thinking aloud. He said: "Well, what do you think? Who could be the one to make the motion? Who could nominate him as a candidate?"

This was genuine diplomatic style, asking questions whose answers were likely to be known beforehand. Nor was Gromyko mistaken this time, either.

"It would be very good, Andrei Andreyevich, if you would be the one to do that," I said.

"Do you think so?" Gromyko asked, still reflecting.

"Yes, that would be best. . . ."

At the end of the conversation, when Gromyko's position was finally clear, he said: "I suppose I am ready to make the motion about Gorbachev. But Yegor Kuzmich, help me prepare for my speech, and please send me more detailed biographical information on Gorbachev."

Gromyko's phone call had enormous significance. His opinion was heeded in the Politburo, and the fact that he had taken Gorbachev's side could determine to a decisive extent the outcome of the vote on the general secretary. Apparently, after last evening's Politburo session, Gromyko had thoroughly analyzed not only the current situation but also the historical prospects. By morning he had come to his conclusion. I do not rule out the possibility that he called some of the other members of the highest political leadership, but I think—no, I'm convinced—that his phone call to me was the first. After making a firm decision, Gromyko wanted Gorbachev to find out about that decision immediately. He knew that the most direct way of informing Gorbachev about his intentions was through me.

In finishing our conversation, Gromyko said: "At ten o'clock I am meeting with Dumas, the French foreign minister. But if you need me, call me right away, anytime. I'll be informed, and I'll leave the minister and come right to the phone. I'll warn my people of your telephone call."

We said good-bye, and I immediately dialed Gorbachev's number. "Mikhail Sergeyevich, Gromyko called. . . ."

Gorbachev attentively heard my report, then said: "Thank you, Yegor, for that news. Okay, let's get to work."

I called in my deputy, E. N. Razumov, and my aide, V. N. Sharkov, and together we quickly prepared the necessary background about Gorbachev. We sealed the envelope and sent it immediately by courier to Gromyko at the Foreign Ministry on Smolensk Square.

It was about noon. Five hours remained until the plenum.

Meanwhile, more and more people were collecting in my office waiting room. From all over the country, by car or plane, members of the Central Committee were coming to Moscow. Many provincial first secretaries came to my office to find out what was happening and express their own opinions.

I knew many of them well. In two years of work at the Central Committee, my ties with them had grown even stronger, since work with the provincial committees first went through the Organization Department. I had close, even confidential relations with some of the first secretaries. Upon arriving for an extremely important Central Committee meeting—a watershed, I would say—it was natural that they come to the department to see me.

And although I had many matters to attend to concerning the funeral arrangements, I thought it was important, an obligation, for me to speak with each one who came to see me.

Of course, I could have received all of the provincial secretaries at once, in a group, as Brezhnev often did during plenums. The whole gang of secretaries would cram into his office; sometimes there wasn't even room to sit down. I remember Gorbachev, then a territorial Party committee secretary, and I once being forced to sit on the windowsill. A general group discussion would then begin, which I must say I disliked, because no concrete issue could be resolved in such an atmosphere. True, we could hear some useful thoughts, but more often they were paeans addressed to Brezhnev. And on that score, I must say, there were some virtuosos, although not a great many.

To make a long story short, on 11 March I immediately rejected the idea of receiving all these people in my waiting room in one group. I invited them in one by one, on a first-come-first-served basis. Our conversations necessarily were brief, about five minutes, and all very similar. They all asked the same question: "Yegor Kuzmich, whom are we going to choose?"

And of course I was prepared for this question, and asked each one in return: "And what do you think: in your view, whom should we choose?"

To a man, all the provincial secretaries named Gorbachev.

With some of the secretaries, the conversation was more confidential: I explained the situation in more detail and described the previous day's Politburo meeting. I warned them that a nomination of another candidate was possible, and much would depend on what would happen at the Politburo session scheduled for three o'clock.

Some of the first secretaries told me that if necessary they were prepared to speak at the Central Committee plenum in support of Gorbachev. And not just based on their own opinion, but also on behalf of a whole group of secretaries and Central Committee members. A kind of initiative group emerged spontaneously. It was decided that during the Politburo session they would stay near my office waiting room. I promised to call them on the telephone and tell them about the turn of events at the Politburo.

Everyone was anticipating important changes. I also understood what Gorbachev was going through. At about two o'clock, I phoned him: "Mikhail Sergeyevich, the provincial secretaries—about fifteen to twenty people—were here to see me. A group of them would like to speak in support at the plenum. If it's needed, of course."

Gorbachev answered tersely: "Well, they have the right."

By three o'clock we were back at the Kremlin. Once again, Gorbachev sat at the end of the conference table; again, not in the center, but moved slightly away from the chairman's place. He understood that the conversation would be about him but that he was the one who would have to begin it.

After a short pause, Gorbachev said: "Now we must decide the question of the general secretary. The plenum is scheduled for five o'clock, and we must review this issue within two hours." And here Gromyko rose from his seat.

Everything happened unexpectedly, in an instant. I don't even recall whether he asked for the floor. The main thing, at least for me, given that morning's phone call from Gromyko, was that he stood up. Everyone was sitting, but he was standing: that meant he would get the first word and that the first nomination of a candidate for the *gensek* would come from him.

The large figure of Gromyko loomed over the table—I would say, even bore down upon it. He spoke in a well-phrased, professional, diplomatic voice:

"Allow me to speak," he began. "I have thought a great deal, and would like to make a motion to consider as candidate for the post of the general secretary of the Communist Party, Mikhail Sergeyevich Gorbachev."

Gromyko spoke weightily, convincingly, and gave a brief political portrait of Gorbachev. I had accumulated a good bit of political experience over the decades. From 1983 to 1985 I had regularly taken part in the Politburo and Central Committee Secretariat sessions and had understood the peculiar "rules of the game" at the highest echelons of power, the manner of behavior of many of the Politburo members. I can say with assurance that Gromyko's speech caught some of them by surprise. I believed that at the moment, when I was a direct witness and participant, and I still believe this today, many years later. And I can still say with absolute certainty that there were people in the Politburo who clearly did not approve of Gorbachev's nomination and understood that they would have to resign.

In fact, at that time conversations would surface about Chernenko's alleged "last will and testament," supposedly in favor of Grishin. Although such a "testament" would not necessarily have had a decisive influence on the selection of the new general secretary, it certainly would have made the nomination of Gorbachev more difficult, and the votes could have been split. As it turned out later, there was no such testament.

A person like Grishin, with his many years of work with Brezhnev, of course would have been closer in spirit to Chernenko than Gorbachev. Yet Chernenko did not take Grishin's side—otherwise he might have left some document. This was a man of the apparat who would hardly have been called a major political figure but upon whom, by the whim of fate, the selection of the new general secretary depended. With one foot in the grave, he displayed a strong sense of civic responsibility in his choice of successor, and did not succumb to flattery.

This was even more true of Gromyko. He, too, was a figure of the Brezhnev era; and proceeding from personal considerations, it would have been more advantageous to see in the post of general secretary a person who was more obedient, closer in age and spirit, who would have guaranteed the aging minister of foreign affairs a few more relatively quiet years. But Gromyko took a different stand on principle and essentially preordained the choice of Gorbachev. Apparently, he also sensed the mood of many Central Committee members.

This could also be said about Dmitri Ustinov, with whom Gorbachev had good relations. When Gorbachev phoned the minister of defense, he would sometimes salute him lightly: "Hello, Comrade Marshal! What orders do you have today on the agricultural front?"

Ustinov was well known to be severe, even brutal at times. He could criticize people very harshly, although he would allow them to stick up for themselves and knew how to defend an intelligent person. He knew the defense industry very well and was personally acquainted with many of the leading designers and scientists. To this day, Ustinov is remembered well in the factories. For me, he was a personification of the generation that forged the victory and glory of the Fatherland. He and I established very good relations. He once said to me: "Yegor, you're one of us. You're in our circle. . . ."

As to what "circle" and what "one of us" meant, I did not know. But I can say for sure that after Ustinov died in December 1984, we really missed his support.[36]

---

[36]*Literaturnaya gazeta* published an interview with one of Chernenko's former aides, who claimed that Ustinov, if he were alive in March 1985, would have opposed the choice of Gorbachev as general secretary. This is a faulty conclusion, based on ignorance of the true facts. In fact, it is not difficult to suppose that many people from the inner circle around the leaders will try to present their version of what happened in the stormy 1980s. As this example illustrates, such assertions should be treated with caution.— AUTHOR

I am making this point for the following reason.

Gromyko, Ustinov, Chernenko, the politicians from the previous generation, the so-called Brezhnev old guard, can and should be reproached for many things. They are largely to blame for the fact that by the beginning of the 1980s the country was on the verge of a crisis. But in the historical sense, political figures must be evaluated impartially. They were all people of their day, with all the major flaws that go with it, but also with certain virtues. While giving them the criticism they deserve, we can see the positive contribution they made to the balance sheet of history.

It must be noted that in the twilight hour of its era, the old guard displayed a high sense of duty and responsibility. When the question of the selection of a new general secretary was raised with the utmost urgency, these wise politicians were not bound by their personal ambitions, but actually flew in the face of their previous philosophy, which would have dictated that they continue the Brezhnev dynasty. They looked ahead. No matter how much we criticize them—and let me reiterate that there are reasons to criticize them severely— we cannot forget that final responsible deed, evincing their fear for the country's future.

Their sense of duty to the future helped them to rise above personal ambitions and considerations. This is the mark of serious politicians with rich experience, in vivid contrast to *nouveaux riches* politicians who have ascended rapidly on the crest of popularity or careerist intrigues. At a crucial moment for the Motherland, these old men acted in spite of themselves, in opposition to their own posthumous interests. As greatly experienced people, they could not help but understand that under Gorbachev, a new political course could be taken. But even so, they supported Gorbachev.

Returning to that historic Politburo session, I recall that moment, what an impression Gromyko made with his appearance, his very pose, expressing firmness and decisiveness as he was the first to rise. Frankly, I don't even remember what he said then, as opposed to his vivid speech about Gorbachev two hours later at the Central Committee plenum. Only something about how Gorbachev was a man of great potential has stuck in my memory.

But it was not a question of words. At the Politburo conference table were people of the greatest experience in politics and "palace" affairs. Gromyko's position was a determining factor; the array of forces became clear, and resistance did not bode well.

Tikhonov rose after Gromyko and also supported Gorbachev's candidacy. Then the other Politburo members and candidates and Central Committee secretaries began to speak. How different this was from the session the night before, when opposition to Gorbachev was clearly in the air. Then, statements were meant to sink the issue. But on 11 March, after the firm and clear statement by Gromyko, the rest of the Politburo members were forced to speak either in favor or against.

They all spoke in favor.

Later, quite a few rumors circulated around Moscow that the votes at the Politburo session were split and that everything was decided by Shcherbitsky's absence. There were many theories about who voted for and who against. But these were just rumors. In fact, all Politburo members and Central Committee secretaries voted for Gorbachev.

Within approximately an hour, when the situation was finally determined, I went to the outer office of the Politburo conference hall and called my secretary:

"Tell the comrades who still want to meet with me that they should be at the Central Committee plenary by five o'clock." And I added, "Tell them that everything's going as it should."

What happened directly at the plenum is widely known. Gromyko moved on behalf of the Politburo to elect Gorbachev. He was supported, and no one else spoke. Gorbachev was unanimously elected general secretary of the Central Committee of the Communist Party.

That evening I congratulated Gorbachev heartily, and he replied: "Can you imagine, Yegor, what an enormous burden we have shouldered?"

"Of course I can," I exclaimed.

During those days, I thought a great deal about difficulties of an objective, "external" nature, in the sense of the whole web of political and socioeconomic conditions that had evolved in and around the country. I was certain that in working together in a new way, by nominating Mikhail Gorbachev for the cutting edge of this work, we would manage to overcome these difficulties. Of course, I could not have foreseen that within three years, "internal" difficulties would begin to accumulate directly within the highest echelons of power and that these very difficulties would prove insurmountable, and finally jeopardize all the original intentions.

So that was how Gorbachev was elected general secretary. Knowing well the circumstances that had evolved within the top leadership during the last months of Chernenko's life, I thought then, as I do now, that events could have followed another scenario. That is why in 1988, at the 19th Party Conference, I said that in this period we went through many worried days, and there had been a real danger of another choice.

That was the comment Yeltsin was reacting to in his book. He said that I offended Gorbachev with this remark, and that there had been no problems with the selection of the *gensek*. Of course, at the Central Committee plenum, everything did run smoothly. Yeltsin, former first secretary of the Sverdlovsk Province Party Committee, took part in that plenum, and writes about what he saw. But with regard to the events behind the scenes, and the struggle that was waged for several months in the Kremlin and on Old Square, I have no call to debate this topic with Yeltsin. I can only reiterate what I said earlier, that it seems that, in Sverdlovsk, they knew better about what was happening in Moscow—better not only than I, but also better than Gorbachev. But before the 28th Party Congress, at a meeting with provincial secretaries, Gorbachev confirmed that the situation in March 1985 was complicated. He said that Ligachev was right when he said at the Party conference that the choice of general secretary could have turned out very differently.

But Yeltsin from Sverdlovsk knows better. . . .

Yeltsin's claim is his own personal business, and perhaps not even worthy of attention. But historical facts require careful treatment. They cannot be distorted in favor of transitory political considerations. When the dust settles and the clouds of smoke rise from the current political battles, history will set everyone in their true places.

In March 1985 the Party was left without a general secretary, and the country without a leader, for less than a day. And that unusually rapid development of events was a foretaste of the coming changes. True, when Gorbachev spoke at the March plenum, he assured the Central Committee that he would guarantee continuity in policy. But within a month, at the April plenum, he was more precise. Continuity is movement ahead without fail, identification and resolution of new problems, elimination of everything that hinders development. This meant, among other things, that a new political team was in formation.

This had become clear in the first minutes of the April plenum. Despite tradition, it began not with a report but with personnel matters. In matters related to the highest-ranking cadres, the initiative always belonged to the general secretary. Gorbachev thus moved that I be elected a member of the Politburo.

It was not often that a secretary of the Central Committee was elected directly to the Politburo, passing over the candidate status. That already signified the style of the new leadership, and it was supported by the plenum participants. Gorbachev invited me to come forward from the hall up to the presidium, where only Politburo members were seated. I went up to the platform where the presidium table was and wanted to take a seat near the end. But Gorbachev called out: "Yegor Kuzmich, come here and sit next to me."

A free place had been left next to Gorbachev, but I think none of those present had paid attention to it. But it turned out that the free seat was meant for me. When I took it, Gorbachev leaned over and explained to me: "You and I are going to run the plenum. . . ."

After that, when all the organizational questions were completed, he said in a fairly loud voice, so that those in the hall could hear him: "Yegor Kuzmich, give me the floor, I am going up to the podium."

With that phrase, the general secretary essentially designated the

No. 2 man in the Politburo. The people in the Plenum Hall were not naive. They knew what was what.

In fact, Ryzhkov was also elected to the Politburo at the same plenum, right from the ranks of the Central Committee secretaries, passing over the rank of candidate. We two were destined to become the closest comrades of Gorbachev in implementing the new political course that became known as perestroika, and were to take key posts in the Gorbachev team. Soon Ryzhkov was promoted to chairman of the USSR Council of Ministers, and I was assigned to run the meetings of the Central Committee Secretariat, which in fact meant promotion to the unofficial second post in the Party.

Subsequently, a particularly fierce attack was launched against Ryzhkov and myself—Gorbachev's two closest comrades—by the new political forces that appeared in the public arena thanks to the rapid and beneficial perestroika processes launched in 1985–88. These political forces, employing the slogans of glasnost and democracy that had been on the banners of perestroika, were waging an open battle for power. First and foremost, they had to remove from the highest echelon of leadership those who had begun the changes.

This subject is very familiar and has been repeated numerous times throughout history. It was tragically played out by Stalin, when at first he smeared, then destroyed Lenin's comrades-at-arms.

Two
THE GORBACHEV ENIGMA: IN THE TRAP OF RADICALISM

Shock Therapy

In 1985, right after the May holidays (May Day and 9 May, the anniversary of victory in World War II), and just a few days after the April Central Committee plenum, Gorbachev called me.

"Yegor, I'm moving into Office No. 6, so you move into this one, No. 2. You have to handle the Secretariat; we'll give the Organization Department to someone else. Think who it should be."

Gorbachev raised the question at the Politburo soon after, and I was officially assigned to lead the Secretariat of the Central Committee and chair Politburo sessions in the general secretary's absence. I moved to Entrance No. 1 in the Central Committee buildings and settled into the famous Office No. 2—"Suslov's office"—on the fifth floor. I don't know who worked there before Suslov; but the occupants after him were Andropov, Chernenko, and Gorbachev.

I have many memories of Office No. 2 in the days when Suslov used it, most of them unpleasant. The point is that this was traditionally the office of the No. 2 man in the top political leadership, in charge of the Secretariat. This permanent working body of the Central Committee was provided for in the Party's bylaws. The Secretariat was created to deal with current affairs; personnel questions; and, perhaps most importantly, to supervise execution of the decisions made by the Politburo, Central Committee plenums, and Party congresses. Simply put, the Secretariat was the operations staff of the Party leadership. In those years of Party-government control, the Secretariat meetings dealt with a wide range of problems encompassing all spheres of life, from ideology and economics to culture, Party-building, and military construction.

Gorbachev never participated in these meetings, but he often convened the Secretariat for an exchange of opinions on actual problems. He and I immediately set up a system in which the general secretary would thoroughly review the Secretariat's work plan for the upcoming six months and make any necessary changes and comments. The plan was formulated from below, incorporating suggestions of the Central Committee departments. Every time, there were seventy or eighty preliminary suggestions; it was impossible to digest them all, and so many questions were deleted. After Gorbachev approved the plan and the Secretariat confirmed it, this would become the blueprint for action.

With rare exceptions, the Secretariat met on Old Square every Tuesday at 4:00 P.M. I generally informed Gorbachev of the agenda the day before, and I *always* reported to the general secretary after the meeting, usually by telephone, but in person for important issues. In that way, Gorbachev was fully informed of the Secretariat's affairs. And from his reactions, I could tell that he was getting information on the Secretariat from other sources as well.

I considered that normal. And I might add that keeping the general secretary and other members of the highest political leadership informed was not a simple matter.

A steady stream of memos, reports, bulletins, reviews, analytical reports, and other work and secret documents flowed to the Politburo and general secretary from such organizations as the Ministry of Defense, the Ministry of Foreign Affairs, the KGB, the Ministry of Internal Affairs, the State Committee on Statistics, and TASS (the news agency). Information from the local Party committees also fell into this category. Members of the top political leadership needed exhaustive information about all domestic and international issues to make responsible decisions. And truth to tell, the special services feeding the leadership with current and analytical information had long been functioning at a good level.

It is understandable that the rank of a leader determines the volume and confidentiality of the information that reaches him. The higher the rank, the more varied and in-depth it is. For instance, I spent more than two hours a day reading such documents. It gave me a good idea of the connections among processes occurring domestically and abroad, and allowed me to respond to current events and to forecast general developments.

I asked to receive the usual materials even on my days off. Following them without interruption helped me catch trends as they developed, and I could hit the ground running when I got back to work. Naturally, I studied materials in all areas, and did not change that habit when I concentrated on agricultural problems. I must mention that traveling around the country was also a very important source of facts and direct observation. Starting in 1985, I made almost eighty business trips in the USSR, a record among Politburo members.

I considered this travel an important part of my work. It gave me the opportunity to take part personally in implementing Party decisions as well as to obtain firsthand information about the people's mood. When circumstances kept me in Moscow longer than usual, the isolation from real life bothered me. Often, the mood in the capital did not correspond to the prevailing attitudes in other regions. I'd return to Moscow after each trip and meetings with locals refreshed and full of energy. Even though the trips were pressured, even though I got tired physically, travel in the country eased my spirit, and I felt more confident in my policies afterward.

Disagreements between me and some members of the top political leadership began to surface in the second half of 1987. Some were on specific matters, others touched on fundamental issues.

Increasingly, they involved analysis of socioeconomic processes of the current moment and the immediate future. Without going into detail about the disagreements, I will say that, in my opinion, they often arose because these people did not have a full picture of what was going on in the country. Some Politburo members studied thoroughly "their" information—on the issues that fell directly into the range of their responsibilities—but merely glanced at the rest. You could see this at the meetings of the Politburo and Secretariat sessions.

In particular, Yakovlev, who had dealt with ideology, then with international policy, obviously was lost when it came to discussing major economic issues. It is known for a fact that he never went to factories, construction sites, villages—where economics becomes real. He didn't know how economic innovations were introduced into life, nor did he care to find out. Nevertheless, Yakovlev was extremely active in shaping the main trends of economic policy. But because of his clearly inadequate attention to actual processes taking place in concrete economic situations, his opinion often suffered from a narrow perspective and radicalism.

Incomplete or one-sided information is one of the main traps awaiting a politician. Unfortunately, I cannot say that the "standard" selection of factual and analytical materials placed on the desks of the top political leadership was always unprejudiced.

Reference documents' "salt" is objectivity. But they are prepared and signed by people, and some of these people, attempting to pander to the moods of the leaders, arrange the materials to suit the point of view reigning upstairs instead of giving straight facts. This highly dangerous and not always recognized phenomenon can push a politician into making a serious mistake. It is vital that one make a comparative analysis of data coming from various sources and place them against real life. I tried to keep that in mind, and if I noticed discrepancies on an important issue, I immediately sounded the alarm—right up to putting the question on the agenda of the Secretariat or even the Politburo, as I did in 1988 with the evaluation of the situation in Lithuania.

But the question of informing high-ranking leaders has another side, urgent in the case of the general secretary. The flow of information intended for the general secretary is so great that it requires selection and regulation. And it raises these questions: Who selects the information? How is it selected? It can be shaped in a very specific way, both in the purely factual materials (by stressing, or, on the contrary, camouflaging certain facts) and in evaluations and analyses.

In addition, there exists an unwritten psychological law of primacy: The first impression of a fact or event is the fullest, while subsequent ones, if they contradict the first, merely seem to be in conflict with it. This leads to an important practical conclusion: if there is a problem, you must rush to present your version of events to the boss, to influence his opinion. And keep in mind that a leader's advisers, both official and ad hoc, can have a noticeable effect on the thinking of their boss.

In ancient times, the wise peoples of the East used to say that more may depend on the adviser than on the shah. Today's aides and advisers enjoy the same advantage. The ones struggling for influence over the leader put maximum effort into putting their people into his inner circle.

That is why the choice of aides and advisers is such a crucial issue. Numerous examples from history teach us that it is not enough to base the selection of a team simply on the principle of personal loyalty. If the inner circle is biased when it interprets facts and events, personalities, and phenomena, it can give a leader an erroneous impression of what is happening at home and abroad. This relates to every general secretary of the Party, and perhaps especially to Gorbachev.

When I returned to Moscow in 1983 after seventeen years in Siberia, I didn't have any of "my" people in the apparat of the Central Committee. I wasn't "hitched" to anyone, which kept me independent and, frankly, made my work much easier. In general, I don't like office intrigues, and so I didn't even think about how Gorbachev would form his closest circle of advisers. I considered that a question only for him. I didn't recommend anyone to the general secretary as an aide or adviser, and I didn't slip anyone into these key positions from an apparat point of view.

Gorbachev and I discussed the major personnel issues that

determined the array of forces in the Central Committee and the Party as a whole. (Naturally, they were approved collectively, in the Politburo, Secretariat, and Central Committee plenums.) And just as in 1983 under Andropov, we had to start with a search for a new head of the Organization Department, since I could not combine that duty with the post of second secretary.

Our choice was Georgy Razumovsky. The Party later formed a negative opinion of Razumovsky, and it was openly expressed at the 28th Congress. I retain a sad picture of Razumovsky, who had been proposed as a candidate for the new Central Committee, and was hurrying to the rostrum to withdraw, aware that he would be blackballed.

Things were more complex than they seemed on the surface—Razumovsky was an outstanding figure, not nearly so simple as he appeared to some at the Congress. He was a politician with a complex fate who showed weakness at one point and was broken.

As chairman of the Krasnodar Territory Executive Committee,[1] Razumovsky demonstrated strong character, managing to rid himself of interference from a local Party leader, Sergei Medunov, who made an effort to get closer to Razumovsky and involve him in his affairs. Razumovsky held firm and rejected all personal contact. Not surprisingly, a conflict developed in the area's leadership of the Kuban area. Razumovsky stated his position firmly to the Central Committee (under Brezhnev), and asked to be transferred because of incompatibility with Medunov. The request was granted, and in 1981 Razumovsky took charge of the Agricultural Department at the USSR Council of Ministers.

After Medunov's activities were exposed, Vorotnikov worked as Party first secretary in Krasnodar. He soon became chairman of the Council of Ministers of Russia, and once again the question arose of the position of first secretary. At that time I was head of the Central Committee Organization Department, and we thought of

---

[1]That is, of the territorial soviet, or government office, which was nominally distinct from the Party.—TRANS.

Razumovsky. I was also charged with running the plenum of the Krasnodar Territory Committee, at which I could see personally that the locals received Razumovsky well, remembering his differences with Medunov.

In May 1985, as Gorbachev and I went over candidates for head of the Organization Department, Gorbachev named Razumovsky, and I concurred. I knew that Razumovsky had worked well with Ivan Polozkov, who was then head of a Central Committee division and whom he'd invited to come to Krasnodar as second secretary,[2] to clean up the region. We saw Razumovsky as a decent man actively fighting corruption, and that was a great factor in his appointment to the Central Committee. When he left Krasnodar, Razumovsky proposed Polozkov for first secretary in light of his good work there. I seconded his proposal: I had gotten to know Polozkov well and had a very positive view of him.

Razumovsky got off to a great start in the Central Committee. He was unafraid to state his opinion, and he liked to make issues more pointed rather than round off the corners. You could see that he had no intention of selling out. At the Secretariat Central Committee meetings, Razumovsky showed himself at his best. This lasted until the fall of 1988, when things began to go wrong.

Some explanation is needed here.

Thoroughgoing reform of our political system was proceeding at an accelerating pace following the 19th Party Conference. The Party proclaimed a genuine *Party* slogan: More socialism, more democracy. Radical changes in the electoral system that had developed during the Stalin years were called for so that we could move to the principle of contested elections.

Over the decades, the elections of people's deputies had become a mere formality, resulting in a passive electorate. Everything was planned down to the letter, and no one was allowed to be listed as a candidate without permission of the Party regional committees.

---

[2]Ivan Polozkov subsequently became leader of the Russian Communist Party before it was disbanded.—TRANS.

Of course, this doesn't mean that there were no decent people among the deputies; in fact, there were quite a few. Moreover, this system did ensure that all classes and social groups were represented in the soviets: people of all nationalities; women; young people. But the principle of uncontested elections unquestionably was obsolete, undemocratic, and in need of change.

The top Party leadership had no quarrel with this basic approach, but the process of transforming the electoral system accelerated too swiftly and radically. There was practically no public discussion of the new law on elections, which was of vital importance, and for the first time in our history introduced the practice of competing candidates. It was passed hurriedly, in just a month. Such a rush does not allow for all the details to be thought through—unacceptable for the development of such a fundamental document.

To tell the truth, I already had my doubts about the need to rush through this law. But just recall the fall of 1988: there had been a powerful attack on me in connection with Nina Andreyeva's article,[3] and I had more or less been removed from directing the Secretariat. Under those conditions it was difficult to speak out against the opinion of the general secretary and those who were clamoring for a maximum pace of political transformation.

But it must be said—and my duty here is to be completely frank—that at this time I did not fully understand the motives for this political radicalization and accelerated pace, nor, most importantly, their harmful consequences. Only later, when there was sufficient evidence, did I realize that this was a kind of political "shock therapy," in another form of *Sturm und Drang* methods. The idea was not to let people catch their breath under the onslaught of innovations, just to present them as a *fait accompli*.

Here I must clarify what "radicalize" means in politics. Contemporary radicals, or pseudodemocrats, are seeking to replace economic and political systems, to turn around our social development, and to move toward capitalism, which entails the impoverishment

---

[3]See Chapter 7 for a discussion of the controversy surrounding this article.—TRANS.

of the majority and the enrichment of the few. The aims the radicals set for themselves make them right-wing, antisocialist forces.

There are also leftist radical elements, who within the framework of the socialist option demand quick implementation of urgently needed changes in society without taking into account realities or common sense. But I am speaking primarily of the right-wing radicals who in the perestroika years were particularly active in the public arena. When I say "radical," I mean the right-wingers.

The pseudodemocrats (i.e., the radicals) used the political inexperience and naiveté of a society awakening after many years of the personality cult and the era of stagnation to impose a wild tempo of political change. Under the guise of democracy, a new form of dictatorship inevitably would arise—the dictatorship of anarchy, of "anything goes." We were always working against time, but the Party could have proposed a more reasonable pace and scope for transformation.

Shock therapy led to deep schisms and social destabilization. This had a deleterious effect on economic reform and brought the country to a state of crisis.

It soon became clear that the new electoral law was imperfect. The haste showed. But this was just a prelude to the pressures and damaging events that flared up during the election campaign.

While the Party had supervised the electoral process to the tiniest detail in the past, now that there were contested elections, it backed away from political struggle almost completely. In every country with a developed democracy, the party structures become most active during the election period, when things get tough and exciting. But here, astonishingly, it was just the opposite.

The Central Committee sent out one directive after another to local Party offices: Don't interfere. Keep your distance. Confusion reigned in a number of Party committees. They saw that many unworthy people had announced their candidacies, even former convicts who had committed serious crimes, including murder. As for loudmouths and demagogues who built their platform only on anti-Soviet and anti-Communist planks, their numbers were legion. You would think that under these conditions, Party propaganda would be increased, providing more support for its candidates and exposing groundless and unrealistic populist promises.

But the Central Committee offered no political orientation, and the local Party offices were helpless. For the first time, there were no clear directions from the center on how to behave. And this came during an election campaign when the question of power was being decided. The soviets are the political base of our system. Now their role should have been strengthened and management functions passed to them in full—and the Party sharply reduced its activity. Once they let loose the election campaign, the people on top thought that everything would work out by itself. The Party's non-interference in the elections was presented as an expression of democracy. The Party was faithful to the idea of struggle with former ways, but they threw the baby out with the bathwater.

Things became so bad that the Communist candidates began fighting among themselves, making it easier for their ideological foes to get elected. On the wave of rallies and demonstrations, anti-Communism reared its head. As an election maneuver, our democrats denigrated our entire history.

When the registration of candidates came to a close, there were disastrously few workers and peasants on the lists. This was without a doubt the Party organizations' most serious mistake, when it allowed the elections to go unsupervised. A false understanding of democracy might have led to the actual absence of workers and peasants from the highest-level soviet.[4] The question came up with increasing frequency at Politburo sessions; Gorbachev himself raised it several times. But it never went beyond expressions of concern. Moreover, an episode took place in that period that left me with a very unpleasant feeling.

Gorbachev had gone to Leningrad to visit the Izhorsky Plant. There, right on the shop floor, the workers raised a question about having elections based not only on residence in territorial districts, but also on workplaces, which would guarantee representation for

---

[4]The Supreme Soviet, or Parliament.—TRANS.

the working class in the soviets. Gorbachev supported this Leninist idea, and it was reported in press accounts of the general secretary's trip to Leningrad.

A few days later, the so-called radical press, as if on command, attacked the "workplace principle" of elections. A storm of newspaper and television protests demanded that the elections be held solely by residential district and accused the Izhorsky workers and their supporters of trying to get Party apparatchiks into the soviets. The Leningrad Province Party Committee immediately announced that no Party workers would be on the ballots in the workplace lists—but no one had any intention of heeding this important statement. The hysteria continued unabated in many publications.

Gorbachev never again supported the Izhorsky workers in public. Nevertheless, I remember we discussed their commonsense idea at the Politburo with approbation, and concluded that it made sense to create workplace districts in some cities and areas *if* the local authorities wanted it. This did not contradict the law on elections in any way.

But this rational beginning was doomed. Foes of the workplace principle used the radical press to bury this important proposal. The position of noninterference in election campaigns triumphed. As a result, the representation of workers and peasants at the USSR Congress of People's Deputies did not reflect the leading role played by the working class and peasantry in society.

All of us in the Politburo underestimated the situation then. The first contested election in our lives was unfolding heatedly, and we were told: Hold your peace.

Traditionally, the department headed by Razumovsky led the election campaign. And so Razumovsky himself had to call local Party committees to tell them not to interfere. A man of great experience who had been through a long education in leadership, Razumovsky must have known what such orders could bring about.

It was during this period that Razumovsky became unrecognizable. He suddenly stopped taking a position during discussions of various issues, although previously he had always had an opinion. He was no longer heard from. Whenever you called him—and I had to call the head of the Organization Department often—his secretary would say, "Georgy Petrovich is in Yakovlev's office. . . ." (Or, sometimes, ". . . in Medvedev's office.")[5]

Razumovsky often called in sick, complaining of moodiness and not feeling well. This strong independent voice suddenly seemed broken. His authority plunged among Communists.

In my opinion, Razumovsky was acting against his own convictions. A strong-minded man who had not feared conflict with a powerful local boss now displayed weakness, completed his assigned role, and left the political stage unnoticed.

Much remains unclear in this story, including this question: Why did Yakovlev, who during this period was charged with dealing with international affairs, take such an active part in domestic ones, including the elections?

Éminence Grise

Yakovlev was one of the most experienced apparatchiks in the Central Committee. Starting out in the mid-1950s, he went through the whole route from instructor to secretary of the Central Committee and Politburo member, leaving Old Square only for the ambassadorship in Canada, study at the Academy of Social Sciences,[6] and a year's internship at Columbia University in New York.

We met in the early 1960s, when I "passed through" the Central Committee for four years on my way from Siberia to Siberia. Our relationship was unproblematic, and afterward he always sent me New Year's greeting cards, even from Canada.

As ambassador to Canada under Andropov, Yakovlev met our delegation headed by Gorbachev. Shortly afterward, Yakovlev was

---

[5]Vadim Medvedev took over Politburo supervision of ideology after Ligachev was moved to agricultural affairs.—TRANS.

[6]The Central Committee's academy, which trained the Party and government leaders. —TRANS.

recalled from his foreign "exile" and for a brief period headed the Institute of World Economy and International Relations (IMEMO) of the USSR Academy of Sciences. In July 1985, Gorbachev proposed Yakovlev for the post of head of the Central Committee Agitprop.[7] It was clear to me that this job was merely a launching pad and that Gorbachev wanted to bring Yakovlev into the Central Committee as quickly as possible. I had a positive response to the general secretary's proposal: he was forming a new political team, and a man with ideological, apparat, and foreign work experience was needed.

Naturally, I couldn't have guessed then that Yakovlev's brand of radicalism would help distort the perestroika course we had set out on after the April 1985 plenum.

A few months later, Yakovlev was elected a secretary of the Central Committee and took charge of ideological matters. I supervised them as a Politburo member, but soon an unspoken division of duties took shape. I dealt with questions of culture, science, and education, while Yakovlev concentrated on work with the mass media. This happened spontaneously, but with the approval of the general secretary. Of course, at Gorbachev's behest I often met with newspaper and magazine editors.

But the main point of this division was that Yakovlev was in charge of replacing editors in chief. Objectively speaking, the new political course demanded appropriate propaganda support, and many mass media leaders were in no shape to achieve "self-perestroika." I remember jokingly recalling Lenin's statement that a revolution begins with the seizure of the post office and the telegraph station, never suspecting that a seizure of the mass media indeed was intended. Alas, my joke turned out to be the bitter truth.

Yakovlev, who had been acting director of the Central Committee Agitprop from 1967 to 1972, knew the ideological cadres very well. He didn't just know their professional abilities, he also understood them personally. I must say that my observations lead me to think

---

[7]Department of Agitation and Propaganda.—TRANS.

that Yakovlev—to give him his due—has great psychological insight. And, he also had longstanding friendships with some of these people.

I am profoundly convinced that friendly relations are not at all reprehensible but are of great help in politics. However, the question is a delicate one, and it all depends on what goals the relationship serves. The candidates proposed by Yakovlev were completely acceptable for those times. Almost all had gone through the Central Committee school, and many had worked under Yakovlev in Agitprop or "general" cultural affairs. How could I have suspected that Yakovlev was forming a radical media team that would have a very special role in the coming events?

Of course, for fairness' sake, I must relate my own mistake involving the appointment of an editor for one of the most radical, hardhitting publications, the magazine *Ogonyok*.

In this case, too, the propaganda department took the intitiative, proposing Vitaly Korotich as a candidate. When I asked them for a sample of his work, they said, "The journal *Roman Gazeta* recently published his book *The Face of Hatred*. Korotich sets out his political credo in it."

I read *The Face of Hatred* closely, and concluded that the author had stable ideological positions. It seemed to me that in places he was overdoing it: he was too much of an extremist when it came to America. But that kind of excess could be remedied, and I decided to meet with Korotich.

Korotich was very pleased by my basically positive reaction to his book, and promised that if he were appointed editor of *Ogonyok*, he would serve the Party truly and faithfully. His assurances were fervent, and the book was powerful. And you would think the best way to judge a writer was by his work.

Yakovlev and I together prepared the resolution appointing Korotich editor in chief of *Ogonyok*. He was transferred from Kiev to Moscow and given an apartment.

And then it started. Everyone remembers *Ogonyok*'s aggressive publications, which sowed dissent among the intelligentsia and were often criticized, some at Gorbachev's meetings with media editors.

I met with Korotich several times, on some occasions at his request. He invariably repented, insisted that he had been let down by his colleagues, swore that he would improve, that nothing like it would ever appear again. But in another issue I would read more extremist, antisocialist pieces stirring up the social atmosphere, insulting the army, or attacking the Party.

Korotich would come to see me again; he'd swear, over and over . . . and would go back to sin once more.

That's the kind of man the author of the harshly anti-American *The Face of Hatred* turned out to be. (By the way, the Americans have forgiven him for it. Korotich spent more time in the United States than in his office in Moscow.[8]) And one more footnote: when the antisocialist press was attacking me, *Ogonyok* was in the forefront. But that didn't keep Korotich from sending me touching New Year's cards; in 1990, he actually sent me one thanking me for all I'd taught him.

I'm prepared to take the blame for Korotich, at least in part. But it was Yakovlev who promoted the other radical editors. Of course, he started with the calmer ones. If I'm not mistaken, his first editorial replacement was the head of the Party journal *Kommunist*. Richard Kosolapov was replaced at *Kommunist* by Ivan Frolov, who had worked with Yakovlev in the Central Committee apparat. And then Frolov, who was a corresponding member when he was confirmed as an assistant to the general secretary, was made a full academician. I raise this point because around 1987, I sensed that Gorbachev was gradually being surrounded by people who were personally dependent on Yakovlev.

Another tendency was very obvious: people who knew the practical life of the country were gradually moving away from the general secretary and being replaced by scholars with an academic turn of mind.

Naturally, the leader needs such assistants and advisers; indeed,

---

[8]Vitaly Korotich resigned from *Ogonyok* after the coup and came to the United States as a visiting scholar.—TRANS.

they are irreplaceable. But in politics as in art, everything depends on proportion. Gorbachev was clearly attracted to the aura of the "enlightened monarch." In the end, this academic overbalance led to an excessive focus on political problems and a lack of practical work on leading the country. Innumerable meetings and gatherings were led by the "Gorbachev team," but daily work by the general secretary to make sure those decisions were implemented dwindled to an unacceptable level.

This flaw, typical of many political leaders, can be compensated for easily by selecting the right assistants, advisers, and colleagues. Ideally, Gorbachev's team should have combined practical realists and academic thinkers. But alas, such a group combining political realism and academic thinking was not to be.

Yet people like that were there: all the leader had to do was make rational use of this potential for true perestroika.

But Gorbachev chose another path. Or it might be more correct to put it this way: Gorbachev was directed onto a different path.

But before I recount how that happened, I would like to mention a few events connected with the struggle over the media.

In September 1987, the newspaper *Moscow News* distressed the Central Committee by publishing the obituary of the writer Viktor Nekrasov,[9] who had died in Paris. One must recall that back then, new views about our compatriots who had moved abroad for various reasons had not yet been established. The Politburo criticized *Moscow News,* and Gorbachev, on vacation in the Crimea, called and assigned me the task of announcing our position at one of our usual meetings with newspapers and magazine editors. A memo from Sergei Slobodenyuk, deputy head of the newspaper division, was also made public at that meeting.

It turned out that Yegor Voronov, then head of the culture department of the Central Committee, had called up Slobodenyuk and told him that both *Literaturnaya gazeta* and *Moscow News* were

---

[9]Viktor Nekrasov (1911–87) was a prominent writer who emigrated in 1974 and published his works abroad and in *samizdat.*—TRANS.

planning to print an obituary of Nekrasov. Slobodenyuk informed Yakovlev, secretary of the Central Committee, and then told both Voronov and *Moscow News* that the secretary's orders were not to print the obituary. But Yegor Yakovlev, editor in chief of *Moscow News,* did not obey Central Committee secretary Alexander Yakovlev.

This was discussed at a meeting of editors on 14 September, the day after the obituary was published. Yegor Yakovlev, however, contradicted Slobodenyuk, saying that he had not received any instruction from the Central Committee. This led to a brouhaha.

Gorbachev, Alexander Yakovlev, and I took a united position on publication of the obituary. We never touched on the artistic side of the writer's work, and dealt only with his political position as an émigré. At that time we had a completely different opinion of compatriots who had emigrated; all of us, top political leaders along with the rest of society, have rethought many things since then. As is only normal.

An analogous process was taking place in the consciousness of the editor in chief of *Moscow News.* It was about then that his newspaper reprinted from *Le Figaro* a letter from nine émigrés in the arts, which Yegor Yakovlev followed with his own article, a direct blast at Yuri Lyubimov, Vasily Aksyanov, Ernst Neizvestny, Vladimir Maximov, and the other signatories. From today's position, such rebukes look ridiculous. But it would be just as ridiculous to rebuke him for lines he wrote several years ago. I wouldn't even bring up the incident if it weren't for its interesting sequel.

Following the meeting Yegor Yakovlev wrote a complaint to the Central Committee addressed to me. Why to me? Because I had run the meeting? I had expressed not just my own opinion, but also that of Gorbachev. And the obituary had been banned by Alexander Yakovlev, not by me. So why did the editor of the right-wing radical newspaper address his objections to me alone?

I admit that at first I didn't pay any attention to this. Within a few days, however, circumstances forced me to give it some serious thought. Gorbachev treated the accusation in a curious way: he sent it to all the members of the Politburo. No one, neither

Gorbachev nor anyone else, made any comments to the editor. The way this complaint had been used made me think. This was clearly support for Yegor Yakovlev—and a slight slap for me. I could see someone's hand behind this.

It left an unpleasant impression on me, and I gradually moved away from running the media. This was clearly a big mistake, since in those days magazines and newspapers were still forming their positions and I could have influenced the process. The result was that Gorbachev and Alexander Yakovlev completely took the press in hand. Gorbachev had regular meetings with the editors, would call them up. There was nothing surprising about this; Gorbachev was then preoccupied with the ideological work of the Party.

But there were some peculiarities in the general secretary's meetings with the media. Despite the presence of almost all the members of the Politburo, Gorbachev was the only one who spoke, while we were relegated to the odd role of extras. And these meetings began to turn into long hours of Gorbachev yakking away, criticizing, instructing, and exhorting the editors to promote the cohesiveness of society, while no one paid any attention. The extremist press continued its destructive work, favoring negative articles that tore apart our whole past.

I remember speaking several times with Gorbachev about the uselessness of these meetings. He would get angry and order the ideology department to improve its work with the media. Those orders would come to naught. I think that Gorbachev at first underestimated the social consequences of the destructive work of press, television, and radio. But the role of the media in the destabilization of the Baltics was very clear, as in the popular front press Lithuania, Latvia, and Estonia became battering rams, shaking the pillars of socialism and the Union state. *Pravda* warned of this while Viktor Afanasev was still in charge there, one of the few editors of national papers who was not within Yakovlev's sphere of influence. (This is why no effort was spared in the successful effort to get rid of Afanasev.)

Many people warned that the Baltics, and Lithuania in particular, were being used as a testing ground for destructive radical models.

Unfortunately, neither Gorbachev nor the Politburo as a whole listened to those warnings. It was clear even then that glasnost and democracy were being used by certain radicals to incite social tensions, disorient the public consciousness, and destabilize the state. In the meantime, the perestroika we had created in 1985 was acutely in need of civil consensus and national unity. To keep the Party and country from falling apart, to prevent anarchy, we had to manage the mass media in a new way—not through *diktat,* but through comradely work and discussions, bearing in mind the socialist pluralism of newspapers, magazines, and television programs. But the radical publications were running amok with their attacks. It's hard to recall a Politburo meeting at which media questions did not appear. They were raised by almost all the members of the Politburo, especially Ryzhkov, Kryuchkov, and Lukyanov,[10] and the secretaries of the Central Committee, with the exception of Yakovlev and Medvedev.

The Central Committee began to receive letters from people outraged by publications insulting our Party, army, and veterans. Naturally, it was impossible not to react to such letters. Sometimes Gorbachev himself would express outrage at certain articles or programs. But every time, it was nothing more than a tempest in a teapot, all words and no action. Occasionally the Politburo would assign Medvedev to "deal with the situation," but no one ever followed up on this, and Medvedev never reported his results. I think—no, I am certain—that this policy was well known to the captains of the right-radical press and was an inspiration to them.

The situation was made even more acute by the fact that at all the Central Committee plenums of that period, at all the meetings of workers, peasants, teachers, and industrialists, there was very loud and strong criticism of the media. Rereading the transcripts of those plenums today, I am amazed by the positions that Gorbachev

---

[10]Gennady Kryuchkov, head of the KGB, and Anatoly Lukyanov, chairman of the USSR Supreme Soviet, were subsequently arrested on charges of plotting the coup. —TRANS.

took. He either did not notice the criticism, or interpreted it as an attempt on someone's part to evade the scrutiny of society and the press. The general secretary was making a serious mistake. A dictatorship of the right-wing mass media clearly was on the way— propaganda terrorism in which there could be no talk of diversity of ideas. On a single day, as if reacting to a starter's gun, five or six of the leading Moscow publications, along with TV and Radio Mayak, and with the powerful support of foreign stations, let loose a coordinated wave of attacks against all their foes in a destabilizing propaganda campaign.

People who called themselves democrats were giving off dictatorial signals and striving to monopolize minds, a dangerous tendency that threatened genuine democracy.[11] But Gorbachev underestimated it, and in the final analysis, the inevitable occurred. The evil genie let out of the bottle attacked its liberator. The radical press treacherously spoke out against Gorbachev at the most difficult and most critical moment of perestroika.

It took Gorbachev two years, until the October 1990 Central Committee plenum, to put on the agenda the question of "responsibility of the mass media" for "trying to impose one-sided, subjective views and passing them off as the opinion of the people." He justly accused the media of "abusing glasnost in order to incite trouble." In the long time it took him to reach this conclusion, perestroika, the process of democratization, and all of society had been dealt a hard blow.

The increasingly harsh criticism of the radical media from all segments of society, particularly the Party, forced Alexander Yakovlev to provide a theoretical underpinning for the destructive

---

[11]The true intentions of the "radical democrats" were revealed by subsequent events in Georgia. Coming to power on a wave of anti-Communism and anti-Sovietism, the local informal organizers, who were actively supported by Sobchak and others, first shut down the newspapers that disagreed with them and decided to dissolve the legally elected local soviets, appointing prefects in their place. Some "democrats": in the Western countries of civilized democracy, people were shocked by these untamed political mores.—AUTHOR

activity of the newspapers and magazines he protected. And so appeared the mysterious thesis that the press and television are merely a mirror reflecting life: as life is, so are the media. Yakovlev actually said at one Politburo meeting: "The main goal of the mass media is to reflect what is happening in life, in society. No wonder they are this way today."

Everyone buzzed in outrage, and the hostile reception forced Yakovlev to be quiet. But the question remained: How could Yakovlev, who had been in charge of ideology for many years at the Central Committee, speak of "mirroring" as the main function of the media? Everyone, including Yakovlev himself, knew very well that the press and television were the mightiest levers in forming public opinion.

This was my first encounter with Yakovlev's astonishing ability to call white black and black white. Later, I came to see that this was a polemical trick dear to this politician. I remember the May Day parade in Red Square in 1990. After the columns of trade union members marched past the Lenin mausoleum, an alternative demonstration of "crazies" took place on the square. With prompting and support from the Moscow City Council, it had been organized by the Moscow Voters' Club, Democratic Platform, and other so-called leftist groups, who carried slogans directed against the Politburo and Gorbachev.

I remember Gorbachev coming over to me and saying, "Yegor, I see it's time to put an end to this. Let's go."

"Yes, it's time," I replied.

And we all left the viewing platform on the mausoleum.[12]

It seemed so obvious. There was the array of political forces for all to see. But suddenly, at a press conference aired on Central Television, Yakovlev announced imperturbably that the anti-Gorbachev demonstration on Red Square had been organized by none

---

[12]That time, in the presence of the other Politburo members, I once again told Gorbachev that these events were confusing the country. But he waved off my warning and reproached me for harping on the same old thing.—AUTHOR

other than conservative forces. His statement, published in *Pravda,* elicited a feeling of extreme bewilderment. But it was clearer than ever what forces Yakovlev himself represented in the Politburo.

Ignoring the Politburo's negative reception of the "mirror theory," Yakovlev defended his thesis in the press and in a speech to a group of editors of youth newspapers at the Higher Komsomol School. Medvedev, echoing him, tried to instill the mirror idea at the Central Committee plenum, provoking a storm of negative reaction from the audience.

Politburo members expressed their collective indignation with the mirror thesis at several meetings. But, alas, Gorbachev's tepid position slid into noninterference with the media. The radicals used the press and TV to manipulate public opinion, persecuting people they didn't like and violating the Law on Elections during the campaign by giving priority time to their candidates.

I am talking not just about a difference of opinion in the press. A dictatorship of destructive forces reigned in the mass media. This accelerated economic collapse and intensified ethnic conflicts. Blows from the radical press seriously weakened the police, giving rise to an increase in crime, including organized crime. In general, their blows weakened society's immune system. Future historians will have no trouble finding a direct connection between destructive publications and the severe illnesses of our society—they will simply leaf through the radical press of the perestroika period.

I hope I am making myself clear. I am not trying to cast a shadow on all journalists whose publications willfully or accidentally aided the general destabilization of our life. I am certain that the great majority of them, especially the young ones, manipulated by politically sophisticated adults, knew not what they did. And my indictment of the destructive press should not be construed as lack of respect or trust for the mass media. I value them to the highest degree, a fact well known to the many Soviet and foreign journalists with whom I met readily. Many publications and entire journalist collectives met the demands of the times and held principled positions, giving a truthful picture of the past and the present.

And I don't feel any vengeful anger against the publications that wrote so many unfair and often slanderous things about me. Today, when the political passions that swirled around my name for several years have died down, I am often approached by the very newspapers and magazines that had "hunted" me so recently. I try not to refuse them, because only a fool could hold a grudge against the press.

No, my musing on the role of the media in perestroika was not prompted by insult or injury. This is a serious political analysis of what happened to the country in recent years, and the crucial role of the mass media cannot be overlooked. We in the USSR always knew that. But we had no idea what a powerful and dangerous weapon the media could be in glasnost and pluralism. Alexander Yakovlev, who had spent many years in the West, naturally had a much better understanding of this than the other members of the Politburo. From the very beginning he established a personal control over the right radical press. This is not speculation; the most "daring" newspapers often wrote about Yakovlev's patronage. Eventually he joined the constituent council of *Moscow News,* a clear indication of his closeness to the right radicals. Everything falls into place.

The truly radical media started using Yakovlev as a secret, then an open weapon in the power struggle on Old Square. And with their help, he directed public opinion against his opponents.[13]

My first open clash with Yakovlev goes back to fall 1987. During his vacation, Gorbachev, as usual, came up with a series of basic proposals for the further development of political processes in the country. Right after his return to Moscow, there was a meeting of the Politburo to discuss the issue of "range and pace of perestroika." The discussions were interesting and diverse. The meeting lasted a long time, and Yakovlev, several other comrades, and I were charged with drafting a resolution based on its conclusions.

I prepared the document, signed off on it, and handed it over to the General Department, to be sent out to all Politburo members. A day or two later I was given Gorbachev's draft of the resolution,

---

[13]Here it might be interesting to quote Svetlana Goryacheva, deputy chairman of the RSFSR Supreme Soviet, in an interview in *Pravda* given later on the role of the media: "I think that our propaganda has become a terrible weapon in terrible hands." —AUTHOR

which lacked many of the original points. In particular, the draft's criticism of the mass media and condemnation of people who blackened our history had been deleted. It turned out that Yakovlev, without telling anyone, had changed the resolution's text, and on the most fundamental issues.

This was a powerful surprise, since it violated the usual procedure for passing resolutions through the Politburo. Most importantly, it signified an attempt to ignore the collective opinion of the Politburo. After all, there had been strong criticism of the media at the meeting, and we had spent a lot of time on the negative effects of blackening Soviet history, because the Central Committee had been flooded with angry letters on that topic.

I immediately wrote my comments on the draft and sent them to Gorbachev, accompanied by a special note. I kept the draft in my files, and I feel I should give the entire note here.

> Mikhail Sergeyevich!
>
> Re the comments of Comrade Yakovlev, A. N., on the draft of the resolution of the Party Central Committee "On key issues of perestroika in the country and the goals of Party organizations in its activization."
>
> As you can see, everything that condemns the press's sensationalism or attempts at blackening everything achieved by our society has been deleted from the resolution's draft. Members of the Politburo Central Committee talked about this sort of phenomenon in discussing the present stage of perestroika. Workers are writing about it in their letters, and publications are printing this. How can we ignore such facts?
>
> There are things that can be dropped or added (the text is attached). These are my comments on the substance. And now about the form. I learned of the proposals of Comrade Yakovlev, A. N., only after we sent the draft on for voting, although my signature is also on the document.
>
> Respectfully,
>
> Ye. Ligachev
> 10/6/87.

I soon received a handwritten note from Gorbachev: "Yegor Kuzmich. I'm asking you to meet once more and discuss it calmly. And then come to see me. Maybe we should think more about what should be written and what should be borne in mind. M. Gorbachev"

That phrase, "think more about what should be written and what should be borne in mind," stunned me. Society was boiling, the demands from citizens and the public to bring democratic order into the press were increasing—and we were supposed to "bear it in mind" and nothing more?

I knew further discussion was pointless. Gorbachev did not take my comments into account. The text with Yakovlev's emendation was printed.

That fall, the press criticism of Yakovlev's "On Antihistoricism," published in *Literaturnaya gazeta* in 1972, was mounting. Their complaint was that the author had spoken out against the rebirth of Russian national consciousness, accused the peasantry of being patriarchal, and considered the publication of Karamzin's *History of the Russian State*[14] to be dangerous, although some writers were insisting on its being reprinted. Perestroika-era publications revealed that Yakovlev's 1972 article had upset the writer Mikhail Sholokhov, who had complained to Suslov. As a result, Yakovlev had been removed as head of the Central Committee Propaganda Department and as "punishment" sent as ambassador to Canada. Gorbachev asked me to meet with Yakovlev. He was aware that a fundamental conflict was ripening between the two of us, and I doubt that he expected us to make up and compromise.

Our conversation somehow began with Yakovlev demanding why I hadn't defended him when the criticism of his article appeared long ago. I hadn't even read the article, I admitted.

"I'll send it to you," Yakovlev said. "Read it and tell me your opinion. I think you'll support me. I'm being accused unjustly."

Then the conversation switched to current events, and it became

---

[14]*History of the Russian State* by Nikolai Karamzin (1766–1826), a conservative historian.—TRANS.

obvious that we had different positions. We disagreed on history, the Party, and the processes of democratization. I must say that Yakovlev has the gift of persuasion and follows the thread of conversation with precise logic. He couldn't affect me, however; his scythe kept hitting stone, as the saying goes.

For ninety minutes, we talked alone in my office. Neither of us changed his point of view, but our relationship became crystal clear.

Of course, there still remained a faint hope that once I read "On Antihistoricism" I would take Yakovlev's side. He was very grateful for any personal support. But after I read the article, I called him up and said, "I don't think we need to get into a long discussion. There are quite a few errors in your article and a peculiar way of looking at the past. . . . There's a lot I don't agree with."

It was a serious article. It wasn't simply an evaluation of some facts, it also was an expression of a world-view. And here I could not yield, couldn't make an alliance with Yakovlev on the unprincipled basis of "you scratch my back, I'll scratch yours."

I called Gorbachev and told him that I had met with Yakovlev but had come to the conclusion that we had different views on many important matters and held different positions.

"In general, Mikhail Sergeyevich," I summed up, "Yakovlev and I could not come up with a unified position. We have to face up to the truth."

From that moment on, I had no doubt that there would be a difficult battle in which the main attacking force against me would be the radical media. Of course, I didn't know that I would be made the fall guy in the Tbilisi Affair, the Gdlyan Affair, and even the Kolpashevo Incident[15] or that I would be branded "chief conservative"; or that Nina Andreyeva's article would prompt people to look for the "antiperestroika group" in the Politburo. But I did realize that a difficult period was coming. I knew in whose way I stood. And I consciously went forward, because I saw the storm clouds gathering over the country.

---

[15]See Chapters 4, 5, and 6, respectively, for discussions on these charges against Ligachev.—TRANS.

The radicalism embodied by Yakovlev at the highest level of Soviet leadership threatened to disrupt the tempo of perestroika and accelerate the pace of transformation without taking reality into account. I had to do everything in my power to block these ruinous attempts. Just as career considerations had not bothered me in 1983, they did not worry me in 1987; I perceived the coming struggle not as a struggle for power but for an idea, and I faced it unswervingly.

But even in that watershed autumn, I could not have imagined in my wildest dreams that I would be defending not only the concept of perestroika accepted in 1985, but also what was most sacred—socialism and the Communist Party—as the right radicals, the pseudodemocrats, mounted an attack against them.

I could not have foreseen the tension and urgency of developments right on Old Square. The attempt to diminish Ligachev's influence had negative consequences for the entire Party. Not because of me personally; it was just the way circumstances unfolded. But as a Central Committee member noted correctly, the Party seemed to be suffering from sleeping sickness.

Exactly a year after the events I have described, in September 1988, again during his regular vacation, Gorbachev worked out a plan for the reorganization of the Central Committee's work. He proposed the creation of commissions on ideology, organization, economics, agriculture, international affairs, and other issues, each to be headed by a Politburo member. This reorganization was motivated by a desire to improve the Central Committee's work. But its ultimate aim was very clear.

Given the atmosphere of confrontation created by the fact that the two people in the Politburo dealing with ideology, Ligachev and Yakovlev, held opposing positions, the situation truly did need to be eased. But the path chosen to do so was at best strange: the creation of commissions automatically buried the Secretariat. This was a very serious violation of the Party's bylaws, unprecedented in recent decades. The cleverness, whether intentional or not, lay in the fact that no one made any mention of eliminating Secretariat meetings or seemed to be attacking them. The commissions were established, and the Secretariat's meetings simply ended of their own accord. The Party was deprived of an operating staff for its leaders.

This had a deleterious effect on the activity of both the Central Committee and the regional Party committees. Executive discipline decreased sharply, and control weakened. One of the Secretariat's most important functions was to spread useful experience throughout the Party. But the division of commissions by branch forced the Party workers to deal with problems on their own. The center seemed to vanish and vertical ties as well.

Almost a year had gone by without a meeting of the Secretariat, and although there had been no official announcement, it was no secret. At home and abroad, I had to answer many questions. Central Committee commissions were now dealing with basic issues, I explained. I feel now that I was mistaken in not raising the question of the Secretariat at a Politburo meeting or Central Committee plenum. To tell the truth, I did not do so for the sole reason that the question dealt with me personally. False modesty led me to ignore my principles and make concessions where I should not have done so. Even when Alexandra Biryukova, candidate member of the Politburo, asked Gorbachev why the Secretariat was not doing its work, I held my tongue. Gorbachev passed the question to me: Ask Ligachev whether he needs a Secretariat, he said. And I did not reply. Well, so be it.

In the new, incredibly more complex political situation, the Communists at the local level waited in vain for directions from Moscow. The Central Committee plenums heard many requests, even demands, for the formulation of a clear Party position on what was happening. These were fair and legitimate demands; the Central Committee existed to serve the main Party headquarters. It was supposed to perform the function of the central body of any political party in the world: direct its members through pitched political battles, especially elections. But the answer from the Central Committee was always the same: "Decide for yourselves how to act. Don't wait for prompting from the center; decide for yourselves."

This mistaken thesis disarmed the Party in the face of a new danger, anti-Communism. And was very cleverly done, given the verbal exhortations that had been made during the election campaign ("Don't interfere!"). The hands of the Party committees that had believed the "decide for yourselves" directive and that were trying to have an active effect on the campaign were being tied. And the fact that the Secretariat Central Committee did not meet during the elections made things worse.

The cessation of the Secretariat meetings also undermined the principle of collective leadership, including the collective discussion of personnel questions. Technically, decisions of the Secretariat still came out of the Central Committee buildings. But this was a matter of formality, of sending papers from office to office for signatures.

Party history shows that violations of the principle of collective leadership have always led to unfortunate consequences for the country. The reasons for these violations have varied with the times; in Yakovlev's case, the Secretariat obviously was in his way. At meetings he usually had nothing to say. I sensed that he did not always read the materials the Secretariat had prepared. Beginning in spring 1988, he began missing the meetings entirely, sometimes without letting me know that he would be absent. I reprimanded him once, and Yakovlev replied, "I had orders from Mikhail Sergeyevich. I was working out of town." I mentioned this to Gorbachev, and he avoided a straight answer. I could see it clearly: the Secretariat was in the way.

After about a year, matters forced a resumption of Secretariat meetings; the work of the apparat was in danger of paralysis. But these meetings, presided over by Medvedev, were sporadic and did not examine serious issues. Regular meetings were reinstituted only after the 28th Party Congress. The commissions of the Central Committee maintained their existence as well. Experience showed that they were not mutually exclusive, which merely goes to show that getting rid of the Secretariat's meetings was a premeditated ploy.

After the commissions were formed, I was assigned agricultural policy, Yakovlev international affairs, and Medvedev ideology.[16]

---

[16]I plan to deal thoroughly with the 28th Party Congress in the second volume of my memoirs.—AUTHOR

How and why did Medvedev become chief ideologist? The answer need not be sought in mistakes or carelessness; on the contrary, it was done consciously and neatly. Medvedev's personality made him a very convenient person. His clockwork obedience ensured that as chief ideologist he would promote firmly, without any deviation, whatever line he was instructed to push.

And Gorbachev was not the only one who gave instructions. Often it was Yakovlev. The end of the Secretariat meetings and the confirmation of Medvedev as chief Party ideologist meant that Yakovlev became the man who determined ideological policy in the Central Committee. From that moment, his role as *éminence grise* was clear.

Yakovlev, who had managed to surround Gorbachev with his people, stood invisibly behind many of the unexpected turns and zigzags in the policies of recent years. It was he, running the radical press, who tried to manipulate public opinion.

How could Yakovlev have gotten rid of such a serious obstacle as the permanent collective Secretariat without getting rid of Ligachev? The answer is very simple. Both Yakovlev and Gorbachev knew well that they could not raise the question of removing me from the Politburo at the Central Committee plenum. The plenum would not have supported it. Moreover, the very attempt could have brought unexpected consequences for its initiators. Gorbachev was well aware of how much influence I had among the active members of the Party.

The very fact of the unceasing attacks against me make me ponder their ulterior motive. Let me reiterate that there were no personal motivations behind them, no hostility or old scores to settle. My relationship with Yakovlev remained stable, that with Gorbachev quite friendly. We had moved together toward April 1985 and we had started perestroika together. As for the struggle for power that Yakovlev was waging, the question had been decided in the fall of 1988, when I was *de facto* removed from the post of second secretary and put in charge of agricultural matters. Why start such furious propaganda attacks against me after that?

From the point of view of the antiperestroika forces, it was absolutely necessary, because the ideological struggle had continued to grow. My firm position interfered with the radicals' plans to drag the country into ruin. I continued to defend the socialist choice and the class interests of the workers and to struggle against the ideological destruction of the Party.

That is why I never considered tendering my resignation, which some people must have been hoping for. The writer Oles Adamovich, one of the radicals who could be considered an "ultra" radical and who tried hard to create a schism in society, in fact called for me to do so. But there were hundreds of letters from all over the country demanding that I not retire. And these came not only from rank-and-file Communists but also from many non-Party members. People called on me to stand firm—and I did.

By spring 1990, when the threat of an all-encompassing crisis hung over the country and many of the things I had warned about had unfortunately come to pass, I began to sense the public atmosphere around me changing. The radical press, which had accused me of all the mortal sins, was losing public confidence. In addition, the slanderous charges made by Gdlyan and Ivanov had been seen by everyone as the provocation they were. Overall, I felt a noticeable lightening. And during that same period I took numerous measures right in the Central Committee, in particular demanding the immediate convocation of the Central Committee plenum to discuss the situation in the Party and the country.

Many Party organizations were insisting on such a plenum. Resolutions to this effect were put forward by the Moscow City and Leningrad Province Party committees as well as by several committees in the RSFSR, Ukraine, Byelorussia, and other republics whose leaders were part of the Central Committee. The flood of resolutions coming into the Central Committee increased, but it never went beyond letting the Politburo members and the Central Committee secretaries know about it. I kept asking myself how a member of the political leadership should be acting in this situation. All attempts to examine the issue at the Politburo failed. And then I used the right of a Communist guaranteed by the bylaws—I wrote a letter to the Central Committee. I cite it without cuts.

To General Secretary of the CPSU Central Committee,
Comrade Gorbachev, M. S.

After painful thought, I decided to appeal to you, Mikhail
Sergeyevich, with questions on the situation in the CPSU.

In the first three years of perestroika the situation in society changed for the better and the Party's authority increased. Then a retrograde movement began. Now, as many
say with anxiety, the country has reached a limit. There is a
real threat to the unity of the Soviet federation, to the unity
of the CPSU. Our society, which tends to have historical
optimism, peace, and quiet, is being overwhelmed with uncertainty, torment, and interethnic conflict. There are thousands of refugees in the country. Great mistakes were made
in the implementation of economic reform, discipline and responsibility have fallen, and the lives of many people have
grown worse. Forces contrary to socialism are at large in
society.

The CPSU Central Committee receives resolutions, letters,
and telegrams from Party organizations, work collectives,
groups, and individual citizens in which, while supporting
the policy of perestroika, Soviet people express profound
anxiety and great pain for our Motherland and the Communist Party. I have formed the same impression from my
meeting with work collectives. People are constantly asking
each of us, and what do we tell them?

I always felt and continue to feel—and I am not alone in
this—that the main force that is capable of bringing the
country out of this acute situation and to implement reform
in society are the CPSU and the soviets. But only if the
Party is united and organized and its policies respond to the
interests of the working class and the laboring masses. Only
in that case can it preserve its political leadership.

In my opinion, the great danger lies in the fact that we
allowed the weakening of the Party. That, I believe, is the
mistake of the political leadership, the Politburo Central
Committee. Of course, the burden of the past has its effect
on the Party's authority—the severe consequences of Stalin-

ism and the stagnation period and the fact of moral corruption of some leaders.

Even now there are factions, groups, and opposition tendencies within the Party. Based on the Democratic Platform, the revisionists (who call themselves radicals) are trying to transform the CPSU from within into a parliamentary party, removing it from organization work with the masses and in work collectives. Entire groups of Communists not only participate in, but lead nationalistic, separatist organizations.

An avalanche of lies is falling on the Party. So many worthy Communists, leaders, prominent representatives of science, culture, and literature have been slandered in recent times. The Soviet Army and the security agencies are subjected to constant attacks and slander.

Under the flag of democracy and glasnost, the ideological and moral pillars of society are being washed away. The destructive work of the opposition forces coincides with the hostile forces from outside. They have set as their goal the breakup of socialism in the USSR, after Eastern Europe, to ruin the social transformation along the lines of scientific socialism, and switch our country to the tracks of capitalist development.

As for the mass media, along with the great creative work that they are doing, some publications, television studios, and radio programs openly trample our past and present, inciting tension in society, hushing up the positive processes of perestroika, and paying no attention to the daily work of millions of Soviet people. There is no pluralism of opinion; this is dictatorship.

And there is a lot of talk about this, including at the Central Committee plenums and Politburo sessions and in the USSR Supreme Soviet, but the situation is not improving. It goes no farther than an exchange of opinion.

In connection with the decision of the Lithuanian Supreme Soviet to leave the USSR, the situation in the Soviet federation has grown more acute and the tendency toward separatism in the other Union republics has increased. State and international interests are being pushed into the background.

All the issues I have listed have been raised frequently by many Central Committee members at plenums. It cannot be said that I am writing about the problems of the unity of the Party for the first time, suddenly, or unexpectedly. I have spoken about them openly and honestly at the Central Committee plenums, at meetings of the first secretaries of the Union republics' Party Central Committees, at Territory and Province Party committee meetings, and at the Politburo. Letters and resolutions come to the Central Committee in which Communists and Party committees criticize the Politburo of the Central Committee for inconsistency. They express the opinion of the Party masses, the workers, and demand increased struggle against destructive forces.

Throughout the Party, along with democratization and strengthening ties with the masses, there was the goal of purging the ranks of those who hold positions of revisionism, social democratism, and nationalism. Otherwise the Party may break up. And then the CPSU can expect the fate of the Communist Party of Lithuania. Why are we delaying? Naturally this work must take place strictly within the framework of the bylaws of the CPSU and USSR Constitution.

I feel that this is the time to examine the political situation in the Party at the Central Committee plenum. If we turn to history, we see that the current moment was examined collectively at plenums under Lenin. We must convene an extraordinary CPSU Central Committee plenum. The Party's goals in strengthening its unity and the unity of the Soviet state could be discussed there. We had agreed at the Politburo to send a letter on this issue to the Party organizations. I am certain that that is not enough.

Among other issues, I feel we must pay attention to the question of particular political importance, the participation of the working class and the peasantry in government agencies and Party committees. As you know, things have reached the point that only one worker each from Moscow and from Leningrad was elected as a people's deputy of the RSFSR. Another urgent matter is an open and direct talk and a decision on increasing the influence of the Party on Communists working in the mass media.

The Party expects an analysis of the events in Eastern Europe from the Central Committee. The socialist community is falling apart and NATO is growing stronger. The German question is a priority. I think that in a historical plane, this is a temporary setback for socialism and I am convinced that the Communist idea will be victorious.

You know me and my character, Mikhail Sergeyevich, and you must understand that I had to write this letter. The situation demands immediate action. The Party and the Motherland are in danger, I would say in great danger. The possible breakup of our federation would be a world shock, an irreparable blow against socialism and the international Communist and workers' movement.

I am convinced that an examination of these questions at a Central Committee plenum would be of great benefit.

I would ask you to bring my letter to the attention of the comrades of the Politburo and the Central Committee of the Party.

Respectfully yours,

Ye. Ligachev
17 March 1990

Subsequent events fully confirmed the analysis made in this letter. If Gorbachev had yielded to the demands from local Party committees and convened a Central Committee plenum to discuss the situation in the Party and in the country, it is quite possible that the developments could have been controlled and a profound crisis avoided. Alas, the plenum was not convened. Despite the loud pronouncements about perfecting internal Party democracy, the members of the Central Committee were not shown my letter. It simply fell into a crevasse.

That was Gorbachev's method. Under Stalin, you would have lost your head for a letter like that. Under Khrushchev, you would have been fired. Under Brezhnev, you would be made an ambassador to Africa. And under Gorbachev, you were simply ignored.

Be that as it may, by the 28th Congress the attacks on me had diminished and my position in the Party had strengthened considerably. Gorbachev and Yakovlev of course understood this.

And on the eve of the Congress an incredible proposal was put forward: to replace the Party leadership entirely. In reality, this idea meant eliminating the entire notion of succession. It is possible, even necessary, to replace a third, or half, or even two-thirds of the leadership at the congresses. But remove almost all of them at once? That had never happened in the history of our Party, and never abroad, in Communist, socialist, or bourgeois parties. A complete change of all the members of the Politburo was an antidemocratic, violent measure. But they didn't care.

I will not go now into the stormy events of the 28th Congress, where I fought to the bloody end. But I must mention one curious episode that occurred the day before the Congress ended, when I had lost the election for deputy general secretary, which in effect meant retirement. During one of the breaks I was in the vestibule of the Palace of Congresses, discussing events with a couple of writers, Vladimir Karpov and Anatoly Salutsky. Unexpectedly, the famous American Sovietologist Stephen Cohen came up to me with a cameraman. I had read his book on Nikolai Bukharin, and we had met before. During these meetings, I realized that I did not share Cohen's views on the processes taking place in the USSR and that he was not among those who shared my position.

And suddenly Stephen Cohen, whose Russian isn't bad, exclaimed, "Yegor Kuzmich, let me shake your hand. You are a bold man, a very brave man! You made a handsome exit!"

Well, Stephen Cohen is entitled to evaluate my actions as he wishes. But actually, I had not thought about "making a handsome exit." The issue was otherwise. I realized that I would not be elected deputy general secretary, if only because Gorbachev was opposed. Then why did I agree to run? With only one aim: to state my position and my perception of the situation as fully as possible to the Congress delegates, the Communists of the land. I used my last chance to the utmost.

I was not the only one sounding the alarm, but it dissipated like water in the sand. Yakovlev kept soothing people, saying, "We're all so nervous today. Is it worth it? This is a normal perestroika period, a normal process. These are the inevitable difficulties of a transitional stage, and there is no need to worry so much."

I remember once at a Politburo meeting responding harshly, "Don't lull us. There are no men with weak nerves at this table. A crisis is developing in the country."

But Yakovlev went on smoothing corners. He behaved this way in every urgent situation, whether the issue was the radical media or Lithuania. That was his position: Don't worry. It reminded me of the old vaudeville song "Everything's Fine, Lovely Marquise!" Flames were raging in one spot after another, but Yakovlev calmly drawled his "Don't worry." Was it lack of contact with reality? Absence of political acumen? Shortsightedness? Or, on the contrary, far-reaching calculation? I was frankly amazed by the combination of strong political radicalism and his attempts to lull us on the eve of the most critical situations.

In many moments of fundamental crisis, when Gorbachev seemed to take a sane position, Yakovlev's approach eventually won out. The *éminence grise* knew how to get his own way. One of the most vivid and telling illustrations of this is an incident that occurred on the eve of the 28th Party Congress. Preparations were fully under way when the question arose of inviting foreign delegations. This was a longstanding tradition of our congresses, and it seemed to me that at our landmark stage of perestroika, the need for foreign guests was even greater. The threat of schism hung over the Party, and we had to seek new paths of consolidation. Moreover, we would now have to live in a multiparty system, and we could use the experience and advice of those who had been functioning under those conditions for a long time.

And, in general, how could we hide the struggle inside the Party from our comrades in ideology?

But the International Department of the Central Committee, headed by Yakovlev, unexpectedly sent the Politburo members a document stating baldly that foreign delegations should not be invited. Once I read it, I instantly wrote Gorbachev a short note expressing my position: this was a serious question, and I was all for inviting them; it was useful both for us and for our foreign comrades.

A few days later Gorbachev went off on an official visit to the United States. As usual, all the members of the political leadership met at Vnukovo-2 Airport. As he said good-bye, Gorbachev returned to the question I had raised.

"Well, are we going to invite foreign delegations or not? Yegor Kuzmich insists on it. I think that he is right, and I support him."

Everyone agreed. There was no disagreement from Yakovlev, either.

A few days after that, we convened in the Secretariat's meeting room on Old Square, and I turned to Medvedev. "How are things going with the invitations for foreign delegations to the Congress?"

Instead of Medvedev, Yakovlev replied. "It's expensive—we'd have to spend millions."

Nikolai Slyunkov[17] replied indignantly, "What are you saying, Alexander Nikolayevich? How can you use such a yardstick in this important issue?"

Slyunkov was doubly right, because in recent years we had spent a lot of money on receiving numerous foreign delegations invited by Yakovlev and just as much on trips abroad by our people, usually the radicals. But no sooner did the conversation turn to Communist delegations than Yakovlev brought up the lack of funds. Yet even that trivial aspect could have been settled by compromise: unlike previous congresses, we could have received the delegations modestly this time, with minimal expenses.

So I strongly supported Slyunkov: "This is a political question. We have always invited comrades from abroad. We will not be understood if now, in the era of glasnost, we act differently."

A discussion of sorts ensued. But having learned from the past

---

[17]Nikolai Slyunkov was first secretary of the Byelorussian Central Committee until his dismissal over the Chernobyl disaster, after which he was made a Politburo member. —TRANS.

two years, I knew that Yakovlev would silently stand his ground and do nothing. Or rather, do something quietly—that was his favorite way, his usual tactic. Days passed. In the end, the question of inviting foreign delegations was buried. For the first time in many decades, there were no delegations from friendly parties at the Congress.

Why had Yakovlev been so opposed to the presence of foreign guests? I think he was afraid of what they would say. The Congress promised to be very heated. It was expected that the right-wingers who called themselves the Democratic Platform and were supported by Yakovlev would try to overthrow the Party or, at least, split it up. Without a doubt, the foreign delegations would not have hailed this turn of events and would have supported the healthy forces in the Party.

But more important, for the first time in many years, if not in all of Soviet history, the 28th Congress did not reflect the international workers' and Communist movement, and the new bylaws of the Party excluded the paragraph stating that the Party is an integral part of that movement. Even in the most difficult times, when the Party was underground, it had never hidden its programmatic ideas.

These questions came up at the Politburo when we discussed the draft of the bylaws. And every time I proposed retaining this important position, the proposal was declined without debate.

Analysis of the contemporary international Communist and workers' movements is a complex matter, of course, and demands great knowledge, political acumen, and profound thinking. The Communist movement has borne great losses and is in crisis. That is all the more reason for a collective analysis and development of measures to overcome the crisis. Our Party has adequate intellectual power to do this work jointly with foreign friends on the basis of discussion and free exchange of opinion. In the early years of perestroika, serious attempts were made in this line, by Gorbachev, among others. But then it was dropped. Why? What explains the lowered interest in ties with Communist and workers' parties? What objective and subjective factors have led to this? Perhaps our participation in the Communist movement is an obstacle to someone abroad?

I still have not found the answers to many of these questions. This is another enigma about Gorbachev.

Certainly, almost every speech the general secretary made on international affairs (and not only international affairs) was prepared by Yakovlev. In general, Gorbachev is a politician who works on his own speeches. But he inevitably brought in Yakovlev, who was thus able to influence him.

The second volume of this book will deal with how Yakovlev handled his own job, international politics. It will examine questions relating to the events in Eastern Europe. Yakovlev calls the changes that occurred there a "great movement forward," but in my opinion that statement is merely an attempt to make a defeat look like a victory. And the events in Eastern Europe are far from over.

I have spoken here of the concrete instances in which Gorbachev changed his position. But that was just the tip of the iceberg.

The Khrushchev Syndrome

The composition of the Secretariat in the period when I ran its meetings was consistently held at seven of the total of twelve Politburo members—a hefty percentage. But in mid-1987 I began to feel that the Secretariat's precise and efficient work, especially given its numerical clout, was making some people, including Gorbachev, uneasy. The signs were elusive, but in my daily meetings with him I could sense them. For me, my own, inner promptings are always most important, and they were pure. I saw in Gorbachev a leader of the processes of renewal who held firm to the ethics of the workplace, did not indulge in intrigues, and worked truly hard in the name of perestroika. And so I had no intention of changing my style of working.

A writer once said, "Evil tongues are worse than a pistol." The growth of the Secretariat's influence and authority apparently were misrepresented by some. The following may have had something to do with it.

There were people in my office waiting room from morning until night. And not because I was "marinating" them—I saw everyone, usually on a first-come, first-served basis, making exceptions only for those who had come from afar, who were allowed in sooner. But many people wanted to see me, and so there was always a crowd near my office. Of course, the first secretaries of provincial committees also made a point of coming up to Office No. 2 whenever they were in Moscow, and I was always ready to receive them.

I have reason to suspect that Gorbachev was given a slanted picture of this human bustle in my waiting room. I worked long, hard, and intensely, solving many specific and vitally important matters with the people who came to see me. After all, that was my practical contribution to perestroika. But someone apparently tried to persuade Gorbachev that Ligachev was taking too much upon himself and was forging too many strong ties in the Party and among the Central Committee members. The press began hinting at a "Ligachev conspiracy" in the Central Committee.

I have no direct proof, nor can I have, that this persuasion of Gorbachev came from Yakovlev. But my indirect evidence is impressive. Yakovlev never rejected the insinuations about a "Ligachev conspiracy" in the Central Committee either verbally or in writing, nor any other inflated talk of conspiracy. Furthermore, the radical press would start a fuss about a so-called conspiracy on my part virtually every time Gorbachev left the country. The very fact that the word "conspiracy" was widely used by the very media closest to Yakovlev is clear evidence that it was coming from the political top.

I'll say more. At some point, talk of "October 1964"—when Khrushchev was removed at the Central Committee plenum—spread through the offices on Old Square, all the way from the staff offices to the top. It was even picked up by the press. I don't know who initiated those "symbolic" reminiscences, but they created an atmosphere of anxiety. And they corresponded clearly in time with the growing criticism of the radical mass media in the Central Committee plenums and other meetings.

The steady repetition of the conspiracy theory in the newspapers heightened tensions (it's easier to catch fish in murky waters) and had the additional effect of turning Gorbachev's thoughts to conspiracy, although I did not think for a moment that the general secretary might believe seriously in the possibility of a conspiracy on my part; he knew me too well. And he's not a meek fellow himself; he's psychologically steadfast and not that impressionable. It was more a question of Gorbachev being attracted to the role of "enlightened monarch," and showing greater interest in abstract philosophical, political, and ethical categories, and less in the dull and thankless but imperative work of running an enormous country. I am drawn to real, practical work and defended its priority, and therefore was out of place on the team that had formed with Yakovlev's arrival and that was changing the orientation of perestroika. So the rumors of a conspiracy were useful.

Furthermore, perestroika, which had started out so well, began to experience great difficulties in 1989. The sharp radicalization of political change, combined with the mess in the economy, confused many people. The notion of a gradual mastery of innovation associated with so-called conservative thinking is, in fact, society's defense reaction against political extremism. People throughout the world understand this, and it is one reason why conservative parties are so popular in developed bourgeois countries.

But instead of realizing the inevitability and fruitfulness of this gradual process, right-wing radical Alexander Yakovlev followed the worst traditions of the past and invented an imaginary enemy—in this case, of perestroika. Tellingly, the term "enemy of perestroika" appeared first on the pages of *Moscow News*. On the philosophical level, this policy shift meant that the very concept of perestroika was being replaced silently by the concept of the "great leap." Those who exhibited caution before such a leap and preferred the process of restructuring—which is what "perestroika" means—were declared proponents of the old command bureaucratic methods and the forces of obstruction, and were given the political label of conservatives.

Here I must shift ahead in time to Foreign Minister Shevardnadze's speech at the 4th Congress of People's Deputies in December 1990, when he resigned and suddenly—*very* suddenly—

announced that healthy conservatism was not such a terrible thing. Gorbachev soon started echoing Shevardnadze: the "reactionaries," as it turned out, were those who called themselves democrats. It was the reactionaries who were the problem.

It was an amazing metamorphosis, but why hadn't they talked that way two years earlier? There had been enough material to come to this conclusion even then. But the tantalizing all-permissiveness of the radical press was presented as the highest manifestation of democracy. That's when the manipulation of the mass consciousness began.

In one speech, Gorbachev spoke of "the various forms of the realization of socialist property." In my opinion, this was fully in keeping with the restructuring of economic relations and represented a definite step forward from the days of total state ownership. The press immediately latched onto this thesis and actively propagandized for it, which in itself was fine. But with the passage of time it became clear that the word "realization" was being removed from Gorbachev's formula, greatly changing the meaning. That was merely the beginning of the transformation.

Later, without any theoretical basis, the word "socialist" also disappeared. That left "various forms of property"—which brought public consciousness to the point of accepting the naturalness of private property. The concept of "socialist pluralism" was turned into "political pluralism." The thesis of the priority of universal values, first used by Gorbachev in reference to peace, underwent a similar transformation. In a discussion of the nuclear standoff, this was a progressive thesis, and an important element in the policy of peaceful coexistence of countries with different social systems. But the radical mass media again subtly transferred this concept to the sphere of social relations, counterposing it to class interests.

Leafing through newspaper clippings, you can find that this transfer as well was done without any theoretical basis. Far from noncontroversial clichés were simply drummed into people's minds.

Returning to the conspiracy theme, let me say that even if Gorbachev could not have been mistaken about me personally, could not have believed such a danger from me, under the influence of the massive propaganda in the media, he must have felt anxiety about "conservative forces" in general. The shadow of the October 1964 plenum hovered over Gorbachev, putting the "conservative menace" in the forefront of Gorbachev's consciousness and influencing him to trust unknown radicals.

The Central Committee elected at the 28th Party Congress was very powerful and included quite a few new people recently moved up to the top. In my view it was an able and judicious Central Committee. It stood firmly for perestroika. That is precisely why it was wary of the "great leap"—the radical idea in "democratic" guise—that changed radically the original goals of perestroika. At every plenum, discussion and criticism were heard of the radical media, of the scattershot attempts in economics, and of Gorbachev himself.

Every plenum was now a serious trial for the general secretary, and Gorbachev repeatedly told me he was planning to quit.

At many plenums, after harsh criticism, Gorbachev would say during the breaks to the inner circle of the Politburo members: "The composition of the Central Committee is extremely conservative, and it is impossible to work with them. I'm going to quit. I'll go out there and tell them that."

In practice, however, Gorbachev took little account of the Central Committee's opinion. So no one has the right to put the blame for the subsequent crisis on the "conservative composition of the Central Committee." But the strained relations of the general secretary with part of the Central Committee created by the "Khrushchev syndrome" did lead a large number of Central Committee members, who for various reasons had been removed from their Party or economic sector posts, to submit their resignations collectively at the May 1989 plenum. According to the leadership, this move obviated the danger of a coup and freed them to proceed with accelerated political reform.

I was close to many of the first secretaries of provincial committees, knew their moods, and saw them frequently. I am prepared to swear that throughout this period all those people, despite their concern about the radicalization of perestroika, definitely supported Gorbachev, and him alone. Not just in words or public speeches, but in their hearts and minds and actions, they considered him the leader of the new course. They had given him his 1985 landslide victory as general secretary, pinning their hopes for change and renewal to him.

Could these first secretaries really have wanted Gorbachev removed just two years later? Impossible; and it did not happen. The dissent at the plenums stemmed from Central Committee members' belief that extreme radicalization was diverting perestroika from its original path. With all their political experience, they could see who was rushing Gorbachev and why, and they foresaw the consequences of that haste.

If Gorbachev had marched in step with these realists, we would be much farther along today. We would not have landed in this crisis and political destabilization, and we would not have to go backward to restore foolishly disrupted contractual economic ties. And I have no doubt that the Party would not have been removed from economic life.

Instead, the Central Committee's unwillingness to turn perestroika into the "great leap" was presented to Gorbachev as a danger of a coup. It was clear that the radicals' clamor of "conspiracy" was an artifice, a treacherous attempt to lead the Party and society's sound forces far away from the real danger: nationalist separatism and anti-Communism. Life soon proved the truth of this. As the political atmosphere grew even more heated, the radicals again spluttered about a conspiracy—this time, of "the generals." And the press repeated such ridiculous rumors, for instance, describing the work of soldiers in picking potatoes around Moscow as deliberate troop movements toward the capital to seize power.

And recall Shevardnadze's stormy December 1990 warning of a possible dictatorship, which was immediately picked up by the radical press. Paradoxically, this time the propaganda campaign about a conspiracy to set up a dictatorship was now directed against Gorbachev. Or rather, not paradoxically, but logically—destructive radical logic.

One of the answers to the "Gorbachev enigma" that puzzled so many people in the USSR and abroad lies in the "Khrushchev syndrome" implanted in his consciousness, the bitter lesson of the October 1964 plenum at which the reformist leader Khrushchev was removed from his post.[18] But the Khrushchev syndrome alone cannot explain the zigzags of the political course associated so closely with Gorbachev's name. There was an entire complex of interrelated causes, including Gorbachev's personal qualities.

Here I am approaching the answer to one of the most important and interesting questions relating to the "enigma of Gorbachev"— the question of being too late.

Being late, or reacting too slowly to events, was one of the most characteristic traits of Gorbachev's policies. There were numerous examples, ranging from Nagorno-Karabakh and Lithuania to price reform and economic and financial measures to overtake the crisis. He was justly criticized more than once for this lateness by the Politburo, and in thousands of letters to the Central Committee and newspapers. Being too late with concrete practical actions has, in fact, become something of a symbol of perestroika.

Why didn't we take timely action when things began to go wrong? I don't pretend to have an exhaustive answer, but here are a few of my thoughts:

In the final years of Brezhnev's administration, social and political developments were marked by a gap between word and deed. They said one thing and did another. For example, they propagandized an "economical economy" but devoured hundreds of billions in hard currency and rubles obtained through the sale of oil and alcoholic products. After the April 1985 Central Committee plenum,

---

[18]In an article about Khrushchev, Fyodor Burlatsky wrote openly that Khrushchev had been defeated by his foes and removed from his post because he did not depend on the intelligentsia and did not deem it necessary to attract them to his side. This, of course, is a highly primitive look at history and the causes of Khrushchev's removal. However, what was important for Burlatsky was not historical accuracy but historical parallel. His thoughts about Khrushchev, published in *Literaturnaya gazeta,* were obviously meant as a hint for Gorbachev. And this confirms the fact that Khrushchev's story was put into circulation to create a certain position on Gorbachev's part toward the "forces of obstruction."—AUTHOR

this gap between word and deed began to be narrowed in both politics and the economy. We soberly and realistically reevaluated the economy and on that basis developed the concept of perestroika. There were mistakes in perestroika as we sought the right path, errors and political zigzags, but there were never any intentionally false dead ends or vicious circles.

It was an honest policy. And this was the fundamental government and political approach. But if we descend from these heights to the sphere of concrete decisions, we see a completely different picture. Here the gap between word and deed was actually growing. Not because one thing was said and another was done; now, much was said and little got done.

Of course, some of this was due to the newness and scope of the transformations and to lack of political experience. The backwardness of social sciences, including economics, had a deleterious effect. But the delay in making decisions was decisive.

So many just words were spoken at Politburo meetings and on television in reference to one crisis or another. How correctly Gorbachev had spoken on the state of the Party and the media! The widespread opinion that the top political leadership was not in the know about certain events is deeply mistaken. The Politburo had virtually exhaustive information on all situations of conflict—political, economic, financial, interethnic.

I remember someone once saying to me about Gorbachev, "Mikhail Sergeyevich is a president who wants to go down in history as a clean man, whom no one can accuse of dictatorship."

Perhaps this concern about his "historical image" did sometimes keep Gorbachev from taking decisive, necessary, but unpopular measures. As a result, problems grew, contradictions mounted, and crises escalated. And in the long run, this line led to a slowdown in perestroika. But having analyzed a large number of facts and conversations with Gorbachev, I have come to the conclusion that it was also a tactical measure of a special kind.

Gorbachev is one of those politicians who takes decisive measures when the situation is overripe; he waits for the apple to drop. He always worried about how the country and the world would accept the solutions he offered for some conflict; that's natural in politics. But I wouldn't say he was overly concerned about using unpopular measures—like any politician, he considered this, but it did not predominate. When a conflict situation came to a peak, when the thunder rolled—then Gorbachev would begin to act. He preferred reproaches for being too late to attacks for making mistakes. Being late is not as dangerous as being wrong for a political reputation, at least at first. Besides, intervening after the fact creates the image of a "savior" who comes to straighten out a situation. As for the colossal losses, human and material, caused by the conflict, which could and should have been avoided, those were brushed over, and stress was laid on "clearing up the consequences."

Yes, Gorbachev was often forced to fix his own mistakes. "Someone" led the Party out of the economy, weakened the principle of democratic centralism and Party discipline . . . then Gorbachev sounded the call for Communists to take up economics and strengthen discipline in the Party. "Someone" overradicalized the development of the economy, trying in 1988 to introduce market relations, and by running too far ahead led to catastrophic disruption of economic ties and a decrease in production and problems in monetary circulation . . . and then the president proposed rational measures to get out of the crisis. "Someone" did not appreciate the dangers of nationalism, let it emerge, and as a result the very existence of our state was threatened . . . and only then did Gorbachev make desperate, if noble efforts to save the Union.

This list of mistakes and corrective measures could be extended, for after 1988, the policies of perestroika turned into "chasing its own tail," and the country gradually slipped toward the brink. The guilt lay with the tactic of being late: that "someone" was Gorbachev himself.

We can't say he didn't know the situation or was ignorant of the dangers. Gorbachev and all of us were warned many times, and fierce fighting was going on over these questions at the plenums and in the Politburo. The most important moments of that struggle—over the economy, Party unity, and nationalism are reflected in this book. But Gorbachev was under the influence of the radicals.[19] They called themselves the "foremen of perestroika,"[20] but they were actually its gravediggers.

My main conclusion is absolutely objective, based on analysis and checked against all known facts and events. Beginning in 1988, the original concept of perestroika, under the influence of radical ideas, underwent significant changes. Zigzags, ad hoc adjustments, and the undermining of the Party and the state began. The country was being shaken feverishly to the point of destructive flutter.[21] And in that truly extreme situation, Gorbachev turned to the sources of perestroika, to conclusions he had rejected or underestimated earlier. This was very clear in economics, when he suddenly saw the light: You can't destroy the old without first building the new. This also affected his rational approach to the Union treaty, and to the very nature of our system—after all, Gorbachev suggested changing the meaning of the second "S" in USSR from "Socialist" to "Sovereign" to make the Union of Soviet Sovereign Republics. And he finally gave a clear opinion on that grave danger, nationalism. (As recently as 1989, many people, notably Yakovlev, preferred not to use the word and spoke of a vague "extremism.")

The radicals' attempt to accuse Gorbachev of moving toward dictatorship was another cheap propaganda trick in the campaign to bring Gorbachev over to their side. Finding himself in a dead-end situation, loyal to the radicals, Gorbachev realized that while he had made the right strategic decision in 1985—perestroika—he

---

[19]In the spring of 1991, speaking in Byelorussia, Gorbachev justly criticized the radicals by saying that "someone" had given the radicals full freedom, tying the hands of the sound forces in the Party, and now he was putting things in their real place.—AUTHOR

[20]"Foreman of perestroika" was a phrase coined in the perestroika era, often used ironically, to describe those in Gorbachev's team who were promoting the new line, or prominent liberal intellectuals who supported Gorbachev's policies.—TRANS.

[21]I am an aviation engineer by training, and I feel that this specialized term, flutter, is a good description of what happened to the country. It refers to a very strong vibration of an airplane, to the point of total destruction of the machine, when the controls are not properly set.—AUTHOR

also had made serious tactical errors, leading back to the situation where he'd begun.

Whether intentionally or not, the West happened to give powerful propaganda support to the radical forces, who wanted to turn perestroika into a "great leap." This in fact led to destruction, the collapse of a great superpower. A whole complex of factors was at work here: ideological rejection of socialism, geopolitical considerations, and so on.

However, I want to stress that the West was deceived. The radicals could not offer a real movement toward progress for the country. Moreover, having taken power in a few local soviets on the wave of anti-Communist and anti-Soviet speculation, they managed to discredit themselves in just a few months. They were helpless when it came to solving practical questions, and managed to set people against them, even those who had supported them in the West. People who had called themselves democrats turned out to be leaders with a monopolistic turn of mind. They showed themselves unable to accept pluralistic thinking, going so far as to ban alternative newspapers. They began selling off Russia's national wealth for the sake of instant gratification. But it could not have been otherwise: if you "scratch our pluralists," in Alexander Solzhenitsyn's words, you will quickly find that virtually all had made their careers in the stagnation period by hailing "developed socialism."

And turncoats, ideological "defrocked priests," as you know, are the least dependable people. Having betrayed their faith once, they will continue switching and lying forever.

But one way or another, at some point in the perestroika process these turncoats managed to persuade influential people in the West that they were the true political forces capable of taking control and leading the country. And so the West gave them all kinds of aid. I'd like to quote a few examples of the propaganda support they received from the foreign press during various periods of perestroika.

In the middle of 1988, the Japanese newspaper *Asahi Evening News* wrote: "Ligachev, who is sixty-seven, is considered by the Soviet intelligentsia to be a conservative, whose cautious approach

to change has made him the beacon of the enemies of reform. . . ."
In the same period the German newspaper *Die Welt* wrote, "For a
long time now Ligachev has been playing the role that Suslov had
played under Khrushchev and Brezhnev. . . . He appears more and
more frequently, obscuring the leadership position of Mikhail Gorbachev. . . . His theses are marked by toughness and energy. However, he wants to move more cautiously and reject the course of
radical change."

That was the Western press in 1988. But on 17 July 1986, the
Austrian *Die Presse* had said: "Some observers consider Ligachev a
conservative, a 'braking factor' next to Gorbachev. But this is far
from his entire image. In Voronezh, for instance, Ligachev said,
'We have to give freedom to people of initiative, energy, people
who think and act boldly and unusually. People like that are our
enormous wealth and we must support them universally.' And he
condemned those workers 'who try to hold up the process of perestroika, started by the Party, and lower the upswing of independence.' No conservative would say that unless it was to disguise
himself. But if there's anyone who despises hypocrisy and phoniness,
it is Yegor Ligachev. True, Ligachev seems conservative. He is the
embodiment of the most intransigent, militant decency, a phenomenon that first elicits hostility and then a sense of relief in the
Moscow that for almost twenty years dealt with the moral insou-
ciance of the Brezhnev era. In Mikhail Gorbachev's eyes this energetic man is the ideal companion for a new beginning, a
wholehearted and modest fighter with no ambitions for first place,
a morally invincible and implacable battering ram in personnel policy, an accolade to be entrusted with 'clearing the territory' of the
personnel legacy of Brezhnev. Chasing the moneylenders out of the
temple for Ligachev is not only a political but a moral duty."

And this is what the Canadian journalist David Levy had to say
on Radio Canada about a Yakovlev press conference: "Alexander
Yakovlev's angry reaction to questions from Western journalists at
his press conference dedicated to glasnost is probably evidence of
the influence Canadian democracy had on him during his long stay
on Ottawa. However, this influence had a negative effect and was

a classic example of using half truths. . . . Judging from the position that Yakovlev took, he must not be averse to a return to the former days."

In just a year and a half, the opinion of the Western press had changed diametrically: Yakovlev, who was not averse to a return to the former days, had turned into one of Gorbachev's closest aides, while Ligachev suffered a reversal—from a wholehearted and modest fighter without any ambitions for first place to someone obscuring Gorbachev's leadership position. For people who understand politics, there is no mystery in this change: the West helped the radical, pseudodemocrats pit me against Gorbachev, while supporting Yakovlev in every way.

But destroying perestroika was not in either country's interests. That is why I feel that the West made a mistake in falling for the radicals' line and allowing itself to be disinformed about the true goals of the various political forces in the USSR and their array during perestroika.

Gorbachev often pointed out correctly that Soviet perestroika was a very important component of modern world history; it was created in the interests not only of the Soviet people, but also for universal benefit. Why, then, was the West tempted by the radicalization of political and economic processes in the USSR, which in the long run threatened the entire movement that had begun so well? It appears that the West was unable to give up its ideological and propaganda approaches to global and international cooperation.

During his March 1991 trip to Byelorussia, Gorbachev proposed a concept of centralism that he tied to political common sense, a solution of problems in the interests of all society, to achieve civil and national consensus.

He devoted considerable attention to the radicals, condemning them for not taking social processes into account and for proposing false slogans. The president of the USSR decisively dissociated himself from radicalism, although he avoided any close examination of how radicalism had taken over perestroika in both the top echelon of the leadership and public opinion, and as a result was on the brink of failure. Gorbachev completely and unambiguously confirmed the political analysis of radicalism made in this chapter, stopping short, however, of naming the actual bearers of this dangerous "virus."

I was struck even more by something else in his speech. In analyzing the traits of political centrism, Gorbachev declared himself for the socialist option, consolidation of society's sound forces, care for historical traditions, concern for national morality, and a heightened attention to questions of patriotism. I listened to this speech of March 1991 and then reread it. I couldn't rid myself of a strange thought: this was exactly what I, and many other Communists, had been trying to achieve ever since 1987, and for which I had been called a "foe of perestroika." The only difference was that this position should be called Communist and not centrist (centrism is a policy of compromise).

After a long silence, Gorbachev turned back to the Party. He spoke about Party unity and about the Party as an active, integrating factor in society. A coalition of social forces in the name of the Motherland and the people's welfare had been achieved only by the Party. A universal formula of civil and national peace had to come out of proposals advanced by the Party.

But isn't this just what many Communists had been trying to get him to say? This was their position in the struggle with the radicals who tried to destroy the Party. And hadn't many directives from the top paralyzed the Party at the most critical moments of electoral and political struggle? Hadn't the general secretary tried to shut down the Secretariat, weakening the organizational and supervisory functions of the Central Committee in the Party, which it now had to work so hard to resurrect? And how can the diminished role of the Politburo after the 28th Party Congress and the breakdown in its activity be explained?

Gorbachev had once again taken his customary position: "someone" had weakened the Party, and he, Gorbachev, would mobilize it. I want to stress that I'm not concerned with myself personally or the fact that the original principles of perestroika, which the Communists defended, now had triumphed. At issue is Gorbachev's sincerity. Many of those who had prepared the trap of radicalism remained close to him; there were grounds for the demand posed at the March 1991 Party Central Control Commission plenum "to examine the political activity of former Politburo member A. N. Yakovlev."

A few years ago, walking next to Gorbachev through the Kremlin, I said, "Mikhail Sergeyevich, you have surrounded yourself with people who are not decent. They will destroy you."

And, unfortunately, I was right. So long as the radicals are in charge, our country cannot be protected from new shocks, and the West will have to wait anxiously to see what new "surprises" our economic and political instability will bring to the world.

Three
HARBINGER OF DISASTER

At the beginning of September 1988, Gorbachev went off for his vacation in the Crimea. He officially left me in charge, and I chaired a session of the Politburo. As usual, there was more than enough business. Among other matters, I found on my desk a report from the KGB on the destabilization of the situation in Lithuania that immediately caught my eye and demanded that I have a better assessment of the meaning of the events there.

A few days after that report, Yakovlev returned from Lithuania. As was the custom, he called me, and I asked how the situation was in Lithuania. Yakovlev answered, "There's nothing special going on. Just the normal processes of perestroika."

I have to admit that I was amazed by the dramatic difference in opinion between this member of the Politburo and the KGB report. I immediately called KGB chairman Viktor Chebrikov, and asked him not to meddle in the situation.

"You say that the situation in Lithuania is taking a dangerous turn, but Yakovlev, who just came back from there, says that there's nothing special going on and no reason to take special measures."

"What do you mean, 'nothing special'?" Chebrikov asked in

astonishment. "I stand by what we wrote in our report for the Central Committee. The situation is alarming, not calm, and a consolidation of nationalistic forces has begun."

Whom should I believe? I knew what to do when there is such a major difference in opinion on an important question—study the matter carefully. True, I would not be candid if I didn't say that the strange contradiction in analyses disturbed me more than the KGB report itself. This was not logic at work, but political instincts.

So I immediately called Gorbachev in the South.

"Mikhail Sergeyevich, I'd like your consent to include in the agenda for the next Politburo session the question of Comrade Yakovlev's trip to Lithuania. According to the KGB report, an unhealthy situation is brewing there."

Gorbachev agreed, and soon after that a memorable session of the Politburo took place.

Yakovlev was the first to give his presentation. He said, "There's nothing dangerous going on in the republic. The same is true of the work and activities of the Lithuanian Communist Party. Yes, there are complications caused by the fact that the center has dictated much that damaged the development of the republic. Union agencies are overloading Lithuania with industry, which has damaged the ecology. Russians are flooding in, unfortunately not the very best people, and migration to the republic is growing. That causes clashes; there is documentation that the Russian-speaking population is treating the native population with disrespect. In connection with that, I suggest the following. First, intensify the work of local agencies with the nonnative population. Second, stop migration. On the whole, the situation in Lithuania is not easy, but it isn't critical. The republic should get through this in the course of perestroika."

I'm not quoting from memory, but from the notes I made during Yakovlev's presentation. Of course, I made no comment on his speech, since I didn't have any reason not to believe a member of the Politburo. But later, when the events in Lithuania first took a threatening and then a catastrophic turn, the events occurred that served as a catalyst for destructive, centrifugal processes and threatened the very existence of the USSR, I kept recalling Yakovlev's presentation.

During this period of heated discussions on the Lithuanian question, when the Lithuanian Communist Party dissolved in front of our very eyes, during the Congress of People's Deputies' debates on the secret protocol to the Molotov-Ribbentrop pact,[1] I might ask why I didn't then make public that conversation in the Politburo. After all, it might have affected the development of events. It's not easy to answer that question, but one mustn't forget that at that time my hands had been tied in the Gdlyan and Tbilisi affairs.

To return to that memorable Politburo session, after Yakovlev spoke, I gave the floor to Chebrikov. The chairman of the KGB said, "I judge the situation in Lithuania to be critical. Nationalist forces are becoming more active, forces that have appeared in the ranks of the Lithuanian Communist Party and will lead to a schism."

A schism did take place within the Lithuanian Communist Party, and rather quickly. That, in turn, precipitated all that followed. But the schism was predicted clearly and unambiguously—and it happened at a time when passions could have been calmed and prevented from causing a bad outcome. Once again, as in many other cases, opposite positions and approaches were in conflict at the Politburo session. And here's what's amazing. Glancing back over the events of the past two years, I see that when various approaches collided, the top leaders often took the approach that in the end led to greater problems and, at times, failure. But reasonable warnings, the rationale of which were confirmed over time, were, for some reason, not heeded.

All the members of the Politburo present at the session were astounded by the dramatic difference in Yakovlev's and Chebrikov's views on the Lithuanian situation. To maintain the peace, I made a suggestion:

"Let's have the Central Committee departments carefully study

---

[1]The Hitler-Stalin pact of 1939, containing secret protocols annexing the Baltic states. —TRANS.

the situation in the republic, especially in the Lithuanian Communist Party, and keep the Central Committee abreast of developments. And Comrade Yakovlev's information will be taken into consideration."

My proposal was accepted. I believe I called Gorbachev in the Crimea that day and told him about the Politburo session, saying in passing, "Yakovlev didn't tell us anything new. I would say that his report was mollifying. It didn't clarify the situation in the Lithuanian Communist Party." Gorbachev had no reaction to that part of my report, so I went on to other matters.

After that incident, the Lithuanian problem never again came up at the Politburo sessions until the split in the Lithuanian Communist Party became a real threat. At that point, the Politburo met with the leaders of the Lithuanian Communist Party, a series of conversations took place with Brazauskas,[2] and Gorbachev went to Lithuania. As we know, those belated measures produced no results. And so there was a split in the Communist Party of the republic, and Landsbergis[3] and his cohorts came to power with the goal of forcibly establishing a bourgeois system in Lithuania and tearing the republic from the Soviet Union. And then came the announcement from the Lithuanian Communist Party that it was (unlawfully) leaving the CPSU.

Could we have avoided such a tragic development of events? Not only was it possible, it also was our obligation. But Yakovlev's mollifying evaluation of the 1988 Lithuanian situation played an insidious role. A social and class-based analysis of processes in Lithuania was replaced by an analysis that manipulated and concealed.

Incidentally, the Central Committee departments carefully studied and analyzed the situation in the Lithuanian Communist Party and sent memoranda with reliable information to the Central Committee. But the top leadership in the Central Committee ignored

---

[2]Algirdas Brazauskas was first secretary of the Lithuanian Communist Party Central Committee.—TRANS.

[3]Vytautas Landsbergis is now president of Lithuania.—TRANS.

these principled analyses and actions; I would say they were playing a game with Brazauskas. Furthermore, the processes taking place in Lithuania were presented as an example of perestroika. As we now know, that benign analysis of the Lithuanian situation cost the country a great deal. In that period, Yakovlev was actively playing the role of the consoler in politics, despite the losses he was incurring. He endlessly placated everyone and told people not to worry. He always reminds me of the character of Luka-the-Consoler in Gorky's *The Lower Depths*.

I could no longer control the Lithuanian question and was essentially prevented from helping to find a solution to it. That memorable session of the Politburo was the last I chaired. Soon after that, the sessions of the Central Committee Secretariat that I had chaired were discontinued. But Yakovlev remained a member of the Politburo and was also appointed to the Presidential Council, which was the highest advisory board of the president.

It is no accident that the Politburo session at which Yakovlev reported on his trip to Lithuania instantly came to mind at the working meeting on Georgia. There was unquestionably a close connection between the two—both were harbingers of nationalist flareups. But in April 1989 the Lithuanian situation was more advanced and suggested a scenario of action for nationalist forces in other republics. In February 1990, when events in Lithuania had gotten out of hand, the subject naturally came up at the next Central Committee plenum. V. Kardamiavicius, the secretary of the Interim Lithuanian Communist Party Central Committee (based on the CPSU platform), spoke at the podium:

"I would like to note that if Comrade Yakovlev has his opinion and right to express it, then we also have our opinion and the right to express it. We want to tell our comrades once more that the arrival of Comrade Yakovlev in Lithuania had an unpleasant effect on our republic. You, Comrade Yakovlev, probably indirectly influenced the decisions of the 20th Congress of the Lithuanian Communist Party. This belief is very widespread in our republic. It is reflected in our meetings with some members of the Lithuanian intelligentsia. And let's speak honestly to Communists."

Amazingly enough, the draft resolution on Lithuania made at the plenum did not provide a political analysis of the events occurring in the republic. Moreover, in writing the draft, an attempt was made not to worsen the situation at any cost. There was already a schism in the Lithuanian Communist Party, but the draft resolution called on people to "smooth things over" nicely. In my view, this was a classic model of the politics of reconciliation, the kind of benign approach that inevitably leads to disaster.

I don't know who prepared the draft resolution. But I can say that as a member of the Politburo, I was not acquainted with the draft ahead of time and didn't expect it. It didn't even condemn the schismatic activities of Brazauskas or support the Communists who still adhered to the positions of the CPSU. Ratifying such a draft would have meant indulging the oppositional forces in the Party; it placated the Party, glossed over differences, and paved the way to opportunism. It is no wonder that when the draft resolution was read, the Plenum Hall hummed with bewilderment and indignation.

I would say that in the situation that had taken shape by February 1990, this draft resolution on Lithuania was in its own way subversive. The position of Gorbachev, who at that time consoled himself with the hope that everything would smooth over and get better, probably played a role as well. But I believed it was utterly impossible to sign this resolution. Twice I asked to be recognized to speak so I could express my strong negative opinion. I moved that we condemn the activities of the leadership of the republic's Communist Party, which wanted a schism, and support those forces that were for the unity of the CPSU.

I was the only member of the Politburo who spoke on this question. But many Central Committee members heartily supported me, and the atmosphere at the plenum became very strained. I recall that Anatoly Logunov, rector of Moscow State University, moved to call a twenty-minute break to prepare another draft resolution.

"This moment is extremely crucial. Why are we rushing? We have to think it over carefully," Logunov said.

It wasn't hard for Gorbachev to catch the mood of the Central

Committee members and orient himself in the situation. He suggested that we take an hour break to work on the resolution. Gorbachev, Anatoly Lukyanov, and I worked on it. The new draft was fundamentally different. It condemned Brazuaskas and supported Mykolas Burokevicius.[4] It was unanimously adopted at the plenum. I say frankly: if we had not supported the Lithuanian Communists who still adhered to the CPSU platform at that moment, their fates would have been very bad indeed in the nationalistic fever that Landsbergis soon created.[5]

Many people other than Kardamiavicius spoke at the plenum of Yakovlev's responsibility for the growing crisis in Lithuania. So Yakovlev had to justify himself.

"It is always uncomfortable to make excuses," he said. "But nevertheless I must make clarifications, since one way or another my name has figured in the plenum concerning events in Lithuania. What do I think about this and what did I say in Lithuania? . . . Is the situation in Lithuania a lost cause? I don't think so. Is there a danger? Without question, and it should be noted. But there is something other than danger. We must admit that in the republic we see the all-too-familiar pattern of Party organizations unable to function. The leadership has demonstrated its shortsightedness."

When I heard those words from Yakovlev about the shortsightedness of the republic's Communist Party leadership, I was beside myself. He wasn't talking about specific people but about the leadership of the Party as a whole—that is, the Central Committee. At the September 1988 Politburo session, Yakovlev had consoled us.

---

[4]Mykolas Burokevicius was head of the Lithuanian Communist Party, which remained faithful to Moscow.—TRANS.

[5]As everyone knows, the Lithuanian Communist Party (adhering to the CPSU platform) not only withstood nationalist attacks but also was winning more and more respect in the republic. One of its leaders, Vladislav Shved, was elected a member of the Lithuanian Supreme Soviet. The growth of its influence was clearly reflected during the referendum to preserve the USSR.—AUTHOR

It was he who was shortsighted, not our comrades in Lithuania, many of whom were already sounding the alarm. And here, at the plenum—not a word of self-criticism, but accusations of others.

I stood up from the presidium table and walked up to Valery Boldin,[6] head of the Central Committee's General Department, who was seated at another table. I asked, "Valery Ivanovich, do you remember that in September 1988 I chaired a Politburo session and Yakovlev reported on his trip to Lithuania? Has his report been saved?"

Boldin nodded affirmatively.

"Of course it has."

"Thank you." I took my place, and when Yakovlev finished his speech, I said to Gorbachev very distinctly, so it could be heard in the hall, "Mikhail Sergeyevich, you can familiarize the plenum with Yakovlev's memorandum on Lithuania."

"Why are you poking into this?" Gorbachev asked me (we were sitting next to each other).

But I repeated, "Mikhail Sergeyevich, I'd like to ask you to familiarize the Central Committee members with the memorandum and the report that Yakovlev gave after his return from Lithuania in August 1988. . . . "

But the issue was dropped. And when I received a copy of the transcript of the plenum for corrections, I decided to cross out my statement concerning Yakovlev's report. Why? Because it was at that plenum that I had an argument with Shevardnadze over the Tbilisi Affair. You can't turn the Central Committee plenum into a squabble between Ligachev and other members of the Politburo. It was enough that the Central Committee heard me.

It goes without saying that at the 28th Party Congress, I had no chance to tell the truth about the memorable Politburo session at which Yakovlev reported on the situation in Lithuania. Like other Politburo members, I had to give my own report before the Con-

---

[6]Valery Boldin, by then Gorbachev's chief of staff, was subsequently arrested in connection with the failed coup attempt.—TRANS.

gress. But I was shocked when Yakovlev, in answer to a direct question about his analysis of the situation in Lithuania in August 1988, said that he hadn't written any report for the Politburo and didn't know what people were talking about. That was not an honest answer.

There is yet another parallel between the working meeting on Tbilisi and the situation in Lithuania. During Gorbachev's trip to Lithuania and his meetings with the Lithuanian intelligentsia on television, you could hear praise for Yakovlev from the supporters of Sajudis [the movement for Lithuanian rights and independence]. Given the subsequent developments in Lithuania, that praise certainly is suggestive—as Kardamiavicius said at the Central Committee plenum.

When the Tbilisi Affair was discussed at the first USSR Congress of People's Deputies and the commission to investigate the tragic events of 9 April was formed, Eldar Shengelaya said, "And finally, I think that it would be very appropriate if the commission were headed by Alexander Nikolaevich Yakovlev, member of the Politburo and secretary of the CPSU Central Committee. This is important because some time ago, in February, in an equally difficult and tense time, he was in Tbilisi and took a certain position. He appeared on television and his speech was received very well by official and unofficial groups, by the entire society. So it would be appropriate if he would agree to head the commission."

The examples of Georgia and Lithuania showed where those "certain positions" led.

Four
THE TBILISI AFFAIR

A Political Typhoon

The Tbilisi Affair is the name popularly given to the tragic events that occurred in Tbilisi on the night of 9 April 1989. Briefly, without getting into details and political analyses: In the capital of Georgia, an unlawful rally had been going on for many days in front of the State House. A decision was made to stop it by using troops. In the process of dispersing the demonstrators from the square, nineteen people died and many were injured. Firearms were not used.

That tragic night in Tbilisi, the death of peaceful citizens upset the country. Sadly, this was neither the first nor the last instance of riot victims during the period of perestroika. Not long before the events in Tbilisi, dozens of innocent people died during terrible pogroms in Sumgait, Azerbaidzhan. After Tbilisi, the country was shocked by outrages in Fergana, Uzbekistan, where there were more casualties. There was an unprecedentedly bloody confrontation in Osha, Kirghizia. Finally, in the Trans-Dniestr Region of Moldavia, the police fired on peaceful residents; again, there were casualties.

But tragic as these events were, and however they so worsened the situation in various regions of the country, none had political reverberations equal to those of the Tbilisi Affair. Only the Tbilisi incident was discussed at the Congress of People's Deputies of the USSR. And no other incident was investigated by so many commissions.

Why did the Tbilisi Affair assume such great political importance? What was it really about, and how did it affect the course of events in the country as a whole? In those days, with passions running high in the mass media and at the Congress over the tragic night in Tbilisi, it was hard to give a fair answer to those important questions. Time was necessary to reveal the true intentions of the participants in the conflict. It is commonly said that history is the harshest judge. With regard to the Tbilisi Affair, this is doubly true. Only now can we make sense out of what happened and draw definite conclusions on the basis of precise facts.

By a whim of fate I was at the very epicenter of the political typhoon that swept the country over the Tbilisi Affair. I knew a great deal, understood a lot even back then, but far from everything. Today, everything has fallen into place. The time has come to fill in the blanks and erase the blank spots in the brutal Tbilisi incident, since a clear understanding of this political matter involving the blood of innocent people helps us to understand better the true import of processes going on under the slogans of perestroika, democratization, and glasnost. These are the strategy, tactics, and true intentions of various political forces that entered the political arena after April 1985; the methods of national separatists and their patrons.

First, I must say that I was drawn into the orbit of the Tbilisi Affair purely by chance. In March 1989, there was a Central Committee plenum on agricultural issues. At that time, Viktor Nikonov and I handled these matters in the Politburo, and the main burden of preparing for the plenum lay on us. The decisions of the plenum were important in determining the basis for the current agricultural policy, and so we discussed how to publicize it among the peasants. I flew to Brest for a major council of agricultural planners from the

Ukraine, Byelorussia, and the Baltic republics, from which I returned on the evening of 6 April. On Saturday, 8 April, I was to go on a short vacation. The burden of the past months had been great, and the Politburo had decided to give me a little breather—needless to say, to be taken out of my allotted vacation time.

A few words about the work schedule of Politburo members may be in order here. When General Secretary Brezhnev became ill, the Politburo decided to limit his workday. Then this indulgence was extended to other members of the Politburo. Friday was considered a day to go over documents at one's dacha; Saturday and Sunday were days off, and they also cut back on work hours. When I would fly to Moscow from Tomsk, the tempo of life in the capital would seem hectic to me. Trying to resolve many problems in three or four days, I'd wear out the soles of my shoes running around agencies and organizations. But I knew that after 5:00 P.M. members of the Politburo didn't receive anyone; they would go home and relax.

First secretaries of provincial Party committees would dash about Moscow, living all day on tea, usually without a chance even to wolf down a sandwich, let alone a normal lunch. Then someone in the Central Committee—probably a former provincial Party committee official—had the brilliant idea of opening up a cafeteria for people on business trips so that any time during the day you could get a quick bite to eat. But these are just reminiscences. . . . In those years, the only Politburo member you could catch at work until late in the evening was Gorbachev. Everyone else followed doctor's orders and tried not to get overtired.

When Andropov became general secretary, this work regime vanished. No decrees were issued, but everyone went from an abbreviated workday to a longer one. I personally had to work until 9:00, even 11:00 P.M. All the rest of the top leaders worked a great deal. In a word, the situation was the same as in the provincial Party committees, where people were used to working long hours.

Vacation schedules were approved by the Politburo. Usually Gorbachev, Yakovlev, Shevardnadze, Medvedev, and Lukyanov took their vacations at the same time, although there were cases when vacations fell during different months. Gorbachev and I always vacationed at different times.

I recall that the day of 7 April 1989 was very pressured for me. I'd just returned that evening from a business trip; the next day, I was going on vacation. Meanwhile, I had a lot to do. I always brought back from business trips a notebook filled with facts, observations, and requests from local leaders. The practice in those years was for members of the top Party leadership to fulfill requests from comrades at the local level to help them through the central ministries and agencies, usually with regard to economic matters. So I had to get in contact with various agencies to convince or pressure them to do various things.

The situation is different now, as we all know. But I used to come back from business trips with a pile of papers. My first task was always to systematize the requests from the provinces and put them in motion. This time I had to do it all in one day.

In the morning, I asked my secretary to hold all calls and say I couldn't see anyone, so I could concentrate on the questions that had been put before the Central Committee in Byelorussia.

As a member of the Politburo, I generally received many visitors. There were always people in my waiting room, where my secretaries (V. G. Agapov and A. V. Startsev, extremely competent comrades) worked. There was the usual preliminary waiting list for meetings, but if the matter was urgent or the person had come in from the provinces or another republic, I would see him immediately, regardless of rank or position. Everyone in the Central Committee knew this. But when I had to think over a question, prepare for a speech, or work on documents, I would sometimes unplug the telephone to my outer office and ask that no one be let in to see me—but only in extreme circumstances.

I had Office No. 2 at the Central Committee. It was a spacious and bright corner office on the fifth floor, looking out on Old Square. In addition to the desk, it had a long table at which I always talked with visitors. Some of the Western correspondents who visited me wrote things like: "I talked with Mr. Ligachev in his gloomy office in the Central Committee building opposite the KGB. . . . "

Why "gloomy"? The office was bright. Why "opposite the KGB"? The Committee for State Security building was located at a respectable distance. Apparently these several journalists felt they could distort the real situation and use that device to create atmosphere.

The office was considered comfortable, rather quiet, and conducive to concentrated effort. Submerged in my work, I didn't notice that the morning hours had flown by. Then the door opened unexpectedly and my secretary walked in.

"Yegor Kuzmich, Comrade Chebrikov is calling. He insists I connect him to you."

At that time, Viktor Chebrikov was a member of the Politburo and secretary of the Central Committee overseeing administrative agencies and nationalities policy. He was a reserved and tactful man, and I immediately realized that he wouldn't be so persistent except under extraordinary circumstances. The General Department had already informed us that Gorbachev was scheduled to return from his visit to London that evening. This served to intensify my concern over Chebrikov's call: the *gensek* was arriving that evening, but Chebrikov insisted he had to talk to me right away.

I asked to be connected with Chebrikov. After saying hello, Chebrikov immediately got to the matter at hand: "The situation in Georgia is getting complicated. . . . " He said abruptly, "Yegor Kuzmich, if you don't mind, I'd better come over to your office."

Waiting for Chebrikov, I recalled what had happened in Georgia in November 1988, when only a message from Gorbachev and the immediate trip of Shevardnadze to Tbilisi had allowed us to avoid an unpredictable outcome. The situation must be starting to get out of control . . . and Chebrikov's first word confirmed this assumption. "Things are bad in Tbilisi," he began. "Haven't you been informed?"

"I only got in from Byelorussia last night. I'm not at all up to date."

"The events are even stormier than in November and February. There are constant rallies, threats to settle the score with the Communists, demands that Georgia secede from the USSR, and preparation of an appeal to the UN to send in troops."

Yegor Ligachev (second row, far left) with a delegation from Novosibirsk Province at a Komsomol Congress. In the first row center is A. Pokryshkin, a celebrated World War II pilot and thrice Hero of the Soviet Union.

Ligachev, then deputy chairman of the Novosibirsk Province Party Executive Committee, with Mao Zedong during a visit to Peking in October 1957.

Ligachev with Academicians Mikhail Lavrentyev and V. A. Kirillin at the construction site of Academic City outside Tomsk in 1967.

Ligachev, then first secretary of the Tomsk Province Party Committee, first met Mikhail Gorbachev in Prague in November 1969. At that time Gorbachev was first secretary of the Stavropol Territory Party Committee.

*Ligachev with his wife,
Zinaida, in Tomsk in
1974.*

*Ligachev in his office
in Tomsk (1975).*

At an art exhibition in 1975.

Visiting oil workers in Tomsk Province in 1977.

Alexei Kosigyn (center), chairman of the USSR Council of Ministers, came to Tomsk in 1978 to discuss the development of the petroleum industry in Siberia. Ligachev is second from the right.

Ligachev with the writer G. M. Markov at the Memorial to the Battle and Labor Glory of the People of Tomsk (1979).

Ligachev in a Siberian wheat field in Tomsk Province.

Cross-country skiing in Siberia. Ligachev (far right) enjoys the popular sport with (left to right) Prof. A. V. Lirman of the Tomsk Medical Institute; Prof. M. P. Kortusov; P. A. Slezko, Province Party Committee secretary; and A. G. Melnikov.

Dressed as a miner, Ligachev (fourth from left) prepares to descend into a mine in Donbass (1983).

At a school in the Ural Mountains in 1985.

Ligachev and Nikolai Ryzhkov visit the site of the Chernobyl nuclear plant disaster in Kiev Province on 2 May 1986.

At a naval parade in Sevastopol in 1986.

Meeting U.S. congressmen in the Kremlin in 1987. Former Speaker of the House James Wright is on the left.

Ligachev talks with citizens on a street in Tbilisi, capital of Georgia (1987).

Ligachev, his wife, Zinaida, and other family members with G. T. Beregov and P. I. Klimuk, heads of the Soviet Center for Cosmonaut Training in Star City (1988).

On the tribune of Lenin's mausoleum in Red Square, May Day 1988. Left to right: Ligachev, Gorbachev, Eduard Shevardnadze.

Ligachev meets with farmers in Rostov Province in 1988.

In a Kirghizian village in 1989.

Ligachev in 1990 at the grave of his brother, who was killed during World War II at the front near Weimar, Germany.

Ligachev and Gorbachev at the presidium of the 27th Party Congress in 1986. In the second row are former East German and Polish Communist Party leaders Erich Honecker (left) and Wojciech Jaruzelski.

Members of the press crowd around Ligachev during a break at the People's Deputies Congress in December 1990.

Yegor Ligachev.

"Whose information is that, Viktor Mikhailovich?"

"Patiashvili.[1] I'm in constant phone communication with him. Mikhail Sergeyevich is arriving this evening, but Patiashvili insists that the situation is heating up every hour. We have to get together to discuss the current situation, work out recommendations, so that by the time the general secretary flies in from England it will be clear what we should do. I want to ask you to convene a working session."

Unscheduled working meetings of the Politburo and the Secretariat of the Central Committee on various urgent questions were normal work practice for the entire top Party leadership. Usually such sessions were convened either by the *gensek* himself or by whomever he had delegated. In the absence of the general secretary, the session would be chaired by the person he had left in charge. These meetings differed from official sessions of the Politburo in that they did not have the authority to pass decrees. They could only work out recommendations subject to later confirmation.

This practice had been worked out decades earlier, but by the spring of 1989 there had been many breaks with the custom in the Central Committee. When he flew off to his meeting with Margaret Thatcher, Gorbachev, contrary to his usual practice, didn't authorize anyone to be in charge. So it wasn't in my hands to convene and chair a meeting of the top Party leadership in Gorbachev's absence. I told Chebrikov this frankly.

But he insisted, "Please, Yegor Kuzmich. The situation requires immediate discussion."

I knew that Chebrikov was a very responsible person. Such insistence meant that things were really in a bad way. But why should *I* chair the meeting? In the absence of Secretariat meetings, there had been snarls in Central Committee procedures. I had chaired the sessions of the Secretariat, and Chebrikov apparently seized upon this tradition in asking me to convene a working meeting.

But if the general secretary hadn't asked me, I didn't want to do

---

[1]Dzhumber Patiashvili was in 1989 first secretary of the Georgian Central Committee and a member of the CPSU Central Committee.—TRANS.

it. I was attempting to adhere strictly to workplace etiquette to avoid giving rise to gossip or provocative rumors that the "democrats" could spread. They would allege publicly and through the mass media that in Gorbachev's absence, Ligachev was plotting a coup. Besides, in that period I was handling only agricultural issues. I wasn't informed about what was happening in Tbilisi.

I had strong reasons for declining to chair the meeting. But if I disregarded personal considerations and looked at the matter from the governmental point of view, things looked different. By April 1989, Secretariat sessions, at which we could and should have discussed such a question, had long since ceased. The elections of people's deputies of the USSR had already been held—elections held in a fundamentally new way. I suddenly realized how strangely weak government authority in the country was becoming. The *gensek* was abroad and hadn't left a deputy. The Secretariat of the Central Committee had stopped functioning. The Supreme Soviet had essentially lost its power after the elections and in our system of Party-government rule, the old government was not used to making political decisions. A huge country setting forth on a very complicated period in its development was confronted with weak authority.

Yes, that gap had appeared for just a few days, but philosophically as well as practically, the breakdown was extremely serious. It testified to hastiness, to disinclination to think through possible consequences, even fleeting irresponsibility. Scarcely having begun to build something new, people were rushing to destroy the old.

As to the immediate situation, I simply juxtaposed the personal with the social. On the one hand, possible verbal and tacit castigation for once again taking the initiative; and on the other, the overall situation in the sphere of power and the danger of inaction during dangerous events. Not to boast, but in this situation I acted as I usually do: I instantly shook off my hesitation and did what I had to do.

I gave Chebrikov my consent to conduct a working meeting. We quickly drew up the list of participants, but I asked him to emphasize to them that my role was only chairman, not initiator.

Several minutes after Chebrikov left, Medvedev called. "Yegor Kuzmich, did you hear about the events in Georgia?"

"Viktor Mikhailovich informed me."

"So we're convening, Yegor Kuzmich?"

I had the impression that Medvedev already knew about my conversation with Chebrikov, but I nevertheless asked, "Do you think we should convene?"

"We have to; we absolutely must have a working meeting," Medvedev said.

Soon everyone whom Chebrikov had told gathered in the Secretariat Conference Hall on the fifth floor. I opened that 7 April 1989 working meeting on the events in Georgia recalling briefly the last Politburo session (September 1988) that I had chaired, where Lithuania was on the agenda. The memory was not formally or personally associated with the present. Some unseen thread united that session of the Politburo and the working meeting in the Central Committee. In the tense atmosphere of that day, it was hard to grasp the connection, difficult to formulate it clearly. But there was no doubt that it existed.

The Secret Is Out

Chebrikov reported to the meeting details of his conversations with Patiashvili, described the evolving situation, and reported that the Georgian leaders were asking the center to take immediate measures.

Then all the meeting's participants spoke—several times each. I recall very well that everyone mentioned Sumgait,[2] where the authorities didn't act and where dozens of peaceful citizens died. The shadow of that tragedy certainly hung over the 7 April meeting, and prompted us all to treat the warnings of Patiashvili very seriously. Each speaker tried to determine what precautionary measures might be taken to avoid a dramatic outcome.

The most hard-line positions were taken by Slyunkov and Lukyanov, who, because of their anxieties that Sumgait would be repeated, suggested getting troops ready so no riots could occur.

---

[2]Sumgait, an Azerbaidzhani town largely populated by Armenians, was the site of a massacre of Armenians in February 1988.—TRANS.

Chebrikov had reported that the slogans at the illegal rallies included "USSR—prison of nations!" "Russian conquerors go home!" "Stop the discrimination of Georgians in Georgia!" "Down with the Turkish agents!" and others with a clearly defined nationalist slant. This prompted the Politburo members to insist on preemptive movement of troops into Georgia. The leitmotif of all the speeches, which were received with approval, was to prevent ethnic conflict and more victims. We had to learn a lesson from Sumgait—not to be late again.

Medvedev spoke more carefully, in his characteristic style, asserting facts without proposing anything specific. Razumovsky, who like Chebrikov was in constant phone communication with Patiashvili, completely supported Chebrikov's conclusions, concluding that it was good that the Georgian leadership had informed us of what was going on but that our Georgian comrades should take measures themselves. We also noticed a tendency for the local leaders to disavow responsibility and pass on all decisions to the center. In addition, several top officials had just returned from Georgia. Their conclusions and observations coincided with what Chebrikov had said.

I did not speak at the meeting. At the end, I summarized the opinions: "We can't make any serious decisions until we learn the opinion of all the Georgian leaders. Right now all we know is the personal point of view of Patiashvili. We must recommend that he discuss the situation in the Georgian Communist Party Central Committee, in the republican Supreme Soviet, and in the Council of Ministers." Then I added, "Besides, all we have is telephone information—that is, you, Comrade Chebrikov, and you, Comrade Razumovsky, base your conclusion on telephone conversations with Patiashvili. But we need at least telegrams in order to make specific decisions. Let our Georgian comrades convene, discuss the situation collegially, and immediately telegraph their opinion to the Central Committee."

I was absolutely certain that only a collegial opinion could put the situation in its true light.

Everyone supported me. In the end the meeting adopted the

following recommendations: First, the Party and soviet leaders of Georgia should not sit in their offices but immediately go to the rally and speak before the people to clarify their positions. Yes, it would be uncomfortable, and people might boo them, but all the same, they had to go and talk with the people directly. Second, given the danger of riots, it was crucial to reinforce security at critical public facilities and safeguard people from unpredictable events that might lead to flareups of nationalist antagonism. To that end we must move military units to Tbilisi, even if that meant taking them out of Armenia.

Those were the recommendations of the working meeting. We did not discuss questions of when to move the military units and in what numbers. We made only political recommendations.[3]

I ended the meeting with this thought: "We believe that we have worked out our recommendations, and in the evening, when Mikhail Sergeyevich returns, we'll tell the general secretary about them."

Everyone approved that decision and parted.

It was about 3:00 P.M.

I received no additional reports from Tbilisi that day. No one called me on the subject, nor did I talk with Patiashvili on the phone. I worked through the pile of agricultural matters I had brought back from my business trip until late in the evening, and didn't set off for Vnukovo-2 until after 10:00 P.M.—Gorbachev's arrival had been delayed three times.

The next morning, I flew to Sochi for my vacation. Only there did I learn from Central Television about the tragic night in Tbilisi. I called Gorbachev right away.

"What happened in Tbilisi, Mikhail Sergeyevich?"

"It's not yet clear. They're sorting it out. Apparently Patiashvili made some terrible mistake," Gorbachev answered.

When I came back from my vacation I began to get a sense of

---

[3]The recommendations were meant to deal with the situation through influence among Communists; the author is emphasizing that military or judicial measures were not to be implemented.—TRANS.

what had happened. Without getting into an analysis of whether troops should have been used to stop an unauthorized rally, I will say that the political intrigues regarding what took place interested me. In my view, they were the root cause of the tragedy and the death of innocent people. The singular use of troops against a civilian population deserves scrupulous investigation to prevent similar future events. But the political position and intentions of the forces that held the unauthorized rally are of some significance. I learned that the leaders of several unofficial Georgian movements who headed the rally advocated clearly nationalist and anti-Soviet positions and demanded the secession of Georgia from the USSR. In other words, we're talking about outright calls to bring down the government. In analyzing the events of Georgia, we mustn't ignore the political goals of the rally.

Anatoly Sobchak, in his speech to the second Congress of People's Deputies in December 1989, said openly on that score: "The political, moral, and other responsibilities, including legal, for the actions must be borne by the organizers of the unauthorized rally in front of the State House." Later, Sobchak named them: "Tsereteli, Gamsakhurdia, Chanturia,[4] and other leaders of unofficial organizations who allowed violations of public order during the rally and appealed for the people to ignore the legitimate demands of the authorities. When there was a real threat that armed forces might be used, they did not take measures to stop the rally and thus did not try to prevent the tragic outcome of events."

Sobchak's words are crucial to analysis of the subsequent events. But first I would like to recall for the reader how the subject of the Tbilisi tragedy had come up unexpectedly at the first USSR Congress of People's Deputies, and how it was dealt with.

The Congress essentially began with the issue; scarcely had the

---

[4]All three were political prisoners before perestroika. Irakli Tsereteli was a Georgian independence movement leader. Zviad Gamsakhurdia was subsequently elected president of Georgia, came under attack for his dictatorial rule, and was forced to flee during an armed insurrection in January 1992. Giya Chanturia was one of the leaders of the opposition to Gamsakhurdia.—TRANS.

chairman finished his opening statement when one of the deputies proposed that we honor the memory of those who died in Tbilisi. That was unquestionably a noble proposal, although later many people said that we should have honored the tragic losses in Sumgait at the same time. But I was particularly astonished by something else: when the minute of mourning was over, the deputy switched from a tone of compassion to a clearly political one and announced, "I introduce the following parliamentary inquiry: At the request of my constituents I demand that a public statement be made now, at the Congress of People's Deputies of the USSR, telling us who gave the order to beat peaceful demonstrators and use poisonous substances against them in the city of Tbilisi on 9 April 1989. I also demand that we be informed of the names of those poisonous substances."

And so it all began. Georgian deputy Eldar Shengelaya referred to the tragic events in Tbilisi as a "punitive military action" and demanded that General Igor Rodionov, commander of the Transcaucasian Military District, be removed from his parliamentary seat. Another Georgian deputy, Tamaz Gamkrelidze, spoke on the same day: "On 9 April at 4:00 A.M. under the pretext of dispersing an unauthorized rally of peaceful demonstrators in Tbilisi, innocent people were beaten with unprecedented brutality, causing loss of human life. . . . This military operation, which was led by troop commander Lt. Gen. I. N. Rodionov of the Transcaucasian Military District, was apparently planned ahead of time—not as an operation to disperse a peaceful rally but as a punitive operation to kill people that was planned in advance. . . . A planned action on that scale with such political consequences must have been known ahead of time by the top leadership of the country."

I listened to the speakers in bewilderment. What was happening at the Congress? Yes, the tragedy in Tbilisi had to be carefully investigated—and we needed to punish severely those whose unconsidered actions led to people's deaths. There was no doubt about that. At the same time, it was necessary to analyze calmly what the organizers of the rally had been trying to achieve. But the emphasis was clearly shifting; the army was being defamed and the top leaders of the country were being attacked, while the political goals of the demonstrators were declared *a priori* sacred. I knew very well that the accusation of "preplanned punitive actions" was unbelievable nonsense. Why did it spread with such persistence? The tragic events in Tbilisi certainly began to acquire the features of a political "Tbilisi Affair." But what was the motivation for this?

The virulent attack on the army was fraternally picked up by the radical right-wing press. Public opinion was directed against the armed forces. General Rodionov's attempts to put forth his understanding of the tragic events was rebuffed, and demands to strip him of his parliamentary seat resounded not only at the Congress but also in the press and on television.

In those days it wasn't easy to evaluate the possible consequences of such a widespread campaign against the army. But suddenly life gave us another example of how unpredictable and tragic the repercussions could be of this irresponsible, deliberate attempt to accuse the army of punitive functions.

This was the catastrophe in Fergana.[5]

The terrible pogroms there exceeded even Sumgait in scale. They mobilized an entire people—the long-suffering Meskhetian Turks, who had already suffered a tragic resettlement from Georgia. In Sumgait, when riots began, the army—the only force capable of quickly quelling the situation when the events are so fiery and large in scale—had not acted. The same thing happened in Fergana. For two days the wave of pogroms grew worse as the entire country watched in horror. The army, which might have stopped the violence by resolute action, remained on the sidelines.

But this time the reasons for inaction were different. In Sumgait we had seen confusion in the face of the first bloody flareup of nationalism. In Fergana it was the psychological shock from the first Congress of People's Deputies. After such virulent and unjust attacks on the army, who would dare give the order to stop the rioting?

---

[5]The Fergana Valley in Uzbekistan was the site of massacres in 1990 when Uzbeks clashed with Turkic minorities who had been forcibly resettled by Stalin.—TRANS.

Newspapers later wrote (and many deputies said) that the political Tbilisi Affair instigated at the first Congress of People's Deputies had tied the army's hands and caused it to move too slowly into Fergana. It was no accident that after the Fergana catastrophe the radical press suddenly turned down the heat on the Tbilisi Affair, and demands for political reprisals against General Rodionov quieted down.

For a while, public attention to the Tbilisi incident waned, although the political process in Georgia continued. I don't make any secret of the fact that I had alarming premonitions that the Georgian situation might erupt into an anti-Soviet, antisocialist explosion.

I thought about the atmosphere in which the Tbilisi Affair surfaced at the Congress and the general course of affairs in the country, and realized the Tbilisi Affair was not the worst tragedy here; the political "affair" was serving as a cover for unofficial forces seeking power, and it wasn't difficult to figure out who they were. The Georgian nationalists who organized the rally in Tbilisi to split Georgia off from the Soviet Union later crushed the republic's Communist Party. Back then, however, I was handling completely different issues. After the working meeting I chaired on 7 April, I never once had occasion to take part in a review of the Georgian problems. It is clear that they were not my direct concern at the first Congress of People's Deputies of the USSR.

How could I have guessed at that moment that I would soon be the central figure in that affair and that Sobchak would address his main political accusations against me?

Why Did Shevardnadze Disobey Gorbachev?

The Commission on the Tbilisi Affair created at the first Congress of People's Deputies of the USSR went to work. One morning, Anatoly Sobchak, chairman of the commission, called to say that the commission members wanted to meet with me.

"Fine, I'm ready. When and where?" I asked.

That very day, I was told, in the USSR Supreme Soviet building on the corner of Kalinin Avenue, where the commission convened.

I recall that conversation with commission members especially well because they asked me less about the circumstances of the Tbilisi Affair than about the situation in the country—in particular, my views of separatism and my opinion of the nationalities policy. They asked how I felt about the "blackening" of our history, the defamation of monuments to revolutionary and military glory. And they asked what my attitude was toward Party organizations in factories and mines. To explain why they were asking questions that had nothing at all to do with the Tbilisi Affair, someone said, "Yegor Kuzmich, we're taking advantage of this meeting to learn your political position as a member of the Politburo." The commission had about twenty members, and they asked a great number of such questions. The conversation went on for more than an hour. There were only two questions about the Tbilisi incident:

"Who convened the meeting on 7 April?"

"I did."

"Were there minutes of the meeting?"

"No, it was a working meeting, and meetings like that are not transcribed and minutes are not kept. That's the common practice in the Central Committee."

That was it. True, Veniamin Yakovlev, minister of justice, added, "Those questions should have been resolved in state and not Party agencies."

I agreed completely with him.

"Of course. But then we still lived under a Party-government leadership—that was reality. The current Supreme Soviet didn't exist."

The minister of justice and the other commission members were satisfied with my answers and didn't ask any more questions on that topic. The entire conversation left me with the impression of a dispassionate, analytical study of the Tbilisi Affair. I sensed the wish of the commission to sort out the circumstances of the tragedy in Tbilisi without inflaming political passions.

I want to stress that I wasn't asked any other questions about Tbilisi. I imagined that the commission would meet with other people who were at the Central Committee meeting. I had no doubt that the people who had been directly involved would tell them what had happened at Vnukovo-2 Airport on 7 April.

The usual procedure for greeting the general secretary upon his return from a trip abroad had developed more or less spontaneously. After greeting the general secretary, all the members of the Politburo and secretaries of the Central Committee would gather either in the vestibule or in one of the rooms of Vnukovo-2 Airport to hear Gorbachev's opinion of his meeting as well as to bring him up to date on what had been happening at home as soon as he stepped on native soil. This correct and reasonable practice was followed faithfully and would last as long as an hour or two.

The General Department had postponed Gorbachev's time of arrival from London on 7 April three times, and it wasn't until about 8:00 P.M. that we finally heard that the plane had taken off. I stayed at work until 10:00 P.M. and went directly to the airport from the Central Committee building to meet our delegation.

As usual, Gorbachev spoke in general terms about the trip and his negotiations with Thatcher, and then turned to domestic problems. "So what's new with you? How are things going?"

Chebrikov and I had agreed ahead of time that at the airport he would report on what was happening in Georgia and our meeting. The main thing was that we had done our jobs and worked out our recommendations. What difference did it make which one of us reported to the general secretary? Without getting into details I should say that at Politburo and Central Committee Secretariat sessions I was always forthcoming on specifics and expressed my point of view, which sometimes differed from the position of Gorbachev or my other comrades. But that's another story. In any case, after the spring of 1989 I tried not to stick my nose into matters that did not concern agriculture unless I really had to, although that wasn't always possible. Enormous questions arose, such as the situation in the country and the Party, in Eastern Europe—and, needless to say, I didn't have the right to remain silent. Nor did I.

But I think it's clear why Chebrikov and I had agreed that he should present the information at the airport. "The situation in Tbilisi is really complicated," Chebrikov began. After briefly reporting on the situation, he added, "Patiashvili insists on help from the center. We had a meeting, which Yegor Kuzmich chaired, and discussed various actions. We would like to report our recommendations to you."

"Go ahead."

Chebrikov precisely presented the conclusions of our working meeting, and Gorbachev confirmed them immediately and resolutely: "That's all correct."

Then we discussed additional measures. The Politburo and Secretariat were all gathered, as was customary when greeting the general secretary upon his return from a trip abroad. I recall that in the course of the conversation Medvedev said, "A coded telegram has come in from Tbilisi, but I haven't had a chance to read it yet."

In the end, we all agreed that the recommendations were wise and preventative. They gave us time to try a broad range of political methods. After summarizing the exchange of opinions, Gorbachev suggested additional measures. "Tomorrow morning, Comrades Shevardnadze and Razumovsky must go to Tbilisi. You must sort out the situation there on the spot. I realize that there is much to be done, but you have to go. We have to do everything in our power to defuse the conflict by political means. If necessary, you must meet with the demonstrators."

I understood Gorbachev, based on the experience of November 1988. Shevardnadze knew the situation and people there very well, was highly respected in Georgia. His presence in Tbilisi had done much to stem the tide of political passions. There's no question that the general secretary made an absolutely correct—perhaps the only correct—decision. Gorbachev also asked Chebrikov to convene a working meeting the next morning at which we would again review the developments, this time with the benefit of the coded information.

I recall that Gorbachev added, "Yegor Kuzmich will go away on vacation as planned."

In conclusion, I can say with certainty that late in the evening of 7 April at Vnukovo-2 Airport, the top political leaders of the country, with the participation of the general secretary, clearly outlined a course to resolve the conflict through political means.

And suddenly, at the first USSR Congress of People's Deputies, Shengelaya announced: "A preplanned action of such scale, with such political consequences, must have been known ahead of time by the country's top leaders."

Returning to the events that took place at the first Congress, I recall that I was bewildered. What was his goal in inciting hysteria? Why did several Georgian deputies start to concoct a political Tbilisi Affair right before our eyes? Why did the radical right-wing press instantly try to shape the appropriate public opinion and set the public against the army?

I must repeat that the recommendations of the working meeting confirmed on the evening of 7 April were designed to regulate the conflict by peaceful means. And the additional measures assigned by Gorbachev that evening were sane and farsighted; they permitted us to maintain complete control of the situation. There's no question that if on the morning of 8 April Shevardnadze had gone to Tbilisi as Gorbachev suggested, the tragic night of 9 April never would have happened.

The main question is not who gave the order to disperse the demonstrators at State House Square; we all know the answer to that. The true mystery is why the one and only time Shevardnadze disobeyed Gorbachev in all those years of work in the Politburo was in regard to Tbilisi.

I left for my vacation the next morning, and therefore can only judge subsequent events based on documents that I have studied carefully.

In accordance with Gorbachev's proposal, a new meeting on the situation in Georgia was held on 8 April at the Central Committee and chaired by Chebrikov. The same people who met the previous evening were there—"with the exception of Ye. K. Ligachev, who had left on vacation," as noted in the conclusions of the Congressional Commission. Vadim Bakatin, minister of internal affairs of the USSR, and Politburo member Shevardnadze also were in attendance. In other words, contrary to Gorbachev's order, Shevardnadze did not rush to Tbilisi the next morning, but remained in Moscow. It is interesting to look at the text of the coded telegram sent by Patiashvili the night before that Medvedev had mentioned at the airport. It was made public by Lukyanov at the first Congress, but he didn't read the entire text; and I therefore want to reproduce it here in its entirety:

> Recently the situation in the republic has drastically worsened. It is almost out of control. Extremist elements are stirring up nationalism, appealing for strikes and civil disobedience, organizing unrest, discrediting the Party organizations and soviets. In this situation we must take extraordinary measures.

The Congress was not informed of all the extraordinary measures that Patiashvili proposed, and that merit particular attention. The telegram read:

> We consider it necessary to:
>
> 1. immediately charge with felonies and misdemeanors the extremists who are making anti-Soviet, antisocialist, and anti-Party slogans and appeals (there is a legal basis to do so);
> 2. declare a state of emergency in Tbilisi (curfew) by moving additional internal security forces and troops from the TransCaucasian Military District;
> 3. implement a series of political, organizational, and administrative measures to stabilize the situation using Party, soviet, and economic leaders;
> 4. prevent the publication of information that would worsen the situation in the Union-level and republican mass media.

The telegram concluded: "We request approval on points one, two, and four."

When I read the full text of the telegram later, I realized that the situation in Tbilisi had deteriorated more than we thought during the day of 7 April, based on Patiashvili's telephone report. But even without the telegram, Gorbachev apparently had a good idea of how events might develop. Six months earlier, he had successfully defused the November crisis in Georgia, and he was completely "up to speed" on the situation. That's why he ordered Shevardnadze to fly to Tbilisi and suggested meeting with the demonstrators even without written documentation supporting the decision.

I should note that the telegram was sent from Tbilisi on 7 April at 8:35 P.M. The top leaders, including Shevardnadze, did not have a chance to read it until after midnight; Medvedev first mentioned it during our meeting with Gorbachev, who left London at 11:00 P.M. Furthermore, we talked for more than an hour at the airport. There were no other official communications from Georgia until morning.

Such an alarming telegram—together with a direct order from Gorbachev and the existing practice of obeying the general secretary's orders—should have prompted an immediate departure to Tbilisi.

But the situation unfolded differently. I would like to quote a passage from the above-mentioned conclusion of the Congressional Commission: "By that time (the Central Committee meeting on 8 April) a telegram had already been received on 8 April 1989, signed by D. Patiashvili, stating that the situation in the city had stabilized and was under control. Comrades E. A. Shevardnadze and D. I. Patiashvili talked on the telephone. Citing the stabilization of the situation on the night of 7–8 April, Patiashvili believed the travel of Comrades Shevardnadze and Razumovsky was redundant. The participants in the meeting agreed."

It is interesting to compare the statement with the conclusions of the Commission of the Georgian Supreme Soviet, according to which a meeting with the intelligentsia was held on 7 April in the Georgian Central Committee at which Patiashvili "called the situation disastrous." On 8 April, a meeting of the Georgian Party activists was held in Tbilisi, where Patiashvili noted: "There is an extremely tense and explosive political atmosphere in the republic. Extremist leaders are calling for the overthrow of Soviet power and the socialist system." The Party officials decided to use military units to disperse the demonstrators from the square. That day, a group of women rallied before Patiashvili's house. On the morning of 8 April there was a show of military force—helicopters flew over the city and three columns of personnel carriers went through Tbilisi. Instead of the expected effect of calming the population, that action drew yet more demonstrators to the State House.[6] In other words, on 8 April the situation in the city became increasingly confused. Patiashvili's speeches in Tbilisi acquired an increasingly alarmed, if not panicky, tone.

But suddenly, coded telegrams were coming into Moscow with an entirely different, far more optimistic tone from the previous evening: "The situation is normalizing."

Those tones could also be heard in the telephone conversations with Moscow. Why did Patiashvili change his mind so abruptly? The very night before, he had insisted on help from the center, indicating that the situation was "practically out of control." Furthermore, the center did not give him permission to carry out the first or fourth points of the extraordinary measures.

Did the unexpected and excessive optimism of Patiashvili, who turned down Shevardnadze's offer to help, cause us to miss an opportunity to regulate the situation peacefully by political means?

The question, by no means rhetorical, is directly answered in the conclusions of the Georgian Commission, which reads:

"During the meeting (of Party activists) D. Patiashvili spoke with Moscow. Patiashvili reported the proposals of the Politburo to send

---

[6]The *Memorandum* of the USSR prosecutor testifies that the demonstrators started to throw stones at the troop carriers and six soldiers were injured. In front of the Rustaveli movie theater, a group of unaffiliated youths captured a traffic patrol car, placed it across the road, and after beating the driver, Senior Officer Metaldadze, tried to make him lie in front of a personnel carrier. The memorandum, which cites 140 volumes of investigative materials, contains many other facts confirming that on the morning of 8 April the situation had become threatening.—AUTHOR

Comrades Shevardnadze and Razumovsky to Tbilisi to help. Patiashvili did not think it necessary, as a result of which another opportunity to regulate the situation in the republic by political means was not used." That is the opinion of Georgians themselves.

But that's not all. That day, 8 April, Patiashvili sent a coded telegram to Moscow in which he asserted optimistically: "As a whole the Georgian Central Committee, the government, local Party and Soviet offices have the situation under control and are taking the necessary measures to stabilize the situation. . . . At the moment no measures supplemental to those already taken by the CPSU Central Committee and government of the USSR are required."

That telegram was sent on 8 April at 8:50 P.M., after the group of youths attacked the personnel carriers, when six soldiers had already been wounded and the situation had become explosive.

The next morning, after the tragedy had already taken place in Tbilisi, Patiashvili sent a telegram: "Despite all the measures taken by Party and Soviet officials and the law-enforcement agencies, after 9:00 P.M. on 8 April, extremists began to incite the 15,000 people demonstrating at the Georgian State House, as well as in other parts of the city. They pushed them to the limit and it got out of control. The leaders of the so-called national liberation movement began to make public their plans to take power in the republic. . . . "

What was that? At 8:50 P.M. they "had the situation under control," but after 9:00 P.M. the situation "began to get out of control." Patiashvili's optimism, which people were sharing in conversations in Moscow on 8 April, did not withstand the test of real events.

In my view, the conclusions of the Georgian Commission are totally just: because Shevardnadze and Razumovsky didn't fly to Tbilisi on 8 April, at Gorbachev's behest, an opportunity was missed to regulate the conflict peacefully. But the question of why they didn't go remains unanswered, at least for now.

Nevertheless, the question of why Shevardnadze didn't obey Gorbachev is fascinating. The atmosphere in the Politburo chaired by Gorbachev was democratic. Politburo sessions were never automatic votes by ukase of the general secretary. It was fairly common to have debates and arguments. Gorbachev sometimes had to retract his proposals. But I don't recall a single case when Shevardnadze contradicted the *gensek*. During the years when Brezhnev was seriously ill and barely functioning, there was a kind of ritual glorification of him by the other leaders. This ritual didn't just appear; it was deftly created. All politicians had to take part in this ritual, even foreign politicians, and not only from socialist countries. From the vantage point of hindsight, we justly condemn this, but we should recall that at that time anyone who tried to violate the ritual was banished immediately. Politics is politics, and in those years anyone who wanted to do his job honestly—and that refers to Gorbachev, Yeltsin, and Ligachev—had to pay tribute in this ritual created by Brezhnev's entourage. But there were true virtuosi who based their careers on this ritual, and among them, Shevardnadze was the best.

I must quote for the public record several of Shevardnadze's characteristic—although far from the most colorful—characterizations of Brezhnev. In March 1981, at a meeting of Georgian Party activists to discuss the results of the 26th Congress, Shevardnadze—then a Hero of Socialist Labor—said, "Comrade Brezhnev's speech opened up to the world a broad panorama of the progress of our country in economics, science, and culture. It is as if he gathered unto himself all the power of our Party, its unity and solidarity. We could sense in it the sure footstep of our great homeland into the future, to the shining summits of Communism.

"Every proposal and every conclusion of Leonid Ilyich's speech, every word resounds with Leninist professionalism, Leninist purposefulness, Leninist objectivity, self-criticism, a truly Leninist, profoundly scholarly approach to an analysis of contemporary life. On the podium stood Leonid Ilyich Brezhnev, so close and dear to each of us. And each of us saw and felt with all our hearts how he thought and forged at the Congress."

Without quoting Shevardnadze's speech at the 26th Congress, let me just say that it was one of the speeches most filled with praise for Brezhnev.

I mention it because this was not simply praise of the *gensek*— this was a passionate, heartfelt support for all his actions, as witness

Shevardnadze's speech on 7 June 1980, at a meeting of Georgian Party activists, at which he said, "We were all terribly concerned about the fate of the Afghan people, the fate of our southern borders, and the bold and correct step taken in regard to Afghanistan was expected by every Soviet citizen in his heart. The Soviet people actively support the measures taken by the Party and Soviet government to preserve and develop the achievements of the Afghan revolution and secure our southern borders. And subsequent events have confirmed that this was the only correct decision."

To be honest, I was amazed at the elasticity of Shevardnadze's political views, his constant readiness to support the leaders in everything, and to carry out their orders with dispatch. That's why I was astounded when I learned that on 8 April Shevardnadze went against Gorbachev's orders. True, Patiashvili unexpectedly began to send optimistic telegrams; and at the meeting chaired by Chebrikov, we decided, after conferring with Patiashvili, that it wasn't necessary to fly there immediately. But all of that happened during the day of 8 April, when Shevardnadze was already supposed to be in Tbilisi! And as a result of his delay, "another opportunity to regulate the situation in the republic by political means was not used," as stated in the conclusion of the commission of the Georgian Supreme Soviet.

But time showed that the optimism was false. The unreliable analysis of the situation in Tbilisi made on 8 April not only led to that tragic night in which innocent people died but also, through a long chain of circumstances, including the emergence of the political Tbilisi Affair at the first Congress, the initial mistake facilitated an anti-Soviet coup in Georgia. Power in Georgia was grabbed by the leaders who skillfully ran the rally at the State House, taking advantage of the nationalist fever, the leaders who were named by Sobchak in his speech at the second Congress as he blamed them for shirking their political, moral, and legal responsibility by violating public order.

Before I continue my discussion about the intrigues of the Tbilisi Affair, I believe it is necessary to answer some key questions that allow us to understand the central drama of perestroika.

The Tragedy of Perestroika

Politics is a complicated matter that reflects the interests of classes, social groups, entire governments, and much, much more. It is a serious discipline, not easy to define in full. But it has its main pillars, several basic postulates that every major political figure in every nation and epoch must address.

We must leave to scholars the listing of all these postulates. But I must single one out for mention: on the rough shoals of history we must define, precisely and without error, the chief threat faced by each country and its people.

To understand and formulate that chief threat is to evince true political wisdom. A reformer who is distracted by battle against fleeting or minor threats will mistake the reasons for the difficulties he faces and will make inevitable errors in overcoming them.

Over time, as social processes develop, the chief threat to the normal course of reform naturally changes. A sagacious politician foresees the changes in the way people think and eases or eliminates unfavorable tendencies.

These are general theoretical positions. Turning to real life, we recall that the initial phase of perestroika was characterized by opposition between the proreform forces who made up the majority of the population, and conservative forces opposed to social change.

It was a correct initial orientation. Of course, even today there are people who long for the days of Stalinism, lawlessness, and mass purges. They exist not only among adherents of the past but also among the new "ultrademocrats" who call for "hanging Communists from the lampposts." But the majority of the people have welcomed perestroika with enthusiasm. At the same time, they weren't ready for the radical change that began in 1987, led by destructive forces who called themselves democrats and "foremen of perestroika." Using their advantage in the mass media, they began to concoct an image of the "enemy of perestroika"—everyone who disagreed with them and adhered to the principle of gradual change and continuity in social reform.

The radical right-wing press called those who didn't agree with

them conservatives and tried to blame them for the failures of perestroika. But putting aside political labels, it is appropriate to ask:
What do conservatives have to do with the upheaval of the consumer
market and monetary relations? Did they really abet the catastrophic
growth of crime and the black market, the appearance of a new
breed of operators? Did they organize flareups of ethnic conflict or
the wave of rallies that kept people from doing their jobs? No—
that's all the work of anti-Communist, nationalist, and separatist
forces, revisionists of every stripe and hue. The so-called conservatives in fact did all they could to prevent such a negative turn of
events.

The so-called conservatives have turned out to be the greatest
realists. If their advice had been heeded, if we had checked the
radicalism from running amok in economics and politics, the country might have avoided many misfortunes. But the realists were
barraged with accusations of being "antiperestroika" when they
cautioned foresight against these mistakes.

The true drama—indeed, the tragedy—of perestroika is that instead of normal, sane polemics with the so-called conservatives, the
leaders of perestroika were distracted by a battle with them and
didn't see (or didn't want to see) the true threat gaining ground—
the chief, terrible threat: nationalism and separatism.

Later Gorbachev and other leading politicians would be heard
saying repeatedly: We underestimated the danger of nationalist
movements. But just who was that "we"? The time has come to
ascertain the sources and advocates of nationalism and to understand
that the distracting political battle with conservatives and leniency
toward the nationalist movements were two sides of the same coin.
This was the fatal error of perestroika.

I do not wish to torment everyone with Russia's traditional question: "Who is to blame?" But unless we understand what happened,
we cannot count on success in our battle against nationalism.

History and world experience bear witness to the inevitability of
the danger of an upsurge of nationalism in the process of reform.
It was not hard to foresee that the first unofficial movements that
appeared during the democratization of public life would use the

national factor to consolidate their forces—it is the simplest, the most accessible to the masses. And in the past there were many distortions, especially in the development of national cultures and languages. All the leading unofficial movements in the Union republics began by harkening to national awareness. National awareness always leads the way, acceding to civic concepts only as the working class acquires political experience.

I personally see nothing wrong in national awareness serving as a catalyst for the rebirth of political activism among citizens. In fact, I'd say it is splendid. The main thing is to ensure that the growth of national consciousness does not turn into the idea of national exclusiveness or the dominance of the native population. Applying this to the political situation in 1988, when popular fronts appeared everywhere in the republics, the question for me was how to encourage activism without allowing it to turn into a nationalistic, anti-Soviet movement.

The first warning signal, the events in Nagorno-Karabakh, showed the explosiveness of the national issue and warned of the bloody demise of social development if nationalism's growth was not checked in time. Naturally, we discussed the situation in Nagorno-Karabakh and the demands of Armenia and Azerbaidzhan many times at many early 1988 Politburo sessions. We reached a unanimous and correct decision: it was impermissible to redraw national and territorial borders at that time. To violate that principle even once would open up a path for a multitude of bloody conflicts.

Somewhat later, in May 1988, we decided other tactical issues, in part to replace the Party leaders in Azerbaidzhan and Armenia. To conduct a Central Committee plenum, Gorbachev proposed that we send members of the Politburo to the republics. I would go to Baku, Azerbaidzhan; Yakovlev, to Yerevan, Armenia. Everyone supported the idea. We decided that Razumovsky would be added to my party, while Dolgikh would accompany Yakovlev.

I familiarized myself with the situation in Azerbaidzhan and began to prepare my report. I finished it at about 11:00 P.M.—the manuscript is still in my files, owing to my old habit of writing my speeches in longhand and keeping the original. The situation in

Baku was complicated, and despite the late hour, I decided to consult with Gorbachev on the phone.

"Mikhail Sergeyevich, I would like your consent on the main point of my speech at tomorrow's plenum."

"Let's hear it."

"The basis is the Politburo decree on Nagorno-Karabakh. The point is that we cannot resolve national issues by changing territorial borders without the republics' consent. We must preserve the status quo. But I add that the lawful demands of all national and ethnic groups in the population, of every person, regardless of his nationality, must be fully satisfied. . . . "

"Yes, that's the basic principle," Gorbachev approved. "Good luck."

The next day I presented this position to the plenum of the Azerbaidzhan Communist Party Central Committee. I had no doubts that Yakovlev would do exactly the same in Yerevan, since this was a decree of principle by the Politburo. But when I later saw Yakovlev's speech at the plenum of the Armenian Central Committee, I discovered with amazement that he had completely ignored the problem of Nagorno-Karabakh. Yakovlev has had much to say about the danger of conservatism. But not once did he even utter the name Nagorno-Karabakh, nor mention the center's firm position on the question of national-territorial borders—as if that important document, or this burning problem, did not exist.

I have already mentioned the memorable September 1988 session of the Politburo at which Yakovlev reported on his trip to Lithuania. By that autumn, our evaluations regarding the intentions of the Baltic republics had diverged completely. Many factors indicated that it was rapidly becoming an active nationalist, anti-Soviet movement.

Yakovlev appealed for calm, asserting that in the Baltic republics the normal processes of democratization characteristic of perestroika were developing.

But what actually happened and who was right?

Today we can draw a graph showing clearly how the unofficial movements of the Baltics turned to radical nationalism and went from republican *khozraschet*[7] to secession from the USSR. During this entire period, a virulent war was being waged on the political front against true Communists, who were labeled "conservatives." At the same time the "foremen," renegades, and revisionists rapidly changed their affiliation from Communists to "national democrats," pinning national colors to their lapels to hold on to power and privileges.

In Latvia and Estonia, former high Party functionaries became leaders of the nationalist forces. In Lithuania, the honors for splitting the Communist Party and creating rich soil for nationalism belong to the former first secretary of the Lithuanian Communist Party Central Committee, the classic Liquidator,[8] Brazauskas.

True Communists, learning from the lessons of the past and carrying out the legal demands of the people, have been relinquishing their past privileges and monopoly on power. Meanwhile, the Baltic "national democrats" who came to power passed dictatorial laws and widened the sphere of illicit privileges. They voted themselves exorbitantly high salaries in the manner of "grand princes"— inviting the Russian republic's pseudodemocrats to join them. That's the way it has been wherever democrats have come to power—in Russia, including Moscow and Leningrad.

The nationalist wave in the Baltics began to grow rapidly at the end of 1989, after the second Congress of People's Deputies and the memorable fiery debates over Yakovlev's speech on the Molotov-Ribbentrop pact and the secret protocol. I'd like to remind the reader of some prophetic words that resounded from the podium when one of the deputies shouted in anger, "What are you doing? Come to your senses! You're giving a green light to the dissolution of the Soviet Union!"

---

[7]The cost-accounting system, which meant the producers covered their losses and expenses by managing profits independently of central directives.—TRANS.

[8]The Liquidators were a faction of the prerevolutionary Russian Communist Party who advocated the eventual "liquidation" of the Party—not just the "withering away" of the state, but of the Party as well.—TRANS.

But they didn't listen.

The tense, mudslinging atmosphere at the second Congress was a harbinger of crisis in perestroika. In the political heat fanned by the Western and domestic mass media, it was hard to be certain of wise decisions being made. I, of course, realized the danger. I don't mean this as an alibi; as a member of the top Party leadership I share full responsibility for what happened in that period. But history demands a precise accounting of the actions of every politician.

At the end of 1988, Gorbachev, Yakovlev, and several other members of the Politburo shied away from uttering the word "nationalism," replacing it with the concept "extremism." The words "internationalism" and "international solidarity" completely disappeared from our political lexicon. This was reflected in the press and official reports on disturbances. This reflected the tendency to forgo mention of the danger of nationalism even as it eroded the unity of the Soviet Union. I preferred to call a spade a spade. I saw the growing wave of separatism as the chief threat to perestroika. I believed we could not tolerate any catering to or indulgence of nationalist elements; this would only bring grief to millions of people.

Since Yakovlev's memorable report on his trip to Lithuania, I had been following events in the Communist parties of the Baltic republics with particular interest. A party infected with nationalism is a dying one—there was no doubt about that. The alarming statements being made in the Baltics were discussed many times at Politburo sessions. They disturbed many members of the Politburo, and these questions were raised by the Communists at the Central Committee plenum. As a result, the newspaper *Pravda* began to publish materials revealing the nationalist essence of the popular fronts.

As the situation in the Baltics heated up in the summer of 1989 I made a special statement at the Central Committee. A flood of bad news was coming to us from the Baltic republics about discrimination against the nonnative population and the upsurge of interethnic tension. My statement recognized with approval and hope the healthy forces in the Baltics and elsewhere. This could have become a turning point in the development of national processes. I wanted to get rid of the remnants of the past, provide opportunities for the development of national cultures and languages and complete freedom for the national traditions and customs, to heed the lawful demands of the native population. At the same time, the statement noted the danger of nationalism and defended the interests of all nationalities living in the Baltics. It was a platform to revitalize the political situation; furthermore, it wasn't an abstract program worked out in an ivory tower, but took into account the real situation developing there.

I'm sure that if the center and the mass media had begun to work in the spirit of the statement, later developments would have been completely different and would not have led to a political crisis in the Baltics. Alas, the leaders, supported by several of the central press organizations, opened fire on the statement—and the Central Committee again displayed unpardonable passivity. I had the impression that for some the statement was simply words on paper, while its sad fate seemed to inspire yet further the Baltic separatists.

Seeing the direction in which things were headed, I decided to address a special memorandum to the Politburo. This was my automatic right as a Party member, but it is interesting that since the beginning of the 1930s the members of the Politburo hadn't once used it. Understandably; it was the most dangerous of actions. But I had no choice: all my attempts in 1988 and 1989 to initiate a serious discussion at Central Committee and Politburo sessions on nationalism and separatism, the position of the Party and its unity, had been in vain. So I decided to put my thoughts in writing.

I was compelled to address the Central Committee several times. But I would like to include here just one letter, sent in May 1990. For reasons discussed below, I would like to print the entire text.

To the CPSU Central Committee, and Comrade M. S. Gorbachev, general secretary of the CPSU Central Committee:

In March of this year I addressed you, Mikhail Sergeyevich, on the question of the unity of the Party, the political situation in the country, and on the convention of the Central Committee plenum.

We all know that to avoid errors in evaluating the political situation, it is essential to determine correctly the trends as events develop and determine what we are moving from and what we are moving toward.

Two months have passed since I sent that letter to the Central Committee. In that short time the situation in society has worsened considerably. The country is in a depressed state. This is the question: Either everything that has been achieved by the efforts of many generations will be preserved and developed, restructured and revitalized on a true, socialist basis, or the Soviet Union will cease its existence and be replaced by dozens of states with a different social system.

Bourgeois nationalists have taken the upper hand in Lithuania, and the republic is drifting to the West. Estonia and Latvia are moving in that direction. Virulent nationalists are leading the soviets in several western provinces of the Ukraine. An internecine war is being waged in the Caucasus and there is a duality of authority in a number of regions there. The socialist community in Europe has dissolved. The country is losing its allies. The positions of imperialism are being consolidated.

It is becoming clear that in these conditions of political instability, it is impossible to carry out a deepgoing reform of society and introduce perestroika. It is impossible.

Interethnic conflicts and centrifugal forces in the federation, strikes, the failure to carry out important presidential ukases and the laws of the USSR Supreme Soviet, and the slackening of discipline in the economy are virtually blocking the implementation of the government's program to revitalize the economy and making it impossible to conduct economic reforms. Judging by the real situation, the policy of revitalization in a number of republics and in a number of indicators is collapsing under the onslaught of nationalist and separatist forces.

Trips around the country, conversations with workers, and meetings with Communists have shown that a gap has opened between the public opinion created in the mass media and the true mood of the workers. You can see this in the letters to the Central Committee. But we often don't notice that or react appropriately.

Many Communists and workers demand that the CPSU Central Committee realistically evaluate the political situation and take effective measures, since our socialist Motherland is in danger. It is a fact that there are forces in the Soviet Union acting against socialism. They are coordinated and have foreign connections. Now the main thing is to save the USSR as a single state. To do that the CPSU must unite the working class, peasants, intelligentsia, and everyone for whom our socialist Union is dear.

I believe it is necessary to convene an extended Central Committee plenum, including Party activists of the country, to discuss the present moment, review the course of the pre-Congress discussions, the preparations for the 28th Party Congress, and the implementation of the recommendations in the letter of the Central Committee to Communists in the country.

A plenum should also be convened to review the government's measures for the transition to a market economy. These questions have still not been discussed at the Politburo. Thus the political leaders of the country are on the sidelines of these programs that concern the entire Motherland and touch the interests of every person.

The most important thing is to draft at the Central Committee plenum and then carry out specific measures to rebuff antisocialist, national-separatist forces, to unite the Party rank and file, and maintain the unity of the Soviet Union. Many provincial and district Party committees demand that a Central Committee plenum be convened. We must not disregard this. Individual members of the Politburo have also called for a plenum.

Yesterday on 27 May I spoke with you about this memorandum. Today I am sending it to you. I ask that you read this letter as well as the letter to the Central Committee of 27 March (which has still not been distributed) by comrades in the CPSU Central Committee, the Central Oversight Commission, the first secretaries of the Central Committees of the Union republics, territorial and provincial Party committees.

Respectfully yours,
Ye. Ligachev
28 May 1990

As I reread that May 1990 letter today, I see with a heavy heart how unfortunately prophetic it was. And its conclusions were not the personal opinions of one Communist; this was an official letter sent by a member of the Politburo to the general secretary of the CPSU Central Committee.

That was the official letter I sent as a Politburo member to Gorbachev. But something so unbelievable and astounding happened that I still can't grasp it. For all the increasingly raucous proclamations about pluralism, glasnost, and democratization of the Party, the situation in its top echelons seemed in actual fact to be reverting to the dark years of the past: in violation of the Party Charter—and, indeed, contrary to common sense and clearly to the detriment of perestroika—my letters were shelved. Politburo members did not see them.

Yevgeny Sokolov, who became first secretary of the Byelorussian Central Committee after Slyunkov, told me about a meeting during the 28th Party Congress to discuss candidates for the new Central Committee. Someone asked Gorbachev, "Why isn't Ligachev on the list?" Gorbachev answered, "Lately he's been writing too many letters. . . . "

I did write Gorbachev letters analyzing the situation in the country and demanding a plenum to discuss the situation collectively. Like many Central Committee members, I foresaw the tragic course of events and could not remain silent. I did all I could to prevent misfortune. Unfortunately, for various reasons, my capabilities were limited. To keep my voice from being heard, Gorbachev went against his promises and the Party Charter and quashed my letters to the Central Committee members. To make me "behave" and tie my hands in the political battle, my political opponents—political opportunists such as Gdlyan—never stopped their preposterous attacks on me. And to some extent those attacks were successful: I couldn't change the course of events.

But who won, and who suffered?

Because the chief threat to perestroika was not perceived in time, a great power found itself on the brink of dissolution. Many ethnic groups were living in poverty, the blood of innocent people was shed, and there were hundreds of thousands of refugees in the country.

Communists, the entire Soviet people, and our supporters abroad must know the following.

As the points in the final report to the 28th Party Congress were being discussed, I insisted that we state clearly the chief threat to the process of perestroika. As usual, Yakovlev and Medvedev wanted to cite this as conservatism, and that was how the version of the final report reviewed in the Politburo read. After looking it over, I sent Gorbachev my view that conservatism, national-separatism, and forces pushing the country to a bourgeois system constituted three lesser dangers. To my mind, conservatism wasn't the chief threat to perestroika. But I compromised politically on this question, since the most important thing for me was to indicate the danger of nationalism.

Unfortunately, the danger of intensified nationalist forces was presented in the report only as a "serious complication" in the implementation of the tasks of perestroika. In other words, even in mid-1990, when the process of dissolving the USSR had already begun, the danger of national separatism was still being downplayed.

Nevertheless, all three dangers were noted in Gorbachev's final report of the 28th Party Congress. But just a month after the Congress, when Gorbachev spoke at the maneuvers of the Odessa Military District, he again cited only conservatism as a threat to perestroika.

Only a year later, at the December 1990 Central Committee plenum, did Gorbachev say in his report:

"Today it is more than clear that the separatists are not interested in the genuine aspirations of their people; they are using sacred feelings to fulfill their own plans. We cannot ignore the fact that some nationalist leaders proclaim the greatness of Lithuania, the Ukraine, Moldavia, and so on, as they declare openly their claim to various territories. We all know what this can lead to and has led to. I say it directly: Today in the country there is no more serious danger than dyed-in-the-wool extremist nationalism that stirs up interethnic discord."

I sat in the Plenum Hall listening to those words, bitterly recalling what I recounted in this chapter. Once again, we were late—and this time disastrously so. How bitter to have been correct. But why didn't Gorbachev and those close to him heed my persistent warnings? Why were they silent? Why did they shelve my letters to the Central Committee members and thereby violate the very principles of collective leadership?

I don't doubt that time will provide the answers to these questions. I can say that Gorbachev was skillfully drawn into this profoundly political battle by those—primarily Yakovlev—who frightened him with the danger from the right, hinting at Khrushchev's fate.

What is more, in the letter to the Central Committee members and Gorbachev, I indicated that the ethnic conflicts and centrifugal forces in the federation were hampering implementation of the economic program and would lead the country into economic disaster. I believed the main issue was to preserve the USSR as a single state.

The question of why Gorbachev constantly acted too late is not simple. It would be untrue to say that he didn't have accurate information about events in the country. But why did the leaders of the country always act too late and allow everything to slip from their control?

Sobchak's Move

Returning to the Tbilisi Affair, I want to reiterate that until the second Congress of People's Deputies, in December 1989, I merely followed it as an outsider. I was particularly worried by Georgia's political evolution during that period. The nationalist wave began to turn into a political typhoon. Exploiting the tragedy of 9 April 1989, in their election campaigning, antisocialist and anti-Soviet forces aggravated the situation. The scenario already tested in the Baltics, especially Lithuania, was being followed—even the Georgian Communist Party's first secretary seemed to be following in his Lithuanian counterpart's footsteps.

Strange things were going on a few days before the opening of the second Congress. Anatoly Sobchak, the chairman of the commission of people's deputies of the USSR investigating the Tbilisi Affair, appeared on a long program on Leningrad television[9] in which he presented viewers with some information from his commission's work and even showed excerpts from film shot by the Georgian KGB. The program was a serious violation of congressional ethics. Even more striking, however, was the fact that Sobchak rejected an objective, substantive analysis in favor of a prejudiced incitement of passion around the use of military gasses and shovels, even though he already knew that experts had determined that the deaths had been caused by crowding, not wounds and asphyxiation.

By then I was familiar with the report of the Sobchak Commission. It seemed a substantial document, which presented the various aspects of the Tbilisi Affair and the tragedy that occurred that night and drew profound and important conclusions. My only objections were to the section containing tendentious criticism of the army. The findings mentioned the meetings at the Central Committee CPSU on 7 and 8 April and that the situation in Tbilisi had been discussed late in the evening of 7 April, in a meeting at the airport with Gorbachev, just as he arrived from London.

---

[9]Sobchak later became mayor of Leningrad, now renamed St. Petersburg.—TRANS.

That is why I was rather taken aback by Sobchak's television performance. It made me wary; I remembered only too well how the Gdlyan Affair had started. Leningrad television, obviously working for the pseudodemocrats in upsetting the nation with distracting maneuvers, clearly had some ulterior motive in inviting Sobchak to its studios.

Military prosecutors objected strenuously to the broadcast; they felt Sobchak was distorting the facts. Leningrad television, again the seedbed of public scandal, was forced to give equal time to military investigators, who presented their version of the incident.

The Tbilisi Affair began to snowball.

By that time, however, many deputies had learned from the various provocations upsetting the country and had matured politically. Demands were made to hear the commission's report at the Congress. And contrary to the objections of Sobchak, the Georgian delegation, and the Interregional Group,[10] the Congress decided to put Chairman Sobchak's report on the agenda as well as a presentation from the chief army prosecutor, Katusev.

Here, something totally unexpected occurred: Sobchak's oral report was quite different from the commission's written conclusion, signed by all its members. The stress was shifted sharply, with many facts not mentioned at all and others thoroughly distorted. Sobchak's report was devised to make it look as if Ligachev was the main villain of the Tbilisi tragedy.

Sobchak's appearance had been the subject of previous hot debate. He was allowed to speak at a closed session. It was not televised, and the full text of the report and the commission's conclusions were not published in *Izvestia*. If you add that the radical mass media instantly picked up the name Ligachev from Sobchak's report and began smearing it not only with the Gdlyan Affair but with Tbilisi as well, Sobchak's unexpected move most certainly achieved its goal.

I would rather not remember what I went through in those hours

---

[10]The Interregional Deputies' Group was a liberal caucus in the USSR Supreme Soviet, of which Sobchak was a member.—TRANS.

and days immediately following the false accusations of the investigators, when I was engulfed by equally absurd and untrue accusations of involvement in the Tbilisi tragedy. This is no time for false modesty. It really did take courage to put up with it all, not to put away my guns, and to keep fighting—not for myself, but against the separatism threatening the country with schism and bloodshed, against the "Liquidators" within the Party.

Now, when the spiritual pain has abated and all the false charges against me have turned to dust; now that the course of events has shown that I was right, I sometimes muse about Sobchak's move. I have no doubt that someone had "put the fix in" with Sobchak. But I am more concerned by another question of basic morality.

I am used to trusting people, to believing in their spiritual purity. Of course, I've come across all kinds in my long life—deceivers, liars, and outright bastards. And yet, on the whole I have always considered people to be good and pure. I met everyone with whom life has brought me into contact amiably, with an open heart and good intentions. I'll admit, I have sometimes suffered disappointment. But frankly I've never sought revenge against those who have hurt me, as people who have worked with me know. Perhaps I developed that trait in the difficult Stalinist years, when our family suffered harsh persecution and I myself was on the very brink of disaster.

Deep down, I trust people. I am confused and terribly tormented when I suddenly come across a manifestation of indecency, especially from people I considered decent and intelligent. And I had placed Sobchak in just that category. Yes, we disagreed on many things, often on major issues of principle. But I was not unaware of his ability to conduct himself correctly, his fidelity to the law, and his desire to follow moral criteria. All that was part of him. As it turned out, however, this was merely an outer shell, while inside was something else. In his speech, Sobchak shifted around the commission's official findings with a crudeness that bordered on indecency.

Yes, this is an emotional reaction. Since Sobchak's speech wasn't published in the press, I should mention a few of its "idiosyncrasies."

Unlike the official findings, Sobchak did not list the participants of the working meeting at the Central Committee on 7 April, but merely reduced it to "taking place under Ligachev's chairmanship." But that was not all. I was astonished that he failed to mention the meeting at the Central Committee on 8 April. Moreover, he did not mention that the Tbilisi situation was discussed with Gorbachev at the airport. I repeat, all those facts figure in the official conclusions of the commission. But according to his report, I was the only representative of the center who had anything to do with the Tbilisi Affair; no other member of the Politburo was mentioned.

All these unconscionable oversights pale, however, in contrast with the effective trick Sobchak pulled at the end of the report. Rather, they were a prelude, a warmup.

During the commission's investigation of the Tbilisi tragedy I wrote a letter to Sobchak that I would like to quote in full.

Dear Anatoly Alexandrovich!

Recently I learned of the findings of the Commission of the Georgian Supreme Soviet on the Investigation of the Events of 9 April 1989, in the city of Tbilisi, published in the republic newspaper *Kommunist* (23 September 1989). I feel it is my duty to call your attention to the following. The authors of that document maintain that during the meeting of the CPSU Central Committee chaired by Ligachev, "the decision was made to accede to the request of the Georgian Communist Party's Central Committee to send help in the form of armed forces." It goes on to say that this was "corroborated by the material evidence of the commission appointed by the Congress of People's Deputies."

However, as far as I know, the commission you head has not made its findings public. This is the circumstance that prompted me to write to you personally. I want to reassert what I said at the commission's meeting. Yes, an exchange of opinion on the situation in Tbilisi did take place on 7 April at the Central Committee CPSU with the participation of members of the Politburo, candidate members of the Politburo, [and] secretaries of the Central Committee. At the

end of the meeting I pointed out that the request for troops
in order to maintain order and the introduction of a curfew
had not been discussed collectively in Georgia's government
agencies and came in fact verbally from Comrade Patiashvili.
Therefore, I proposed recommending that the Georgian
Communist Party Central Committee examine the situation
in Tbilisi as well as the leading soviet and Party bodies, the
presidium of the Supreme Soviet, the Council of Ministers,
and the Party's Central Committee. I stressed the necessity
of acting politically, increasing the work with participants in
rallies and in the workplace, and not sitting around in offices. My proposal was passed along by the secretaries of the
Central Committee to Comrade Patiashvili.

Unfortunately, these fundamentally important directions
of the CPSU Central Committee were not reflected in the
commission's conclusions. Soon after, the Georgian Central
Committee sent several encoded telegrams to Moscow. They
were read by Comrade Lukyanov at the first Congress of
People's Deputies. By that time—that is, the morning of 8
April—I had left for a scheduled vacation. In discussing the
issue on 7 April a request was expressed and the Ministry of
Internal Affairs and the Ministry of Defense were instructed
to be prepared in case of a dangerous, life-threatening turn
of events. They did not want to repeat the mistakes that led
to the failure to prevent the tragedy in Sumgait. Unfortunately, our anxieties were confirmed by subsequent events in
Abkhazia and Fergana, when troops had to be moved urgently from other regions, and even so, deaths and casualties, sorrow and suffering could not be avoided. I would like
to remind you that according to information from the Georgian Central Committee, the USSR Ministry of Internal Affairs, and CPSU Central Committee divisions, the situation
in Tbilisi was already growing complicated and dangerous
extremism was on the rise. I categorically reject the conclusion of the Georgian commission in the same newspaper
that the events of 9 April were not a secret from the leaders
of the country, including Ligachev. The leadership of the
country learned about the tragic events after they occurred.

As for me, I can say that I learned about it from the television. Strictly speaking, before 7 April and after that day I
did not participate in discussions of Georgia. Those are the
facts. I would ask you to familiarize the members of the
commission with this note.

This is the letter I sent to the commission, briefly setting out
everything that the reader now knows. It doesn't seem like much.
How could it be used against me?

However, Sobchak managed to squeeze out of the letter an effective ending for his report. He did it with real virtuosity, I must
admit. He reported everything in my letter and then said, "I would
like to add something. If a political or government leader makes a
decision, he bears responsibility for the results of that decision
whether he knew about the results of that decision or not—whether
he's on vacation or in his office."

With those words, the report was over. The deputies of the
Interregional Group applauded.

After all, I hadn't made any decisions, and that was clearly noted
in the official conclusions of the parliamentary commission. This
was the lawyer's personal trick, based on courtroom practice. He
did it to create the impression that Ligachev was at fault for the
Tbilisi Affair and bore the responsibility for it. That's what was said
at the end: "bears responsibility."

In the life of every political and public figure there are deeds that
have a decisive effect on how his contemporaries and future generations see him and that form his image in history. Our stormy
times brought to the fore many new names who two or three years
earlier were completely unknown. This is characteristic of watershed
years. Some of the new politicians will manage to stay in the mainstream of events; others will simply be flashes in the pan. But in
the final analysis, each will have to stand before the court of history.

That unexpected and sudden move by this professor and experienced lawyer, wreaking violence on the truth and distorting the
essence of his own commission's conclusions, was a true drama for

Sobchak himself. Perhaps in the heat of battle he did not notice it, but the mark of Tbilisi is written ineradicably into his political biography and inevitably will emerge in the future.

The Tbilisi Affair is too important and memorable not to become part of history, and Sobchak with it. He will enter history as a sophisticated lawyer and orator who turned his craft to covering up the truth.

Only later did I learn with astonishment that Sobchak had not joined the Party until 1987, and left it in 1990. No comment is needed. I must note sadly that the presidium said nothing in response to Sobchak's speech. There were people in the presidium who knew perfectly well how events had developed; they had taken part in them personally. And yet they said nothing. Just the day before, in that same hall, passions had raged over the bribery case in which the unconscientious investigators Gdlyan and Ivanov tried to implicate me. And now there was Tbilisi; and once more it was Ligachev. Wouldn't anyone clear things up, reestablish justice? I had worked side by side with those people for several years, and we had often spoken of Party comradeship.

But the presidium was silent.[11] After the speeches of Katusev, the chief army prosecutor, and Gumbaridze, first secretary of the Georgian Central Committee, a break was announced, and I went into the presidium's room. If you look at the stage of the Palace of Congresses, you may notice a small door built into the massive wall on the right. Beyond that door is a good-sized room where the Politburo members usually gathered to rest. It had all kinds of communications facilities and directories to all the hot lines, and you could also get a quick snack.

Apparently I wasn't the only one upset by what was happening at the Congress. Almost the entire Politburo was there. Everyone

---

[11]At the April 1991 plenum of the CPSU Central Committee, where Gorbachev was harshly criticized, he mentioned Party comradeship many times in his concluding speech. Why had the general secretary forgotten about it earlier, when political adventurers of various stripes were slinging mud on many members of the Politburo? —AUTHOR

was nervous. No one talked to anyone else, no one asked questions, everyone felt awkward. Gorbachev drank tea silently, with concentration.

Suddenly Shevardnadze walked in, looked over the room quickly, threw his file down on the table, and exclaimed in agitation, "That's it! Mikhail Sergeyevich, I quit. I'm outraged by what's going on here. Consider this a firm decision."

The very next day the Western press was carrying the story of Shevardnadze's decision to quit. I was surprised how quickly the foreign correspondents had learned about it. After all, he had spoken in an intimate circle, behind closed doors.

I didn't have a second's doubt that Shevardnadze's threat to quit was feigned; he merely needed it to save face with the Georgian deputies who had walked out during the chief army prosecutor's speech. And perhaps not only with the Georgian deputies.

I will admit that in those minutes, in the presidium room, I considered appealing to someone individually or to them all at once: "Comrades! What is happening? Why are you all silent? You know what the real situation is. You can see that Sobchak shifted around the facts!" But, naturally, I refrained from such exclamations. Politics is a tough game, built on calculation, not emotion. I also knew that Sobchak's move had other, broader goals besides getting rid of Ligachev at any cost.

The Tbilisi case continued to develop, reaping huge dividends for Georgia's nationalist leaders and elevating them to the heights of power. Until those heights were reached, it did not pay for them to enter into open conflict with the country's leadership. They were following the path beaten by the Lithuanian Sajudis, inflaming passions and preparing for a future revolt. That is why, even as they attacked the army, they softened their attacks on the central authorities. And the center, for reasons I have described, preferred not to notice the rapid growth of Georgian nationalism.

Sobchak was given a very specific role in this well-planned business, although not a very significant one. His services were used because the findings of the Congress of People's Deputies Commission were objective and did not allow for political manipulation. But another brouhaha was desperately needed to heat up nationalist passions and focus the attention of millions on the Tbilisi Affair. That's what lay behind Sobchak's appearance on Leningrad TV.

I must note that I never felt any hostility from Georgians, for in Tbilisi they understood that I had nothing to do with the tragic events of that night. The subtext of Sobchak's speech, aimed personally against me, was not part of Georgian games; it came from Moscow. And Sobchak did not limit himself to the speech; he also offered his own version in an interview in *Ogonyok*.

Overall, our fledgling glasnost presented a truly amazing picture. The Congress of People's Deputies had elected a special commission to investigate the Tbilisi tragedy. The commission had presented its findings. But so as not to agitate people, that conclusion was kept secret, while the commission's chairman, Sobchak, freely presented his version in the mass media, creating a public uproar and distorting the commission's conclusions. It goes without saying that this would be impossible in any country with a developed democracy. In America, England, and France, glasnost has long passed through this wild period. Any lawyer who behaved this way in a civilized state would lose his political credibility and his clients forever.

Be that as it may, in his interview Sobchak maintained, "The meeting chaired by Ligachev, in which the fateful decision was made to send troops to help the republic, was not even a Politburo but merely a group of people (albeit of responsible members), who had gathered without the country's president, who was in England at the time, and without the head of the government, even though Nikolai Ivanovich Ryzhkov was in Moscow. Do you see what was going on? That's where the real danger lies!"

A wild stretch of the imagination . . . Well, of course, it's not really imagination, but calculation, an intentional pumping up of passion. Constantly warned about mythical conspiracies, the people are distracted from the real threat. Society's vigilance is being lulled deliberately; I'm convinced of that.

It had been noted many times that no decisions were made at that working meeting. We spoke only of drafting recommendations, which were soon ratified by Gorbachev and all the other members of the Politburo, including Ryzhkov, Shevardnadze, and Yakovlev. But amazingly, in that lengthy interview in the magazine *Ogonyok,* Sobchak never mentioned the evening meeting at Vnukovo-2 Airport. Using the fact that the commission's findings were not published, Sobchak obviously tried to hide the fact that Gorbachev was fully informed of the Tbilisi Affair by the evening of 7 April. Sobchak was clearly trying to keep Gorbachev and Shevardnadze out of the game.

Moreover, Sobchak never mentioned that Gorbachev ordered Shevardnadze to fly out to Tbilisi immediately. Perhaps that was the real point of Sobchak's full-fledged campaign—to cast a shadow on Ligachev to distract people from Gorbachev's actions and, most importantly, from Shevardnadze's. Although, to be precise, the main point must have been to get Shevardnadze out of the Tbilisi Affair, since he did not obey Gorbachev's very important and, I feel, correct order.

A thinking person should have no trouble understanding Sobchak's role. But he clearly overdid it in the *Ogonyok* interview. He wanted to show how hard he was trying, but instead he made it possible for me to state the truth publicly.

In that regard, I want to quote a small section from my February 1990 speech at the Central Committee plenum, in which I once more clearly stated my position on the chief threat to perestroika. I touched on the Tbilisi Affair. I quote from the transcript:

> A serious oversight is that we did not see the main danger to perestroika. Life has shown that the main, the mortal threat, to perestroika and to the Soviet Union are the powerful forces of a nationalistic, separatist, and antisocialist leaning. That is where the real danger to socialism and to the homeland lies in wait.
>
> Of course, some people try to distract the nation's attention and create false impressions in society. They divide many of us into radicals and conservatives, they consciously spread slander and inspire rumors.
>
> I would like to mention one fact to the members of the Central Committee. Recently the magazine *Ogonyok* announced

that a group of Politburo members and Central Committee secretaries headed by Ligachev, behind the backs of the general secretary of the Central Committee and the chairman of the Council of Ministers, met at the CPSU Central Committee on 7 April and discussed issues dealing with the situation in Georgia and made appropriate decisions.

But it is obvious that questions of that level are not decided by a group. Many comrades know that on that day—that is, 7 April—the Politburo in full complement, with the participation of Gorbachev, Ryzhkov, and Comrades Yakovlev and Shevardnadze, who had flown in from abroad, unanimously, and I stress unanimously, approved and passed political recommendations dealing with the development of events in Tbilisi.

I wonder: why are suspicions being raised? why these hints at a conspiracy? I said it before and I'll say it again: with only one goal—to distract society from the main threat to perestroika, from the destructive work being done in the country and in the Party by, I dare to say it, political demagogues and intriguers.

This part of my talk prompted a stormy reaction from Shevardnadze, who took the floor soon after me. Again, I quote from the transcript:

SHEVARDNADZE: A few words of clarification in connection with Yegor Kuzmich's remarks.

I do not know why it was necessary to return to this discussion after there have been parliamentary and special and detective investigations of the events in Tbilisi, especially after this issue was examined at the USSR Congress of People's Deputies.

In order to try once more to reestablish the truth I want to say that there was no Politburo session, there was an ordinary meeting at the airport. Among other things, there was a report on the upsetting telegrams from Tbilisi and it was said that the requests of our Georgian comrades for the necessary aid in maintaining order had been fulfilled, including the return of those units of internal troops that had been stationed on the territory of Georgia and had previously been transferred to Armenia.

It was stated categorically, the general secretary gave his categoric statement, that the Politburo would resolve the issue politically, through political dialogue. Those recommendations were given. That is all that happened at the airport.

GORBACHEV: No, that's not all. We also instructed Comrade Shevardnadze, despite all his trips and so on, as well as someone else—

VOICES: Razumovsky—

GORBACHEV: Razumovsky to fly to Tbilisi.

SHEVARDNADZE: And that happened, too, there was such a conversation, but the Georgian comrades said that there was no need for such a trip. That is the whole truth.

LIGACHEV [TO SHEVARDNADZE]: Eduard Amvrosiyevich, there is no contradiction between us. . . .

SHEVARDNADZE: No, I'm not saying there is a contradiction.

LIGACHEV: Listen, what was I supposed to do if a magazine with a circulation of four million is distorting the issue? After all, I have the opportunity to express my point of view. Especially, since you are all silent, dear comrades.

GORBACHEV: I think that we can end the first part on this and move on.

SHEVARDNADZE: I think that such a morbid reaction is unnecessary. First of all, I did not keep silent. I gave explanations to the commission of the USSR Supreme Soviet and said everything that was necessary. Secondly, I am not having a discussion with you, I am asking a question: Why is it necessary at all to start this discussion after the Congress of People's Deputies?

LIGACHEV: I didn't start it.

SHEVARDNADZE: I'm not accusing you.

GORBACHEV: This shows yet again the circumstances in which we struggle for the realization of our policies and that we must certainly remain cool.

I'm sure that in light of what I have revealed in this chapter, everything is clear to the reader. I do want to stress that when I spoke of no contradictions between Shevardnadze and myself, I meant the following:

Is the question really whether that evening session at Vnukovo-2 Airport was officially called a session of the Politburo? What's more to the point is that the Tbilisi issue was discussed by the full complement of the top political leadership, including the general secretary of the Central Committee. The political recommendations developed at it were collegially supported; not a single person objected. That includes Shevardnadze. And yet he, of all people, could have said, "Comrades, I am very familiar with the situation in Georgia, I know the Georgian people, their character and mood, and I do not agree with the decisions made. Why don't we do this instead. . . ."

But Shevardnadze said nothing. Moreover, he didn't object when Gorbachev instructed him to leave for Tbilisi first thing in the morning—but neither did he go. And then at the Central Committee plenum he tried to forget about his strange disobedience, admitting it only after Gorbachev had spoken.

Incidentally, the Politburo didn't always meet at the Kremlin. Often, it was when seeing Gorbachev off or meeting him that we collectively discussed matters and made highly important political decisions. Circumstances often called for urgency. Why put a premium on formalities?

As for the essense of our "squabble" with Shevardnadze, there were differences. Exploiting Sobchak's ambition and vanity, as well as the antiperestroika press, somebody tried to blame the entire Tbilisi tragedy on Ligachev.[12] In fact, it had worked, because as far

---

[12]In this connection, it is interesting to quote from the transcript of the October 1987 Central Committee plenum, when Boris Yeltsin raised the question of being released

as Shevardnadze was concerned, the matter was closed—why re-open it? The interview in *Ogonyok* gave me the chance to reestablish the truth and at last speak out publicly about what had really happened. This announcement forced Shevardnadze and Gorbachev to admit publicly that Ligachev was telling the truth.

The transcript of the Central Committee plenum was published in *Pravda*. This time, glasnost prevailed. Ever since then, no one has ever again tried to "stick" the Tbilisi tragedy on me.

When Shevardnadze said that the Georgian comrades did not see the need for his trip to Tbilisi, I suddenly remembered that the telephone conversation between Shevardnadze and Patiashvili took place during a working session of the Central Committee on 8 April and during a Party session in Georgia.[13] This was the session at which they decided to use the troops to force the demonstrators out of the square. Did Patiashvili mention this to Shevardnadze? Did Shevardnadze know about the intention to use the troops?

Bearing in mind the rules of interaction between the Central Committee of republic Parties and the CPSU Central Committee, Patiashvili did not have the right to hold back a report to the center of a decision made at the Georgian Party session on 8 April.

That meant that Shevardnadze knew that military units were going to be used against the demonstrators. But in that case, in accordance with Gorbachev's orders, he should have flown out to Tbilisi immediately to be present personally at such a delicate operation—or object to such a decision and to protest against it.

But Shevardnadze did neither. He preferred to behave as if he knew nothing of the decision made at the Georgian Party session on 8 April.

---

from his duties as candidate member of the Politburo. Shevardnadze also spoke at the plenum. Calling Yeltsin's statement "completely irresponsible," he added, "Who in this room doubts that Comrade Ligachev is a crystal-pure man? A man of the highest morals and principles, loyal, as they say, with his body and soul to perestroika."—AUTHOR

[13]This is clear from putting together the official reports of the commissions of the USSR Congress of People's Deputies and of the Georgian Supreme Soviet.—AUTHOR

After the Central Committee plenum that restored the truth, I certainly could have felt a sense of satisfaction, if it weren't for the fact that the whole business damaged the authority of the Politburo. In hundreds of letters and at many meetings, I was asked why Gorbachev and Shevardnadze were silent at the second Congress of People's Deputies, when Sobchak tried to shift the blame onto me. And I know that the question was asked of others. A normal person with common sense and at far remove from the corridors of power thinks this way. It would have been wonderful if Gorbachev, say, had taken the floor after Sobchak and said, "No, comrades, this is not right. It is not correct to bring it down to Ligachev. This is too simplified a way of looking at the situation. We all participated in the discussion of the Tbilisi issue; the events require a deeper analysis. . . ." A statement like that would have been met with understanding by the deputies and the people; it would have sounded noble and would have promoted a growth in the authority and respect accorded to the state and Party leadership. But, alas, politicians of world rank behaved differently that time. There was no such statement at the 28th Party Congress, either, when I answered that question in my report to the delegates.

Of course, this didn't keep Shevardnadze from talking about Party comradeship during his personal report to the 28th Party Congress.

How did events develop in Georgia? How did they affect the fate of the Soviet Union? The illegal rally that led to the tragedy on 9 April had been provoked by events in Abkhazia, which had wanted to leave the Georgian SSR to become part of the RSFSR. The bloody confrontations between Georgians and Abkhazians were stopped only with the intervention of troops from the USSR Ministry of Internal Affairs. The interethnic situation in Georgia is not simple, and when the authorities are rabid nationalists, the probability of new bloody conflicts is very high. Of course, I really do not want to be a prophet once again.[14]

---

[14]These lines were written before real civil war broke out in South Ossetia. My worst fears have come to pass.—AUTHOR

The basis of the Communist Party's nationalities policy was the guarantee of the rights and freedoms of citizens regardless of their nationality and place of residence, the right of nations to self-determination, the sovereignty of republics, and a renewed powerful Soviet federative state. And the main connecting link of the Soviet Federation was not the market, which some people are trying to impose, but a united, interconnected economic complex.

Often the desire to weaken the ties of the republics with the center and to leave the USSR expressed the claims and ambitions of those who sought undivided leadership in a republic as authoritarian prophets in politics. A strong impulse toward disunion came from the Declaration of the RSFSR on the Sovereignty of Russia, which declared the supremacy of republic laws and which contradicted the USSR Constitution, then the fundamental law of the land. This had an insidious effect not only on the situation in the USSR but in the Russian federation as well, which did not want sovereignty for autonomous territorial units. Yeltsin's proclamations about a single union were one thing; his actions set Russia apart, breaking up the Union as he struggled against the president and the central authorities.

It is incumbent on Russians above all others to support internationalism and unity of the Union—that is our predestined role. That does not mean I am calling on Russians to sacrifice without adequate reason. I am certain that the peoples of our country properly appreciate the role of the Russian people. But the growing threat to society of nationalism and chauvinism includes Russia, and we Russians must be internationalists, patriots of Russia, the Land of the Soviets.

The true intentions of the local nationalists and of their patrons in the center are absolutely clear.

A new appraisal is needed of the political and moral positions of those who furiously supported the Georgian nationalists and attacked the army. This may put the cheap politicians, whose main concern is to go along with the latest political fashion, into a difficult position. But the direct and honest position is worthy of respect—and that is supported even by those who do not share it.

In conclusion, a few words about a curious thing that took place in January 1990 and seemingly had no relation to the Tbilisi business.

On 23 January during the tragic events in Baku, some Western radio stations announced that Ligachev was in the Azerbaidzhani capital. Moreover, the Soviet radio station Mayak picked up that information.

And the next day, at a briefing for journalists at the Ministry of Foreign Affairs press center, they apparently hurled a blizzard of questions about Ligachev at the press department. My assistant, R. Romanov, was called at two-thirty that afternoon from the ministry and officially asked, "Foreign correspondents are wondering where Mr. Ligachev is right now."

"He is in his office," Romanov replied.

An hour later, there was a new phone call from the press center. "Tell us: at what time will Ligachev fly out of Baku?"

I wasn't in Baku then, but in Moscow. But when I was informed of the calls from the Ministry of Foreign Affairs, I thought that there might be someone who was not adverse to starting a Baku Affair involving me to follow the Tbilisi Affair.

Very little time has passed since the tragic days of Tbilisi, but life, like a tightly plotted play, has revealed the true intentions and goals of the inspirers of the Georgian disturbances and of their supporters. Gamsakhurdia came to power for a time on the wave of anti-Communism and nationalism and established a "democratic dictatorship" in Georgia that upset not only Georgians but many people in the West. In the West, Gamsakhurdia's rule was referred to as "fascist." And the Tbilisi ruler dealt with his opposition in the manner of Stalinist times. He announced that there was no political opposition in Georgia but only criminals in prison. Incidentally, he said this to a cowed correspondent from Radio Liberty.

What all this really adds up to is genocide of the Ossetian population and the desire to rid Georgia of all non-Georgians.

But was this turn of events a total surprise? According to the investigation by the USSR Prosecutor's Office, Gamsakhurdia,

Tsereteli, and others organized a rally even before the tragic night of 9 April, in the village of Leselidze (Abkhazian ASSR), where demands were voiced for appointing only Georgian nationals to leading posts in Abkhazia and for doing away with Abkhazian autonomy. And at a rally in Tbilisi on 5 April 1989, Gamsakhurdia announced: "The Abkhazian nation never existed historically. . . . They are fighting with Georgians, with Georgia, so they can become Russified." The notorious Memorandum to the Government of Georgia, written by the separatists, states:

1. End the Russification and Armenianization of Adzharia.
2. End the Armenianization of Meskhetia-Dzhavankhetia.
3. Stop settling Armenians and Russians in Georgia, Mengrelia, and Imereti.
4. Stop settling Dagestanis in the Kvareli region.
5. Take measures in the Telava, Lagodekhi, and Sagaredzhoi regions, where Azerbaidzhanization is taking place.
6. Repatriate Georgians who had migrated to Krasnodarsk Krai.

Further on the memorandum said: "All organizations . . . of Abkhazians, Ossetians, Armenians, Azerbaidzhanis, and Meshkhetian Turks are condemned by our movement and are declared anti-Georgian criminal groups, against whom implacable war will be waged." Gamsakhurdia himself announced at that time: "As long as Soviet power remains, we will not be able to rescind the autonomy of Abkhazia, Adzharia, or Southern Ossetia."

The 140 volumes of the investigation's files hold many such testimonies. All these ultranationalist statements, which brought blood and tears to the peoples of Georgia, were made before the events of 9 April. Why hadn't anyone paid attention to them? What is the moral and political responsibility of those who turned the flywheel of the Tbilisi Affair, elevating Gamsakhurdia and his people to the highest authority?

A significant part of the Georgian intelligentsia remained in shock, deceived by Gamsakhurdia's "democratic toga." Showing no political maturity, having fallen for anti-Soviet, antisocialist lines, the intelligentsia was left in a difficult position as creative freedom disappeared in Georgia. Unfortunately, this is far from the first such lesson that history has given to people in the arts and literature. And it will be very bitter if even this lesson is of no avail, and if in other Union republics the intelligentsia builds a national-separatist trap for itself.

I am firmly convinced that true democracy will triumph in Georgia, that the nationalist fumes fanned by ambitious politicians who usurped power will blow away. But for this to happen as quickly as possible, they need close unity with the intelligentsia of other regions, particularly with the Russian intelligentsia.

And this raises in a new light the question of the moral and political responsibility of Sobchak, who announced to the second USSR Congress of People's Deputies: "The commission finds an absence of facts confirming General Rodionov's assertion at the first USSR Congress of People's Deputies that a real threat existed by 9 April of a takeover of vital sites in the republic." The investigation of the USSR Prosecutor's Office compellingly showed that there was such a threat. Time showed all too graphically that it was real. How could an experienced lawyer have missed the statements of Gamsakhurdia and his cohorts quoted earlier? Why then did Sobchak remain so stubbornly silent, when even the West came to consider Georgia's regime fascist? If Sobchak had drawn attention to the ultranationalistic ideas of the organizers of the illegal rally in Tbilisi, there might not have been the bloody nightmare of South Ossetia, nor the threat of civil war in other autonomous areas of Georgia.

History is a strict examiner. Sooner or later it grades the politicians who trim facts to suit political fashion. In this case one might say that history summed up only too quickly. Later events in Georgia clearly bore "the mark of Sobchak."

After the events in Lithuania, Sobchak frequently attacked the "unconstitutional committees of public salvation." But why did he overlook the "United Committee of National Movement," created by Gamsakhurdia for illegal actions before 9 April 1989? Why didn't he sound the alarm about the plans for the creation of a "temporary transitional government," also mentioned in the prosecutor's investigation? Over and over we become witnesses to unprincipled political games that helped create a crisis.

In studying the history of the French and October revolutions, we can see from the distance of time how certain politicians behaved. Some of them became celebrated personalities; others entered history as odious figures, symbols of political flaws. No doubt many of the active participants in the processes of perestroika will have a place in history. The lawyer Sobchak, who joined the Party for political reasons and left the Party for the same reasons two years later, who willingly took part in unprincipled political games, will acquire his historical image, too.

In concluding this discussion of the Tbilisi Affair, I must mention Shevardnadze, who exactly one year after his first threat to resign relinquished the duties of the minister of foreign affairs, noisily slamming the door behind him by standing at the podium of the USSR Congress of People's Deputies and warning of the threat of dictatorship. Some believe in light of the events of August 1991 that this "clairvoyance" was justified. But the reader should be aware that the coup d'état was not a manifestation of dictatorship.

I must also mention that as minister of foreign affairs, Shevardnadze never made a single trip in our country. He never spoke to a group of workers to provide an unofficial account of Soviet foreign policy—even in Moscow. Even in the Brezhnev years, the leaders of important ministries, including Foreign Minister Gromyko, spoke to Party organizations and at factories. Alas, in the period of glasnost and democratization, Shevardnadze totally rejected the counsel of the people. And in the years of perestroika, there was never a report at the Central Committee plenums on foreign policy.

After his retirement, Shevardnadze continued foreign policy activity without portfolio, traveling widely abroad but avoiding his native Georgia,[15] even when a powerful earthquake occurred that

---

[15] Shevardnadze returned to Georgia in March 1992 after the ouster of Gamsakhurdia to head the Temporary State Council.—TRANS.

caused enormous damage and took many lives. You would think that in this hour of need, Eduard Shevardnadze would have been with his people, using his world renown to obtain humanitarian aid for Georgia. But Shevardnadze was traveling around America then, and not to raise funds for the victims of the earthquake.

Finally, and perhaps most important, the Memorandum of the USSR Prosecutor's Office to the USSR Supreme Soviet, sent in March 1991, states that "the criminal case against officials and troops of the Ministry of Internal Affairs and the Soviet army . . . is dropped for lack of evidence of criminal action on their part." As for the charges against the center, witness Dzhumber Patiashvili explained: no orders or instructions from central agencies or Union ministries were issued on using force against the demonstrators.

And so the memorandum of the USSR Prosecutor's Office about the Tbilisi Affair became history. As it turned out, there was no case at all. The nationalist-separatists had attempted a provocation against the legitimate authorities and then with the help of certain people's deputies of the USSR and the right-wing radical mass media turned it against the Party, the army, and the Soviet Union. The conclusions of the investigation of the USSR Prosecutor's Office state clearly that all the charges were false.

> In the course of the investigation we checked the reports in the central and republic media on the cruelty of the military, the use of gas, and so on. The investigation has determined that those facts do not correspond to reality and were based on rumor and false testimony. The materials of the case include a film by director E. Shengelaya, with a tendentious treatment of the events of 9 April 1989.

The history of perestroika has taken a meandering path. The accusations in the Tbilisi Affair turned out to be false, but the political case, falsified by the radicals, had an enormous influence on the course of events in the country and in fact led to Georgia's exit from the USSR. The main organizers and inspirers of the bloody provocation in Tbilisi are in power in the republic. And the deputies and journalists who spared no efforts to blow up a scandal and actually helped bring about a profound crisis in South Ossetia are now flourishing, building a career on lies. And while they call on the entire Communist Party to repent for the sins of the Stalinist leadership, they themselves are in no hurry to repent for their political hysteria, which led to the bloody events in the Caucasus.

I want to reiterate that I have no intention of playing judge. History is the true judge. But my view on events and the facts known to me will help our descendants establish the whole truth.

Five

GDLYAN AND OTHERS

A Stab in the Back

Disaster always strikes when you least expect it.

In May 1989, I traveled to Tashkent for a meeting of leaders from Moscow and Leningrad, Siberian industrialists, and Central Asian agronomists. The Soviet economy was developing in a new way, and we were discussing mutually beneficial contacts among regions. For example, Siberian oilmen were using their own resources to build modern food storage facilities in Central Asia; they would send timber and cement directly to a collective farm in the South and receive fruit in return. Of course, such barter deals cannot be called an ideal economic system. I understood that perfectly well. But in the transition to new economic relations they might support agriculture and improve the supply of foodstuffs to industrial centers. No one at that round table gave orders or undertook any obligations; there was no "strong-arming." We put our faith in initiative and resourcefulness, and we parted in good spirits.

I returned to Moscow on the evening of 13 May. It took me half an hour to drive home from Vnukovo-2 Airport. My first words with my family were about the weather in the South and my impressions. Everything seemed normal, but all the same, I immediately sensed some reserve, some concern in the family. And sure enough, my wife, Zinaida, said, "Yesterday, investigator Ivanov appeared on Leningrad TV. He said the Uzbek mafia is tied to Moscow and the highest echelons of power. And you were named."

"What do you mean—me? He mentioned my name?" I didn't understand what was going on.

My wife said she hadn't watched the show. Our son, Alexander, had seen it, and he explained.

"It was said that all the mafia is tied into the Kremlin and the Politburo. Ivanov reported that the names of Romanov, Solomentsev,[1] and Ligachev have come up in a criminal investigation he was working on. I think someone else was named, but as soon as I heard our name I stopped listening. You can imagine . . ."

Of course, I already knew about the investigative group under Gdlyan and Ivanov. But I couldn't take Ivanov's report seriously. My first thought was only about the confusion that would spread by Monday. I knew the domestic political situation and how public opinion was being shaped in a certain direction, and it wasn't hard to imagine how much gossip there would be. My good mood disappeared.

No one in the family panicked. Our scrupulous refusal to ask for favors was well known. As for various "offerings," I always paid for any kind of household service if we couldn't wait for the apartment supervisor to handle it, and simply returned gifts given as "souvenirs." It was my firm rule, an ironclad, unwavering position. Everyone who worked with me in Novosibirsk and Tomsk provinces knew it well and didn't complicate relations with me. No one tried to get on my good side by providing favors or bringing me "offerings"— it would have produced the opposite effect. And it made my life easier: I wasn't obligated to anyone, a guarantee of independence.

---

[1]Mikhail Solomentsev became a member of the Politburo in 1983 and served as head of the Party Control Commission.—TRANS.

Nor did I back down from this principle in Moscow, although in the capital it was far more difficult than in Siberia to maintain independence and not get snagged by people who had mastered the art of gift-giving. And people didn't know right away what I was like. Sometimes I literally had to fight off people who—back we all know when—had figured out cleverly how to entangle leaders in obligations by offering all manner of gifts and then calling in the IOU.

I recall going to Ukraine in the fall of 1983, soon after I was transferred from Tomsk to the Central Committee. When I came home on Saturday evening, my wife said, "A crate was sent from Kiev. They said it was your baggage."

"What crate? What baggage?" I asked in astonishment. "I have all my luggage with me. A briefcase and suitcase."

Strange as it seemed there was a crate in my apartment. What was the crate? What was it for? I opened it and gasped—it was filled with everything imaginable, electronic equipment, tableware . . . I don't remember it all. We had traveled lightly when we moved from Tomsk to Moscow. We hadn't amassed any valuables. I mentioned that to someone in Kiev, half joking and half proud, but my words apparently had been interpreted otherwise, and they had decided to help me set up my household.

I was beside myself. On Monday morning I asked the director of our department's secretariat, along with a few other department members, to take the crate, make an inventory of its contents, and immediately send it back to Kiev. I myself called Shcherbitsky and announced that I perceived the gift as a personal insult. I asked him to straighten things out with his people who handled the giving of gifts to the right people. Although at the time I was just a department director and Shcherbitsky was a member of the Politburo, my sharp tone apparently made an impression. He promised to get to the bottom of the incident. Knowing the ways and habits of the apparat, I said that I would wait a while and then call the Central Committee of the Ukrainian Communist Party to find out the results of the investigation.

I recall Shcherbitsky saying that this deplorable incident had been beyond his control. But I knew that this would not have happened unless the republic's top Party leadership approved—apparently they had wanted to get on good terms with the new director of the Organization Department.

Two or three weeks later, I did indeed call Kiev and was told that measures had been taken. The modest store of gifts for highly placed guests had been eliminated. It was only then that I, a naive Siberian, found out that the republican Party committee, and some provincial ones, kept stock of this sort. Storerooms were filled with goods from local factories—like peasants' taxes to the landowner—and officials were ensnared through this dubious practice. There was an entire network. Carpets and crystal were brought in from other regions.

After I had figured out the system, I went to Andropov and told him about my investigations, expecting that he would eliminate this amoral legacy of the Brezhnev years. Andropov supported my proposals to combat the practice of making offerings to the leaders and arranging banquets for them during business trips. We were able to do away with all that, and people in the provinces gave a sigh of relief. They no longer had to seek out funds for gifts or struggle to pay for their luxurious hospitality.

The Kiev incident became very well known. After that, no one tried to give me anything. I brought home only flowers and souvenir photographs from my business trips.

Over time, I began to see that my tough stance on these offerings made me distinctly unpopular with some people. I don't want to name names; that would be tantamount to accusing them of bribery, and I don't have the right to make allegations. But I became more aware of how my categorical refusal to accept any offerings got under some people's skins. What kind of a strange bird was this? It would have given them great pleasure to sully my name.[2]

---

[2]My dislike of corruption also stuck in the throats of those who later called themselves "democrats" (in quotes, of course). When they came to power in some places they dipped their hands in the till and started machinations on a scale that was beyond the dreams of previous figures.—AUTHOR

Yes, everyone I'd had occasion to work with more recently in the Central Committee or on business trips knew how scrupulous I was. I don't drink alcohol, and have no desire to "live it up." It took a filthy imagination to accuse me of corruption. Unbelievable or not, the investigator's appearance on Leningrad TV was a fact. Could he really make people doubt my honesty? How did the Politburo members react? What did Gorbachev think? I was certain that he would give me support and encouragement.

That Saturday evening with the family was spoiled irreparably. Gorbachev was scheduled to fly to China on Sunday. The Politburo members were to meet at Vnukovo-2 Airport to see him off. I decided that the next day, right at the airport, I would try to clarify what had happened.

By 1985, the long-established protocol for seeing off the general secretary had begun to grate on people, and the Central Committee received indignant letters protesting the large farewell parties where not only Politburo members but also candidate members and Central Committee secretaries went to the airport each time. Gorbachev raised the issue at one of the Politburo sessions and suggested the old protocol be changed. At that time we decided that only Politburo members would see off the general secretary when he traveled within the country, but when he went abroad, the entire top Party leadership would continue to see him off.

The General Department usually announced the day and hour of departure the night before. We'd generally drive there on our own about half an hour before departure time. In the lobby of the small governmental airport of Vnukovo-2, intensive work would begin— that's right, work. We'd discuss various problems and decide how to resolve questions that required the joint actions of several Politburo members. We would share ideas and clarify issues. In general, those were extraordinarily valuable moments for all the Politburo members. It is no exaggeration to say that we turned the protocol for sending off the general secretary into a true working meeting.

Gorbachev arrived at the scheduled time. We spent about ten minutes settling a few questions concerning the trip. He shared some thoughts on the matters he intended to raise. We told him our opinion. And then we all escorted him to the plane.

Official photographs of send-offs were always published the day after, and were studied carefully both in our country and abroad. People would try to determine the power politics at the top by how Politburo members were arranged around the general secretary. Under Brezhnev, every member of the Politburo had his immutable place on Lenin's mausoleum for political and state holidays and official ceremonies.

People who knew the Kremlin "rules" during the years of stagnation tried to use the same approach as they studied official photographs after 1985. But frankly, my comrades on the Politburo and I made no attempt to stand closer to the general secretary to show our influence. Everything happened spontaneously. Gorbachev had another tactic: he would simply take one of the Politburo members by the arm or strike up a conversation on the way to the plane, and that would determine our places in the photograph. Brezhnev let his entourage compete to get closer to him; Gorbachev picked his close associates himself.

Need I explain my feelings on 14 May as I drove to Vnukovo-2 to see Gorbachev off to China? I mentally rehearsed my conversation with Gorbachev, but everything turned out differently from what I expected.

Gorbachev arrived a few minutes before takeoff. He greeted everyone and exchanged a few words. Just before going out on the tarmac, he came up to me and said, "Yegor, I know about the TV broadcast. Well, what can you do but live through it . . ." And that was it.

I admit I expected something more definite. What did he mean, "live through it"? Did Gorbachev believe the accusation made against me, or reject it? I've had to go through many difficult experiences in my life; they had made me strong, and I wasn't about to fall apart now. I didn't need advice; I needed moral support. I wanted to hear that he didn't doubt my honesty and that he thought the investigator had been irresponsible in making that statement.

Alas, I heard neither.

Later, driving home, my heart was heavy. I couldn't articulate what I felt. Nor could I foresee what would happen. But I remember that feeling as if I had been stabbed in the back.

Rashidov

To understand the background to the Gdlyan Affair, I have to take the reader back to the days of April 1983, when Andropov named me director of the Party Organization Department of the Central Committee. As I began to learn more about my new job and the situation around the country, the real problem areas quickly began to stand out, crystallizing out of what seemed a primeval chaos of new problems.

The problem of Uzbekistan was brought to my attention by the director of the Central Asian Republics Division in our department, Viktor Smirnov. It took a good deal of persistence for Smirnov to bring his concerns and suspicions to my attention—he was, as they say, "hitched" to his immediate superior, and should have reported to him. But Smirnov ignored the hierarchy and risked getting into his direct boss's bad graces. Smirnov came directly to me and painfully poured out all his woes.

It turned out that thousands of letters were coming in from ordinary Uzbeks, complaining about lawlessness and arbitrary and unfair actions. Those letters had to be sent to the Uzbek Communist Party Central Committee for investigation, and we would immediately receive back the reply either that the complaints were unfounded or that measures had been taken. But people continued to write to Moscow, crying that they were being punished for their criticism. Smirnov showed me one outraged letter after another from simple peasants, rural teachers, agriculturalists, and chairmen of collective farms.

"You're a new man," he said. "You were brought into the Central Committee by Andropov, and I'm certain you'll deal with this matter."[3]

---

[3] I later stood by Smirnov when he was arrested and charged with taking bribes, as I always did when I knew the person, regardless of how it might affect me. I knew he couldn't have taken bribes. Why on earth would he have been so persistent in reporting the misuse of power in Uzbekistan, sounding the alarms and drawing attention to

Word of the conversation got all around the department, and I had the feeling that my entire staff was looking to see how I would react. Would I put the question on ice or make the grade?

I began to study the question carefully. I had worked in Tomsk Province since the mid-sixties, and I didn't know enough about what was going on in the other republics. I didn't fully realize how they were being destroyed by falsification of economic indicators, deceit, corruption, and bribery. The living standards of ordinary people were low, while those in power flourished. Uzbekistan was particularly worrisome in that regard. Everything, or almost everything, was decided by one man: Sharaf Rashidov. For twenty years he had been the first secretary of Uzbekistan's Central Committee. He was a candidate member of the Politburo, had been awarded two gold stars as Hero of Socialist Labor, and had received the Order of Lenin ten times. I think this latter was a record; in any case, I don't know of anything comparable.[4]

Rashidov had considerable influence in Moscow. Brezhnev had shown him every imaginable kindness. The Uzbek Republic was "sacrosanct"; only flattering articles about it were allowed in the press.

I had realized all that quickly. As head of the Organization Department, I was concerned with another matter: in Uzbekistan, the Party, soviet, management, and law enforcement personnel were chosen largely on the basis of personal loyalty to Rashidov. No fewer than fourteen of his relatives worked in the republican Central Committee apparat.

My study of the problem involved a great deal of work. First I had to read the many letters from Uzbekistan. In three years, 1980 to 1983, the Central Committee received tens of thousands of letters

---

himself? People with dirty hands don't do that. After all, not knowing me, he had no idea how I would respond.—AUTHOR

[4]Later in Uzbekistan another "record" was discovered: falsified figures for cotton sales to the government reached 600,000 tons, which cost the government hundreds of millions of rubles every year.—AUTHOR

from that republic. People complained that justice was impossible, that many of the leaders behaved like *bai*—ancient Central Asian landowners. Nothing could get done without a bribe. After reading those letters I went home depressed and in a terrible mood: no matter which letter you picked up, it was about arbitrary and unfair actions, lawlessness, ruined lives. These were cries from the heart. After Brezhnev's death the flood of letters from Uzbekistan to Moscow descended with new force. But everything remained as before: Rashidov was invulnerable and sacrosanct.

To make a long story short, I realized that I needed a chat with Andropov at the Central Committee. I wasn't in the habit of burdening Andropov with my visits—I didn't "report in," like some people. But when it was necessary, Andropov would see me just as soon as a window opened in his schedule. Although at that time I wasn't a member of the Politburo or a secretary of the Central Committee, simply head of a department, the department was extremely important and therefore my office had a *kukushka*, a direct line to the general secretary. When the telephones were modernized later, their "voices" changed—became more lilting.

Incidentally, there was an unwritten rule in the Central Committee: whenever the *kukushka* "cuckooed"—in other words, when the general secretary called—anybody present other than the person whose office it was would leave the room. After all, the direct line was for talking with the general secretary alone.

I picked up the *kukushka* and asked Andropov to receive me. He received me right away, and I explained the essence of the matter to him, showed him the most alarming letters, and said it was high time to put an end to the official replies and start a serious, in-depth review of the facts. Things certainly seemed to have gotten way out of hand in Tashkent. It had all been worked out cunningly: the Union offices expose specific facts of arbitrary and unfair actions or falsification of figures, the guilty party would be severely punished (as if to say, since you got caught, you have to answer for it), but the phenomenon itself—the system—remained unscathed.

I was upset and indignant—the facts were appalling. Andropov listened calmly and attentively. I think he must have known the basic outline of the situation in Uzbekistan, the KGB must have informed him of what was going on in the republic when he was chairman of the KGB. But what could Andropov have done under Brezhnev? Apparently he had to pretend that he didn't know anything. Or perhaps he had reported it all, but no action had been taken.

Whatever the case, I had the sense that Andropov was prepared for my report. After hearing me out, he immediately told me, "Let's do it this way. You meet with Rashidov. Yes, you have to meet with him. Invite him in to see you and have a chat. I don't have to teach you how to ask questions."

I hadn't expected this suggestion, and, of course, I hardly found it appealing. Everyone knew how obstinate Rashidov was; he wouldn't deal with someone at the level of a department director, and he came to Politburo members only when he had a problem. The invitation from the Organization Department probably would be enough to irritate him.

I expressed my doubts about the wisdom of this decision. Was a conversation with a candidate member of the Politburo the right level? But Andropov insisted. I saw what he was up to: he wanted to put Rashidov in his place.

Soon afterward Rashidov came to Moscow on business and was immediately informed that the new director of the Organization Department wanted to meet with him. A day was scheduled, and the time tentatively arranged. Despite the very polite form of the invitation, there was no doubt that this would be a serious talk.

I had never met Rashidov before, though I had seen him at plenums and in Brezhnev's office. First secretaries from the provinces who had made appointments were accustomed to waiting for hours on the hard vinyl couches in the waiting room at Entrance No. 1, Office No. 6. But Rashidov didn't have to wait. Of course, he was a candidate member of the Politburo; but there was something other than protocol in the speed with which he would be ushered into Brezhnev's office. Such unhampered access to the general secretary seemed testimony of political power and influence.

And now suddenly he was being invited to chat with a department director—one Ligachev he'd never heard of, who'd worked in Siberia and just recently transferred to the Central Committee. Apparently this naive Ligachev hadn't figured out what was what, didn't understand high-level power politics. As we began to talk, I could see that this was Rashidov's attitude.

But let me tell the story in sequence. At that time, you had to go through an underground passage across a road to get from Entrance No. 1 to Entrance No. 6. Rashidov, who probably never had been in this building, had to be escorted to my office. I was informed that Rashidov had arrived, went out to greet him, and invited him to sit down at the table in my office.

It was an old habit of mine to receive visitors at this conference table, so we could sit across from each other. I had deliberately placed on the table tall piles of letters from Uzbekistan. Rashidov was an old hand and immediately realized what the letters were. And after the initial pleasantries he got rather flustered and began to glance from time to time at the piles of letters, as if trying to guess what threat those envelopes concealed.

Sensing that, I soon got down to business.

"Sharaf Rashidovich, the Central Committee is receiving many letters about the outrages in your republic. People are complaining—on major issues—more and more. We send the letters to you to be checked, but you and your comrades reply that the allegations are unfounded. That's hard to believe. Look at how many letters there are. And this is only a small selection of them. The Central Committee has been deluged with letters from Uzbekistan."

Rashidov began to fidget in his chair and even moved to get up several times. He clearly did not expect me to be so bold or direct, or ask the question outright. After quickly sizing up the situation, he decided to go on the offensive and put me in my place. Without responding to the substance of my questions, he frowned, and unceremoniously demanded, "Who do you think you're talking to?"

The situation was getting tricky. I'd gone through similar incidents in the past—a particularly memorable one in 1965, right after I was named first secretary of the Tomsk Province Party Committee.

In those days, Tomsk Province was insignificant; the word was that it had no future. My predecessor had even come up with a plan to abolish the province by merging it with the Novosibirsk or Kemerovo provinces. On the other had, a major, primarily military construction unit from the Ministry of Medium Machine-Building had moved to the region. It wasn't subordinate to us but dealt directly with Moscow, and the people running it were completely autonomous. I decided to invite the general who headed military construction in and ask for his help. "I have a great favor to ask you: help us with construction in the countryside. We're stuck without roads, and you know how bad it is."

But the general was not accustomed to carrying out the requests of provincial officials. He only shrugged and said didactically, "The homeland has given us different tasks, Yegor Kuzmich. We can't get distracted by helping the agricultural sector."

"I understand. But this isn't simply my personal request. It's the request of the Province Party Committee bureau. We don't have any other options. You have to help us."

The conversation quickly became heated. Our voices rose with every new argument. Finally I stated my case. "Well, if that's the way it is, we'll convene the bureau. Don't forget that you're registered as a member of the local Party. We'll decide what to do."[5]

But the general turned out to be tough. He jumped up and barked: "It wasn't you who gave me my Party card, and you don't have the right to take it away!" He strode to the door.

"Just one minute!" I picked up the receiver of the high-frequency governmental communications line and dialed the number of Yefim Slavsky, the USSR minister of medium machine-building.

Slavsky dominated an entire epoch of the Soviet nuclear industry's development. He was a powerful man in both personality and figure, and a brilliant organizer—the credit was his for our country's creating of nuclear weapons that allowed us to establish military-

---

[5]The general would have lost his position if he were dismissed from the Communist Party.—TRANS.

strategic parity with the United States. Under Slavsky, Medium Machine-Building was a state within a state, an industrial empire with its own factories, institutes, even cities, one in Tomsk Province. And, of course, it had its own construction units, which used military construction corps. Slavsky enjoyed extraordinary respect in the Central Committee and the Council of Ministers. He was truly a Soviet industrial baron—and I mean that only in the positive sense.

A big man with a deep bass voice, he kept his empire in exemplary order. He retained his professional demeanor even in old age, and he kept in shape. It was said that even when he was eighty years old Slavsky could down a tumbler of wine and make the trickiest pool shot on the first try.

In 1965 Slavsky was at the peak of his success. When I called him, he didn't immediately understand what the problem was or what I was talking about. It's possible he had never heard my name before—what was a greenhorn provincial Party secretary from Siberia to a powerful man like him? All the same, he was polite. But he essentially gave me the same answer as the general: "The Party and government have entrusted us with critical defense duties and we can't get distracted by tangential matters."

Then I said, "Well, then, in that case your subordinate will come back to you without his Party card."

On that we said good-bye—rather coldly. The entire conversation had taken place in the general's presence.

Slavsky apparently weighed all the circumstances and considered the unbending personality of the new Party leader. About a week later Slavsky withdrew the general and replaced him with someone who had a profound understanding of the province's needs. We worked well together, and builders from the Atomic Ministry helped the people of Tomsk construct major dairy complexes, poultry farms, a greenhouse complex, a scientific center, and the facilities for a huge petrochemical complex, and outfit the institutions of higher education. They made a capital investment of hundreds of millions of rubles in economic and agricultural aid in what could be called a step on the road to conversion of the military industry.

That's the incident that instantly sprang to mind when Rashidov asked sharply, even threateningly, "Who do you think you're talking to?"

The question could be understood this way: "You, Comrade Ligachev, haven't forgotten who you're dealing with here? Before you sits a candidate member of the Politburo, not to mention everything else. And just who are you?"

Unlike the heated discussion with the Tomsk general, this time voices could not be raised. I had to restrain myself. So I answered calmly, emphasizing that I wasn't troubled. "I'm talking with Comrade Rashidov."

Rashidov seemed ready to make another pointed comment and apply more pressure, but this time I beat him to it.

"Sharaf Rashidovich, this is a serious matter. Yuri Vladimirovich Andropov has been informed about the letters. I am speaking with you at the request of the general secretary."

Rashidov deflated instantly. It may be that this was the first time his threatening tactic—"Who do you think you're talking to?"—didn't work. Brezhnev was gone, and it was clear that he couldn't count on patronage from Andropov. I continued. "The department is going to propose that a commission authorized by the Central Committee be sent to Uzbekistan."

Times certainly had changed. Nothing like this had ever happened before. Rashidov changed his tone. "You know, Yegor Kuzmich," he said, trying to keep calm and glancing at the letters, "those letters are full of slander. We have to protect our leaders and give them a chance to work in peace. Uzbekistan must give the country cotton, and not . . . you know, letters."

The conversation had calmed down, so I could state my position, which amounted to this: the commission will sort out what's going on there on the spot. Slander is slander; if the authors of those letters are exaggerating, then we'll announce that publicly, and the situation in the republic will improve. If everything is in order, we'll be pleased. So what's there to fear from the commission?

I added that I held Uzbekistan in high esteem, that the Uzbek people truly had been heroic as they turned barren, arid deserts into cotton fields. Those weren't niceties—I truly believe that transforming the desert was a feat of national heroism. But it was for that very reason that we could not allow corrupt elements to prey on the people's self-sacrifice.

Rashidov realized that it was impossible to persuade me to join his side. I'm sure that before the meeting he'd made some inquiries about me. I would have done the same in his place; that's the way you prepare for a difficult conversation. After making inquiries, he knew that the keys in his arsenal would not work with me. So he didn't even try to use them.

Our good-byes seemed calm on the surface, but our attitudes were different. I was thinking of the hard work that lay ahead in Uzbekistan. Rashidov, I'm sure, was worried.

This happened in late August 1983. I don't remember the exact date, but I recall that at the beginning of our talk we discussed the fact that the cotton harvest was beginning and the country needed a good crop, etc., which means it was nearly September. The conversation is as clear in my mind's eye as if it happened yesterday. I know why the situation took a dangerous turn. One of my well-wishers—I use the term in its literal sense, with no irony intended—in the Central Committee believed I was taking a huge risk when I crossed Rashidov. Some people thought Andropov had set me up. But Andropov didn't operate like that. I simply had no interest in that kind of talk; it was the product of the mentality and morality of the Brezhnev years, which were foreign to me. I did what my job required; it was my Party duty. As for the bureaucrat's instinct of self-preservation, I don't have it. Everyone who worked with me in Novosibirsk, Tomsk, and in the Central Committee knows that.

After my talk with Rashidov, I put my thoughts in order and reached my conclusions. Then I picked up the *kukushka*. Andropov received me almost immediately, listened to me carefully, and agreed to send a Central Committee Commission to Uzbekistan. In particular, he asked me not to compromise the highest principles while examining all the questions. I took his parting words to mean that he wanted to get to the bottom of the matter.

I began to prepare to meet again with Rashidov. I decided to delay slightly sending the commission to Uzbekistan; it was better not to make people nervous at the toughest time of year, the harvest season. I wanted to wait until the cotton crop was picked. But events took a different turn. Two months later I received news that shocked me: Rashidov was dead.

What really happened to him? What went on? I can put my hand on my heart and swear that I truly don't know. Other comrades from the Politburo went to Rashidov's funeral in Tashkent. At that time I was only a department director, so if they knew something at the top, they didn't tell me. The official story was that Rashidov's heart gave out. So it was a sudden illness? But when we met he gave the impression of a man in robust good health. The writer Georgy Markov, who saw Rashidov in Tashkent not long before his death, later told me he had the impression that Rashidov was extremely depressed about something. I also know that after our talk at the Central Committee, Rashidov traveled a great deal around Uzbekistan and was very involved in the cotton harvest.

These are all the facts I have for a conclusion about Rashidov's death. As you see, there aren't many facts at all. But if you ask about hunches and judgments concerning Rashidov's tragic demise, I think that the Moloch of deceit, intrigue, and demagoguery ultimately consumes its creators.

The Central Committee Commission, headed by K. N. Mogilnichenko, the department's deputy director—a principled, extremely honest man—uncovered heinous violations of the law in Uzbekistan. What were we to do with the material from the investigation? Someone suggested that we put it before the Politburo. But after discussion, we decided to pass on the commission's conclusions for review by Communist Party activists in the republic— let them straighten it out themselves. This was a fundamentally new approach. The center didn't dictate policy and play the role of the "Supreme Court."

This decision was passed at the June 1984 plenum of the Central Committee of the Uzbek Communist Party.

By that time I had been named secretary of the Central Committee. The Politburo decided to send me to Tashkent to chair the plenum. It was a heated meeting. I was among the speakers, and my speech was extremely demanding. At that time, the first secretary of the Uzbek Communist Party was Inomzhon Usmankhodzhaev. I'd first met him in 1983, when he was appointed to his post by Chernenko, who was handling personnel matters for the hospitalized Andropov. Five years later, I was accused of accepting a bribe while chairing the Tashkent plenum, which had been aimed at stopping corruption and misuse of power. And the man who was said to have offered me the bribe was Usmankhodzhaev. It was offensive and absurd. It didn't make any sense. It stank of the likes of Yezhov and Beria.[6]

In 1989, when the campaign against the members of the leadership began, an acquaintance joked, "Yegor Kuzmich, so how much does Gdlyan say Usmankhodzhaev slipped to you? He says thirty thousand? . . . Well, you're a strange one, Yegor Kuzmich. You sold yourself too cheap, way too cheap . . ."

Needless to say, I didn't feel like joking.

Counterattack

The Central Committee Commission uncovered tremendous misuse of power by the Uzbek leaders. The commission members acted through political channels in close connection with Communists, primarily using the Party organizations in the republic. The Central Committee decided to strengthen the republican Party personnel by bringing in people from other regions who weren't connected with the compromised top Uzbek leadership. We sent many Party and government economic officials from various regions of Russia, Ukraine, and Byelorussia to normalize the situation.

I reminded these people that we had to help the republic free itself from the embrace of the mafia and resume normal develop-

---

[6]Nikolai Yezhov and Lavrenti Beria successively headed the secret police under Stalin and were responsible for the worst of the purges.—TRANS.

ment. Meanwhile, the KGB started to dig into the corruption in cotton production. Its scale was shocking. We realized we couldn't do the job with low-level law-enforcement personnel. The prosecutor of the USSR thereupon formed investigative groups, one of which was headed by Telman Gdlyan.

I don't know why he was given this position, although he'd apparently distinguished himself in past investigations, in particular, the Hint[7] case in Estonia. It turned out that Gdlyan had railroaded this innocent man (his conviction was overturned—but it was too late for Gdlyan's victim, who had died in prison).

But Hint was acquitted much later. In 1984 the "Hint case" that Gdlyan railroaded through—exposing the political "innards" of the accused in the process—probably facilitated his career advancement.

The investigative group began intensive work as soon as it arrived in Tashkent. However, in addition to the group's purely professional efforts, a new quality of "perestroika"—in quotes, of course—soon appeared in the investigators. They had a real knack for working with the press and TV, publicizing sensational materials before trials, sometimes signing their own names to articles. I don't know what kind of professional ethics you'd call that. But given the lack of full disclosure—glasnost—among investigative bodies, Gdlyan and Nikolai Ivanov, who actively sought out contact with the press, emerged as winners. They were popular, and people began to attribute all the achievements of a collective of almost two hundred investigators to the two of them alone.

The press and narrow-minded people hungered for more sensations and exposés. To get fast results, Gdlyan and Ivanov began to go outside the law.

The innocent people they investigated were subjected to mental and physical harassment. The terms of detention stipulated by law were violated, and threats of reprisals against families and close relatives were used as pressure to elicit the testimony they needed.

---

[7]Johannes Hint, Estonian physicist and mathematician, arrested for reformist *samizdat* writings in 1983, died in detention from mistreatment in 1984.—TRANS.

I should say right off that in those May days, when Ivanov appeared on Leningrad TV and cast the shadow of suspicion on me, I didn't know about these illegal methods. I was far away from Uzbek problems, completely absorbed by agricultural issues. I only realized who they were on 24 May, when I opened *Literaturnaya gazeta* and read an article by Olga Chaikovskaya called "The Myth."

The article was the first to expose publicly the truth about their methods. Considering time requirements in the publication of a weekly, the essay must have been submitted to the editorial board before Ivanov's TV appearance. This is of considerable significance—I don't exclude the possibility that Gdlyan and Ivanov found out that they were about to be attacked and planned a counterblow.

"The Myth" contained a letter from the director of a state farm from whom the investigators had tried to extract a confession that he had bribed the secretary of the Karakalpak Province Party Committee. The investigators, he wrote, "began to threaten me that they would put me in prison with felons and tell them to do with me whatever they wanted—'let them trample you, kill you (I can't write what they really said). After that you'll be a sweetheart and write whatever we tell you to.' Vulgarity, vile slang, gutter language, and lewdness were the norm for the investigators. If you had told me that something like this could happen in our time, I probably wouldn't have believed you."

Chaikovskaya wrote about cases when people under investigation couldn't stand the threats and torture and signed whatever the investigators handed them. Some committed suicide during the investigation.

Later, in the fall of 1990, Chaikovskaya wrote another very critical article exposing the methods of Gdlyan and Ivanov. Alas, to paraphrase the Latin, times and morals had changed—and newspapers along with them. This time, *Literaturnaya gazeta* refused to publish Chaikovskaya's exposé, which was printed in *Vestnik Akademii nauk SSSR (Bulletin of the Academy of Sciences of the USSR),* which has a much smaller circulation (No. 8, 1990).

But to return to the May 1989 days that were so dramatic for me, my work in the Politburo then had nothing to do with the investigation of the Uzbekistan mafia. I began to check around and discovered that the situation of 1983 was repeating itself: a flood of letters about arbitrary and unfair actions, lawlessness, and legal violations were pouring from that republic into the Central Committee, the USSR Prosecutor's Office, and the presidium of the USSR Supreme Soviet. This time people were not accusing the republican leaders: they were accusing the investigators Gdlyan and Ivanov. Many letters actually called them "the executioners of Uzbekistan."

Rashidov, who had influential contacts in the top echelons of power, earlier had interfered with an objective review of complaints. Now a calm, substantive analysis of the letters was impeded by, of all things, public opinion, formed by a certain part of the mass media. It isn't difficult to see that both situations were profoundly inappropriate for a law-based government. Earlier people in the top Party leadership were sacrosanct; now Gdlyan and Ivanov had become equally "untouchable."

In the final analysis, the consequences for perestroika and the entire society were tragic. We realized that Gdlyan and Ivanov were pawns with an exaggerated sense of their own importance, who thought they could break off from the queen. The fact is that society couldn't deal with those accused by Gdlyan and Ivanov objectively and substantively, without hysterics, but instead knuckled under to them. Responsibility for this must be shared by parts of the mass media: either in their quest for sensation or out of special political interests, they created the instant myth of "heroic investigators."

The ballyhoo that accompanied the creation of that myth drowned out the reports and complaints about the investigators' unlawful methods, which only a few newspapers picked up. Cheers drowned out the moans of the tortured in the investigators' offices of Uzbekistan. The press even attacked the special commission created by the presidium of the USSR Supreme Soviet to investigate complaints from Uzbekistan.

This was essentially a return to the old days. The old methods were still in force under the new veneer of glasnost and democracy.

The commission had been established before Ivanov's appearance on Leningrad TV. I had heard something about it, but I didn't pay particularly close attention to it. But Gdlyan and Ivanov knew the flames were getting closer. The main thesis of their electoral platform was as simple as could be: Moscow was interfering in the exposure of the Uzbek mafia, since the top leaders in the Central Committee and, of course, in the USSR Prosecutor's Office, were corrupt.

The country was up in arms. In Moscow? In the Kremlin? On Old Square? The investigators' primitive technique worked. They gained popularity by attacking the Party leadership, accusing one and all of taking bribes, hinting at more. Riding on that wave, Gdlyan was elected deputy in the first round in Moscow's Tushino District. In Leningrad, Ivanov didn't muster a majority of the votes, but he would still have a chance to try again in the runoffs. The second round of elections of People's Deputies of the USSR was scheduled for 14 May 1989. And Ivanov appeared on Leningrad TV on 12 May.

That Sunday, when we were seeing off Gorbachev on his trip to China, I did my homework and came to the realization that this had to be an unscrupulous election maneuver. Ivanov was certainly cunning. He appeared on TV Friday evening. The elections were on Sunday, and on Saturday no one would have a chance to investigate or even issue a rebuttal. He began his citation of well-known names with Romanov, who was particularly "dear" to Leningraders. And finally, he cited Ligachev in an attempt to curry favor among my political opponents and get the support of certain sectors of the mass media.

It really was cannily thought out. Before I had even seen the text of Ivanov's speech, I realized that two investigators acting alone could not have planned this multilevel, propagandistic electoral ploy.

On Monday morning I set out to find the text. I called one person, then another—no one knew much of anything. I was given only excerpts from a report over Western radio stations that immediately announced what had happened to the entire world. For example, French international radio announced: "Soviet prosecutor Nikolai Ivanov announced that several highly placed officials, including the leader of the conservatives in the Politburo, Yegor Ligachev, Grigory Romanov, and Mikhail Solomentsev, are involved in a major scandal, and that the authorities are trying to block the investigation. Today the newspaper *Pravda* began a counterattack on Ivanov."

As I read the announcement, I noted two important issues. The first person Ivanov named was Romanov, but the French immediately picked up on the "leader of the conservatives, Ligachev." Ivanov was playing the role of a little boy tossing a ball; the decision on how to hit it was made by other, far more influential forces. Second, I noticed the word "involved." What does that mean? What's behind it?

I should also say a few words about the reference to the newspaper *Pravda*. Ivanov went on TV late in the evening on 12 May. Like the other central newspapers, *Pravda* on the morning of 13 May printed its regular column "In the Presidium of the Supreme Soviet of the USSR," which mentioned that a special commission was looking into the many complaints and allegations of serious misuse of power by Gdlyan and Ivanov. It's clear that this could only be a coincidence. But the foreign radio stations played it for all it was worth. ("The newspaper *Pravda* counterattacked Ivanov" really sounds like something. That's how propaganda works.)

The Voice of America broadcast an even more curious statement: "Prosecutor Nikolai Ivanov announced that in the course of an investigation into corruption in governmental bodies, the name of Yegor Ligachev, a member of the Politburo of the CPSU Central Committee, surfaced. Ivanov didn't report any details in connection with his investigation. Yegor Ligachev, who has the reputation as a conservative political figure, is sometimes considered competition to Gorbachev."

Now, they're getting closer to the mark; the Voice of America doesn't care about Romanov or Solomentsev, it's only interested in Ligachev. My last doubts disappeared. Ivanov was just a minor figure in a political game concerning me that was being played not only in this country, but also in coordination with certain foreign forces. "Conservative"; "sometimes considered competition to Gorbachev": could it be any clearer?

I finally was able to get a copy of Ivanov's statement. Transcribed, it turned out to be less than one page of typed text. I believe it's essential to reprint it here in full, word for word, because in light of the events that subsequently swept the country like a tornado, this text has taken on new and greater importance.

> Many voters are asking why the mafia in Leningrad isn't being routed and who at the top in Moscow is being investigated for felony violations. There's no attempt to fight the mafia because it is state policy to curtail the battle against organized crime. But it could be fought everywhere. For the information of Leningraders, I can say that among those whose names have come up in our felony case is the former leader of Leningrad, Comrade Romanov. Other names that have come up are members of the Politburo, such as Comrade Solomentsev and Comrade Ligachev, and Terebilov, the former chairman of the Supreme Court. Today the situation concerning Ligachev is very worrisome. We are very concerned to see the consolidation of his position in light of the move to the right that we are observing in today's politics. That naturally raises serious concern. I'm not speaking about the innocence or guilt of these people. Today all I can say is that the case will be investigated in the future. I am speaking very deliberately. And I'm prepared to take full responsibility for my words. Thank you."

To be honest, I was heartened. I had no doubt that more powerful figures were behind Ivanov. He was simply carrying out the political orders of those "disturbed by the consolidation of this person's position" while at the same time investing some electoral capital.

But a year later, when socioeconomic processes in the country had reached a critical point, I realized that it wasn't pure politics that guided the investigator. He incited the country with rumors about corruption at the top echelons of power and directed society's attention in that direction. He did not reveal any facts, and his entire campaign turned to dust. But under the cover of his shouts about the "bribe-takers in the Politburo," the new perestroika mafia quickly gathered strength. As this new mafia—which created the critical shortage of cigarettes, matches, salt, and other goods—became far richer and its influence on the development of the crisis became clear, we could see that it had held the economic levers during the period when the smear campaign against me began.

In his speech on Leningrad TV Ivanov shot down one other bird. He blocked the commission of the Supreme Soviet of the USSR as if by saying, "At the top you are also involved in corruption, and that's why you have started your attacks on us investigators." Every word of his statement was beautifully chosen. He probably knew it by heart; it was very carefully crafted, perfectly formulated; you can tell it was worked over many times.

It was completely clear to me that Gdlyan and Ivanov were hardly courageous loners fighting against a corrupt system. And no matter how difficult it was for me later, however many unjust words I heard from those investigators, I felt no hatred for them, only compassion. Taking advantage of their arrogance and, needless to say, their lack of political scruples, they were deftly drawn into a major game, the true significance and goal of which they couldn't initially perceive—an unenviable fate. Our long-suffering history knows the names of our own Herostrates—we had them during the Stalinist persecutions when they served as detonators in the "doctor's plot" . . .

I'll have occasion to return to the tragedy of Gdlyan and Ivanov. But now I'll try to re-create the course of events at that time, information significant to understanding their true import.

I wrote a list of several words from the press reports about the affair. Ivanov said "came up." The Americans said "surfaced." The French reported "involvement." That's how a propaganda campaign gets going—like an avalanche! After all, Ivanov said nothing—absolutely nothing—accusatory, but the entire world knows that Ligachev is "involved" in corruption and "under felony investigation."

Believe me, I couldn't shake the sense that there was some kind of tacit accord here. Even without instructions, each member of that accord knew perfectly well how he should act in regard to the "conservative Ligachev." Taking advantage of the people's ignorance of the true facts, someone was betting on political impact—there weren't any other dividends to be had here.

I had to act quickly. But how? Primarily by demanding an open investigation, since I had nothing to hide.

I took a clean sheet of paper and wrote:

> To the Commission of the presidium of the USSR Supreme Soviet and prosecutor general.
>
> My name was among those mentioned by investigator Ivanov in his statement that new figures had "come up" in a felony investigation. This is subversion with an ulterior motive. Somewhat less importantly it casts the shadow of suspicion on me that I committed a crime. This was done above all to further his own career as well as to disavow responsibility for the many accusations against him that have been presented in letters from citizens. I request that my petition be reviewed and the results of the review be widely published in the press.

I signed and dated it: 15 May 1989.

I reread it. It had turned out well. The most important thing was to publish an announcement of my statement as soon as possible so that people wouldn't think I was afraid of something. I had nothing to fear.

I soon learned that Solomentsev had also appealed to the USSR Prosecutor's Office. Naturally, we discussed this matter and decided to send statements to the Commission of the Presidium of the Supreme Soviet and the USSR prosecutor general and ask them to publish them immediately in the press. But since unsavory rumors were intensifying and the shadow of suspicion lay on the Politburo as a whole, for purely ethical considerations I decided to make the final text available to all members of the Politburo.

There were no objections or corrections. The Prosecutor's Office was about to pass on the text to TASS when Vadim Medvedev called.

"Yegor Kuzmich," he began, "perhaps you shouldn't rush to publish your statement. Why stir up excitement? Let's wait for

Mikhail Sergeyevich to return, consult with him, and discuss it from every angle."

To be honest, I wasn't surprised by the call. Medvedev was indecisive, indefinite, and preferred to wait things out.

"Why wait?" I contradicted Medvedev brusquely. "My honor has been sullied along with the honor of the Central Committee and the Politburo. Why should we be silent and let our silence encourage idle gossip?"

But Medvedev dragged his feet and didn't give his consent. Meanwhile, TASS and the press were picking up the story. I didn't want to be unfaithful to myself in dealing with Medvedev. I knew the system. The editors in chief of the newspapers would get the statements from Solomentsev and me and call Medvedev for his instructions.

But Medvedev wanted to see "how things went." Gorbachev was gone, and Medvedev didn't want to make a decision on his own. If he had consulted with someone unofficially—and I couldn't exclude that possibility—his persistence was all the more understandable. Since there was no point in pursuing it with him, I said good-bye.

Time was passing and I still hadn't said anything since Ivanov's statement. Where was Gorbachev? The General Department informed me that the general secretary was returning from China that very day. But the plane was arriving very late, in the middle of the night. If I waited for his arrival, the newspapers wouldn't have time to publish my rebuttal in tomorrow's edition. Of course, a day or two would make no difference. But Medvedev's call put me on my guard. I recalled Gorbachev's terse phrase at the airport and my political instincts told me that I had to act decisively. No one could hold me back at that moment. I understood clearly and precisely what I had to do. I had to publish my rebuttal the next day: my rapid response would serve as a moral basis for subsequent actions. In military terminology, I had to launch a counterattack.

I picked up the receiver of the top-secret communications (TSC) phone.

General Secretary Gorbachev's communications system was top

of the line. That makes sense: there can't be a single minute in a huge country like ours when the *gensek* and the chairman of the Defense Council can't be contacted. It's the same in the United States. In that regard the Americans don't have anything on us.

I picked up the receiver and asked the women at the switchboard, "Where is Mikhail Sergeyevich now? Please try to connect me with him. As soon as possible."

The satellite connection worked reliably. In three minutes, the TSC began to ring.

I had estimated that the plane was somewhere near the border. I could hear beautifully. I explained the heart of the matter to Gorbachev and read him my short statement.

"I understand it all," Gorbachev said. "Of course you should publish it. See you in Moscow."

On 19 May *Pravda* and *Izvestia* published my statement with the headline "Categorical Protest." In part it said, "On 15 May Ye. K. Ligachev sent a petition to the USSR prosecutor general regarding the speech by investigator N. V. Ivanov on Leningrad TV. . . . Ye. K. Ligachev categorically refutes what was said, regards it as slander and a provocation. He asks that the facts be investigated and that the results be published in the press."

I believed then and still believe now that I acted absolutely correctly by refuting publicly Ivanov's statement. First, it was pure slander, and I showed that I wasn't afraid of an investigation. And second, these actions were in accord with my open, direct, and, I confess, sometimes rather single-minded nature. I don't like intrigue or influence-peddling.

When Gdlyan and Ivanov played the "Ligachev card" and got the sense that they should stop there, they tried to stay in the public eye by attacking Gorbachev publicly. At rallies they accused him of being involved in the so-called Stavropol Affair. After the first attacks, at a session of the Politburo I suggested to Gorbachev that he should immediately fight back and refute the slander. But Gorbachev decided to act otherwise; he decided not to say anything and not draw attention to the investigators' statement.

I think that was wrong. That kind of action by political opponents against a leader isn't just a personal matter.

Tactic or Strategy?

The regular plenum of the Central Committee took place on 22 May 1989.

By then the smear campaign in the mass media had gained speed. Rumors were circulating that Usmankhodzhaev had given me a briefcase containing thirty thousand rubles.

Several newspapers were obviously following political instructions. I decided to take a new counterstep, this time through the Party.

The Party Charter gave every member the right to address any question, petition, or suggestion to any level of the Party, right up to the Central Committee, and to demand a substantive reply. I decided to use this right and sent a petition to the Central Committee. I wrote that the accusations made by the investigators Gdlyan and Ivanov against me were a subversion against the Politburo as a whole, and testified to a growing tendency toward political careerism that had to be acknowledged and fought since it could only lead to harm.

I also wrote that although the press was doing much to advance perestroika, unfortunately sections of the mass media were making their pages available for smear campaigns that convicted people before trials and turned public opinion against them. The press was vilifying people who were not even under investigation. There were many examples of this, and the Central Committee was receiving letters about it. Our attempt to create a law-based government was being accompanied by a slide toward lawlessness. I wrote: "The atmosphere is growing similar to that during the purges of 1937." If the press continued to make the social and political atmosphere more tense and inflammatory, conditions conducive to mass lawlessness might appear.

My petition was read by Gorbachev at the Central Committee plenum on 22 May. This was reported in the information bulletin on the plenum. Although the right to such petition was stipulated in the charter, there had been nothing like it in fifty years. And yet there was scarcely any reaction to it at all. I thought there was serious cause to discuss the worsening political situation and the extremist forces that were gaining strength throughout the country. But no, the opportunity to discuss the situation again was ignored. Gorbachev made no comment on my petition. He simply read the previous resolution asking the prosecutor general to review the facts.

At the first Congress of People's Deputies, which took place soon afterward, it became utterly clear that the slander against me from Gdlyan and Ivanov was merely serving as the background for purely political attacks. By accusing me of taking bribes, they tied my hands in the political battle. Unfortunately, I wasn't even given the floor at the Congress.

The speeches of some of the deputies were painfully insulting. Deputy Yuri Chernichenko, a journalist, distinguished himself in particular in that regard. He changed from an enthusiastic adherent of the collective farms into an ardent enemy of the collective farm system. Chernichenko, whom the press was calling a "progressive" at that time, was clearly trying to win points by criticizing Ligachev. As I listened I recalled that the journalist Yuri Chernichenko had in his time been assistant to none other than Sergei Medunov.[8]

Insulting speeches by some deputies melded with Gdlyan's slanderous attacks. This all created obvious and heavy pressure not only on me but also on the entire Politburo and the Communist Party. Several times I sent the presidium notes requesting an opportunity to reply, and once I wrote to Gorbachev personally. But days went

---

[8]Sergei Medunov, in 1962 first secretary of the Sochi City Party Committee, had become incensed at an article in *Literaturnaya gazeta* by Alexei Kapler about the daughter of the head of the Sochi Militia who had become friends with a boy her father didn't like. As a result the father put the boy in prison and sent his daughter to a mental asylum. What made the article particularly heartrending was the fact that Kapler had suffered a similar tragedy: he had planned to marry Stalin's daughter Svetlana Alliluyeva, for which he was arrested. Some weeks later *Sovetskaya Rossiya* published an article violently attacking Kapler for blackening the reputation of the valiant Sochi Militia and slinging mud at decent people. The article was signed by Yuri Chernichenko; in effect, it supported Medunov, who had threatened legal action against Kapler. Later Chernichenko served as public defender in the trial of Smirnov-Ostashvili, who was convicted of anti-Semitic acts at the Writer's Union and who committed suicide in prison. God preserve us from advocates like Chernichenko.—AUTHOR

by, the situation at the Congress continued to develop in a single direction, and I wasn't given a chance to speak.

At first I thought Gorbachev wanted to clarify things himself and respond personally to the exaggerations certain speakers had allowed themselves to use. There was more than enough cause for such a reply. During several speeches indignant outcries resounded in the hall. This would be just the time to intervene.

But Gorbachev said nothing, even though an entire group of deputies spoke in my defense at the Congress. He didn't even speak out when the writer Valentin Rasputin addressed him directly from the Congress podium. As the deputies applauded, he asked Gorbachev how he would comment on the allegations by some of the press and individual speakers that while the general secretary was out of the country Ligachev was practically preparing an overthrow. Why didn't Gorbachev respond to groundless attacks on Ligachev? Wasn't it abundantly clear who the next target would be?

Rasputin's speech was bold, utterly candid, and politically accurate. It contained a direct, unambiguous question for Gorbachev. But Gorbachev didn't reply.

I must admit that I congratulated myself for getting in touch with Gorbachev by satellite communications on 18 May to ask about publishing my "Categorical Protest." I was resolute, and it would have caused a scandal if he had refused. At the Congress I realized that my political instinct had not failed me: if the question about publishing the protest had been decided by "thinking it through from every angle," as Medvedev suggested, the matter would have evaporated.

I began to think about the question events were forcing me to confront, one that began to occupy me more and more: was Gorbachev's silence over the slanderous attacks on me tactical or strategic? If the point was to draw less attention to the Ligachev Affair, this kind of tactic doesn't lower the fever pitch of passions, but has quite the opposite effect of indulging the slanderers.

So was it strategic? If so, what was its point? At that time I still didn't have an answer to these questions or a clear understanding of what was going on. That came later, in the context of the general development of the political situation in the country.

Valentin Rasputin's speech at the Congress turned out to be truly prophetic. Since Gorbachev didn't slap Gdlyan and Ivanov down, they quickly exhausted the array of accusations against me they felt were permissible—and they acted very carefully, I must say. Interest in the "heroic investigators" began to wane. That's when they went after Gorbachev himself.

At one of the Politburo sessions, Gorbachev noted that slander against the Politburo was not ceasing; in fact, it was growing. "Do you know why that's happening?" I asked.

"Why?" Gorbachev replied, curious.

I answered precisely, with utter clarity: "Because we don't have Lenin. He always protected the people working next to him from unjust attacks." There was a dead silence. Gorbachev flipped through the papers on his desk with great absorption. Then, without answering me, he went on to the next point on the agenda.

Only once was the question of Gdlyan's smear campaign raised at a Politburo session. It came up in a strange way, and indirectly, in such a way that it could not be followed up. It was an odd incident. One of the members of the Politburo had been publicly accused of taking bribes, and everyone was pretending that nothing had happened. Of course, I clearly felt the sympathy of some of the other Politburo members: Ryzhkov, Vorotnikov, Zaikov, Lukyanov, Kryuchkov, Vlasov, Yazov, Biryukova, Baklanov. This isn't a matter expressed in words but in human decency. But Medvedev and Yakovlev behaved with exaggerated indifference. The mass media that they oversaw had organized the harassment—those agencies of the mass media whose editors in chief had been confirmed through Yakovlev's support. I remember how it had happened.

At a rally in Tushino—a district of Moscow—Gdlyan viciously attacked a press interview with a KGB colonel. He accused the KGB of going after the wrong Politburo members. "We trust Yakovlev. We've gone to him with problems. He supports us," the investigator announced. What did Yakovlev do to win his sympathy?

I disagree with Yeltsin on many points of principle. I was once
on good terms with him, but the course of politics shifted us to
different sides of the barricades. Furthermore, he betrayed the interests of the Party and left its ranks. Well, that's life. But when we
criticize each other, neither Yeltsin nor I lower ourselves to outright
insults. When I read his book *Against the Grain,* however, and saw
that Yeltsin found a particular rapport with Yakovlev, I instantly
recalled a conversation in the Walnut Room, where the members
of the Politburo met before sessions. Somehow the conversation
turned to Yeltsin and Yakovlev said, "Yeltsin is paranoid."

But at a public meeting in the Cheryomushki District of Moscow,
Yakovlev answered a question with the comment, "Yeltsin is a normal political figure." And after Yeltsin's announcement at the 28th
Congress that he was leaving the Party, Yakovlev called him and
said, "Be strong, Boris Nikolayevich." Meanwhile, the delegates of
the Congress regarded Yeltsin's actions differently, calling out,
"Shame! Traitor!" after Yeltsin as he left the hall.

Historic events that affect the future of the people are taking
place in our country. Gorbachev, Yeltsin, Yakovlev, Ligachev—
these are not individuals, simple mortals. Fate has made too much
depend on them. When I was in the political leadership of the Party,
I maintained ethical relations and restrained myself from talking
about disagreements. Was I correct in doing so? I don't know. It
may have been a mistake. But today I know for certain that our
people, whose fate now hangs in the balance, must know the whole
truth and who is who. So my disclosure of the conversation in the
Walnut Room of the Kremlin should not be regarded as settling
scores or anything of the sort.

Political events in the country during the summer and fall of
1989 were greatly influenced by the Gdlyan campaign. All the same,
at Politburo sessions I continued to insist on my policy. I sounded
the alarm and warned that such a course of events would lead the
country into a deep crisis, to economic decline, the breakdown of
economic ties, political instability, and the dissolution of the federation. It was for that position that our radical propaganda press
and foreign radio stations unmercifully christened me a "conservative." Yes, I spoke about all this many times at Politburo sessions,

at Central Committee plenums, and set it out in letters to Central Committee members (who didn't, alas, receive it). And, to my profound sorrow, I turned out to be right.

But it would have been possible to prevent these events. A powerful country has sufficient reserves and resources to complete the transfer to new economic relations more smoothly and without major losses.

But in that period political considerations clearly took the upper hand over economic ones, and the Gdlyan vs. Ligachev campaign became a political lever for achieving certain goals. At the September Central Committee plenum in 1989, Prosecutor General Alexander Sukharev gave an official report with many substantive examples and facts about Gdlyan's and Ivanov's misuse of office. An oppressive silence hung in the Plenum Hall. I watched the participants in the session and felt that many were disturbed by the same thought: why is this outrage occurring? What on earth is happening in the country? Could this really be perestroika? There was a smear campaign against the Politburo, leading Party workers in the center and in the provinces against scientists, cultural figures, and decent Communists. And no one was even trying to get to the bottom of things. Gdlyan's methods were very reminiscent of the fabrication of cases during the Stalinist purges. Could we really be on the brink of that?

Every day we firmly asserted the establishment of a law-based government, and here before our very eyes one of the most important articles of the Constitution of the USSR was being violated: No one can be declared guilty without a trial and investigation. At that September Central Committee plenum I thought for the first time that the "Gdlyan Affair" would go down in history and stand with such shameful episodes, unthinkable black spots on humankind's conscience, as the Beilis Affair[9] and the "doctor's plot." An enormous game that played with people's fates had begun, and in such games justice, sooner or later, is always victorious.

---

[9]The trial of the Jew Mendel Beilis in Kiev in 1913 for "ritual murder." Although the trial was emblematic of the worst of Russian and Ukrainian anti-Semitism, Beilis was ultimately acquitted.—TRANS.

As usual, Gorbachev chaired the plenum. He and I exchanged comments on the presidium, and I sensed that the general secretary's mood was: "There's nothing to be discussed here; we should sign the resolution and be done with it." But that didn't suit me. I said that I was prepared to speak and would ask for the floor.

"What on earth for? There's no need—everything is obvious. We should sign the resolution," Gorbachev answered.

"No, Mikhail Sergeyevich, I don't agree," I objected firmly. "If you don't give me the floor, I'll go to the podium all the same."

I could sense from the atmosphere in the hall that I had to speak. My silence would be interpreted the wrong way. It was bad enough that I had been silenced at the Congress of People's Deputies; many people thought that I just didn't wish to say anything, not knowing about my notes to the Congress presidium.

Apparently Gorbachev realized that this time I couldn't be restrained. If there were a conflict, I would address the plenum directly and the plenum would support me. So he let me speak.

I spoke candidly about what was bothering me. The hall took my suffering to heart; everyone understood that we weren't just talking about me, but also about the fate of the country. Smear campaigns and moral terror always precede a physical crackdown. We had already gone through that in our history.

I tried to uncover the roots of what was happening and caution of the impending disaster. The investigators were spreading a flood of slander and demagoguery among the people against the Party and the judicial system, deceiving millions of people. There was no need to dramatize. I said that we were dealing with an extraordinarily dangerous political phenomenon. It was clearly gathering strength and becoming an effective device for achieving far-reaching goals that were far from virtuous. People were trying to drive a wedge between the Party and the people, between Communists and non-Party members, to compromise honest workers and put their own people in power.

After my speech, Gorbachev had an objection. The day before, at the start of the plenum, he had spoken about the hardships in the country, yet he again called on people to remain calm. As events have become catastrophic, my fight with Gorbachev at the

September 1989 Central Committee plenum has come to seem symbolic. "Conservative" Ligachev warned against the danger of separatism, flareups of nationalism, and the collapse of the economy and government, and suggested passing a special resolution on the unity of the Party. I said it was necessary now, before it was too late, to prevent the country from sliding into the abyss. But Gorbachev was calling on people "to keep calm."

The course of events—and who was right—are now clear to everyone. This is not a matter of arrogance. As I've asserted repeatedly, it was possible to avoid the catastrophic turn of events.

But at the September 1989 plenum, yet another chance to have a serious discussion of the situation was missed. They simply passed a resolution stating that the accusations of bribe-taking lodged against me were unsubstantiated; in other words, the matter concerned only me. Meanwhile, the smear campaign against honest people—leaders, writers, figures in the art world, staunch Communists—was going on throughout the city and countryside.

There was a curious incident at the plenum. The preliminary draft of the resolution consisted of only one point concerning my innocence. But as an experienced politician, Gorbachev realized that the plenum would unconditionally take my side and suggested including a second point: "The plenum gives the Moscow City Party Committee the task of reviewing the question of the Party responsibilities of T. Kh. Gdlyan and N. V. Ivanov in connection with the report of the USSR Prosecutor's Office."

The plenum's decision was important to me; it skimmed away the fatty layer of slander and calumny under which I had been living for all those difficult months. But the destructive press went up in arms over the plenum's decree. Meanwhile, letters of support for me began to arrive at the Central Committee from all the republics. As I read the mail, I realized that people were beginning to comprehend where events were leading. A tenth-grader from Sverdlovsk wrote with youthful extremism: "I want to assure you that Ivanov's base sensationalist statement didn't succeed in confusing me personally or any decent person." M. P. Pivarelis wrote from Leningrad: "I think that such actions by Ivanov as smear campaigns are not just an election ploy, but purely political maneuvers planned by certain political forces." The leitmotif that Gdlyan was the front-man for certain political forces was repeated in almost every letter.

It's curious that all the letters were positive and supportive. Several times I asked the people working in the Central Committee's Department of Letter Registry, "Why do you only send me kind and reassuring letters? Where are all the rest? The ones that are against me?"

But I was told, "We pass on what we get. All the mail is registered, so you can check if you want."

Considering the negative opinion of me in the ultraradical, anti-Soviet press, I believed that my mail would include meanspirited letters. But for some reason it didn't. After thinking about this strange phenomenon, I have concluded that the so-called left-wing (really the right-wing) press had not been adequately reflecting the nation's mood during the period of perestroika. However, later I did receive several negative letters. One, by the way, was sent from the presidium of the USSR Supreme Soviet handwritten on the letterhead of a USSR people's deputy, and suggested in all deference that, with the Party "losing its authority with every day," no one would believe me even if I went out on Red Square and swore on the purity of my mother's name, that I was innocent. In light of the situation in the Party and government, the letter writer suggested that I retire. "Soon the situation will become clear and everything will fall into place again," he added. The letter was signed: "respectfully yours, T. Avaliani, Kuzbass."

What could I do but take the letter at face value, as an individual's point of view. Another point of view, which was repeated many times in comments, was expressed in a letter from an engineer in Rostov-on-the-Don, who wrote, "Elites of all stripes and foes of socialism cannot forgive you for defending the principles of socialism, collective ownership, and the interests of the working class, and opposing private enterprise and the dismantling of the collective farm system. I am alarmed to see how elites and foes of socialism in the countryside are fanning distrust of you among the masses and presenting you as a compromised bureaucrat whose retirement is imminent. Do you understand the scale of the campaign, headed by certain groups? Under these circumstances, your silence disturbs us. Take an active position as a deputy. Under no circumstances should you retire. And if you've put in your papers, take them back! Be strong! You have nothing to lose. Do not disappoint our hopes."

These hundreds of heartfelt letters were a tonic for me. I cherish them. Ultimately, these were not personal correspondence; they are important political documents of our time, and I think they will be published one day.

In this dark hour, I always had my family, my true friends, and comrades on my side. When things are going well we don't seem to notice each other. But as soon as lightning strikes, you know who your real friends are. I had more friends than I knew. Not one of them shunned me.

I got letters from acquaintances, workers and engineers, military men and teachers, people of all ages and many nationalities—Russians, Ukrainians, Azerbaidzhanis, Armenians, Jews, Tatars. . . . An instructor at the F. E. Dzerzhinsky Military Academy, Lt. Col. V. V. Kruglov, concluded his letter: "Yegor Kuzmich! In the interests of the Party you must, you are obliged to withstand this blow and not surrender your Party positions. Alienation is death for the Party. For the sake of the Party you must withstand it all!"

I selected about fifty letters that contained particularly astute analyses of the situation in the country and asked for copies. I put them in my dossier, and one evening I passed them on to Gorbachev. The selected letters spoke not so much about me as about the situation in the country and the hardships of perestroika. I was sure that when he read those alarming letters, Gorbachev would find a way to discuss the situation, either at the Politburo or in a private conversation.

I waited a day, another, a third. A week went by, then another. Gorbachev didn't say anything. So what was it—tactic, or strategy?

"Ligachev vs. Gdlyan"?

I received a letter on the eve of the 19th Party Conference, 27 June 1988:

> You are very busy with the upcoming conference and it is difficult to make an appointment to see you. Therefore, I ardently request that you read my letter—perhaps later. This is a question of my honor. I used to be a leader and now I have turned into a criminal. This is the public opinion created by several newspapers and journals. Again and again I ask you to believe me, a Communist, that I have never taken any payoffs or bribes and haven't given any. It's all slander! A blow has been dealt me. There is a group of people who have been pushed aside, and they want to destroy me and take revenge for everything that I did, with the great help of the CPSU Central Committee, in the battle against negative elements in the republic. I ask that you carefully review my request and resolve my questions fairly. With great hopes, I will wait and see what our Central Committee will do to safeguard Communists against slander.
>
> Very respectfully yours, Usmankhodzhaev.

Because some questions later were raised about my part in the appointment of Usmankhodzhaev as first secretary of the Uzbek Central Committee in 1983, a few words are necessary about how personnel matters were handled in those days.

I recall that in 1983–84, when I was working as the director of the Organization Department, some Politburo members were trying to influence various appointments. In particular, Romanov called me several times to let me know that he was offended: "For some reason I don't seem to know anything about the nominations for Party positions. . . ."

But I always had a clear answer ready:

"I decide questions about Party positions with Comrade Andropov, and, in his absence, with Comrade Chernenko. And then I propose them at sessions of the Politburo." Then I firmly added, "And that's the way it will be in the future."

Romanov realized that he couldn't get anywhere with me.

In the fall of 1983, when the question of Usmankhodzhaev's appointment was being decided, Chernenko was second secretary of the Central Committee, but Gorbachev's power had already grown noticeably. He was involved in agricultural questions, however, and formally could not have decisive influence on nominations to Party positions. But I often found Gorbachev in Chernenko's office, and he took active part in the discussion of candidates. When Chernenko recommended Usmankhodzhaev, Gorbachev and other members of the Politburo and the Central Committee Secretariat supported him.

Those are the facts. In this light the allegations by some of my critics that I was Usmankhodzhaev's patron are ridiculous. Later I learned from Usmankhodzhaev himself that Gdlyan convinced him to garnish his testimony against me. He, Usmankhodzhaev, was supposed to have thanked Ligachev for the appointment as first secretary. But he didn't know, and couldn't know, the true facts of what really was going on in the top offices on Old Square. And that's why he shot wide of the mark. I wasn't the one who nominated Usmankhodzhaev. The final confirmation of candidates was always done collegially at a Politburo session and in the presence of the nominee.

When I received Usmankhodzhaev's letter before the 19th Party Conference, I believed that everything should be investigated. How could I have imagined that his letter wouldn't be the last, that I would get yet another letter from him? And what a letter it was!

Usmankhodzhaev was arrested on 19 October 1988. At his first interrogation he denied having anything to do with bribes. The interrrogation was continued on Sunday, 23 October, although lawyers know very well that without special need investigative activities do not take place on Sundays. All the same, the investigators conducted an interrogation on Sunday. I think this was done to exert psychological pressure on the accused and create a tense atmosphere. And also to avoid many witnesses.

It was then, on Sunday, in the transcription of the interrogation, that the names of eleven top officials in the Party, the apparat of the Central Committee, and the Union Prosecutor's Office "came up." My name was not among them, but emerged on 25 October, at the next interrogation.

Usmankhodzhaev sent the prosecutor general a petition in which he asked that the investigation of his case be conducted only by Gdlyan, Ivanov, and their direct superior Karakozov, whom he "trusted absolutely." The petition stated, "I will not give in-depth testimony to any other investigators."

And then something happened that apparently Gdlyan did not plan and that essentially ruined his game. When they had the investigation completely in their hands, they apparently moved too quickly and Usmankhodzhaev immediately realized what a horrible mistake he had made when he believed their promises.

My name stayed in the investigation for only eight days. By November, at the next taped interrogation, Usmankhodzhaev retracted his accusations against me. He announced that he hadn't given me any money and asked for my forgiveness.

Naturally, at that time I didn't know anything about Usmankhodzhaev's interrogations. I learned everything written here from a speech by Prosecutor General Sukharev at the September 1989 Central Committee plenum. Sukharev also reported that on 8 March 1989—that is, five months later—Usmankhodzhaev sent the prosecutor general a petition through the prison administration while he was in pretrial detention. He retracted his testimony with regard to other central Party officials as well. Sukharev himself conducted the interrogation on that topic on 8 April in the presence of two of his aides. Usmankhodzhaev stated that he had implicated honest people at the demand of Gdlyan and Ivanov.

The investigators ran the risk of being exposed, so they decided to play their trump cards. That's why Ivanov appeared on Leningrad TV. After all, my name had been in the testimony for all of eight days. Usmankhodzhaev very quickly retracted his incrimination and there was absolutely no indirect evidence of my involvement in bribery. Between November 1988 and May 1989, a half year went by. From the point of view of decency and morality, should he have concealed from television viewers the fact that Usmankhodzhaev had retracted his testimony?

After the September 1989 Central Committee plenum when the investigators' accusation was totally removed from me, attacks from the press didn't stop. Clearly, there were political instructions. They had tied my hands, however, and prevented me from doing anything about actions that I considered destabilizing and destructive. But I kept on fighting. Sooner or later, I believe, the documents from the Central Committee sessions and meetings will be published, and they will make it perfectly clear that my proposals always had the aim of keeping us from sliding into a crisis. If only they had been heeded.

In my view, the first clear symptom of the serious setback to perestroika was the second USSR Congress of People's Deputies, which wasted a lot of time reviewing various scandals. The Gdlyan Affair, the Tbilisi Affair, the Molotov-Ribbentrop pact. Isn't that a lot to cover in one session?

When there was discussion of the report of the commission investigating the Gdlyan group, Gdlyan was, of course, allowed to speak. Everyone expected that he would finally make public specific evidence of my guilt. Tens of millions of people were watching his great moment on TV; it was the highest podium in the country: and foreign correspondents were there. It was truly the perfect moment to expose the "Kremlin mafia" with a flourish. But, alas, Gdlyan once again did not bring forward any specific facts. This really irritated the audience. I recall how E. A. Pamfilova angrily spoke to Gdlyan at the microphone, "Telman Khorenovich, as a lawyer, you must be completely responsible for the statements you make on television and at rallies. I personally saw on Leningrad TV your accusation of Ligachev, saying that you personally had materials that would prove his guilt. I ask you to bring them forward here, at the Congress. You knew that today we would listen to material on your case. You know that the entire country is waiting for it. If you have it—bring it out; if you don't—stop your demagoguery! Stop stirring up the entire country!"

Needless to say, Gdlyan didn't reply, and everyone was extremely disappointed and, moreover, indignant. Deputy Pamfilova expressed the feelings of the deputies.

Concerning me personally and the accusations of the investigators, the Congress of People's Deputies was completely convinced of my innocence, and attention was redirected to the misuse of power by Gdlyan and Ivanov. (Later, in April 1990, the USSR Supreme Soviet reviewed the conclusions of the Parliamentary Commission on Gdlyan's investigative group and condemned their groundless statements "that discredited the Supreme Soviet of the USSR and individual people's deputies and officials." The Supreme Soviet also warned that if such activities continued, proceedings to remove Gdlyan and Ivanov from their parliamentary seats would be started. In addition, the Supreme Soviet consented to remove the investigators from the Prosecutor's Office. They were subsequently fired.)

I might have celebrated. However, my mood was bleak: in my heart, I felt that the country was moving toward disaster.

I recalled how during the 1989 USSR Congress of People's Deputies, the deputies decided to lay a wreath at Lenin's mausoleum. We walked in a closely packed group all the way across the Kremlin to go out onto Red Square through the Spasskaya Tower. Gorbachev walked up to me, took me by the arm, and asked how I was feeling. I was still depressed and astonished by the debate on the Tbilisi Affair that had just taken place, so I countered with a question.

"Why didn't anyone in the top leadership speak out on the Tbilisi Affair and recount the conversation at the airport when you arrived from London and asked Shevardnadze to fly immediately to Tbilisi? Mikhail Sergeyevich, there are dishonorable people close to you. They will do you in."

We were walking quickly across the Kremlin in a tight group and I deliberately spoke loudly so that the other people walking along with us would hear.

"What do you mean—do you think that Lukyanov is like that? He's close to me, too," Gorbachev said, indicating Lukyanov, who was walking next to us.

"Lukyanov—no. I mean Yakovlev—you know that. The time will come and you'll see . . ."

"You're wrong."

"No, *you're* wrong, Mikhail Sergeyevich," I retorted. "The time will come and you'll see . . ."

"You're upset," Gorbachev said, trying to calm me down.

"It's hard to be indifferent when you can feel the storm coming," I replied.

The conversation clearly had not gone well. I realized that and brusquely—perhaps too brusquely—made a show of moving away.

That time I frankly told Gorbachev what I had been thinking about for a long time. Gorbachev's closest advisers, a group Yakovlev had helped to form, had a really strong influence on him. Later some of this entourage ran off as if from a sinking ship, slinging mud at Gorbachev.

In the Politburo many cases logically required that all the members give their opinion on a question under discussion. And naturally, Gorbachev required that of all of us. But Yakovlev didn't say anything. Sometimes Gorbachev would get angry.

"Alexander Nikolayevich, what's your view on this?"

But Yakovlev would sometimes still avoid giving a direct answer.

This is, of course, a peripheral matter. The question of the people closest to the leader was far more serious.

I received many letters and telegrams suggesting that I sue Gdlyan and Ivanov for slander. People I met in my travels around the country encouraged me; they didn't just tell me to do this, they demanded it. And, of course, we talked about it in my family.

So why didn't I sue them?

I don't like to throw myself into a fight without thinking the matter through. First I analyze the situation thoroughly. When I first considered a lawsuit, I asked several Moscow lawyers to help me by giving a legal analysis of the situation. When they studied the investigators' speech scrupulously, word by word, they were not surprised to find that no laws had been broken. Strange and astonishing as it may seem, neither Gdlyan nor Ivanov said anything that might be considered legally incriminating. The people who ran this slander campaign against me were quite skillful. The press pulled out all the stops and spread rumors about the "accusation of bribery," but the accusers skirted the issue. They said my name had "come up" in the case, that I was close to the Kremlin mafia, and so on—but they never once called me a bribe-taker outright. They never used direct accusations, but created the necessary impression indirectly.

These were real political pros.

Actually, there's nothing strange or astonishing in this. After all, special investigators and people in the criminal justice system are knowledgeable and know what would face them if they made a false accusation.[10]

There were other articles in the Criminal Code that I might have used for the basis of a suit—emotional damages, for example. But recall the situation in those days, the deteriorating public atmosphere—I had absolutely no doubts that if I, a Politburo member, had sued for emotional damages, it would have been used by anti-Communist forces to incite hysteria. Therefore, after thinking it over carefully, I decided not to begin a lawsuit.

By then I had in my possession an important document that presented the whole "Gdlyan vs. Ligachev" campaign in an entirely different light. That document has been in my safe awaiting its moment, and now the time to publish it has come. I would like to make public a letter (the second) that I received from Usmankhodzhaev:

---

[10]*Izvestia* (4 February 1991) tried to present its own, clearly fraudulent version of why I didn't sue the investigators for the "unfounded accusation." In its opinion, I was "too long outside and above the law . . . Ligachev would have had to change his spots, his habits and traditions, act against his own dominant 'I.' "

Concerning the claim that I was outside the law, indeed above it (which they define and analyze with such ease!), I consider it a falsehood. As a Communist and Party worker, I may have always been more strict in my observance of the law than others. And that's no problem for me. And in this case *Izvestia* can't "change its spots" and get rid of the distorted image of a Party leader, fabricated by pseudodemocrats, many of whom violate laws, as the press is reporting more frequently.—AUTHOR

23 January 1990
Confidential

To Ye. K. Ligachev, member of the Politburo, secretary of
the CPSU Central Committee:
Esteemed Yegor Kuzmich!

This is being sent to you by Inomzhon Buzurukovich Usmankhodzhaev, former first secretary of the Uzbek Communist Party Central Committee, who has now been sentenced
to twelve years of imprisonment.

First of all, I ask your forgiveness a thousand times for
everything that has happened. You must know—and I say
this sincerely—that I never even considered accusing you of
anything, of humiliating you, or implicating you in a crime.
The investigators Gdlyan and Ivanov needed that, and they
got it.

I was a victim of the political intriguers Gdlyan and Ivanov, who tried to fabricate accusations that a number of
Party and soviet figures committed crimes. As a result of
their illegal actions—blackmail, the threat to execute me and
arrest members of my family and relatives, I hoped to save
the honor of my family and relatives and feared for their
lives. I was not responsible for my actions, but I was compelled to implicate people not guilty of anything at all, including myself. Later, when I came to my senses, in literally
a few days, I retracted my false testimony about giving you
and others bribes. But despite that, the above-mentioned investigators continue to make a hue and cry and sling mud at
decent people who are guilty of nothing. Once again I proclaim, fully aware of my words, that it is all a lie! It is high
time for these investigators, who have completely lost their
souls, these opportunists, to be called on the carpet and the
force of the law to be used against them.

Esteemed Yegor Kuzmich!

I've been imprisoned for over a year now and have suffered a great deal. I had never been in this situation before.
My conscience continues to torment me and I suffer sleep-
less nights and great anxety. While I was under pressure
from the investigators and started down the path of decep-

tion, I implicated innocent people, including you, Yegor
Kuzmich. I will curse that day my whole life. So with all my
heart I ask you again and again to forgive me. I also deeply
apologize to K. N. Mogilnichenko, V. I. Bessarabov, I. Ye.
Ponomarev, and all the officials in the division with whom
I worked on such friendly terms and with such mutual
respect.

> Apologizing once more,
> Respectfully yours,
> Usmankhodzhaev

You have to face the truth head-on. In our life, in the Communist
Party, there are the Medunovs and Shchelokovs[11] of the world. The
nation put up with a lot from them. People saw that they lived by
double standards, hiding behind lofty words as they pursued their
own selfish interests. People naturally thought: if they can get away
with it, then other people, the current leaders, can, too. That's why
Gdlyan's lies and slander fell on fertile soil and were perceived as
truth. This factor must be taken into consideration. But it is unworthy to take advantage of the righteous indignation of the
nation.

Let me relate yet one more act of repentance with regard to the
Ivanov Affair. On the eve of the referendum on preserving the
Union,[12] a *Pravda* correspondent talked with Alexander Nevzorov,
anchor of the Leningrad TV program *600 Seconds,* who had
miraculously survived two shootings. Nevzorov was well known
for his many attacks on the Party and *Pravda.* The popular television
journalist said, "This isn't the time to judge. We must unite in the

---

[11]Sergei Medunov (see footnote 8, p. 232 above) and Nikolai Shchelokov (1910–84),
minister of internal affairs (1968–82), both officials close to Brezhnev who were removed for corruption.—TRANS.

[12]The March 1991 referendum, worded to make it difficult to vote against it, asked if
citizens supported a "renewed Union of sovereign republics." It was passed by a majority
of the population, including in republics that later voted for independence after the
coup.—TRANS.

name of our common task. The Motherland is in danger, and we only have one Motherland. Yes, I was an ardent Communist. But excuse me, they set themselves up. Maybe I've gone overboard in some things, but in this case my conscience doesn't bother me. But there's something else I cannot forgive myself for—this is the sin I cannot wash away: I helped today's democrats come to power in Leningrad. If not all, then most of them. I even stooped to hooliganism. . . . Do you remember when I gave Ivanov airtime? I was deceived along with everyone else. I saw who they really were when they threatened what we hold most sacred—the Motherland—by calling for a boycott of the 17 March referendum and a vote of 'no' to the Union. That is betrayal!"

There's no need to comment on such a candid statement. A display of frankness is always more convincing than commentary.

Here it makes sense to include the opinion of one other person, who was virtually banished from the Party under Brezhnev and Suslov and excluded from the political life of the country, forced to publish his works in the West: the writer and historian Roy Medvedev. To a question by a correspondent from the newspaper *Rabochaya Tribuna (Workers' Tribune)*—"Do you believe the allegation that Ligachev took a bribe from Usmankhodzhaev?"—he answered, "I don't believe it."

I have thought about all this for a long time. I have turned the events of 1989 and 1990 over in my mind many times. Why did Gorbachev take such a strange position? Only once did he briefly note that he believed in Ligachev's honesty—and that was two months after the investigator appeared on Leningrad TV, in answer to persistent questions from workers in Izhorsk. He simply avoided similar questions by foreign correspondents. Why didn't he say anything? After all, it was clear as could be that this wasn't just a discussion about me, but about the Politburo, about him, about the Party as a whole.

Why didn't he say anything?

I am not interested in the fates of Gdlyan and Ivanov. I would like to repeat that I don't hate them, I only pity them. . . . The Communists of low-level Party organizations expelled them from the Party because they slandered the Party and Soviet power. When that happened they joined the "democrats" in Moscow City soviet—anything to attract attention. Their place in history is not to be envied.

But this isn't about them. It's about something else: in 1989–90, the country slipped into an all-encompassing crisis and the domestic political situation became threatening. As someone who until July 1990 pinned his hopes on the inner top Party leadership, I understand very well what occurred. In this book I am trying to answer the many questions that now demand answers. The world is not moved by the arrogance of the memoirist. I want to help my country to the extent of my powers. On the basis of the facts available to a member of the Politburo, I am making my analysis of what has happened.

And the Gdlyan Affair was one of the keys to such an analysis.

My understanding of the events that might be called in English legal terminology "Gdlyan vs. Ligachev" went through several phases.

At first I thought the attacks by the investigators Gdlyan and Ivanov were directed against me personally so they could remove me from the Party's top leadership and make their political careers in one fell swoop.

But as time went by, I realized that they were aiming higher. After anti-Communism was legalized, we could see the target of the political forces supporting Gdlyan and Ivanov. While I am in no way attempting to exalt myself—that's not my nature at all—I have to say that I was the person in the Politburo who constantly came to the defense of socialist principles and spoke against private ownership and unemployment.

For example, I was the one who categorically insisted that the thesis on legalizing private property be excluded from the Central Committee's final report to the 28th Congress. At Politburo sessions and in public statements I repeatedly sounded the alarm about events in Eastern Europe; resolutely supported the current agricultural policy and state-run farms. I demonstrated the need to modernize farming. In the most crucial questions of principle—

private property, collective agriculture, the situation in Eastern Europe, and other matters—I had a great many supporters. On the level of the top Party leadership I voiced particular civic positions that had to at least be taken into consideration. These positions held back the implementation of far-reaching plans to make the country capitalist.

I am convinced that this is why the investigators attacked me.

I had a moment of total, comprehensive insight at the 28th Party Congress, when a heavy attack was launched against me. Not a single person mentioned the accusation of taking bribes. Over 150 written questions were addressed to me during my report on my work, and numerous questions from the delegates in the hall. But there wasn't a single question about the Gdlyan incident, although I had many ideological opponents among the delegates. It was patently obvious to everyone that I was above suspicion.

The situation developed in an astonishing, paradoxical way. It was as if there had never been any uproar over the accusation that I took bribes, as if the radical, anti-Communist press hadn't tormented me for an entire year, pouring oil on the bonfire of public passions. It was as if at rallies no "democrats" had ever carried posters accusing me of corruption. A black tornado had stormed over me, and now everything had quieted down. The shadow of suspicion over my name had disappeared. At the 28th Party Congress, I was rehabilitated not by the conclusions of a commission but by the complete silence of thousands of people who understood that accusing me of bribery was simply nonsense.

I had an inner satisfaction. But other questions didn't give me peace. What on earth had it all been about? What was the nature of the tornado that stormed over me? After all, as I never tire of repeating, this wasn't a matter of settling a personal score. The slander campaign against me had a significant impact on the development of political events in the country. Moreover, it provided impetus to the slander campaign against Communists and the Party. Now it turns out that it was all fiction, slander. Now people understand.

Ligachev can be rehabilitated and suspicion removed from him, but time has passed, the deed is done. You can't turn back the clock on political events.

And here I discovered the treachery of the political forces who were plotting to turn back history. The felony accusations against me burst like a soap bubble, revealing the moral corruption of those who plotted this affair behind the scenes and those who carried it out.

And the conclusions about what happened are important not only to me.

Six

GHOSTS OF
THE PAST

The Kolpashevo Incident

As the whirlwind of political passions started by the radicals engulfed me and the Tbilisi Affair was added to the Gdlyan Affair, yet another report aimed against me appeared in the press. This concerned the so-called Kolpashevo incident. The gist of this tragic event, an echo of the bloody Stalinist persecutions, was as follows.

Kolpashevo, a rather small old town, on the banks of the River Ob, in the northern part of Tomsk Province, was founded by deportees. Its notoriety as a place of Siberian exile was already firmly established in the past century. "Politicals" were brought there by steamship. Given the sweep of the Siberian taiga and the complete absence of roads, the only escape was via the river, where a boat is always visible and there's nowhere to hide. Furthermore, it was no easy task to row hundreds of miles upstream against the current, to more inhabited areas to the south. (Downstream, the boat would be taken straight into the Arctic Ocean, into the lifeless land of white death.)

No wonder a Stalinist place of exile was later established in this wilderness. In the 1930s, Kolpashevo was notorious for the torture chambers of Yezhov's and Beria's NKVD.

But, of course, none of the local people knew what was being done in these torture chambers; there were only vague rumors of cruelty and executions. And then suddenly, in the spring of 1979, something happened in Kolpashevo that was a horrible reminder of the Stalinist terror.

Melting snow made the flooding of the Ob unusually severe that year. The high waters eroded the precipice on which a transit prison had once stood, the bank collapsed, and lo and behold, a mass grave was revealed on the prison grounds.

What was the reaction? Two dredgers raced up the Ob, quickly demolished the remains of the precipice, and washed the secret cemetery, the visible reminder of Stalin's victims, into the river.

Naturally, in those years as before, this event remained unknown; it was concealed from the public. But when the time of glasnost came, when the victims of Stalin's persecution were rehabilitated and monuments were erected everywhere in their memory, the Kolpashevo incident was recalled. Newspapers related the events of 1979 and were appropriately indignant. But in 1979 I had been the first secretary of the Tomsk Province Committee, and so they started trying to convince the public that absolutely everything that went on in the province was done at the behest of the Party committee—including the destruction of the secret cemetery. There were hints that I personally might have given the order for this monstrous effort to cover up all tracks.

Of course, there was absolutely no evidence that I or the committee had been involved, and even the right-wing radical press did not risk making such serious accusations directly. But rumors and allegations started flying, and it was demanded that the Prosecutor's Office investigate the Kolpashevo incident.

At the time I considered it right to investigate what happened. I still believe we must try to establish for posterity the names of those who perished in Kolpashevo. But unfortunately, there were some who began exploiting the incident for immediate political gain. In particular, radicals started insisting that the Novosibirsk

Prosecutor's Office take charge of the Kolpashevo occurrence, since the Tomsk office was possibly biased and might protect the local Party committee and its former first secretary.

Knowing some of the circumstances of the Kolpashevo incident, I was of course confident in regard to any investigation, whether it was conducted by the Prosecutor's Office in Tomsk, Novosibirsk, or Moscow. I was grieved, even deeply oppressed by the fact that the opposition was using what I regarded as a sacred duty, that of immortalizing the memory of the victims of Stalin's persecution, as a chip in their bid for power.

Of all the accusations that people have unsuccessfully tried to hang on me in recent years, reproaches for concealing the Kolpashevo burial have inflicted the deepest spiritual wound. They blasphemed me. And not only because neither the Tomsk Province Committee nor I personally had anything to do with the events of 1979. It is more serious. In the late 1970s, when the beneficial effects of the 20th Party Congress, which exposed the cult of Stalin's personality, began to come to naught, it was I who made great efforts to immortalize the memory of those who had been persecuted.

I had personal reasons for this: I knew what the year 1937 meant, and not from hearsay. I did not study this tragic period in books, but learned of it from the bitter experience of my own life. My father, the Siberian peasant Kuzma Ligachev, who had left his village to work in Novosibirsk, was expelled from the Party in 1937 (true, he was later readmitted). And my wife's father, Ivan Zinoviev, perished during those years—he was arrested on false charges and executed.

He was a Red Army soldier during the Civil War. Later, after obtaining his education, he served in the People's Commissariat for Defense, in the Moscow Military District. By the middle of the 1930s, his military rank was already relatively high—lieutenant general by today's ranking. In 1935, when Stalin began sending generals out of Moscow, Ivan Zinoviev was sent to the Siberian Military District as staff commander. Later, as we know, military personnel were subject to massive persecution. Zinoviev was arrested in December 1936; in June 1937 he was tried, charged with espionage and with activity that was aimed at weakening the military preparedness of the district troops. The whole "trial" lasted ten minutes. And two hours after the "Anglo-Japanese-German spy," who totally denied all charges of betrayal, was sentenced, he was executed by a firing squad.

I learned details of his death only at the end of May 1989, during the first USSR Congress of People's Deputies, when the possibility arose of becoming acquainted with the files of the case brought against Zinoviev in 1936. That Congress in general was a very difficult period for me. Gdlyan came down upon me with slanderous attacks; the radicals started demanding my retirement; my wife, Zinaida, fell ill. It never rains, but it pours. And when my family became acquainted with the files of the 1930s, Zinaida burst into tears:

"Why am I doomed like this? Before, I was the daughter of an 'enemy of the people.' Now I have become the wife of an 'enemy of perestroika.' "

I remember her father very well. He was a lively, interesting, colorful man, a good speaker (I once attended his lecture on international affairs in Novosibirsk); in my opinion, a natural talent. Zinaida and I were in tenth grade together; I visited the Zinoviev home. Their family tragedy took place before my eyes. Zinaida and I got married right after the war. And in this connection I must recall a letter I received at the beginning of the Gdlyan Affair, when hundreds of people felt it necessary to express their support for me. I. A. Spirina wrote from Moscow: "Dear Yegor Kuzmich! It is clear to me who you are and that you are a very decent man if during the Stalin years you were not afraid to marry the daughter of a persecuted 'enemy of the people.' This fact in your biography says a great deal."

I admit openly that this letter touched me to the depths of my soul. Indeed, before 1953, before Stalin's death, I felt very clearly what it meant to be married to the daughter of a persecuted general. Such facts had to remain in your personal dossier. I knew of people who were severely punished for concealing such details of their biography; dossiers at that time were verified very scrupulously. The process took months. A person marked with such an entry in his personal file was considered second-class. One could be reminded of this invisible stigma of "enemy of the people" hanging over a family. And very concrete consequences could follow a reminder.

In 1949 I had quite a reminder. At that time, I was first secretary of the Novosibirsk Province Komsomol Committee, and at our initiative, youth brigades were being organized at factories and on collective farms. This practice was very widespread during the war and yielded good results at production facilities. We felt that youth collectives were also necessary in peacetime. You may ask, What could be wrong with this? But they thought differently in Moscow; I was accused of trying to wrest young people away from the Party and given the menacing label of "Trotskyite."

But after all, I was no rank-and-file Komsomol member, but the first secretary of the provincial committee. Our committee report was reviewed in Moscow, at the bureau meeting of the All-Union Komsomol Central Committee, chaired by N. A. Mikhailov, the first secretary of the Komsomol Central Committee. Moreover, my situation was complicated by one circumstance that was dangerous for me. A year prior to this, the tragic Leningrad Affair unfolded. Ivanov, the second secretary of the All-Union Komsomol Central Committee and the former first secretary of the Leningrad Komsomol Province Committee, an extremely smart man, was charged in this affair. He and I were on good terms, he supported me, and the Central Committee leadership knew about this. Ivanov was slandered and convicted, and perished. What happened to him affected me deeply; I could not believe in his guilt, particularly knowing about the fate of General Zinoviev.

And very soon after, I myself was charged with "Trotskyism." One would think they had reviewed the provincial committee report. Indeed, there was a lot to talk about—we made an effort, we accomplished a lot, but, of course, we had a lot of shortcomings—and then we were reproached with "Trotskyism." At the bureau, Mikhailov, who charged me with attempting to wrest young people away from the Party, started the conversation. He kept emphasizing that we had "behaved in this way like Trotskyites." I tried to defend myself, but no one was listening. The members of the bureau knew, of course, that my wife was the daughter of a persecuted general— nobody said this directly, but I felt this fact hovering in the air. The political sentence was quickly pronounced: Remove him from his post.

Paradoxically, because of my inexperience at that time, I felt absolutely no sense of danger. I apparently did not appreciate the full seriousness of the situation. Or maybe this simply showed my character. Since my conscience was clear, I preferred not to hide but rather to go out on a limb. I wrote an angry letter to the Central Committee in which I presented the essence of the case and asked that it be investigated.

A couple of days later, I was summoned to the Organizational Instructors' Department of the Central Committee. The comrade on whose desk my letter happened to land was in a small room, but not alone; some woman was working at another desk. I remember that the conversation started slowly, with the instructor asking me about my life, about the young people's work brigades.

Then the woman got up and left, carrying some papers. We were left alone. Suddenly the conversation took a totally different turn. The instructor, whose name I deeply regret I do not remember, told me:

"Comrade Ligachev, I strongly advise you not to write any more appeals, and please go home as quickly as possible. Do you understand me? I strongly advise you not to write any more appeals. And I will report that I have had a talk with you."

I apparently looked puzzled, even flabbergasted, so the instructor continued, nodding at the other desk:

"Do you know who that woman was? That was Comrade Mishakova. Well then, good-bye."

It was only on the street that I understood what had happened. Mishakova was the notorious "ultravigilant" person who had "exposed" A. Kosarev, the first secretary of the Komsomol Central Committee. She was being vaunted as a model for us all and if my letter had come to her for investigation, my fate most likely would have been very different. I was terribly lucky. That incident proved that all kinds of people worked in the Central Committee, as in other agencies. Among them were many decent people who understood what was going on and tried to do what they could to help those whom disaster threatened. I was not only helped; in plain terms, I was saved.

Upon returning to Novosibirsk, I heeded the good advice given to me in the Central Committee and did not complain to anyone else or appeal for justice to be done. But no one would hire me, either; I was unemployed for seven months. It was very difficult. My family lived only on Zinaida's salary as an English teacher at the pedagogical institute. The mental oppression was unspeakable.

And exactly forty years later, in 1989, when the newspaper *Komsomolskaya Pravda* published its anniversary issue and included in it material of past years, they again published an old item reporting on the Novosibirsk Province Committee Komsomol plenum that had removed former first secretary Ye. Ligachev from his post.

The item was inserted without any comment and occasioned much idle talk as well as responses in the press and on radio. Some young journalists began referring to it as proof that even when he was still in the Komsomol, Ligachev had been up to something. At first glance, reprinting an item from 1949 in the *Komsomolskaya Pravda* was a trifle, a newspaper curiosity, nothing more. At first I looked at it that way and did not attach any significance to it. But then I understood that this could not be viewed in isolation from all of what was going on in the radical mass media.

All that we are seeing in the destructive radical press has happened before. Specifically during Stalin's time, when just such energetic, young, talented journalists persecuted people demanding reprisals against the "enemies of the people," and so on. Only the external attributes have changed: today the press is directed not by official Agitprop but by the leaders of the so-called democratic movement. The political coloring of the press and the objects of its persecution have changed diametrically, but the psychology of persecution, the same immoral instinct to discredit an inconvenient person at any price, undoubtedly is present.

This was bitter and frightening, a dangerous ghost of the past.

The tone of the radical press, the degree of its irreconcilability with Communists, was quickly and dangerously approaching that which existed during the time of Stalin's personality cult. Then, people were branded "bloody agents of imperialism"; today, they are branded "bloody Bolsheviks." The spiral of hatred again is escalating, and people of the older generation, whose lives have shown them where this can lead, agonize for the young people being drawn into a new era of misfortunes.

As for that old accusation of "Trotskyism," my seven months of living in poverty gave me a chance to find out who was a true friend and who was only a casual fellow traveler. There were people who recoiled from me. But there were others who gave their support, who did not sever ties of friendship—one values this particularly in difficult times. Thanks to them I did not become embittered toward life. On the contrary, I came to believe firmly that sooner or later, good and justice triumph. I believed, and still believe, in people.

Of course, I was turned down at the Chkalov Airplane Plant, where I had worked after finishing my studies; I was rejected because of data in my personal file, since this was a defense enterprise. I had to roam around quite a bit before—finally and very unexpectedly for me—it was suggested that I become a lecturer in the Novosibirsk City Party Committee. But I did not breathe freely, did not straighten my shoulders and believe that the worst years were behind me, even after Stalin's death—not until the 20th Party Congress, which exposed the personality cult.

It seems to me that the above is sufficient for the reader to understand and appreciate fully my attitude toward Stalin's personality cult and the persecutions. I smile bitterly when I read today that I desire a virtual return to Stalinist times. As I have said, my attitude toward history is serious; I perceive it as a whole, in all its fullness and variety. I see its dark and tragic patches very well, but I also see the merit of the great things that our country, our people have achieved. I am a categorical opponent of a black-and-white view of history. But its ambiguity does not make it permissible to exploit it for the political goals of the moment. Those who try to do so are, however unwittingly, true spiritual descendants of Stalinism, no matter what "democratic" togas they may don.

This is why the great civic task of remembering the victims of Stalinism was linked indissolubly with my own deeply personal experiences. And in the years that I was working in Tomsk Province, I happened upon an opportunity, however local in its application, to fulfill my moral duty to those who had suffered persecution.

It is in Tomsk Province that the infamous Narym, the fatal land of political exile, even more harsh and distant than Kolpashevo, is located. Kolpashevo was once the center of the whole Narym territory, and the village called Narym, founded four hundred years ago—older than Tomsk—is almost two hundred kilometers north of Kolpashevo.

As an exile settlement town, Narym traces its history to the Decembrists[1] who served their punishment there. The Petrashevsky circle,[2] participants in the Polish insurrections,[3] the People's Will[4]— all were sent to these same penal territories. Then came the period of the Bolsheviks, whom the Tsarist Government left to rot in Narym. Stalin, [Valerian] Kuibyshev, and Sverdlov were not spared a stay in these parts.[5] In the 1930s, dispossessed kulaks were exiled to Narym. All in all, Narym has a bitter, but glorious history. This territory has seen many tears and sorrows, but it has also known high flights of the soul and courage.[6]

---

[1]Young writers and intellectuals who led a revolt against Tsar Nicholas I in December 1825. Some of them were executed, others were exiled.—TRANS.

[2]Among whom Dostoevsky was numbered.—TRANS.

[3]In 1830 and 1863.—TRANS.

[4]Active revolutionaries, evolved in 1870s from earlier populist groupings, who were responsible for the assassination of Tsar Alexander II in 1881.—TRANS.

[5]Valerian Kuibyshev (1888–1935), president of the State Planning Commission from 1930, and Politburo member. Jacob Sverdlov (1885–1919), chairman, Russian Central Executive Committee.—TRANS.

[6]Today the northern, Narym, parts of Tomsk Province, where geologists and petroleum

"God created paradise; the devil made Narym." I often found myself repeating this Siberian saying. At one time, a small Stalin-era museum was organized in Narym. Later, after the 20th Party Congress, an exposition dedicated to exiled Bolsheviks was opened. But it did not reflect the whole rich and tragic history of Narym, a large taiga village with "classical" Siberian wooden architecture, and the Narym region. As first secretary of the Province Party Committee, I often visited Narym, listened to the stories of the old residents, witnesses of the evil exile years, and became familiar with its past. In 1977 we came up with the idea of turning Narym into a historical museum to preserve for posterity the memory of all the exiles who spent time in this harsh land, from the Decembrists to those repressed by Stalin.

Of course, it was impossible to implement such an idea with a local resolution alone; permission from the center was necessary, and from a very high level.

I set off to see Suslov with a request to consider this issue. I reminded him briefly of the history of Narym and then said: "It is a matter of turning Narym into a memorial village. We would like our request to be considered by the Central Committee and to be given the appropriate instructions."

After a brief pause, Suslov answered: "Yegor Kuzmich, we cannot support you."

"Why not, Mikhail Andreyevich?"

"Because, Yegor Kuzmich, your proposal means that we would also be immortalizing the memory of those exiles who were condemned when the Soviet government was in power."

It would be insincere of me to say that I had not foreseen the possibility of this kind of answer. But I tried to insist and placed the letter from the Province Party Committee on his desk. I understood perfectly that we do not have the moral right to sever the unfortunate history of Narym at the year 1917. And I had not come to Moscow empty-handed; I had brought a detailed report about

---

employees work, are actively being conquered; new cities and workers' settlements are springing up.—AUTHOR

creating the memorial village of Narym; the report was prepared with the help of Tomsk historians.

"Mikhail Andreyevich, what's going on here? Why should we give up creating a historical museum? Our Siberian scholars have prepared a well-grounded report on this matter."

Suslov's response was much harsher than I anticipated. He essentially ignored the question and said dryly: "Go on to the next issue."

Understandably, I have no memory of what the next issue was. Disgruntled at the decisive rebuff, I continued the rest of the conversation with desultory correctness.

The question of creating a memorial village was left in limbo. Could I have known in 1977 that two years later, Suslov himself would be forced to return to the discussion of the victims of Stalinist repressions when an unusually high flood level on the Ob brought down the Kolpashevo precipice and revealed the secret burial ground?

The Closed Circle

I think that the reader can now understand how deeply I was wounded by the suspicion that I'd given the order to destroy the Kolpashevo burial ground on the banks of the Ob.

My first impulse was to speed to the scene of the incident to take control of the situation and try to legitimize what had happened. But more than two years had passed since the failure with the Narym memorial, and it had become increasingly obvious that the work to rehabilitate the victims of the personality cult was being restricted.

The first to call and tell me what had happened in Kolpashevo was the head of the provincial directorate of the KGB. I asked him: "What kind of burial ground is this?"

The answer was vague: "It's still difficult to say anything specific. Perhaps it is a burial ground connected with the interment of White Guard soldiers, deserters. Or else, and most likely, these are people executed in 1937. But we have no documents to this effect; we have already looked."

Archival records concerning those persecuted were kept under lock and key from Party committees. From time to time, Communists would approach me with requests to see the "cases" of their family members who had perished in the 1930s, but I could do nothing to help them. It was not even possible to raise the issue of seeing the 1937 case connected with my own family.

There was a strict procedure: all "nonstandard" situations, and particularly incidents having a political aspect, were to be brought immediately to the attention of the Central Committee. In this case the issue was of supreme importance, so I called Suslov without delay.

But Suslov interrupted me after my very first words: "I have been apprised. Comrade Andropov has already informed me about it."

It became clear that the provincial directorate of the KGB first informed those higher up within its own organization, its direct superiors; only then was the provincial Party committee informed.

Suslov continued: "The KGB will call you. This is not a matter for the Party committee."

Indeed, I soon got a call from Andropov. He, too, was unusually brief: "I know about your conversation with Mikhail Andreyevich," the chairman of the KGB began. "We, and only we, are dealing with this matter." Then he repeated Suslov's statement exactly and with some emphasis: "This is not a matter for the Party committee."

My attempt to get involved in the situation, to try to figure it out, was cut short most decisively. All special projects were dealt with by the KGB. The provincial committee had nothing to do with it.

I am not writing this in an attempt to justify myself. I had every intention of flying to Kolpashevo, in which case events might have developed differently, but business prevented me from doing so.

By the way, I never saw any documents regarding the events in Kolpashevo. However, many years later, certain details unexpectedly came to light. When in 1988 *Pravda* first published the news of the graves that had been washed into the waters of the Ob from the times of the personality cult, Viktor Chebrikov, who was already then working in the Central Committee, told me that a special KGB group had been formed to deal with the Kolpashevo events. The real decision had been made somewhere "at the top"; it was undoubtedly of a political nature. But it was hidden even from the local Party offices, and KGB men were ordered to "carry out the resolution" under conditions of complete secrecy.

It is clear that the sad outcome of the Kolpashevo incident would have been completely different today, under conditions of glasnost and the new appraisal of certain periods in the past. Those same KGB men, along with the population of Kolpashevo, would be organizing the reburial of those who had perished, regardless of who they were or which side of the political barricades they were on. But the decision back then corresponded to the mood of society at the time.

The KGB workers carried out orders from the highest echelons of power. But no decision on this matter was made directly at a Politburo session: everything was decided verbally behind a couple of closed doors.

The circle was closed: the orders to the KGB men working on the "Kolpashevo Affair" referred to instructions given by the Party command; the refusal to allow local Party committees the right to get involved laid the blame on KGB secrecy.

Such manipulation wasn't contingent only on a lack of glasnost; it also was a very vivid, symbolic example of where concentrating Party and state power in one pair of hands leads. It reveals the very essence, the core, of the system of Party-government rule that took shape as early as Stalin's time.

Perhaps the strongest, most serious example of this nature in recent years is the decision made in secret to send troops to Afghanistan. Although the decision was made in secret, and not by all the members of the top leadership, in people's minds the blame lies entirely with the ruling Party.

More recently, many extremely important decisions involving the fate of the country were made without the real participation of the Party, although in people's minds they were connected with the

Party, because Gorbachev was its general secretary. This is what happened with the extremely fundamental issue of making the transition to market relations and with raising prices.

To regain the nation's confidence and win its sympathy, the Communist Party should have entered the social arena as an independent political force not fettered by obligations to the state. Many Communists understood this. It was no accident that they questioned increasingly the expediency of combining the functions of Party general secretary and president of the USSR.

In this regard, let me mention the Politburo session that took place before the 20th Party Congress. We gathered outside the city, in Novo-Ogarevo, at 6:00 P.M. and dispersed at about midnight. All the issues connected with the opening and the work of the Congress were discussed, as well as personnel possibilities. Among other things, there was an exchange of opinions about whether to combine the posts of general secretary and president. Gorbachev asked everyone to speak on this subject. Everyone spoke in favor of combining them, which clearly corresponded to Gorbachev's intentions. I unequivocally said that I objected to combining the functions. A president is one thing; a general secretary, acting energetically and with initiative, is another. I also said that Gorbachev should remain general secretary, and the nation should elect someone else president.

Of course I understood that I would be alone on the issue of dividing the highest functions and that this could not but affect Gorbachev's attitude toward me. But I could not act against my conscience, whatever the cost.

President Gorbachev later strove to distance himself a little from the Party; but how did this accord with the role of the general secretary of the Central Committee, obliged to carry out the Party line?[7]

---

[7]Gorbachev resigned from the post of general secretary in September 1991, after the coup, then resigned from the Soviet presidency in December 1991, when the USSR collapsed.—TRANS.

Was this not simply legalization of the situation that existed secretly before, when a single Politburo member, Suslov, could "in the name of the Party" charge the KGB with destroying a burial ground of victims of Stalin's excesses and conceal this decision from Party agencies, while placing all the blame on the Communists?

Is what emerged here not the situation of Pontius Pilate, in which Pilate referred to Pontius, Pontius placed the blame on Pilate, and Jesus in the meantime was taken to Golgotha to be crucified?

We Got Things Done!

At Central Committee Secretariat meetings we discussed a whole range of current issues regarding the country's socioeconomic development. We invited metallurgists, miners, engineers—from ministers to brigade leaders—and we also devoted considerable attention to preparations for upcoming agricultural campaigns. And, of course, each month we monitored strictly the course of sociocultural development.

In 1990, the volume of housing, school, and clinic construction dropped sharply. Millions of people did not receive promised and long-awaited apartments and other public facilities. The picture had been very different in the years 1985 to 1988, when there was an unprecedented growth in social, consumer, and cultural construction. Never before had so many residential buildings, hospitals, clinics, and school buildings been constructed in our country. Statistics confirmed this, and people felt it.

What happened? Why, after the rapid growth in the first years of perestroika, was there an obvious drop in the level of sociocultural and consumer services? Sad to say, there is no end in sight to this decline. Moreover, we may assume that the quality of life of the Soviet people will grow worse. What happened?

Constant monitoring undoubtedly had a great influence on fulfilling and overfulfilling the plan for housing construction. However, monitoring is, after all, only one of the linchpins of state social policy.

Without going into the essence of the fundamental economic innovations of recent years, I will only say that however much we are told about the need to break up the previous system as soon as possible and make the transition to a planned-regulated market (in principle, I agree with this), we should not have been so hasty in removing controls in the social sphere. Until the new economic conditions were created, this sphere should have remained under centralized control so as not to permit acute deterioration in the living conditions of working people. For, as could have been expected, the sharp decline in the volume of state orders and the transition to contractual ties struck social services first of all. As a result, the economic innovations were felt most painfully in the housing and consumer spheres.

Experiments in these vital areas are unacceptable, and controlled development should have been used to compensate for weakness in the new economic controls. Only as the overall economic situation began to improve should we have made a gradual transition to a planned market in housing construction.

The fundamental issue here is the division of jurisdiction between central and republic agencies. In stormy debates, it soon became obvious that the center was insisting on the need to concentrate in its hands control over such extremely important branches of the economy as the extraction of oil, natural gas, and coal, rail transportation, communication, etc. This clearly is a correct course, guaranteeing the prosperity of the country as a whole. And yet, social services, which in my opinion should have been left under the authority of the center, were dropped unjustifiably from state priorities. It is not a question of planning what, where, and how to build from Moscow. It is a matter of the maximum delivery of resources to social services, and of accountability.

Such an approach would have left working people very much the winners. The mood in the nation would have been different from today's, with social programs sharply reduced and essentially left to their own devices.

My thoughts keep turning to the enormous improvements in social services in the first years of perestroika. Did we have to be so hasty in sacrificing a matter well in hand to new economic—or, more accurately, political—principles? To jeopardize the living conditions of millions of people? I understand that my point will provide grounds to accuse me of a desire to preserve old authoritarian methods of leadership. But if one approaches this issue without prejudice, it becomes clear that in this case, my doubts again relate not to the overall strategy but to tactics.

I am a staunch opponent of "great leaps," including those in the area of economic reforms. To be well grounded and gradual is a major assurance of success. Such an approach in no way implies that the introduction of innovations has to be dragged out. A gradual approach means not a lengthy process, but an orderly, carefully conceived sequence of changes, in sharp contradistinction to both the new "ideological assault" in which everything is to be destroyed for the sake of market principles, and economic romanticism, which fails to take the realities of life into account.

As the saying goes, "Haste makes waste." I am sure that if we had moved ahead gradually—in the above sense—we would have progressed much farther along the road of reform. And we would not have neglected such an important sector as social services.

All in all, when my thoughts return to the first years of perestroika, I recall with pleasure the difficult, but invigorating issues and problems society lived for at that time. The heart rejoiced that the time had come to solve these problems, now that we had discarded the dogmatism of the past.

For example there was the problem of Lake Baikal. My interest in ecology dates back to my time in Siberia. It started with the cedar—the true pearl of the Siberian taiga. This amazing conifer is not only quite beautiful in the decorative sense, its cone is both delicious and extremely useful for medical purposes. But economic planners saw the cedar simply as just another vigorous trunk and felled them in huge numbers, fulfilling their plans easily. Tomsk was responsible for supplying all the country's pencil factories with timber, but the selection of criteria for pencil manufacturing was very stringent, and only a minute amount of the cedar went to pencils. Most of it was used for boards, rail ties, and, strange as it may seem, for ordinary packaging. The Ministry of Timber Industry's insistence on harvesting the cedar forests threatened to lead to their extinction.

This fact disquieted many. A solution had to be found to save the cedar. On one of my trips to Moscow, I gave Brezhnev a report about scientific and public concern in Tomsk about the progressive disappearance of cedar groves. We proposed ways of saving Siberian cedar and using it more efficiently. The first secretary imposed an unusual resolution: "A disgrace. The report from the Tomsk Province Committee must be examined. Guilty parties must be sought out and made answerable."

Active work began. Over the opposition of the Ministry of Timber Industry, a government decree was adopted concerning the rational utilization of cedar and cedar groves. Felling was stopped, and a cedar-farm complex was established. Alas, the measures were not fully carried out, and passions on the subject of cedar forests continue to run high even today. It's not a simple problem to balance the need for this timber with the danger of the cedar's disappearance.

Our family has a respectful, even passionate relationship to our beloved cedar. When we came to Moscow from Tomsk, my son, Alexander, and grandson, Alexei, planted several Siberian cedar saplings outside Moscow. A cedar's intensive seed-bearing begins in 120 to 150 years. The trees are still growing—envoys to future generations.

To return to Lake Baikal, it, too, is a pearl of Siberia. The writer Valentin Rasputin had long fought to save this unique Siberian body of water. But the issue kept drowning in bureaucratic red tape and departmental selfishness. In 1985, when it became clear that the new political leadership intended to heed public opinion, Rasputin turned again to the Central Committee and passed on to me a detailed report on Lake Baikal.

A long-time reader of Rasputin, I owe him special gratitude for his description of the wooden architecture of Tomsk. The old Tomsk wooden lacework, hewn by the axes of our grandfathers and great-grandfathers, is one of the great sights of Siberia, testimony to our ancestors' advanced national culture. Unfortunately, the decades and centuries had left their mark on the wooden architecture, and some unique edifices had become dilapidated. So we in Tomsk created a special new organization to start a thorough restoration of the old buildings. The effort moved ahead well, and a good word from such a master as Valentin Rasputin was a true reward for our residents.

After reading Rasputin's report on Lake Baikal, I invited him over and listened carefully to what he had to say. I then consulted with various academicians and resolved to raise this issue at the Central Committee Secretariat. Gorbachev gave his support, and the Lake Baikal problem soon was reviewed. Advocates of Baikal—many of whom were present and spoke at that meeting—were the first to get professional support from the highest political leadership. Among them, of course, was Rasputin. The issue was clear: to shut down and retool the Baikal cellulose and paper industrial complex. The foresters and paper manufacturers objected and voiced their problems. But reason and emotion were indisputedly on the side of Baikal's defenders. The two sides agreed to start working seriously on retooling the industrial complex.

We met a few more times in the Central Committee after that. Rasputin kept a close eye on the resolution of the Baikal problem and regularly contributed to the press. Irkutsk and Buriat organizations seized the issue. The deadlock appeared to be broken at last, and future success seemed assured. But it has now been a long time, it seems to me, a very long time indeed, since anyone has mentioned Lake Baikal. Society is overwhelmed with political squabbles, a fierce battle for power is being waged, and even Rasputin now has no time for Lake Baikal, although one can imagine how his heart aches for it. The decisions we made back in 1985, whose implementation we closely controlled up to 1989, in effect have been shelved.

There is no time for them. There is no time for Lake Baikal. The most important thing is for our country to survive.

What happened to all of us? Why did we leap hastily from solving the concrete problems troubling society—be they housing construction or saving Lake Baikal—to shaking the foundations, only to find ourselves at the edge of a precipice? Who changed the original political idea of perestroika? Why?

Here I cannot help but recall the stormy debates about Tolstoy's Yasnaya Polyana. After reading several quite contradictory articles in the press, I understood that the historical estate was ecologically threatened and in danger of falling into neglect. Various organizations were charged with looking into the situation: the residents of Tula themselves, the Central Committee Cultural Division, and the Ministries of Culture of the USSR and the RSFSR. At my initiative, the issue of Yasnaya Polyana was discussed several times in the Central Committee. Major decisions were made to preserve the old house and the wooded garden and to build a new modern tourist complex next to it.

But the greatest trouble was caused by the ecological situation around Yasnaya Polyana. Next to the estate, just behind the fence, was a heavily traveled highway. Furthermore, a new route was planned nearby from Moscow to the south. The military, who had planned this part of the highway, protested its rerouting. At the Central Committee we insisted that the new route be moved ten kilometers away from Yasnaya Polyana, which diminished noticeably the ecological threat. Even the Ministry of Defense yielded to the demands of the environmentalists.

That is how we started. I write about this as a reminder of the emotional *esprit* that reigned in our society after April 1985, when we started "humanizing" the economy, altering it to address the spiritual and daily needs of the people.

Most of the polluting factories around Yasnaya Polyana have been closed, including the large chemical fertilizer factory at the Shchekin industrial complex. The thermal stations have been converted to natural gas. Such an approach was a rarity in those days. Departments objected desperately, and the Russian Council of Ministers dragged its heels and made only desultory efforts to preserve Tolstoy's estate. I will not conceal that I had to pressure the Central Committee repeatedly until the general plan for the renovation of Yasnaya Polyana was finally confirmed.

What could be done at once—normalize the ecological situation, limit construction in the vicinity of the museum and nature preserve—was implemented. But after 1988, this issue also receded and was no longer mentioned. Reconstruction has stopped. Why are none of the Russian parliamentarians concerned about the fate of Tolstoy's estate? Yasnaya Polyana is Russia's national pride. All the energy and ardor are going into political squabbles. But concrete deeds need to be attended to as well.

The Party-government system of management undoubtedly must be changed, government functions given to the soviets. But surely this process itself did not have to be a revolutionary crash effort. The mass media—in this case, on orders from Gorbachev himself—had perpetuated the myth that the Party apparat was seizing administrative and economic functions, and we therefore had to take decisive action to wrest power from it. But let us recall that the question of dividing Party and economic functions had been raised much earlier, immediately after the war, and then revisited in the 1960s and 1970s.

It was the proper move. If the Party had transferred management gradually to the soviets, many of our current shocks could have been avoided. But instead of a calm, considered transfer of functions of power from the Party apparat to the soviets, this process became a power struggle—or rather, a squabble. The Party did not pass on any economic functions to anyone; it was simply denied participation in settling extremely important general state matters. Here, too, a restructuring of the management system was replaced by a "leap." The general secretary was criticized more than once for this at Central Committee plenums. Later, when disorder was rampant, when it had become clear that the soviets were not yet ready to take on the full load of power, Gorbachev returned to what he had prematurely rejected, reminding Party committees to intensify their influence on the economy.

There was no disagreement within the Party leadership after 1985 that the Party-government system of management had to be changed, that it had outlived itself. A careful political course was outlined to expand the independence of enterprises and local agencies, and implementation was begun. Of course, these were only the first steps; there was an enormous amount of work to be done, requiring an extended period of time. Management and economic functions had to be transferred systematically to the soviets. Everything should have begun with strengthening the material base and the authority of the soviets. Instead, the opposite was done. Although the soviets were still helpless and inexperienced, the Party was forced to release the reins of government. The result was anarchy. And it later became clear that behind all this was a long-range political maneuver—the creation of opposition parties.

Many of us came from villages. Let us recall how a peasant gathers his resources and his strength and plans a new, spacious house. He continues living in the old house as he proceeds with this complex task. Only later, when everything is ready, does he tear down the old building. We behaved differently: without having created anything new, we hastened to destroy the old. And where were we to live? I am convinced that as the new political system was emerging, the Party committees should not have been cut off from governance, but should have at least been allowed to give some backing to the soviets. Not to replace them, of course; quite the opposite, to help them. In Belgorod Province, for example, Party agencies and soviets were working harmoniously to solve common problems, and things were going well. The local Party first secretary, Alexei Ponomarev, was elected chairman of the local soviet and ended up being given the title Hero of Socialist Labor, a rare occurrence in the years of perestroika.

Where the soviets and Party committees clashed, however, the economy deteriorated. That was just what the "democrats" wanted. Later, they were to call for another demolition, saying that the soviets were inept and demanding that they be replaced with governors.

At this stage of perestroika, how could we disregard the Party committees' great experience in resolving vital problems?

Take the Central Committee's cultural activity, which in my opinion is of considerable interest as an illustration of the relationship that developed after April 1985 between the Party and the intelligentsia.

I had occasion to become well acquainted with the scientific intelligentsia and prominent Soviet academicians during my years in Akademgorodok and Tomsk. I also developed friendly ties with many cultural activists. Between 1954 and 1961 I was deputy chairman of the Novosibirsk Province Executive Committee on Cultural Issues and secretary of the Province Committee on Ideology. It was the splendid time of the "Khrushchev thaw," when restraints disappeared and the initiative of the masses was awakened by the 20th Party Congress. Culturally, Novosibirsk was being transformed before our very eyes: a conservatory, operetta theater, drama and choreography schools, and an art gallery were opened. The famous Siberian National Choir, directed by the composer Valentin Levashov, was finally registered permanently in its own building. It was truly a cultural explosion. Outside Novosibirsk, an academic center was gaining strength. This is, after all, also an important educational environment.

I was besieged by representatives of various branches of the arts, who demanded attention, aid, and support. I remember that the music community displayed particularly great persistence. Even then, Novosibirsk could be considered a city with high musical culture and a vast number of classical music lovers. But it had no conservatory, and building such a complex structure was not possible at that time.

The idea was born to renovate the old, classical-style Siberian Fur Exchange building, where auctions had once been held, and which was at that time occupied by about twenty offices. Certainly, it wasn't an easy task to move them and find new accommodations, but doing so depended solely on the persistence of the Executive Committee, and here we could manage. Obtaining a decision about opening the conservatory was much more difficult. As it turned out, the issue had to be decided not just in Moscow but also at the highest level.

To make a long story short, it became clear after several fruitless efforts that the Novosibirsk conservatory had to be pushed through directly past Nikolai Bulganin.

It was in this connection that I got to meet the then chairman of the USSR Council of Ministers. Compared to large state affairs, our request was insignificant. But its resolution clearly manifested both the character of Bulganin himself, a military man who thought on an expansive scale, and, perhaps, the very governmental style of those years, when the "science" of scrupulously noting down everything from "a" to "z" had not yet taken hold at the top, and issues were approached on the grand scale, in their totality as befit the top leadership.

After listening attentively to me and S. V. Zilmanov, the director of the Novosibirsk opera and ballet theater, Bulganin called the secretary and ordered him to prepare a positive resolution. This resolution consisted of a single item, which Bulganin dictated himself: "A conservatory must be opened in Novosibirsk." That was it. Then Bulganin turned to us and said: "When, how, and how much money is needed for this is not my business. That will be handled by the comrades in the Art Committee. You work with them."

When I went to the Art Committee the next day, the resolution was already in the works. We discussed exhaustively everything connected with setting up the governing body of the conservatory and the renovation of the old building. But the main thing was that we managed to insist on their approaching the issue comprehensively including construction of apartments for the professors and teachers of the conservatory. Frankly speaking, this point was one of the most important for me, because it laid the groundwork for the future Novosibirsk Academy of Music.

These hopes were fully vindicated. Thanks to the apartments, professors from Moscow, Leningrad, Lvov, and other cities came to Novosibirsk. A creative teaching collective was quickly formed, and today the Novosibirsk Academy of Music is known in our country and abroad.

My connections with the artistic intelligentsia became even stronger during my years in Tomsk. In 1966, we began an annual "Northern Lights" festival, to which we invited the country's leading performers. One of our residents of Tomsk joked: "I don't know about other countries, but our 'export' performers tour Tomsk perhaps more often than Moscow."

We had only our hospitality to offer these performers; everything was decided by personal contacts. I myself more than once called prominent artistic and cultural figures in Moscow and invited them to Tomsk. And they came, because they knew and valued highly the grateful Siberian audience.

When I was transferred to work in the capital in 1983, I was at first not officially connected with culture. But on a personal level, my friendship with the creative intelligentsia grew even stronger. During those years, continuing the tradition of my student years, I attended the capital's theaters often. I became familiar with the entire repertoire of the Bolshoi, of course, from *Swan Lake* to *The Tale of the Town of Kitezh*; I attended the Plisetskaya, Maksimova, Vasilyev, and the memorable Ulanova anniversary galas. Even after I became a member of the Politburo, I attended the Bolshoi Theater unofficially, as a regular spectator. I didn't rush backstage after the performance to shake the artist's hand "in the name of the Central Committee and the Politburo": I needed the theater as a contact with true art for its own sake, as a spiritual joy. I also visited Tatyana Doronina at the Moscow Art Theater, the Vakhtangov Theater, and the Sovremennik. But perhaps most often, I attended symphony concerts at the Bolshoi Hall of the Moscow Conservatory, particularly when Yevgeny Svetlanov or Vladimir Fedoseyev was conducting. Orchestral music is my old love from my Novosibirsk days. To tell the truth, from about the end of 1988, I more or less stopped going to the conservatory. I wasn't in the mood to give myself over fully to the power of music. Now I have started going to symphonic concerts again, meeting my good conservatory friends, and immersing myself in the inspiring musical environment.

My old, not at all official, purely spiritual ties with the artistic intelligentsia prompted me, after 1985, to turn serious attention to questions of the development of culture.

At Central Committee sessions we examined questions of concern to the creative intelligentsia, and first of all the need for accelerated funding of the arts, for which large sums were allocated. Strange as it may seem, a particularly bad situation was discovered in Moscow. For all its enormous spiritual reserves, the majority of its theaters, concert halls, and museums were in precarious condition.

At the Central Committee we gathered executives from the construction ministries, the Moscow City Council, and prominent cultural figures, and put the question point blank: What needed to be done to revive the capital's cultural base in the shortest possible time?

It wasn't just an exercise on paper. A group of officials set out one day on a rickety old bus sent at my request from the All-Russian Theatrical Association. We invited builders, directors, and leading actors to join us, and set off to examine the Moscow theaters. We spent two days driving around the city, becoming familiar to the point of tears with theatrical management. But it gave us a full picture, and made clear how we ought to proceed. The decision was made to renovate the Bolshoi Hall of the conservatory. We also agreed that the Maly Theater building and the Moscow Art Theater building on Moskvin Street required basic renovation. The City Party Committee and the City Executive Committee then adopted a decree on renovating the buildings of the entertainment institutions. The Central Committee Secretariat supported this plan; in those days, that meant that Union agencies would be involved in its implementation.

The same was done with the management of museums. I was in the Pushkin Museum twice with builders and designers. At the request of its director, we managed to convince the Council of Ministers to give the museum the adjoining building. We kept a close eye on the Tretyakov Gallery, accelerating its renovation. All in all, we managed to get things done. Cultural renovation picked up speed, and other issues were addressed as well. Funds for building village clubs were increased threefold, a program for erecting concert halls in the country's large cities was implemented, and oversight over the progress of the construction and renovation of sanatoria for people in the arts was established.

But things have almost come to a halt here, too. No one has time for Lake Baikal; for the renovation of museums and theaters; for actors' rest homes.

I recall a memorable conversation at one of the Politburo sessions when I was already involved in agricultural policy. Naturally, I started insisting that more resources and funds be allocated to the countryside. Ryzhkov responded:

"When Ligachev was involved with culture, we put a lot of funds into this area at his insistence. Now he's demanding the same for agriculture. Let's do this, Yegor Kuzmich: we'll take from culture and give to the countryside . . ."

But I objected strenuously: "No! That won't do. We can't do culture out of its fair share."

But alas, the times and the ever-worsening economic situation have led to the rapid impoverishment of culture.

Not long ago, when I had occasion to drive along Moskvin Street, I was grieved to see the building of the Moscow Art Theater in a state of extreme neglect. Renovation was supposed to have begun. The poster boards were torn off the facades and the windows were boarded up from the inside—and that's how it was left. The construction work stopped a good while ago, and no one knows when it will be resumed. The beautiful, unusual building of the former Korsh Theater, which used to adorn Moscow, now stands orphaned and deserted, a symbol of the current attitude toward the needs of culture. In the center of the capital a number of old buildings have been renovated and converted into modern offices for various joint-venture enterprises and foreign firms. But alas, there is almost no money for culture.

To a large degree, theaters, museums, and music groups, once deprived of state support, are now placing their hopes on patrons, both domestic and foreign.

It goes without saying that individual outstanding actors, artists, and musicians in the West are materially better provided for than in our country. But taking culture as a whole, Westerners were always very envious of the large Soviet state subsidies and the stability of the living and working conditions of our cultural figures.

Our cultural figures—and this is no reproof—have become accustomed to depending on state support, and are not well aware of the extremely cruel market conditions under which their Western colleagues have to work. And whatever they may say, whatever examples of limitations and suppression of creativity they may give, I am convinced that generous state support is very beneficial for the development of true art. Hence, after April 1985 I took the following course: get rid of the former suppressions, prohibitions, and limitations and increase funding for the arts.

Was this a bad course to take?

And these were not just words, not appeals, not wishful promises. The reality of this course was felt indeed by cultural figures in 1985–88.

But what have we come to now by discrediting the Party, by pushing it away from power, by striving to tear down the socialist state? To a furious commercialization of culture in which inferiority and artistic tastelessness undoubtedly get the upper hand and in which true art is forced into a destitute existence, daily asking for charity. The Moscow virtuosi have already left to take up residence abroad. Who will be next? Won't the present situation lead to an irreplaceable loss of domestic talent and resulting spiritual impoverishment?

No, this isn't what we were striving for in the first years of perestroika. Nor is it where the Party was leading. The bitter fruit that our great but abandoned and increasingly impoverished culture is now reaping is the result of the political recklessness of the radicals who have appropriated the right to decide the country's fate— whose numbers, it is a shame to say, include some of our artistic figures.

Scarcely a day goes by without the papers carrying news of the progressive impoverishment of culture, but one hears almost nothing about improvements. Things were different in the first years of perestroika. The artistic intelligentsia turned to the Central Committee, and they found help there. They remember this.

In 1987, for example, Igor Moiseyev came to see us. His renowned dance company had essentially no rehearsal space, and Moiseyev was asking for the use of the whole Tchaikovsky Hall on Mayakovsky Square in Moscow. Moiseyev told us an anecdote about the time he went to Bulganin, then chairman of the USSR Council of Ministers, with a request to lower the retirement age of ballet dancers. Bulganin asked, "Up to what age can a ballerina dance? Forty? Fifty?"

"She can even dance until she's sixty, but it's difficult to watch such dancing."

We laughed, Moiseyev told us a few more stories about ballet life, and we helped settle the matter that Igor had raised and improve his dancers' working conditions.

The artist Ilya Glazunov also approached me on several occasions. At his suggestion, we helped found the Russian Academy of Art. The Council of Ministers adopted a resolution assigning it the building on Kirov Street where a renowned art school, the Higher State Art and Technical Studios, had once been located. This all made perfect sense. The resolution was made public, but the various organizations occupying the building did not want to vacate it. Glazunov fought with them, to no avail. He turned to us again for help.

What could be done? Of course it is not the concern of a Central Committee secretary, a member of the Politburo, "personally" to drive people out of offices they had occupied in the center of Moscow. But art requires sacrifices. Moreover, the matter was complicated by the fact that subdepartments of three Union ministries had settled down in the same building, a monument of architecture where artists had once worked. Glazunov would not have been able to cope with them alone, of course.

Finally, I had to go myself. Just to be sure, I had invited the ministers whose workers continued to occupy the building, which already belonged officially to the Academy of Art. On the surface, the conversation was jocular, with laughter and humor:

"Make way for art! Get out!"

In fact, it was not so simple. It is perhaps harder to evict professional people from the center of Moscow than to build them a new building. I will honestly say that I was well served by the experience I had acquired in Novosibirsk, when I practically had to storm the Siberian Fur Exchange building to free it for the conservatory.

I never walked away from personal requests by artistic and literary figures, including instances when it was a question of establishing living and working conditions. How could I? These were world-famous people, after all. They are constantly busy on tours, many of them are very vulnerable and not equipped to deal with issues of everyday life. If I may put it openly and a little bluntly, I have always subscribed to the principle that talent should be helped along in every way possible, while an energetic but talentless person will forge his own path.

The well-known artists, musicians, writers, and actors with whom I met as a Politburo member didn't always come to me with concrete requests; often they simply needed to exchange opinions, discuss an idea. The mood during those years was open, truly creative; everyone was inspired with hopes, and initiative flowed. I will note that when the wave of slander against me was let loose, not a single truly respected actor, artist, scholar, writer, or musician said a single word against me.

I realize that many very worthy and talented artistic and literary figures today are experiencing spiritual confusion. These are people of strong spirit; in spite of all the uncertainty of the times, they remain occupied with creative work. But not everyone has the strength to hold his or her ground in troubled times. Many, inspired by the boldly and successfully initiated perestroika, were naively carried away with radical political phraseology. Once the populist fog started to disperse, it became clearer that our ship was headed for the dangerous reefs of dictatorship, where dissent is unacceptable. There were calls for anticonstitutional actions; lawlessness abounds. Under the banner of anti-Communism, alas, we are being led back to what we'd left behind.

At this new sharp turn in our country's history, the fateful question rises once again to confront the creative intelligentsia, the conscience of the nation: "With whom do you stand, masters of culture?"

Seven

WITCH HUNT

The Rift

By the fall of 1987, the tendency toward distortion and slander of Soviet history in the radical press was well defined.

To better understand the complex past was one of the most important conditions for the process of renewal begun in April 1985. Too many blank spots had accumulated in our history. The 20th Party Congress, which had exposed Stalin's personality cult, undoubtedly shook the public and caused a sharp turnaround in public awareness. But the "Khrushchev thaw" did not last long, and the political leaders of that period, in my view, were still psychologically unprepared to tell the people the full truth.

We still had to fling open the door to our past so that the life's work of the nation's fathers, grandfathers, and great-grandfathers would stand before its eyes in all its limitless sweep and heroism, tragedy as well as greatness.

We took up this task immediately back in 1985. If you look at the newspaper and magazine files of those times, it is easy to see how quickly the press began to be filled with articles with a historical bent. At the same time, scholars and journalists invaded ever more boldly the so-called forbidden topics of the 1930s. Heightened interest in these events was understandable, justified, and completely natural.

To move forward successfully, society had to go through a process of self-cleansing and rethinking much of what had happened in the past. Gradually but very noticeably, censorship limitations started weakening. The explosion of interest in the fates of Bukharin, Tukhachevsky,[1] and other victimized political and military activists, scholars, and writers is still a vivid memory. At first this striving to restore historical justice was salutary: it emancipated people's minds, liberated them from a feeling of fear, and generated initiative.

But gradually the tone of historical publications began to change. Initially it was our task to analyze what had happened and to create the legal mechanisms that would forever eliminate the possibility of a repetition of such persecution. The mistakes of the past were written about with pain and deep feeling. Such an approach, dictated by concern for learning from the past, could only be welcomed. But later, the stress shifted and some writers started talking about past lawlessness caustically, gloatingly; with castigation rather than healing, not for the edification of our posterity and contemporaries but narrow-mindedly relishing the misfortunes that had befallen earlier generations. In so doing, they were leading the readers to a single conclusion: the social system was guilty of everything, and therefore had to be changed.

The cresting flood of denunciatory articles engulfing the mass media began to deform the historical retrospective. The past rose up from the pages of the right-wing radical press not as a diverse and contradictory combination of achievements and errors but in exclusively gloomy if not pitch-black tones. Judging from these publications, there was nothing good in the past; our fathers and

---

[1]Nikolai Bukharin (1887–1938) was a Bolshevik leader executed in Stalin's purges. Mikhail Tukhachevsky (1893–1937), marshal and first deputy defense minister, was accused of treason during World War II and also executed.—Trans.

grandfathers had passed their time on this earth in senseless suffering, mired in travail.

This unfair and slanderous bias did not correspond to the truth; it disturbed and agitated the social atmosphere. And it was directed at Communists, the Party, against the history of the Party (I repeat: a difficult but glorious history), and in the final analysis against the nation, against its historical memory. In this context, how can one not recall Dostoevsky, who had said that we need self-respect, not self-abasement?

There was another deviation from historical truth: one of the sad legacies of the past was the treatment of history itself. The chronology of this great country began primarily with 1917, giving scant attention to the thousand-year path it had traveled before. This was manifest most clearly in the postwar period: everything was, so to speak, "ancestry unknown." But the growth of national self-awareness that began in the period of perestroika gave rise very naturally to an interest in our ancestors' history and culture. This process, which I saw as beneficial, could be observed in all the republics, including the Russian Federation. But there were those who made an exception for Russia and did not approve of its thirst for rebirth.

The counterreaction actually began in 1972, with Alexander Yakovlev's article "On Antihistoricism," which created a sensation. In it, he spoke sharply against the awakening of Russian self-awareness, unjustly labeling it "patriarchal mentality, nationalism, and chauvinism." This line was clearly continued during perestroika, when Yakovlev returned to the Central Committee and once again headed the Propaganda Department. Moreover, in an interview he gave in the academic newspaper *Poisk* [*Inquiry*], he announced that he was still prepared to subscribe to every word in his article of 1972, even today.

The radicals' goal here was to break down society, undermine patriotism, and deprive people of a feeling of pride in their Motherland. The confusion that arose in society, as it destroyed the nations' historical memory (and at the same time, its moral foundations) was the necessary precondition for the large-scale manipulation of mass consciousness that began, aided by the right-wing radical press, in spring 1988.

And there was another, not unimportant, cause movitating the radicals to distort and slander our history: they were sacrificing the past so as to return onto the political stage as heroes.

The newly emerged "foremen" hastily appropriated the noble rights of fighters against the consequences of Stalin's personality cult and set about smashing one thing after another in our history. It was not a thoughtful, serious analysis of our contradictory history that concerned them but primarily their own political image of "fighters against Stalinism." There was an important confirmation of such intentions in the fact that the "foremen" referred far too rarely to the 20th Party Congress, which had exposed the personality cult. They preferred to forget about it as they attempted to give credit for the battle against Stalinist excesses to themselves alone.

Many representatives of the mass media took to this task in a sensationalist style. Naturally, they did not trouble themselves with serious scholarly research, scrupulous verification, or checking of facts. Decades will be insufficient to plow through the piles of historical articles and get to the essence, the truth.

It is a source of bitterness and pain that certain professional historians revamped themselves into newspaper and magazine publicists and started writing in this same vein. With no serious scholarly authority and little known in scholarly circles, they rushed to acquire popularity as civic activists, rushing headlong to crush everything that had been sacred in the past. (Perhaps the most vivid example here is the historian Yuri Afanasev.) They acted like beasts of prey tearing our society to shreds, destroying the historical memory of the nation, spitting upon such sacred concepts as patriotism, and discrediting the feeling of pride in our Motherland.

There was something of a congruence of interests between these ambitious ravages and certain outside forces striving to weaken our state and bring down our social system, and, on a larger scale, to lower our great state to the status of a second-rate country. But the so-called foremen earned the dubious distinction of being more successful than any foreign enemy in the entire history of the Soviet regime in the pernicious deed of undermining the foundations of society, of perverting the historical past.

A nation deprived of its historical memory is a nation of slaves. Even during Stalinist times, the rulers were not able (nor did they try) to destroy the people's feeling of pride in their great state. In fact, they did everything they could to cultivate this feeling (in their own way, to be sure). Thus it is not surprising that the flood of slander disgorged by the pages of the radical press provoked the indignation of millions of people. Tens of thousands of angry letters poured in to newspapers, magazines, and the Central Committee. The nation did not want its history, its Motherland, to be spat upon. In spite of many tragic pages, the nation continued to believe in the greatness of its Fatherland. The protest against spiritual pauperization came from all sides. The patriotic heart of the Soviet people was deeply wounded.

This was what people talked about during my many business trips across the country. I understood that what was going on was wrong. The slandering of our history deformed the original idea of the policy of perestroika, depriving it of historical continuity. This when it was crucial in overcoming the difficulties of the perestroika period to be able to lean on our people's glorious history, our citizens' feeling of pride (as it had been before, during the years of trial that befell the Soviet Union, just recall the harsh times of the Great Patriotic War). The patriotism of the nation unquestionably could be counted among the driving forces of perestroika.

This was our starting point. What had we reached by mid-1987? Only contention, artificially introduced into society, purporting to be a battle with those allegedly acting against perestroika. Only an oppressive "brain washing" by publications that did nothing but vilify, spitting upon patriotism and internationalism.

In the meantime, the decision was made at the Politburo to hold a Central Committee plenum devoted to problems of public education. Unofficially, by prior verbal agreement, Gorbachev had suggested that I give a report at the plenum. This was an important assignment, and I gradually got to work on it.

We made a thorough study of the situation in the schools and institutions of higher learning, looking at what had been actually achieved in this area after the 1984 Central Committee plenum, and what had remained only on paper. Obviously, the processes of democratization were changing the very approaches to childrearing, education, and training. But it was clear to me that in addition to all this, it was essential to include in the report the problem that I formulated as the "problem of the slander of history." It was most directly and immediately related to the upbringing of younger generations.

The plenum was still some time off. The Moscow Province Party Committee had invited me to appear at a meeting of pedagogical activists in the city of Elektrostal in connection with the upcoming Teachers' Day, and I decided to take advantage of this opportunity to talk about our treatment of history.

Every politician experiences moments when he feels a strong need to speak publicly on some important topic. And he looks for an opportunity to do so. The appearance before a pedagogical audience was in my view an extremely appropriate occasion to touch upon the topic of history. And I did so intentionally, knowing my speech undoubtedly would provoke a mixed reaction.

But I could not have predicted the course of events that followed.

I dealt briefly with the topic of history in the Elektrostal speech, intending to expand on this in my report at the Central Committee plenum. But since this speech became the starting point of all later attacks on me, since after this speech a rift appeared in my relations with Gorbachev, it may be appropriate to cite the main historical thesis of the speech. So I quote:

> Much is said these days about the personality cult. It is very important to understand the causes of this phenomenon and particularly to create conditions under which a similar occurrence would be impossible. This is our sacred duty, our obligation. The Party and the nation are now occupied with this task, the crux of which is the process of democratizing the life of society.
>
> But it is impossible not to see something else. There are

those abroad—and certain people in our own country—who are trying to discredit the entire path of the building of socialism in the USSR, to present it as a chain of nothing but errors, to disguise the nations's feat of heroism, which created a powerful socialist state, with the facts of unfounded persecution. . . . Those who were in power at the time should answer for the lawlessness committed in the 1930s. We should proceed from this, to tell our young people about the heroic history of the Party and the country responsibly and competently, as they say, to cherish the truth.

That, essentially, is all. I also allowed myself to say a few words about how I had worked in Siberia:

At that time I lived and worked in Tomsk and Novosibirsk provinces. And if I were to be asked how I feel about that time, I would answer as follows: This was an unforgettable time, a truly great life. There were many difficult days, but not one was a burden. In the expanses of western Siberia, the efforts of the entire country at that time were building a powerful Soviet science center, a world-class petroleum and gas works. . . . But this is one side of the coin. Along with positive changes, negative phenomena were growing in the country, the pace of development of the extensive economy was slowed down, abuse of power became widespread. . . . All of this taken together constitutes the real truth, the dialectical understanding of the essence of the time.

Today I continue to insist on such a measured treatment of history. This truly dialectical approach allows for the full consideration of lessons drawn from the past, neither embellishing history nor turning it into a garbage heap.

Gorbachev was on vacation at that time. I communicated with him by telephone twice a week, informing him of current affairs. Sometimes he called me. During one of these telephone conversations, he mentioned in passing: "I'm sending you a summary of responses to your speech in Elektrostal."

I believe it was that same day that I received by special messenger via the next scheduled flight from the Crimea several pages translated from various languages. On the first page was Gorbachev's resolution—or rather, not a resolution but a note—to me written in large, bold letters covering almost the entire page.

But first, a few citations from the Russian translation of foreign responses to my speech.

The correspondent for the *Times* of London wrote:

> Yegor Ligachev announced that the reevaluation of the Stalin years that is now taking place in the Soviet Union should not slander the whole history of Russia after 1917. Historical truth lies in the fact, he said, that the Party has condemned the personality cult, has removed the label of "enemy" from thousands of Soviet people, and has restored socialist legality. The tone and content of Ligachev's statements differ from that of the majority of commentaries on social and historical issues now appearing and seem to support the fact that Ligachev has serious doubts about the limits and consequences of the reforms of the Soviet leader.

The correspondent then suddenly made a completely unexpected zigzag:

> His views of Stalin and of the necessity of being proud of Soviet achievements followed an article about the value of patriotism published in *Pravda* last week. A number of letters published in the Soviet press recently also characterize Stalin as a leader in a positive way and show the depth of the opposition to some of the changes that are now taking place in the Soviet Union.

I would very much like to believe that this is far from a typical example of Western journalism, for it is hard to imagine a more subtle mockery of common sense. My views on Stalin were expressed extremely clearly—the reader may verify them on the preceding pages—but the *Times* said pride in Soviet achievements and patriotism along with "a positive characterization of Stalin" and "a depth of opposition to perestroika." What it boiled down to was that I was the leading Stalinist standing in the way of Gorbachev's reforms and dragging the country back into the past.

Further on in the summary of the press that I received from Gorbachev was a Reuters dispatch:

> Ligachev introduced a change in the Kremlin debates on the question of Gorbachev's struggle for glasnost by speaking out in defense of a number of aspects of the government of Leonid Brezhnev, foreign affairs specialists claim. Ligachev gave a strikingly different interpretation of the Brezhnev years compared with the picture of inertia and stagnation that Gorbachev often draws. Specialists claim that Ligachev's speech is a most single-minded attempt by this Soviet statesman to depict the Brezhnev government as a period of successes as well as failures. Higher government officials usually repeat what the Kremlin leader, Gorbachev, says, underscoring the failures.

The correspondent continued:

> In talking about the Brezhnev period, Ligachev stated: "The national income rose fourfold. People's lives became richer both materially and spiritually. A military and strategic parity between the USSR and the USA was acheived." In a paragraph that specialists characterize as unusually emotional, Ligachev described the Brezhnev years, which he spent in Siberian cities, and stated that he does not regret a single day of this work. In January Gorbachev said that Brezhnev's government was marked "by a disdain for law, by deception, by bribery, and by the encouragement of a system of spongers and bootlickers." "Ligachev clearly believes that enough has been said, and that an end should be put to talk of dirt and stagnation. He feels it is necessary to emphasize that, as his own experience testifies, there were excellent people even in the Brezhnev era," said one foreign diplomat.

These commentaries, in turn, require emendation. It is clear that only my positive evaluation of past years was seized on in my speech, although I distinctly and specifically talked not only about pluses but about minuses as well, about a dialectical treatment of history. As Western agencies presented it, Gorbachev criticized stagnation, while Ligachev justified it. Here again, the very essence of my position had been distorted very deliberately to bring me head to head with Gorbachev. Moreover, I was labeled a conservative. Why? Because I had allowed myself to criticize demagogues who were self-servingly using glasnost. But the events that followed, when populism burst into full bloom, showed that I was completely right. And is it reprehensible to wish to put an end to muckraking and go on to constructive work?

But the correspondent for the very respectable Reuters agency, whose reports are reprinted all over the world, characterized my speech to present me as an opponent of change, even in opposition to Gorbachev. I could not shake the impression that someone was trying to cause a falling out between Gorbachev and myself. After all, Gorbachev might well not have read the complete text of my speech, published in the *Teachers' Gazette*. But he would have had to come to some very definite conclusions from reading the Reuters evaluation. The many references to anonymous specialists particularly caught my attention. There was an impression that someone was intentionally feeding a certain point of view to this correspondent of an independent agency. And if we note that it coincided strikingly with other analyses from Moscow, the thought arises of a conductor's baton coordinating the pens of some of the Western journalists accredited in the USSR.

Of course, I can't help remembering the British intelligence operation, code-named "Liote," which was designed to provoke friction in the Soviet leadership.

However, in my opinion, another scenario is more likely: the "specialists" were Soviets from radical circles who were in close contact with foreign correspondents. It is no accident that these evaluations, and only these, were selected from the foreign press and obligingly placed on Gorbachev's desk. And they were taken from only three sources: the *Times* of London, Reuters, and the French *Le Monde*.

The newspaper *Le Monde* came right out and said: "Is this speech [in Elektrostal] not a warning for Gorbachev himself? Ligachev is dissociating himself from at least two points of the 'new outlook,' whose pioneer is Gorbachev." Further on, *Le Monde,* not at all disconcerted by the direct falsification of my speech in Elektrostal, wrote: "While for Gorbachev the 1930s are associated with heavy losses, for Ligachev this period is connected with real successes."

What can one say to this? If all this had to do only with me personally, I could have paid no attention to such a gross juggling of facts. But a sharp turn in the policy of perestroika was being planned; at that time the radicals had already started their battle for power. And these were their methods.

I could immediately see that someone close to Gorbachev had done some very, very good "work" on my speech in Elektrostal. The articles were chosen selectively. The aim of the summary was patently clear—to drive a wedge between Gorbachev and Ligachev. A note written in a bold hand on the first page of the summary also proved that the authors had not worked in vain. The general secretary wrote:

"Yegor Kuzmich! Read this. It relates to our last conversation. So our 'friends' abroad are not happy with the unity of the Soviet leadership. This will then be carried by the 'voices'[2] in Russian. M. Gorbachev."

I certainly knew how to read the subtext of such a note. Obviously Gorbachev had taken at face value the thought suggested by the brief summary of the foreign press put together at the request of someone from his inner circle.

There had been nothing remarkable about the "last conversation" mentioned in the note. I had repeated to Gorbachev my views concerning the "history hysteria" in the press and said that the top

---

[2]That is, the Voice of America and other Western radio stations.—TRANS.

leadership should be united in rebutting the slander; the Soviet people and our foreign friends demanded this. We had many conversations of this sort.

Gorbachev turned out to be right about the radio broadcasts. Soon a fierce propaganda campaign was launched on the airwaves to discredit me. This campaign soon evolved into invented rumors about some "conspiracy" planned in Gorbachev's absence. And so forth, all in the same spirit. I am tired of writing about it.

But I would like to make three more brief remarks in connection with the speech in Elektrostal.

Although they knew how to use this speech to create a rift in the relations between Gorbachev and myself, I felt deeply gratified, because I understood that I had hit the nail on the head. I had clearly and pointedly expressed my position, done my moral and political duty. Of course, I had not thought about the consequences of my decisive action. And with my hand on my heart I can say that with all that has happened to me since, with all the anxiety and the unjust calumny heaped on me, I still have no regrets that I held my ground in Elektrostal and did not accommodate myself to the distortion of the course of perestroika.

And, I must note that there was essentially no difference of opinion between Gorbachev and myself in our evaluation of the historical past. For my part, I was highly critical of Stalin's personality cult and of the abuses of the period of stagnation. However, I felt that the past could not be encompassed only within these boundaries but must be approached dialectically. And Gorbachev, while severely criticizing the errors of the past, at the same time emphasized that not one day had been lived in vain, all generations had contributed their efforts in creating the Fatherland. I could subscribe to these words with a clear conscience.

But Gorbachev's words, although in essence true, remained nothing but words; they were not translated into concrete actions. This was one of the many cases in which the right goals were set but practical work did not correspond to them. Gorbachev's thesis that not one day in our history was lived in vain was never the reference point for the ideological activity of the Party or for the press.

Approached from this position, there were serious differences between Gorbachev and myself.

I should note that Gorbachev at times mentioned his position on an issue in his speeches without fighting to implement it in deed. Furthermore, I never noticed the general secretary exhibit any indignation concerning the perversion of our past. His position even expressed a certain duality. On the one hand, he called for a responsible attitude toward our history; on the other, he himself demonstrated the opposite approach. In particular, speaking before the country's prosecutors, Gorbachev said: "In the past everything was essentially done under the lash; man was alienated from the land, from the means of production, from power—from everything . . . 'appanage princes' ruled in regions, provinces, and districts in spite of all prosecutors and laws."

No doubt, such a general accusation cannot be called fair. Of course, there was no dearth of infractions of legality in our recent past—that is precisely what I had talked about in Elektrostal. There were good people and bad people. But it did not in any way contribute to a correct, measured evaluation of the historical past for the leader of the country and the Party to call all Party officials "appanage princes."

I remember a wonderful speech Gorbachev gave in Kiev about the Party, one that could have become the foundation for the energetic Party activity to renew itself and cleanse its ranks. The general secretary, however, never again mentioned this speech: he spoke, signed off, and forgot. When I reminded him of his Kiev speech and of the fact that its theses should be implemented, Gorbachev changed the subject. There were many such occasions. I got the feeling that this was not inadvertent but rather an element of political tactics—to voice some thesis to placate various social strata and political tendencies, but to carry on a different line in deeds.

Forces in our country and abroad wanted to drive a wedge into the Soviet leadership, to destroy the "link" that had proved so efficient under the difficult circumstances of the Chernenko thirteen months. But to Gorbachev's credit, although a rift had appeared in our relations, he did not retract his intention to give me the right to report to the plenum devoted to problems of public education. After he returned from vacation, I was officially confirmed as a speaker.

However, the confirmation of my report did not go smoothly at the Politburo session. The thoughts on the treatment of history that I had expressed in Elektrostal caused reservations, as expected. But since Gorbachev did not see fit to make any comments on the subject, Yakovlev was forced to disclose his position in full at the Politburo. Yes, it was Yakovlev who disagreed with my call for a measured dialectical approach in evaluating the historical retrospective. He, of course, offered no logical evidence and could not express himself bluntly, openly. So he stalled: "This is not connected with the topic of the plenum. Why drag discussions about history into the report? Is it necessary?"

But I held my ground firmly: "No, I insist. This is a fundamental question and is most directly connected with the education of our young people."

No one else objected. Gorbachev, too, supported me. And my report at the February 1988 Central Committee plenum, in which I spoke out against the distortion and slander of history and against the destruction of the historical memory of the nation, presented my position with extreme precision.

But in the case of the Politburo's decree "On the Progress and Scope of Perestroika," adopted soon after Gorbachev returned from vacation in the fall of 1987, Yakovlev, against my protestations, managed to throw out of the draft criticism of the right-wing radical mass media and the slander of history.

What conclusion can we draw from this? That in the extremely important question of the treatment of history, Gorbachev in one instance supported me, but in another, supported Yakovlev, although our positions were mutually exclusive. Such maneuvering corresponded to his makeup as a politician.

Nina Andreyeva's Letter

Everyone in our country and many abroad probably know about the events that took place in connection with Nina Andreyeva's letter "I Cannot Forsake My Principles," published on 13 March 1988 in the newspaper *Sovetskaya Rossiya*. The letter was called a "manifesto of antiperestroika forces," and the name of its author, a teacher at a Leningrad university, was turned into a synonym for "an enemy of perestroika." I am certain that if ten people on the street are asked whether they remember what was written in that letter, nine, perhaps all ten, would answer in the negative. But everyone has heard of Nina Andreyeva.

This is indeed a phenomenon of the manipulation of mass consciousness: people do not know the essence of the matter but they have been inculcated with a firm stereotype, with the help of which opponents can be labeled without any explanations, elucidations, or arguments. A strange situation has developed. Having exposed the lawlessness of the past, we now know very well that, for example, Bukharin was a wrongfully persecuted honest person, but in the 1930s his name was anathema and served as a symbol of betrayal. But today the radical press, while justly unmasking the methods of Stalinist propaganda, itself acts in the same way.

Moreover, almost everyone has heard that the name of Nina Andreyeva was in some way connected with the name of Ligachev. Exactly how, no one is able to say—but it is connected.

What really happened?

Many rumors were spread concerning the letter "I Cannot Forsake My Principles," including the charge that I personally was said to have ordered it to be published. The time has come to tell the truth about what hid behind the unbelievably sensational propagandistic "anti-Andreyeva" campaign, about what political ends she pursued and who was behind her. The time also has come to find out about the events that took place in the top political leadership in connection with Nina Andreyeva's letter.

The letter—or as they started calling it, the article—was published on 13 March. On 14 March, Gorbachev left for a trip to

Yugoslavia. Immediatly afterward, Yakovlev left for Mongolia. I mention these dates to cut off immediately the absurd and thoroughly malicious rumors to the effect that the publication was especially timed to coincide with the absences of Gorbachev and Yakovlev.

Like all readers, I became familiar with "I Cannot Forsake My Principles" only after it was published on the pages of *Sovetskaya Rossiya*. From what I have said, the reader understands my position regarding the slander of history. I openly stated it at the February 1988 Central Committee plenum, which met with the approval of the members. After my statement was published in the papers, the flood of letters condemning the destructive action of the radical press in carelessly slandering our past grew. Public opinion in the Party and the country was obviously inclined in that direction. And I intended to double and triple my efforts to straighten the "historical line," moving from misguided censure to a serious anaylsis of errors and achievements. At the same time I never stopped reminding people about the great significance of the 20th Party Congress, which exposed Stalin's personality cult, and about the fact that our main task was to protect the Soviet people from a repetition of such persecution.

I familiarized myself with Central Committee mail and also asked for a selection of letters sent to newspapers, including *Sovetskaya Rossiya*. Some publications later claimed that Nina Andreyeva's letter was addressed directly to me and that I purportedly sent it to Valentin Chikin, the editor in chief of *Sovetskaya Rossiya*, with instructions to publish it. There is absolutely no truth to this allegation.

The entire selection given to me, I repeat, consisted of letters condemning slander; they all had much in common, repeating each other on many points, and in sum creating a common, unified background refusing to accept the general mudslinging. This was particularly important for me as a reflection of the frame of mind dominant in the nation.

Later, in the process of investigation, it was discovered that Andreyeva had sent her letter simultaneously to three newspapers—*Pravda*, *Sovetskaya Rossiya*, and *Sovetskaya Kultura*. Moreover, the original version of the letter consisted of thirty typewritten pages—a whole study, a treatise. Such voluminous works with an exposition of various concepts were not uncommon in the Central Committee mail. People who despaired of ever publishing them or defending a dissertation based on them turned to the Central Committee as to the highest office of appeal capable, in their opinion, of restoring justice. But more often than not, these letters were the fruit of purely speculative discourse divorced from life. Members of the Politburo and Central Committee secretaries are in no position to study such voluminous correspondence. It was "assigned" to consultants for careful study and response. I, too, was unable to make a careful study of thirty pages of text. This would, after all, require at least an hour's time, a luxury I did not have.

Rumors to the effect that Nina Andreyeva's letter was published at my instruction, upon my resolution, are a primitive invention (later refuted by Gorbachev himself).[3]

Now a few words about the events that developed after the letter was published.

---

[3]V. Denisov, former staff member of *Sovetskaya Rossiya*, who prepared Nina Andreyeva's letter for publication, described it in the magazine *Rodina* [*Motherland*]. Unfortunately, his story is obviously speculative and sensational, as the title itself testifies: "Backing Perestroika with Stalin." Denisov was simply fantasizing, which is not difficult to determine by checking the facts he cites.

In particular he mentions that the photocopy of Andreyeva's letter was brought to him by Valentin Chikin, the editor in chief, whom I supposedly had called. "Apparently," says Denisov, "the conversation with Ligachev had only just taken place." Several paragraphs later he informs us of one more detail: "The most 'striking' phrases and expressions in Andreyeva's letter were underlined. It is unlikely that Chikin did this before sending it to Ligachev." "Apparently," "it is likely"—these are what fantasies are usually built on.

It is self-evident that if Chikin brought Denisov the letter "right after the telephone conversation" with me, the underlinings in the text of the letter physically could not have been mine. This illustrates the speculative nature of Denisov's constructions and his story's frivolous and tendentious nature (not to mention the careless style). But more interesting, as always happens when something is so grossly strained, Denisov in fact only confirms that I had not given any instructions about publishing Andreyeva's letter.—AUTHOR

I held a meeting with editors on 14 or 15 March, at which we talked about many issues, in particular the participation of the press in propagandist support, the sowing campaign and the development of livestock breeding. I also talked about the situation in Nagorno-Karabakh. In general, such meetings were planned in advance, and Central Committee divisions prepared for them by studying publications, so that the conversation would be to the point. And so it was in this case: the meeting was not at all called as an emergency session; it had been scheduled a week before the publication of Andreyeva's letter.

Naturally, when the planned topics were discussed, I dealt with the question I had raised in Elektrostal and in the report at the Central Committee plenum about the dialectical attitude toward the historical past. It is already clear to the reader that this issue was of a fundamental nature and that a fierce political battle was being waged around it reflecting a difference of opinion at the center of the country's leadership.

Developing the thought of my report at the plenum, I recommended that the editors read "I Cannot Forsake My Principles," published only the day before in *Sovetskaya Rossiya*. What was attractive in this letter was precisely what interested me during that time—the refusal to accept the outright slander, the careless censure of the past—what I had mentioned earlier. Many people noted that Andreyeva's article came as a reaction to the turbid stream of anti-historical, anti-Soviet materials in our press and I am convinced that was the case.

The response to Nina Andreyeva's letter was published on 5 April in *Pravda* and stated that there were some valid points in her letter. Everyone has the right to attach importance to what interests him. I noticed those valid points; while Yakovlev, who supervised the preparation of the response in *Pravda*, accentuated the weak points in Andreyeva's letter. The difference is simply that I expressed my thoughts openly, while Yakovlev hid behind editorial anonymity.

This is very characteristic of the differences in our personalities.

Yes, I did mention Andreyeva's letter at this editorial meeting. I see nothing shameful here. We were talking about our treatment of history, a topic that was acutely polemical at that moment. It was in this context, and this context alone, that I spoke about the article in *Sovetskaya Rossiya*. And I certainly did not give any instructions to have it reprinted everywhere.

But this was enough to open up furious attacks, declaring the letter to be a "manifesto of the antiperestroika forces."

They were not after Nina Andreyeva. They were after Ligachev.

The events did not start immediately after Gorbachev and Yakovlev returned from abroad. Some time apparently was necessary to think through the situation and map out a plan of action. The situation was contradictory and ambiguous. A rift undoubtedly had appeared in relations between Gorbachev and myself. At the same time, I remained second secretary of the Central Committee, and Gorbachev had spoken out in favor of granting me the right to report to the plenum. Moreover, my view was supported at the plenum, my positions strengthened. And the 19th Party Conference was to take place very soon, that summer. It was not difficult to presume that at that conference I would again defend the dialectical view of history and criticize the right-wing radical mass media.

New, obviously deliberately planned actions began. First, rumors about some sort of "conspiracy" ostensibly concocted during Gorbachev's absence began to make the rounds. These rumors were directly linked to Nina Andreyeva's "manifesto" and those who had supported her. There were not only verbal rumors but also items in the press. The radical press at that time circulated the thesis of a growth of opposition to perestroika by the conservatives; they even went so far as to start to label people "enemies of perestroika."

All this was, of course, fabricated, artificial, and false. There was no "conspiracy"; I had no connection with Nina Andreyeva's letter; and the so-called conservatives were in reality true supporters of perestroika who were trying to prevent it from falling into the pernicious trap of radicalism.

The alleged "growth of opposition to perestroika" was not supported by anything except emotional passages in the mass media. A special investigation of public opinion and newspaper and magazine publications on this point concluded that the insidious thesis was unsubstantiated. My files contain a document of the investigation of public opinion on this issue, and it is quite interesting to quote a few examples from it.

On 14 April 1988, *Pravda* wrote: "It must be said that the opponents of perestroika are not only waiting for the moment when it chokes. . . . They are now getting bolder and raising their heads." Again on 18 April, *Pravda* noted: "The full-scale program of open and hidden opponents of perestroika intends the mobilization of conservative forces. . . ." And *Sovetskaya Kultura* put it even more sharply on 16 April: "Has the time not come to remove the quotation marks and call by their own names those who, on the threshold of the 19th All-Union Party Conference, endeavor to unite their forces for a battle against the ideas of the 27th Party Congress and landmark Central Committee plenums? Having regrouped after the shock of the first years after April, the adepts of the 'heavy hand' concept are trying . . . to sow uncertainty within our ranks."

As can be seen, not a single fact, not a single concrete argument. But what a style—utterly in the spirit of 1937, when "open and hidden enemies of the people were raising their heads, becoming bold, endeavoring, and sowing uncertainty."[4]

As for the concept of the "heavy hand," it was the radicals who soon invoked it, although they used the phrase "iron hand." It is also amusing to reread the radicals' defense of the ideas of the 27th Congress—the same radicals who later left the Party and proceeded to attack Communists, accusing those who continued to defend the ideas of the 27th Congress, which set the course for perestroika, of all the mortal sins.

The tone and style of these allegations were set by the 5 April 1988 *Pravda* article in which Yakovlev had a hand. In the best tradition of Suslov's Agitprop, which Yakovlev had headed at one time, a large-scale unsubstantiated campaign was launched to discredit people who were inconvenient to him.

---

[4]"Heavy hand" and "dictatorship" accompany all of the years of perestroika like a scarecrow for the people. How primitive!—AUTHOR

It is also very interesting to cite the conclusion of the above-mentioned investigation:

> Whomever we talk to, everyone shrugs his shoulders at the question about the intensified opposition to perestroika. And certain people express the opinion that whipping up such fears is similar to the thesis of the intensification of the class struggle in proportion with the building of socialism. Indeed, who of the top echelon of the economic administration, for example, is in opposition if in the past three years two-thirds of the government has been renewed, and if we take the past four years, then three-fourths? One can speak of the inability of many cadres to accomplish the tasks of perestroika, to get a firm grasp of the unaccustomed levers of cost accounting, self-financing, and self-management. One can also not fail to take into consideration the process of the dismantling of organizational structures, expectations of personnel cutbacks, etc.— all this, of course, has to a certain extent been reflected in the psychological mood and pragmatism of workers at the center and at the local level and, in the final analysis, in the pace of development. So the causes are perfectly understandable, down to earth. Is it worth speculatively looking for others?

This conclusion was very reasonable and plausible. However, the thesis about the growth of opposition to perestroika continued to be spread—truly in the spirit of the those years of bitter memory. In a word, the true antiperestroika radicals, through the press that served them, constantly imposed an environment of suspicion and uncertainty on society. They got their way: all this influenced Gorbachev. Soon decisive actions were taken.

These began with an unscheduled Politburo session that suddenly convened, not in the Kremlin, but right in Old Square. A single issue was on the agenda: discussion of Nina Andreyeva's letter.

Politburo sessions always took place in a very casual style. Opinions would be exchanged in a relaxed manner, and even when there was disagreement, the general atmosphere remained democratic and free and easy. We truly discussed issues rather than "producing resolutions" dictated by the general secretary. But this time it was different. The mood was very tense and nervous, even oppressive. This was unusual and unexpected.

Another thing was that some Politburo members and Central Committee secretaries, exchanging opinions before the session, made some very positive comments about Nina Andreyeva's letter, noting its dialectical treatment of history. Her letter after all had been placed in the "Polemics" column in the paper, so it expressed only one possible view rather than a categorical directive. Some of those present thought it was good that against the background of general slander, a different voice had been heard; it was a manifestation of glasnost, of democratism.

This was the mood when the discussion began. However, it immediately became clear that suddenly, for the first time in all the years of perestroika, the usually reasonable style at Politburo sessions had changed completely and turned punitive. The tone was set by Yakovlev, who came down on Nina Andreyeva's letter and *Sovetskaya Rossiya*. Expressions never used before were unleashed: "manifesto of antiperestroika forces," "opposition to perestroika," "forces of deceleration"—the whole set of labels the radical press then started to exploit. In that unusual, oppressive atmosphere, Yakovlev acted like the master of the situation. He was echoed by Medvedev. They wanted to impose on the entire Politburo their opinion that Andreyeva's letter was no ordinary statement: it was a recurrence of Stalinism, the chief threat to perestroika. They completely ignored the fact that the letter had been published in the "Polemics" column. And yet, how many times had they called for pluralism and discussion?

Clearly, an attempt was being made within the highest Party leadership to guide perestroika away from the real threat of nationalism and separatism. The task was to find the high-level political figure who supposedly stood behind Nina Andreyeva and directed and coordinated the actions of the "enemies of perestroika" who had thought up the "conspiracy," "coup," and whatever else you will. And they were looking not just for someone; they were looking specifically for Ligachev.

They wanted to turn Andreyeva into the symbol of Stalinist excesses, and then tie Ligachev to her and announce him to be the chief advocate of a return to the times of the personality cult. Yakovlev insistently and purposefully kept turning the conversation in that direction, without daring to take the final step of using my name. But he did everything he could to urge, to induce others to do so; so he kept trying to put the idea into their heads.

Even today, when I think about that Politburo session, I feel uncomfortable. It was not fear or confusion that I felt then; my conscience was clear, and I was ready to defend my name resolutely if that became necessary. But the atmosphere itself, the methods that had been set in motion, were oppressive. I involuntarily recalled the 1949 meeting of the bureau of the Komsomol Central Committee, when I was accused of "Trotskyism." In Yakovlev's style, I found much in common with that other punitive mood and actions. It is strange indeed to use the Stalinist method of the witch hunt in the struggle against Stalinism. And there was no doubt that a witch hunt was under way.

However, other Politburo members and Central Committee secretaries, with the exception of Medvedev, did not take Yakovlev's bait. Although the agenda was clearly formulated and consisted of only the one item—the article in *Sovetskaya Rossiya*—the conversation extended into a broad discussion of the problems of perestroika. Some of those who spoke preferred not even to mention Andreyeva's letter. No, on the whole, this was certainly not a recurrence of 1937; these were completely different times and different people. Yakovlev's idea hung fire. The Politburo members did not want to take part in this indecent game and failed to support his efforts to look for an "enemy" among the highest echelons of power.

The real tragedy of perestroika is that those few in the political leadership who were using the old methods under new slogans temporarily got the upper hand. Apparently the reason they managed to get control of the situation in 1987–88 was that our society, which had trustingly opened itself up to the changes, had not yet developed an immunity to the sophisticated devices of the former political game.

As for Gorbachev's position at this Politburo session, in the censure of Nina Andreyeva's letter, I would say he came out unequivocally on the side of Yakovlev in expressing his dissatisfaction with those Politburo members who had been conciliatory. There is no reason to name names here, but I will say that several participants in the session were forced to change their point of view during the course of the discussion under the pretext that they had initially read Andreyeva's letter without sufficient care. Upon subsequent reading, they'd discovered there was something in it that was in opposition to perestroika.

I am not naming names because, as a result of the decisive skirmish that took place at the Politburo "witch hunt," the politicians were forced into a compromise. This was not a failure of principles but a sober calculation. It was important for the condemnation of Andreyeva's letter not to overflow into full-fledged confrontation. Political wisdom was needed to deflect the real purpose of the game undertaken at the Politburo and not allow a new version of the "anti-Party group" of 1957.[5]

Thus Gorbachev literally "broke" those who, in his view, failed to condemn Nina Andreyeva's letter sufficiently. But so far as Yakovlev's main idea was concerned, the general secretary seemed to distance himself. I do not know whether Gorbachev was acting sincerely or whether this was simply caution, an unwillingness to reveal himself as actively participating in an extremist enterprise. But the fact remains that he did not take part in the search for the "enemy" among the top political leadership.

Without such support, Yakovlev could not win, but he revealed his intentions completely.

Incidentally, this unusual Politburo session lasted not one day but two, six or seven hours each day. It is not difficult to imagine the intensity of the passions raging beneath the surface.

In all the years of perestroika, this was the only Politburo session at which an article published in the press was discussed. Everyone

---

[5]Reference to Molotov, Bulganin, Kaganovich, and Shepilov, opponents of the 20th Party Congress and Khrushchev's reforms.—TRANS.

knows very well how many vicious anti-Soviet and antisocialist articles there were in the mass media at that time. But not one caused any reaction whatsoever by Yakovlev, Medvedev, or Gorbachev himself: glasnost, pluralism of opinions, after all. But it was enough for one polemical article to appear in defense of socialist ideals—even if it was written with excessive acrimony, with a lot of juggling of facts, and if it was far from consistently valuable in all respects—for a storm to arise against it in the press. No, Andreyeva's article was not discussed or criticized, which would have been perfectly normal—it was executed, torn to pieces, made into a "manifesto" and then widely used in the battle with those who opposed the destructive radical anti-Soviet idea. What kind of a double standard was this?

I have no doubt that sooner or later, however events develop in our country, the answer to this question will be given for our descendants. It will be an impartial explanation of the true intentions and the moral aspect of the organizers of the witch hunt during the time of perestroika.

But one thing is clear even now. The political accent was displaced; conservatism was declared to be the main threat to perestroika. If in 1987–88 the chief threat to perestroika, growing separatism and nationalism, had been correctly perceived, the country could have avoided bloody conflicts and ferment.

The witch hunt really was in the spirit of the cult years. The morning after the Politburo session, a Central Committee commission suddenly descended on the editorial offices of *Sovetskaya Rossiya,* set about studying the original of Nina Andreyeva's letter and the whole process of preparing it for print, and subjected the workers of the editorial offices to a thorough interrogation about it. The very appearance of the commission was staged in the best traditions of the past. The editor in chief received a call from the Central Committee, notifying him of the intention to send inspectors to his offices, but scarcely had he hung up when these very inspectors walked into his office—they'd been waiting in the reception room. This classic device of the 1930s had the aim of not allowing anyone to "cover his tracks," of "catching him red-handed." The inspiration and direction of this operation came from the "democrat" Yakovlev. It was his style.

But there was nothing from me to "cover" or "catch." The inspectors returned empty-handed.

The editorial offices received many responses to Andreyeva's letter; between 5 and 20 April alone—that is, immediately after the publication of the response in *Pravda*—380 responses were received, with only 80 people condemning Andreyeva while 300 supported her. These are the official statistics cited in the investigation to which I have referred.

However one feels about Andreyeva's article, the principles of glasnost and pluralism proclaimed by perestroika required presentation of the whole palette of readers' opinions. After all, at that time our press—and the right-wing radical press at that—was already publishing quite a few letters making apologies for Stalin, demonstrating that these attitudes, too, can be found in society. The special attention devoted to Andreyeva's letter at the Politburo session would seem to be all the more reason for serious ideological work to be done on it. But nothing of the sort happened. *Sovetskaya Rossiya* was categorically forbidden to publish letters in support of Andreyeva and ordered to print only condemnatory letters. Moreover, the approving letters were taken from the editorial offices. Scandalously, the true picture of readers' opinions was hidden from the public, and the idea imposed of a unanimous condemnation of the article.

What kind of glasnost or pluralism was this? The issue clearly went far beyond Andreyeva's article. What kind of "democrats" were these if they were prepared to trample on the basic principle of freedom of speech?

An offprint of the editorial for the next issue of *Pravda* was sent out to the Politburo members for their information on the eve of its publication, but so late (I, for example, got it at 6:00 P.M.) that there was no time to read it and think it through seriously, much less discuss it. I'm sure there was no intention of providing time for reflection. Otherwise, why the rush? (Regarding this editorial, the editor in chief of the paper, Viktor Afanasev, told me bitterly,

"They twisted my arm and forced me to put the article into the paper. I will never in my life forgive myself for that.")

Even before publication of the editorial article sharply condemning Nina Andreyeva's letter, raising it to the rank of a "manifesto of antiperestroika forces," Gorbachev invited me to come to see him. I remember that it was about noon. I also remember that Gorbachev started speaking almost as soon as I entered the room. Without waiting for me to come up to his desk, he said:

"Well, Yegor, I must tell you that I have been busy with the question of the publication of Andreyeva's letter; I had a long talk with Chikin. He explained everything, told me how it all took place. You really did not have anything to do with this publication!"

My feelings at that moment were very complex and contradictory. It was, of course, gratifying that the suspicions had vanished and that Yakovlev's attempt to "link" me officially to the "antiperestroika manifesto" and to create an "antiperestroika force" in my person had suffered complete failure. On the other hand, I was uncomfortable. How could we work together if we did not trust each other?

If all this was possible at the very highest level of the political leadership, in regard to the second in command in the Party, then what could one say about the rank and file who stood in the way of the radicals, the anti-Soviets?

Yes, the initiators of this campaign were prepared to resort to repressive measures when needed. Those who had dressed themselves in the toga of democracy were in fact "ghosts from the past."

The "foremen of perestroika," without pangs of conscience, without attention to the absence of facts, started stigmatizing the "conservatives" allegedly behind Nina Andreyeva. All their speeches were strikingly reminiscent of the theories Yakovlev had put forth at the Politburo session, creating the impression that the foremen had simply been told what to say. After all, they did not know what Yakovlev had said. But I heard him with my own ears and understood that many of the participants in the campaign against Andreyeva did not realize that they were being dragged involuntarily into executing an idea that smelled strongly of the infamous traditions of Stalinist times.

After that memorable conversation in Gorbachev's office, when the general secretary cleared me of suspicion in connection with the publication of Andreyeva's letter in *Sovetskaya Rossiya,* in spite of the calumny I had been subjected to, Gorbachev never once announced publicly that I'd had nothing to do with this matter. He limited himself to a conversation alone with me—and that was it. In exactly the same way, he failed to come to the defense of Ryzhkov when a storm of unjust accusations hailed down on the chairman of the Council of Ministers.

All in all, Gorbachev remained true to himself.

Eight
OUR OWN PATH

Six years after beginning a sharp turn in its development in 1985, our country found itself in the abyss of a crisis of unprecedented severity that threatened not only a drop in production but also paralysis of the entire economy and social upheaval.

This fleeting but very dramatic round in our nation's history inevitably poses these questions: What happened? Where are we heading? How can we emerge onto the road of progress? Our entire society is agonizing over these questions.

I have already discussed, to the extent that I know the facts, the process of perestroika in the area of politics, the sphere of power. But what concerns people most, what serves as the true measure of the success or failure of the reforms, is the economic outcome.

This outcome is now known, and it is not comforting: this sad but, alas, now no longer avoidable course of events makes a thorough understanding of what happened urgent, for every cure must begin with a diagnosis.

It was with a diagnosis that we began in April 1985, when we reevaluated honestly and openly all previous Soviet history, particularly the years immediately preceding the stage of renewal. As we know, our country's economy approached the year 1985 very short of breath; everyone understood that it was being consumed by disease, but no one suspected how serious it was. And so, after performing a kind of X ray of the economic organism with the help of glasnost, society discovered that the economy was gravely ill, the main reasons for the illness being the command methods of leadership and the suppression of economic initiative and independence.

We then set about developing the economic strategy of perestroika and determined the first steps to overcome stagnation as quickly as possible. The nation soon felt a change for the better. There is no particular need to go into detail: 1985–87, when housing construction accelerated and store shelves began to be filled, is still well within people's memories.

What happened to the reform? Why did the economy take a nosedive and then break into a tailspin? Two diametrically opposed points of view dominate public discourse on the causes of what happened. The so-called radicals (the right wing), to whom I have given much attention in this book, submit that the socialist system of structuring society, which does not yield to renewal, is to blame for everything. There is also another viewpoint, which holds that we were led to the brink of the abyss not only by the scope and complexity of the accumulated problems but also by the gross errors made by the leaders of perestroika. They gave in to these same radicals and rashly destroyed the planned economy and existing economic ties before conditions could be created for the transition to economic management methods.

Is the answer in the crisis of the system, or in the blunders and mistakes of the leaders of perestroika?

Successes and Errors

I am not one of those who consider perestroika to be a Pandora's box, the focus of all evils and ills. But neither do I agree with those who contend that the misfortunes that befell the country are the inevitable accompaniments of renewal. It is possible that this last statement could have been convenient for me, considering the fact that I was a member of the political leadership of the country. But the truth is more precious.

With joy, but also with sadness for what has departed, I recall the country's spiritual élan in the first years of perestroika. The Soviet people received more economic and political freedom. The process of creating guarantees against recurrences of lawlessness and oppression was under way in society. The renewal of all aspects of life, democratization, glasnost—these most important signs of social progress were supplemented by swift economic stabilization and a rapid development of the sociocultural complex. Society remained calm, stable, and united. Although the full satisfaction of needs was still far off, people lived with faith in the future. Truly, a time of great hopes had arrived.

Today, in the midst of crisis, there are those who are inclined to ascribe the economic successes of the first years of perestroika to the so-called inertia of the economy; in other words, arguments have been put forth that the country continued moving forward thanks to the stock of previously completed projects. But what kind of inertia can we talk about if the growth rates of social production in the Eleventh Five-Year Plan were substantially lower than in the first years of perestroika? If one speaks of inertia, then the opposite should be expected. The development of the economy would have continued decelerating in spite of the first perestroika efforts.

But the opposite took place. In 1986–88 the annual growth rates of the gross national product and industrial production significantly surpassed indices for 1981–85. In agriculture they rose from 1 percent to 3 percent; in consumer goods production, from 3.7 percent to 5 percent. The entire increase in industrial and agricultural production was achieved by raising labor productivity. It is important to emphasize that the course of development was amenable to rapid change immediately; the country came out of a dive and headed upward. Politically and psychologically, this was essential.

The announcement of a course toward unification of planning principles and the broad development of commodity-money relations was a key factor here. Of course, this was just a beginning in the enormous task of expanding economic independence and making the transition to economic management controls. Rapid stabilization made it possible to pursue these reforms calmly, systematically, and steadily, with every chance of success.

New priorities in investment policy were adopted, with emphasis placed on accelerating the development of machine-building as the basic foundation of scientific and technological progress, and the reconstruction of the national economy. But there was another important, basic characteristic of those first perestroika years: broad economic experimentation. Various models of cost accounting were implemented in factories, transition to self-financing began, and economic standards were assimilated.

Many of these experiments failed to yield complete success. Some of them gave only a partial return; others were in total contradiction to real life. But it was the tendency itself that was important; the country moved forward on a broad front, feeling out new paths and the most rational economic options not in offices, but directly in the sphere of production. Experimentation on a local scale—without hasty "fundamental revolutions" of the entire economic system at once—in my opinion was the most important task, the prerequisite of future successes.

In those years we changed our overall attitude toward the received wisdom of decades particularly with regard to planning, the cornerstone of our economy.

It is well known from history that a planned economy is advantageous in concentrating vast forces and resources in the resolution of key national problems. I will make the immediate reservation that the system of planning, or large-scale state programs, is not exclusively characteristic of socialist economies, as some politicians of various ranks—including, strangely enough, professors of economics—hotheadedly contend. The planning of such programs is accepted in all developed countries of the world. In the United States, for example, two of the most impressive examples of this type are the state programs for the development of the high-tech industry: NASA and SDI, the Strategic Defense Initiative. This is to say nothing of the programs of a social nature—for example, the struggle with the drug trade.

There is also no dearth of achievements in the history of our country testifying brilliantly to the advantages of state planning. So it was in the period of industrialization in the 1930s, the conquering of space in the 1950s and 1960s, and the creation of the world-class western Siberian oil and gas complex in the 1960s and 1970s. No reasonable person can deny the economic advantages to be gained from planning; attempts to discredit the planning system have been of perfidious indeed. I would go so far as to say that the planned economy, adopted for the first time on a large scale in the USSR, is an achievement of universal human significance; this principle of managing the processes of development is now used all over the world (as is, by the way, the state system of social protection for working people created in our country).

However, command-administrative methods have in many ways distorted the principle of a planned economy, have taken them to the point of absurdity. Those at the top started planning from on high not special programs, not overall directions of development, but literally everything, up to and including the entire distribution of resources and wages. The economy, squeezed by innumerable instructions, started to choke. But the greater the scarcity of resources, the stricter its planning became—although this was no longer planning but willful administrative invasion of the sphere of production.

We realized this very quickly after 1985, as we planned to correct the situation by freeing the national economy from the center's petty guardianship, gradually bringing the share of state planning down to rational limits and giving planning back its primary essence, the large-scale management of material, financial, and labor resources in the interests of society as a whole. Properly understood, centralized planning can be compared to the creativity of an architect who designs a building. The mechanisms and work methods used to erect the structure are the problems of the builders.

When the issue is put this way, centralized planning becomes not a narrowly technical matter but one closely linked to political decisions made by the leadership on the instructions of congresses of soviets or the ruling party. This is how it is done the world over.

But the opponents of socialism have proclaimed the abovementioned distortions of planning the inevitable attributes of the social system and have made it their goal to destroy the planning system completely for the sake of an absolute economic freedom— which does not exist anywhere in the world.

There is one more collapsed item of received wisdom: erroneously understood social justice, which not infrequently turned into primitive egalitarianism.[1]

We discussed this question with particular thoroughness at the Politburo as we prepared for the 27th Congress. What is the true essence of the concept of social justice? The collective answer differed noticeably from the previous crude egalitarianism. Yes, the essence of social justice is contained in the fundamental law of socialism: to each according to the quantity and quality of his work. However, such a definition is insufficient. It must be supplemented with the right of the collective to dispose of its product and the income from its property, if this property is earned by its own honest labor. There is only one criterion, but an unshakable one: the legality of earnings, the social benefit of labor.

This departure from former egalitarianism was a fundamental matter; it was also directed toward the future and gave people room for initiative. The main thing was that a high labor income was rehabilitated in the eyes of society. The rest was a matter of "technique"; we still had to work out the fairest taxation, etc.

I am bitter that this important, fundamental move forward defining the general strategy of perestroika was simply ignored by the new political forces that emerged in the social arena to seize power. Trying to break down an open door, they attributed the old definition of social justice to the Communist Party. As a counterbalance, they advocated the idea of the so-called differentiation of incomes, the division into poor and rich. Publications even appeared to the

---

[1]*Uravnilovka,* literally "leveling off."—TRANS.

effect that in any population of living creatures, including the human population, only 4 percent of individuals are active, while the remainder are only the "biological mass," obliged to service those who are the most enterprising. And if these 4 percent are very well off, then the remainder will be just the tiniest bit better off, too.

In a word, they proposed letting the moneychangers and Pharisees back into the temple. Is this social justice? Is this what the people wanted from perestroika? Idealogues of such changes gradually forced out the original economic strategy and in the final analysis brought the country to economic collapse. They did not ask the people whether they wanted the moneychangers and Pharisees to triumph.

Economic experimentation, freeing economic activity from petty guardianship and regulation, rejection of egalitarianism—these are the steps in the only feasible process to improve the economy. This process is the democratization of economic and social life. In the most important sphere of the rights and freedoms of man, it was supplemented by the development of glasnost, the elimination of censorship restrictions, and striving to rethink the historical past honestly. Only such an approach could guarantee an upsurge in national initiative and emancipation of mass consciousness.

Alas, in recounting the beneficial changes that took place at the start of perestroika, I am forced once again to write that unfortunate word "but." *But* soon something came out that was not quite comprehensible to me. At the January 1987 Central Committee plenum, the need to supplement the economic reforms with political ones was announced. In practice the process of democratization became unmanageable. Society began to lose its political stability; the idea that everything was permitted gained the upper hand. Discipline dropped precipitously, law and order collapsed, and regulations were not enforced. Did it make sense to plunge the country into the stormy upheavals of a political struggle at the most complex stage of economic reform, when social stability is the decisive condition of success?

When one looks back at the spiritual and financial resources wasted in those years for strictly political campaigns, one's heart bleeds. Numerous elections, countless congresses, incessant multi-stage sessional debates—from the USSR Supreme Soviet to the Moscow and Leningrad city soviets—embittered squabbles in the mass media, intoxication with the frenzy of rallies. My God, this is what the potential for renewal that accumulated in society for decades was wasted on? Was there any room for the economy here?

Successful economic reform of course was not possible without changes in forms of ownership and management. The state-dominated economy fettered people's initiative and did not allow such a key factor in production growth as the interests of various professional groups and social strata to start working at full capacity. Of course, it was necessary to introduce new types of property ownership.

And in full accord with the intention of perestroika, the Party introduced a slogan about the improvement of socialist production relations, about the variety of implementing forms of socialist property. It provided for the broad development of cooperative, leasing, joint-stock, and other forms of collective ownership. Nor did this slogan just remain on paper; it was soon being implemented in real life. As early as the spring of 1988, the Law on Cooperatives was adopted. I will not go into an analysis of this ill-thought-out law and its consequences, but merely mention it to establish that the country stepped onto the path of destatifying the economy in reality.

I wish to voice an immediate reservation. Care and circumspection should be used on the question of destatification. The fact that 10 percent of enterprises produce three-fourths of industrial output is an enormous plus, making it possible to construct an economy effectively by concentrating production. This is one manifestation of the advantage of public ownership of the means of production. To be sure, an excessive monopoly over production of certain types has negative sides as well, which rightly puts processes of demonopolization on the agenda. But large enterprises should not be destroyed; rather, we should go the way mainly of creating new small and medium-sized plants and factories.

Most importantly, the transformation of state property should be accomplished only by transferring enterprises to labor collectives.

We cannot allow public property, created through the labor of all
the generations of Soviet people, to be dismantled and expropriated
by petty operators and black-marketeers. The labor collective should
become the basic master of the enterprise and disposer of the results
of its labor.

Along with this, naturally, the powerful state sector of the economy should also be preserved. Its share in the common economic
"pot" will be established by practical experience.

However, in the question of destatifying property, we once again
have not managed without strange and puzzling "degenerations,"
which haunt perestroika. In the right-wing radical mass media, the
principle of a "variety of forms of realizing socialist ownership" put
forth officially by Gorbachev was transformed into a call for a "variety of forms of ownership," which essentially changed the policy
itself. Amazingly, the general secretary, who was holding the main
ideological thread in his hands at the time, did not once react to
the progressive distortion of the slogan proposed by the Party, even
though this was an about-face in social development.

It is difficult for me to judge whether the maneuver of "truncat-
ing" the original formula was planned ahead of time, or whether
Gorbachev simply came under the influence of political forces that
called themselves the "foremen of perestroika." As it later emerged,
they were in fact the political vanguard of private enterprise. But
most significant in this case is the fact of departure from the strategy
chosen collectively in the Politburo.

It entailed decisive changes in the essence of the perestroika processes. Destatification was in many respects reduced to privatization—in other words, to turning the means of production over to
private ownership. This was not a matter of a variety of forms of
ownership but of a type of ownership—private—new for our society. After decades, we are returning the country to what the October Revolution eliminated. Translated into language accessible to
everyone: Instead of renewing and improving socialism, the system
was to be replaced. Why did they raise this age-old and bloody
conflict and make it so acutely political at the height of perestroika?

In doing so, they often refer to capitalist countries, whereas only a small number of the Western countries are thriving. Undoubtedly, to a large extent this is the result of the labor of the people of these countries. But it is impossible not to consider the historical factor. For centuries and to this day, capitalists pump superprofits out of poorly developed countries by using cheap work forces and raw materials. Add to this the millions of foreign dispossessed workers who receive low wages and live in difficult conditions without benefit of many rights and freedoms.

Unlike the leading capitalist countries, the Soviet people created their national wealth with their labor alone. Only through labor was the Soviet Union transformed from a backward country, in which savagery and semisavagery reigned in the vast spaces, into a powerful industrial state with a developed science and culture. And this all took place in a very short period of time and without plundering other nations.

My personal position on the question of private ownership of the means of production is well known. It corresponds to the main original slogan of perestroika, in whose development I participated: More democracy, more socialism! And yet the establishment of private ownership, the introduction of hired labor, and the buying and selling of land contradict the Party's programmatic statute about the socialist option and a Communist future. And adding "labor" to the concept of "private ownership" does not save the situation. One can assume that dragging in private ownership is a concession to the West, to get economic and political aid. Even though plenty of declarations that this is not the case have been made to placate society, the West clearly is counting on the introduction of private ownership to lead our country to a rejection of socialism. With this prospect in mind, it is even agreeing to some political "sacrifices."

It is appropriate to examine the Lithuanian example from this point of view. The nationalist leaders of Lithuania hoped to obtain powerful support from the West, since the capitalist countries did not recognize Lithuania's entry into the Soviet Union. It is natural that they would have expected the Soviet Union to be pressured. The West, and in particular the United States, did not agree to a confrontation with the Soviet Union, not least of all because they feared that this might have led to the disruption of our perestroika, in which they have a particular stake. Lithuania found itself essentially in international isolation, although its leadership was graciously hosted in the capital cities of many states.

Quite a few politicians in the West make economic aid to our country conditional on a series of demands, including the introduction of an unregulated market and private ownership of the means of production. There are those among them who simply hope to turn the Soviet Union into a raw-materials appendage of the West. In other words, we are talking about the openly expressed class nature of Western policy.

An April 1991 roundtable of politicians and economists in Moscow brought together people with different viewpoints on the processes taking place in our society: Gavriil Popov, Vadim Bakatin, Grigory Yavlinsky, Stanislav Shatalin, and I were invited. Afterward, one of the American businessmen present, in answer to my speech (which he judged to be clear, precise, and free of murkiness—of which, in his words "there was no dearth at the roundtable") made the following statement: He has a lot of dollars, but he will not give a single one either to Mr. Ligachev or to President Gorbachev until there is private ownership in the USSR. As we see, the coffer is easily opened: if you want a loan, change your social system.

But this politicized approach is a mistake. And incidentally, the socialist Soviet Union for decades was considered one of the most reliable business partners in the world—it paid its bills on time. Western firms have gained a great deal by doing business with us. The important thing is that in relations among states, mutual benefit, not political and ideological considerations, should be the cornerstone.

An additional consideration is that transition to a market economy will facilitate our integration into the world economy. It would be a serious mistake to link the market exclusively with private producers, however. Such an approach is superficial. After all, in the West as well, cooperatives enter the market as full members. The consumer market is a kind of "service mechanism" for which all forms of ownership are equal. Its chief concern is the degree of economic gain of each economic subject. And in our country, the basic economic subjects are socialist enterprises. They should be given the right to choose their forms of social ownership voluntarily.

State regulation of the market in fact plays a significant role in the world's most developed countries. As the market forms in our country as well, the role of planning will change and its center of gravity will begin to shift in the direction of creating specialized programs and developing economic regulators. For example, special programs are needed in machine-building, agriculture, and conversion of the defense industry.

Specialized planning has political as well as economic significance. It promotes development of an integrated national economy within the framework of a federation of sovereign republics. It was often said that an All-Union market would guarantee an integrated Soviet state. This was clearly an exaggeration; it is not so much a market that unites economically sovereign republics, as cooperation and integration of production. This is understandable; after all, production is primary, but exchange is secondary. The degree of interrepublic cooperation had reached 45 percent in our country, a very high indicator of economic ties that had served the unity of the Union and the development of the sovereign republics.

The fact that some circles in the West, and in our country as well, are trying to replace the problem of forming a regulated market with the problem of introducing private ownership in the USSR is somewhat offensive. The thesis that perestroika is impossible without private enterprise has heated up political passions. It opens up the possibility of changing the social system, and such a course of events naturally leads to social and political instability.

In time, it became clear that preparations were made in advance for the proclamation of the "sacred principle of private ownership." For this it was necessary first to impair and then to destroy the national planned economy. This task, in turn, was begun with a propagandistic blow to the headquarters, the centers of administration, under the pretext of attacking the "command-administrative system." I guarantee that no one, including the inventors of this propagandistic cliché, can explain exactly what this is. True, command-administrative methods of management have evolved in our country over the past decades. And it is indeed necessary to renounce them decisively, making room for independence and initiative. But what is the "command-administrative system"?

The question was soon illuminated: what was intended was a blow against everything central, from the State Planning Committee to the armed forces. Everything that cemented the great power as a state, as a single whole, was declared to be the "command-administrative system," subject to demolition. Under the banner of the repudiation of command methods, the dismantling of state structures began in earnest; economic ties and the unified national economy were being destroyed. Right-wing radical economists advocated breaking large production and agricultural units into small subdivisions, ostensibly to create better conditions for economic independence.

I recall my conversation with an American banker, John Crystal, from Iowa—incidentally a former farmer—whom I met in Moscow in 1989. We had only just started exchanging opinions when he asked me right out: "Mr. Ligachev, you deal with agricultural policy. Tell me, have they really decided to abandon collective and state farms in the USSR and start creating small farms?"

I answered his question with a question: "And how do you view this problem?"

"Whoever wants to break up large farms into small ones is obviously not all there," he said, making an expressive "loco" gesture. "The process of concentrating, amalgamating, individual farms is rapidly taking place in the whole world, America included. Only large farms can fully utilize the new expensive achievements of agronomy and technology."

I have no doubt that our leading economists, who are proposing that we reduce the national economy and break it up into smaller units, to place our stakes on small and medium-sized enterprises in every way possible, understand very well that in fact this goes against the world trend of development, and sidetracks our country from the main road of progress. They understand very well that it throws us back decades, if not a whole century. But these scholars have turned into the most active of politicians; they are motivated not by scholarly or patriotic concerns but by mercenary political advantage. What they passed over in silence in 1988–89 they proclaimed openly in 1991: capitalization, the creation of a social stratum of entrepreneurs based on private ownership. It is this strictly political aim that has been placed at the cornerstone, not economic revival. What is more, its achievement requires that the potential already created must be shattered, that a crisis be created in the country.

And what then, when power has been seized, when the social revolution has been accomplished? Then, of course, feverish efforts will begin to restore the economy to the "mainstream of human civilization" in today's fashionable phrase. Once again, the inevitable process of amalgamation and concentration will take decades, and again, at the cost of enormous national deprivation. We have already been convinced that many of the radicals' calls in fact serve as nothing more than deceptive maneuvers. In particular, under the pretext of depoliticization, they demanded removal of Party organizations from enterprises. But as soon as the democrats got down to forming their own party, calls were heard to create corresponding cells at factories and mines.

These calls, incidentally, came from the mouth of Moscow's Mayor Popov, who earlier had been particularly active in the fight for depoliticization. But in his role as economist, Popov advocated conversion to small family farms, breaking up collective and state farms. And in doing so he did not shy away from gross distortion of the data of world experience, including the American experience the banker from Iowa had cited. It is not difficult to see that once such activists achieve their goals, they will "restructure" themselves, turn over yet again.

I take full responsibility for declaring that demands for the immediate dissolution of collective and state farms to create private farming on the basis of private ownership will lead to famine in our country, as experience has already confirmed. In effect, what they want to do is utilize in reverse the same device that Stalin used in the early 1930s, when an artificially created famine was used to liquidate individual farms and institute universal collectivization. Now they crave the opposite version: to create famine artificially again and, after blaming the collective farms for it, to dissolve them forcibly.

And once again it will be the people who have to pay for these political intrigues.

In their aggregate, the false democrats, the anti-Communists, disclose with sufficient clarity the strategy of those forces striving for the capitalization of our society. They want to disorganize the national economy, bring it to the brink of total collapse, and then blame the social system for this disorder. The reallotment of land and the ruin of collective and state farms were only part of this general strategy. It was also evident in the evolution of the creators of the "500-Day" Program.[2]

When this program was being discussed in Parliament, its authors did not stress the principle of private ownership inherent in it, referring to it merely in passing. But after the "500-Day" Program was rejected, they no longer concealed the fact that they had undertaken to bring the country back to "the bosom of universal human civilization," understood as the complete domination of private ownership.

In my view, what was most immoral was the fact that both the creators of the "500-Day" Program and many other supporters of private ownership also supported the movement toward separatism and the disintegration of the Soviet Union in the ensuing ideological battle. Under conditions of state instability, ethnic conflicts, and even civil war, it is, of course, easier to attempt a replacement of the social system. Political ambitions and love of power turned out to be higher than patriotism, higher than the age-old interests of the state.

---

[2]A blueprint for transition to a market economy drafted in 1990 by economists Stanislav Shatalin, Grigory Yavlinsky, and others. Although Gorbachev and Yeltsin reached a consensus to support the plan, this collapsed under pressure from conservatives. The USSR Supreme Soviet rejected the plan and adopted a much watered-down version; the RSFSR Supreme Soviet approved it but lacked the power to implement it.—TRANS.

Under the extremely difficult conditions of the First World War and civil intervention, Lenin and the Bolsheviks managed to retain the unity of the multinational Russian state bequeathed by our ancestors. In this lies their great service to their Fatherland. And what will today's radicals leave behind? Under the banner of a struggle with "the Bolshevik empire," in the name of a system based on private ownership, they have heartlessly and barbarically shattered the state of their grandfathers and great-grandfathers. They are prepared to leave behind only the shards of a once-great power. The hope cherished for centuries by our foreign enemies turned out to be fulfilled by our false democrats, our nationalists.

After the "500-Day" Program was rejected and its creators fled from the presidential helm, they no longer concealed the fact that this was a program for an about-face of the social and state system, of the whole sociopolitical system, for taking our country back onto the road of capitalism and private ownership, which, in their opinion, is the high road of human civilization. They did not believe in our people, in our country, when they claimed that without the West we "will resolve neither the immediate nor the strategic problem of economic development." A capitulating position! It is enough to look at the history of our country to become convinced of the reverse.

The economists who came out with the "500-Day" Program finally tore off their masks and advocated private ownership of land and its buying and selling, and the dissolution of collective and state farms. What in the "500-Day" Program attracted President Gorbachev, who once proclaimed his adherence to it, remains a mystery. In fact, if one scratches the surface of this program hard enough, one sees that its implementation would have meant an essential change in the social structure of society, in the composition of representative bodies. Private owners and entrepreneurs would occupy the seats in Parliament.

We have the right to borrow a great deal from abroad, such achievements of capitalism as high technology, production organization, and the market infrastructure. But not the principle of private ownership, because this is the basic principle that forms a foundation for changing the essence of the system! It is not a question of dogmas; if we betray our essence, our country will inevitably be thrown back a century, will once again have to traverse the arduous path that the current developed capitalist countries traveled for a long time and that the countries of the Third World (in which the system is also, as we know, based on private ownership) continue to travel.

We are struggling to eliminate the alienation of the producer from the means of production. Private ownership does not resolve this issue at all; it merely aggravates this problem.

But there is another road to progress—through social ownership of the means of production. We embarked on this road after the October Revolution. All the discussions about whether this was a mistake or predestination are now simply boring. History does not use the subjunctive mood; it has already taken place. And indisputable facts exist: in spite of the tragic pages of the Stalinist years, the USSR became the second power of the world. Yes, the nation has suffered great hardships, but the country has managed to create enormous production and scientific and technological potential. And have many generations of working people in capitalist countries suffered fewer deprivations on their road to progress? (Incidentally—this is now recognized throughout the world—they have made use of such achievements of socialism as social guarantees, large-scale planning, etc.)

Transformations of state property should take place without privatization (without turning it into an object of buying and selling). There is only one type of ownership and economic structure, and that is socialist.

I am convinced that socialism also has equal rights as one of the roads of humanity toward progress.

What do I understand socialism to mean? It is a society in which priority is given to man and to democracy. True, other political organizations also proclaim humanism and democratism. The foundations of the society, of true socialism, are also important. The economic foundation of socialism is the public ownership of the means of production, in which man becomes the co-owner, in which there is a combination of planning and the market. And its political foundation is the existence of democratic soviets at all levels, and a law-governed state. On the moral level, it is a society of socialist values, which includes universal human values. On the social level, this is a society of social justice, free of exploitation and ethnic oppression, a society in which there is no unemployment, in which everyone has the right to work.

What comes to mind is the Congress of French Communists in December 1987, at which I was present as the head of the CPSU delegation. In my speech I reported that people laid off from the management apparatus at enterprises during the course of perestroika would get benefits and compensation. Particularly dear to their hearts were my words that they are guaranteed the constitutional right to work. Thousands of participants greeted these words with a standing ovation. When I asked Jacques Marchais, the French Communist Party leader, why the delegates had reacted so warmly to this part of my speech, he answered that many of the delegates had personally experienced unemployment and were constantly in fear of losing their jobs.

Today, when our homegrown proponents of capitalism are in a rush to put an end to socialism as quickly as possible and excessively extol the benefits of the "capitalist paradise," I often recall that Congress in Paris and the real envy the French working people felt toward the Soviet people, who at that time had a constitutional guarantee against unemployment.

In concluding the discussion of the successes and failures of the first years of perestroika, I would like to note two issues that had an important influence on the course of the reforms. The first is connected with the conversion of the defense industry.

After April 1985 we faced the task of curtailing military spending. Without this, large-scale social programs could not have been implemented: the economy could not breathe normally with a military budget that comprised 18 percent of the national income. But at the same time, it must be understood that the growth of military spending during the past decades had been dictated by the need to achieve strategic military parity with the United States. This task was successfully accomplished, and it substantially influenced the fate of the world.

Today the danger of nuclear confrontation has been reduced significantly, based on the principle of sufficient defense. As a result, the military budget has been reduced, and conversion has begun.

However, a great country must be concerned with its defense capability to maintain the strategic military balance. We cannot destroy the unique scientific and technological potential of the defense sectors. Conversion cannot be perceived as adapting large factories to the production of aluminum frying pans. This is a very complex process. That is why the issue of working out a unified comprehensive program for carrying out conversion was placed on the agenda.

The second issue was the intensified efforts of certain forces to push the Communist Party and the Central Committee out of the sphere of economics.

Explanations are necessary here. Over the decades, many Party agencies interfered in effective production activity, sometimes to the point of meddling in petty details. And it is no accident that the question of separating Party from economic functions came up not just yesterday, but also a long time ago. This was understood to mean limiting the actual interference of Party agencies in production activity. There was less and less petty guardianship over economic planners by Party committees.

However, at a certain stage of perestroika this very proper approach was distorted. There were those who started talking about pushing the Party aside altogether from the economy, in essence "depoliticizing" the economy. But this is impossible. The veracity of Lenin's statement that economics is politics in a concentrated form has been confirmed by the course of world development. In all countries of the world, political parties—and only ones in power—design the economic strategy, whereas in our country the separation of economic and Party functions was taken to absurdity. The Party was to be answerable to the nation for decisions made by the general secretary on which he did not consult Communists!

To cite but one example: for a long time the Party was excluded from designing and discussing the program for the country's transition to a market economy, although the USSR Supreme Soviet discussed these problems twice in 1990. Proceeding on this basis, in May 1990 I sent a memo to the Politburo (with a request to make it known to the members of the Central Committee as well) in which I proposed examining government measures for the transition to a market economy at a Central Committee plenum. The memo noted that "these issues were not discussed at the Politburo. Thus the country's political leadership has found itself detached from these programs, which are of concern to all of society and affect the interests of every person." Alas, my memo was shelved. And it was not until October 1990 that the Central Committee plenum took place at which the issue of converting the national economy to the market was discussed, already in retrospect. The same fate was met by the anticrisis program and the resolution on raising prices.

But nature, as we know, does not tolerate a vacuum, and a good seat does not stay empty for long. Since the Party was excluded from participating in a program for the transition to the market at a certain stage, this matter was taken up by the democrats, who proposed the "500-Days" timetable. It was similar to what happened during the pre-election campaign period, when the Communist Party's hands were tied while its opponents were given complete freedom of action.

Why did this happen? Who benefited?

I remember visiting the Sormovo shipbuilding plant in Nizhny Novgorod in the 1960s as it was undergoing reconstruction, dismantling the shop built before the Revolution. In my opinion, the way this was done was well conceived, even symbolic in its own way. A large, tall new building was erected over the old building without touching it. Only after completing the new roof was the old structure inside taken down. Now, this was working intelligently—and a similar method should have been used in transferring authority from Party agencies to the soviets.

How much damage was caused by the pseudodemocratic principle of electing economic leaders? Not a single country in the world

elects managers; they are appointed. But here, too, we found ourselves ahead of the whole planet, demonstrating the immaturity of
our democracy. Many excellent managers were removed from their
posts. (The campaign ended with the chairman of the Council of
Ministers condemning this flawed innovation and with correctives
being introduced in the Law on the Social Enterprise.)

Of course, no one is insured against making mistakes. But the
problem is that serious errors by the highest leadership seemed to
have become a matter of course.

The negative consequences of the political decision about the
economy made near the end of 1987 began to be clearly visible by
the end of 1989. This truly fateful decision was made at a Politburo
session where the concept of the government's plan was discussed.

But before talking about that memorable Politburo session, I feel
it is necessary to discuss one of the most important issues of perestroika: agriculture.

For decades the nation lured human resources away from the
countryside while depriving it of its fair share of resources for social,
cultural, and technological development. This is how it was during
the period of industrialization. During the Great Patriotic War, the
countryside placed everything on the altar of the Fatherland. And
even in later periods, the industrial development of the USSR was
achieved largely at the expense of rural areas. We could do nothing
else; we got no foreign loans. We created everything with our own
labor. We did not loot colonies and dependent countries. There
were mistakes in agricultural policy itself, despite frequent proclamations that agriculture would receive top priority. But, alas, the
countryside was in fact financed and supplied essentially on the
"leftover" principle.

When I was put in charge of agricultural policy in 1988, I attempted to do everything possible to end the mistaken practice of
doing the countryside out of its fair share of funding and resources.

In taking on the food problem, I was guided by the fact that the
Party's policy did not consist of instructions on how to plow, sow,
and milk cows. It wasn't the Party's function. But taking into consideration the interests of the peasantry, of all the laborers of the

agro-industrial complex, and strengthening economic ties between the city and the countryside to supply the country with food resources—this was the province of Party policy. Agriculture provides more than one-fourth of the national income and fixed production assets. This is not only agriculture but also machine-building, construction, storage, processing, science, the reconstruction of rural areas, personnel. The agro-industrial complex supplies 70 percent of commodity turnover. In a word, this is the largest complex in the national economy.

Immediately after being confirmed in the post of chairman of the Central Committee Agricultural Commission, I, along with other concerned officials, set about preparing for the March 1989 Central Committee plenum, which determined the Party's agricultural policy during perestroika, its goals, basic directions, and principles. These included reworking economic relations in agriculture, scientific and technological progress, the reconstruction of the food industry, produce storage, and social reconstruction of the countryside. The farmer finally became the focus of politics.

Right before the plenum, these policy issues were discussed for two days in a small circle of the Party leadership. There were fierce debates, particularly on the problem of material and technical supply of rural areas. The leaders of the government and of the State Planning Committee contended that the full supply of rural areas would not solve the food problem. Several of us—Nikonov, Vorotnikov, Vlasov, and I—demanded that we give the farmer resources at the level established in other developed countries. Maybe not all at once; but let us make a significant increase. We were going on the assumption that for a 1 percent rise in capital investments in agriculture, there is a growth in output of no more than 0.4 to 0.6 percent. (This is supported by domestic and international practice.) Production in the countryside had to be increased by 25 to 30 percent; thus a 50 to 60 percent increase in resources from rural areas was needed.

Our farmer is now technologically equipped approximately at the level of the American farmer of the early 1950s. We must also bear in mind that the natural biological potential of our fields is

2.5 times lower than in the United States. To get harvests comparable to the Americans' we have to be even better equipped technologically.

I had to raise this more than once at Central Committee plenums, in the Politburo, and at the second Congress of People's Deputies. I will say openly that I did not consult with the leadership on this issue because I knew I would not find support for my proposals for a significant increase in resources to rural areas. It is also true that I was not openly criticized for this; I was, as often happened, just ignored.

But this is an either-or issue. Society must find additional material resources for the development of the agro-industrial complex, and above all supply it with effective technology and create good social conditions for rural dwellers or we will not be able to feed the country.

The democrats' call to dissolve collective and state farms and make land privately owned—which allegedly would ensure an adequate food supply within two or three years—was a dangerous illusion. The destruction of collective and state farms is a direct path to ruin. I heard of such projects as early as 1987 from Svetlana Alliluyeva, Stalin's daughter. We had a meeting at her request because she wanted to go abroad once again with her daughter. When I informed her that there were no obstacles to her doing so, I remember she was very much surprised at this; she apparently expected some "trickery" from the Party leadership.

At the end of our meeting I asked her if she had any requests. Her answer, in turn, surprised me: dissolve the collective farms. In the course of our conversation, it came out that she had never been on a collective farm. Finally, she "allowed" us to do as we wished: "Resolve this yourselves along with the collective farm members."

The March 1989 Central Committee plenum made some important decisions: it legalized various forms of working the land, making them equal before the law, and also expanded significantly the independence of collective and state farms. Not enough time has passed since then for the resolution of rural problems. But during this period, collective and state farms got the highest grain crop and milk yields. For the first time, all the grain remained at the disposal of agricultural production units after fulfilling the state order.

But the farmer was squeezed between agricultural and manufacturing prices and the lack of equivalence in exchange between the city and the countryside. Moreover, attention to such problems has waned. The authorities are busy designing all kinds of programs for the "renaissance of the countryside" but production is declining. In words priority is given to the development of the agro-industrial complex, but in deeds we can see a reduction of resources for rural areas.

I recall how during my childhood I had occasion to stand in line for hours for bread. Usually my mother stood in line in the early hours of the morning while it was still dark. My brother and I would take over from her so we could buy "a brick" of bread by afternoon, or sometimes evening.[3] The bread shortages in Moscow have reminded me of those distant Siberian years. True, there is a difference, and a significant one. Then, there was a lack of flour for baking bread; today, it is a matter of irresponsibility and incompetence by the head of the "democratic" Moscow City soviet.

I would like to finish this chapter by addressing an issue in which I have something of a personal stake, since public opinion associates it with my name.

I have in mind the anti-alcohol campaign begun in May 1985.

To recall briefly the background of the campaign, in the early 1980s there was an increase in the number of letters—mostly from wives and mothers—received by the Central Committee, the government, and the editorial offices of newspapers and magazines. In these letters, women, crushed with grief, cursed the drunkenness that took away the lives of their sons and husbands and crippled their children. Alcohol consumption at that time had reached an

---

[3]My older brother, Dmitri, took part in the Great Patriotic War, reaching Germany in battle. He was buried in the military cemetery in Weimar; I visited his grave in 1990. —AUTHOR

annual nine liters per capita; in some regions, up to eleven liters. It was impossible to read these women's bitter outpourings without shuddering. The saying that wives and children have shed as many tears as men have drunk vodka is apt indeed. This was a veritable cry for help. Moreover, many scientists were sounding the alarm and forecasting the threat of degeneration of the nation's genetic stock.

It should be borne in mind that, for example, state revenues from the sale of alcoholic beverages reached 53 billion rubles in 1984, having increased fourfold over twenty years. The Treasury was collecting a huge, excessive tribute from its citizens, and these fiscal objectives were the state's contribution to drunkenness, in my view immoral. These revenues were essentially obtained at the expense of people's health and material wellbeing.

It was impossible to ignore the countless letters, the nation's groans. In 1984, the Politburo established a commission to draft effective measures for overcoming drunkenness and alcoholism. The May decrees and the 1985 edict were the outcome of its work.

I was not a member of that commission and did not participate in the preparation of its documents. However, as a member of the Politburo, I became actively involved in the cause; we discussed this issue many times at the Central Committee Secretariat. My official responsibilities and my personal refusal to tolerate drunkenness coincided in this case.

There is no need to recount in detail the events connected with the anti-alcohol campaign. I will only say that the central agencies were immediately inundated with letters of thanks: millions of families heaved sighs of relief. And it was certainly pertinent that the report at the 19th Party Conference in 1988 noted that the country's "birth rate had risen and mortality had declined, which in no small measure is connected with the battle against drunkenness and alcoholism."

Subsequent events are also well known. Along with positive results, the anti-alcohol campaign also brought considerable costs— a sharp increase in home-distilled vodka production, and a black market in alcoholic beverages. Obviously it would not be possible to overcome this age-old ailment immediately. An emphasis on prohibition, on administrative measures without the adequate support of educational measures, without the organization of healthy leisure, could not bring about the desired results. In addition, quickly mounting financial difficulties caused the government to rely again on the production of vodka. And in 1989 the state pumped 54 billion rubles out of the people's pockets from the sale of alcoholic beverages, which was higher than the 1984 level. And the 1991 sum probably exceeded 65 billion rubles. We have reverted to rampant drunkenness, with its harvest of victims and misfortune across the country.

But the anti-alcoholic campaign unexpectedly acquired a certain political tinge as well—it was linked with my name.

What can I say? I want to repeat that the decision to declare war on drunkenness was collective; formally, I did not even take part in drafting the decree. However, this doesn't mean that I want to evade the issue. As a leader of the Secretariat, I indeed had to take an active part in drafting practical measures for the struggle with drunkenness. And I am not dodging responsibility for the fact that these measures initially turned out to be excessively harsh and bureaucratic. Apparently a certain involuntary personal element was at work here. As a nondrinker, I was psychologically unprepared to accept the fact that someone would not be able to "kick" drinking if the possibility of obtaining alcohol were sharply curtailed. This was undoubtedly a mistake on my part. And I will add frankly that initially I appeared as a radical in the anti-alcohol campaign, even though I myself condemn radicalism and extremism. It seemed to be that if you went at it with a will, drunkenness could be eliminated quickly. The slogan "For a sober way of life" was put into circulation—as it turned out, prematurely.

But the insight came fairly quickly; the battle with drunkenness is a long-term, gradual task. This made it necessary to change tactics, to switch the emphasis from prohibition and working in spurts to educational work calculated for the long term. I see nothing terrible in this evolution from directive to education; it is natural. If we remember this campaign, then particular attention should be paid to the fact that protests against it coincided with an aggravation of the political situation in society. The protests were far from universal (the majority of people were solid backers of the battle against drunkenness and alcoholism), and came primarily from the "foremen of perestroika" and the government, for which it was easier to patch up the budget by selling vodka. I don't mean they had no reasonable arguments; they did. But the pseudodemocrats were clearly pursuing a political agenda in the "anti-anti-alcohol" campaign, primarily against its "initiator," Ligachev. Reproaches for destroying vineyards became widespread, and then, of all things, for disrupting the monetary system.

Naturally, neither corresponds to the facts. Neither I personally nor the Central Committee as a whole ever gave verbal or written orders to uproot vines. The official statistics completely disprove claims of a reduction in the number of vineyards. Incidentally, I cited these statistics in my report at the 28th Party Congress, and no one even tried to refute me.

Unfortunately, this did not stop Sobchak from continuing his "vineyard" reproaches at the Russian Communist Congress. But he was immediately cut short sharply by the Kuban Cossacks, to whose territory he was referring. (It would seem that a self-respecting individual who has mistakenly accused another would feel obliged to ask that person's pardon. But Sobchak apparently respects neither himself nor others.)

It is equally unseemly to blame the anti-alcohol campaign for disrupting monetary circulation. First, it began in May 1985 and continued in its acute form less than two years, and during that time the population's rise in income was not yet excessive, which is once again confirmed by statistics. But more important is another indisputable fact: the battle against drunkenness allowed labor productivity to rise, lowered absenteeism and accidents, and noticeably lowered sick-leave payments—in other words, it produced a tangible material effect. And how can one measure thousands of saved lives?

Again, I do not shirk responsibility for the excessively harsh approach during the initial stage of this struggle. But I have no intention of covering my head in ashes. We are talking about saving the people's health, about easing the suffering of tens of millions of individuals. This is a sacred goal, and even failures along the path of its attainment will also bring benefits, will save us from similar mistakes in the future. And if any are guilty before the people, it is precisely those who completely buried the battle with drunkenness for purely political goals.

Why, in spite of the vociferous campaign for the battle against crime, is persistent violation of law and order not decreasing but actually constantly increasing? To a significant degree this is because the battle against crime today is not tied to the elimination of drunkenness, which has become the primary cause of almost half of crime. It is commonly known that lowering the incidence of crime and securing the tranquillity of citizens have become the most urgent problems of our society.

The initial mistakes of the anti-alcohol campaign should have been corrected, the prohibition softened, educational work intensified. Everything can be forgiven except the malicious glee at the failure of one more attempt to cope with a chronic national ailment. Drunkenness is our misfortune. He who attempts to accommodate this national pain to his own political goals commits a crime against society.

The Fateful Error

How was the economy brought to a state of crisis? Why is the unified national economic complex disintegrating?

What brought about the collapse of the economy and the breakdown of the consumer market?

Events evolved as follows:

In the second half of 1987, the USSR government, on the basis of a general conception of economic perestroika, prepared its proposals for the plan for 1988. In particular, there was provision for completion of the transfer of industry and agriculture to the new economic mechanism. The rigid plan was transformed into the state-order system, which was fully covered by material and financial resources. However, a radical innovation was also introduced, which clearly pointed to the direction of development of the national economy: the state order for 1988 was lowered to 90 to 95 percent of the general volume of production, and in some branches even lower. Thus enterprises for the first time acquired the official right to dispose of a certain portion of their output at their own discretion. The new era of contractual relations was upon us.

The government's tactic was very definitely visible. Since contractual relations were radically new, the transfer to them had to be instituted carefully and with circumspection. There was still no free wholesale trade for providing users with resources; after all, the supply system was geared almost exclusively to centralized deliveries. Moreover, how free contractual prices would develop had to be studied—this, too, was a radical innovation. Finally, we are, after all, talking about the enterprises producing everything considered necessary beyond the limits of the state order, being guided only by demand. But there were essentially no instruments for studying demand. In a word, the economy was entering a completely new phase, and the government correctly assumed that this process should be gradual. As experience was acquired, in 1989 the share of the state order was to be lowered even farther. And so forth, up to reasonable proportions, established by experience itself.

This was the proposal of the state plan for socioeconomic development for 1988—in my view, on the whole a very measured, soundly conceived, and clearly delineated strategy for the further reform of the whole economic system. It developed the tactic of economic experimentation established in the years of perestroika that could now be called the "tactic of great trials and small errors." Radical innovations were eschewed, and possible breakdowns would have been restricted to the local level.

This tactic correctly took into consideration real processes and the unknown nature of the new economic paths. It was developed by people well versed in the complexity and contradictory nature of the country's economic organism, aware of the psychology of our economic planners and their "economic tempers."

But politicians had to confirm the proposal. By late 1987 the political situation in the country was very different from that at the beginning of perestroika. Processes in the sphere of power had shifted direction from the democratization of all aspects of life, to attempts to change the political system as quickly as possible. Society was divided into the "foremen of perestroika" and the "forces of deceleration."

In taking up long-term issues of changing the political system, radical circles let the current problems of the country slide. The situation in society was heating up before our very eyes. Complications also started arising among the top political leaders, attested to by the events surrounding my speech in Elektrostal. Yakovlev and I had it out. Positions were finally defined, and the confrontation with the radicals was out in the open at last. Everything indicated that Gorbachev was already in the trap they had set. This prompted the radicals to act energetically to attain success.

And act they did.

The proposal for the state plan was presented for discussion to the Politburo at the end of 1987. As was often the case in such situations, the meeting was attended by leaders of the Council of Ministers and many ministers. Naturally, the plan was not prepared in secret; all the documents were sent out ahead of time to Politburo members and Central Committee secretaries so they could familiarize themselves with them. Quite a few amendments were usually made to the proposal in such discussions, since every member of the political leadership studied it beforehand along with the Central Committee departments, consulting ministers, and sometimes republics or provinces, by telephone when necessary. Amendments more often than not reflected a collective opinion, the interests of various social or professional groups.

But never before had the proposal for the plan been rejected essentially in its entirety; the very concept of the plan was deemed unacceptable.

This time this is exactly what happened.

When Ryzhkov finished his report, Yakovlev took up the attack on the plan as a whole. He spoke sarcastically about the command-administrative system and demanded that the pace of economic reform be accelerated and economic reform be radicalized. In conclusion, he announced that the proposal presented by the Council of Ministers was conservative and "decelerating" and did not take into account the demands of life.

As often happened at Politburo sessions, Yakovlev was actively seconded by Medvedev. (I recall Medvedev's theoretical articles in the magazine *Kommunist,* in which, on the eve of the 1980s, he ardently—there is no other word for it—defended the concept of developed socialism. Now Medvedev, without explanation or repentance, diametrically changed his point of view and supported the "foremen of perestroika." But his approach to business remained the same as before.) Medvedev, like Yakovlev, was far removed from the practical necessities of life, and therefore Medvedev's demands for a sharp reduction in the state order were speculative and obviously sketchy, and caused bewilderment among those present in the meeting room.

Against the background of the propagandistic squabbles of that time, it was not difficult to know where this was heading. Voices were immediately heard calling for circumspection and a gradual approach. This view was expressed by those members of the Politburo, Central Committee secretaries (Vorotnikov, Zaikov, Nikonov, and Slyunkov), and ministers who constantly had to deal with practical issues of management, who were well acquainted with real life and the most complex interconnections in the economy.

Gorbachev took another position. One rarely heard Gorbachev called a weak-willed man, nor is he (although at times he gives that impression). This time he spoke energetically, vigorously, and with a peremptory tone. Reproaches of conservatism and a return to old approaches were leveled at the proposal. Naturally, the general secretary referred to foreign experience and insisted that economic relations must be changed quickly. Perestroika demanded this, otherwise "the people would not understand," would not forgive sluggishness. Right away, as was his wont, he reminded us that there was no time for experiments. His words had categorical overtones, dismissing the possibility of any other decision. In such a situation, direct opposition could have been viewed as a lack of confidence in him.

Gorbachev truly displayed his character that time. Apparently he was absolutely convinced that he was right, that all economic problems would be solved as soon as we implemented a radical reform, the sooner the better.

One may ask, Who was echoing whom—Yakovlev, echoing Gorbachev, or vice versa? This is not a rhetorical question; it arises because on the eve of the 28th Party Congress, *Moscow News* published an article titled "The Good Man from the Politburo," in which the whole development of the perestroika policy was attributed directly and exclusively to Yakovlev; Gorbachev was only "voicing" his ideas.

At that Politburo session, we were talking about such fundamental problems in the policy of renewal as the depth and rate of social reforms. At the June 1987 Central Committee plenum, when we discussed a radical economic reform, the word "radical" was taken as a synonym of the depth of the reforms and did not elicit objections. But at the memorable Politburo session at the end of 1987, it was used as a kind of "whip" for sharply accelerated transition of contractual relations. But the depth of reforms and their rate of implementation are not equivalent. What is more, life and even political experience show us that the more serious the decisions being implemented, the more fundamental preparations they require, so as not to damage the cause in making haste.

To get a full picture, we need to recall what was taking place outside the Kremlin walls. The radicals' star was rising. Having cranked public opinion into high gear, they directed it against the central government, accusing it of conservatism, deceleration, attempting to return to the period of stagnation. The right-wing radicals of the mass media beat into the national consciousness each day that only government and ministerial officials stood in the way of a new life. If they were removed, the gates to paradise on earth would immediately be thrown open.

Only the agro-industrial complex was standing in the way of the country's being fed to satiation; if it were liquidated, store shelves would crumble under the abundance of food products. The public image of the old management structures (which indeed needed reforming, and had themselves embarked on this road by mapping out a gradual, smooth transition of the national economy to contractual relations), was turned into that of "enemies of perestroika." They were not criticized, they were reviled.

But the powerful propaganda machine of the radical mass media did more than create an image of the enemy of perestroika in the person of ministers and departments. With its unqualified promises, it even muddled the minds of some sophisticated economic planners, primarily directors of large plants that held a monopoly position in industry, playing on their lack of practical experience. In 1987, captains of industry were often invited to express their views in newspapers and on television. They complained, not without justification, of the pressure of independence and initiative, but at the same time they demanded that the pressure of the plan be lifted from them and that they be given almost complete economic freedom immediately.

They rashly felt that their monopolistic position would bring them huge winnings in making the transition to contractual relations; the demand for output was high, and they could establish contractual (free) prices and sharply increase profits in the process. At that time television showed the first auctions at which a Zil truck, whose state price was about 5,000 rubles, sold for 85,000 rubles. The directors did not take into account that an excessively fast disruption of established cooperative ties would hit first of all those plants that needed a large quantity of spare parts.

The directors of large production facilities now curse the day and hour when they began disrupting economic ties with factories producing parts for use by others.

In general, in the discussion at the Politburo of the conception of the plan for 1988, when the very fate of economic perestroika was being decided, and along with it the fate of the country, intense pressure was being invisibly exerted by public opinion that had been misguided. Considering the particular, fundamental importance of the decisions made at that time, here was a classic model of skillful manipulation of mass consciousness through the controlled medium of the press. This example will undoubtedly go down in history.

It was difficult for a government that was universally reproached for "conservatism" to stand up to the strong political pressure. As a result of very tense debates, the conception of the plan for 1988 was deemed unsatisfactory and was essentially rejected.

The government retreated. In the report at the Politburo session, it was briefly and vaguely stated that the USSR Council of Ministers had been charged with continuing work on the proposal for the plan for 1988. Neither the nation nor the community found out about the dramatic upheavals of that Politburo session.

At this critical moment the fate of the country was being decided: it was precisely then that the worsening of the economic situation was irreversibly predetermined, that the disruption of finances and the ultimate decline into deep crisis became inevitable.

The radical, or rather, ultraradical, option prevailed: the state order for many ministries was immediately lowered by one-third; in some branches by one-half or more. In effect, an attempt was made to implant contractual, in essence commodity-market, relations in a planned system without the legal and economic groundwork, without creating a tax system and a market infrastructure. Given the extremely monopolized structure of the national economy, with many products manufactured by only one or two enterprises, contractual economic relations were in fact commodity-market, based fundamentally on the law of supply and demand. Moreover, antimonopoly measures had not yet been drafted, and the taxing of superprofits had not yet started. As a result, collective greed burst into full bloom, cooperative ties started to break, and supply became unbalanced.

Taking advantage of free contractual prices, many enterprises, especially those in machine-building, in the initial stages began to "reap" huge amounts of money—superprofits, not due to a growth in production but exclusively to their monopoly position, which allowed them literally to grab the consumer by the throat. These profits, which were not really earned but acquired instead with the aid of monopolistically high contractual prices, then largely went toward wages, which caused a spasmodic rise in the population's income. In the 1970s, the annual rise of income was 8 billion to 10 billion rubles. For the first seven years of the 1980s it was 12 billion to 15 billion rubles. In 1988 income suddenly rose by more than 40 billion rubles, and the consumer market ballooned.

I remember that exactly a year after the memorable Politburo session on the eve of 1989, I went into the general secretary's office to wish him a happy New Year. I said with sorrow: "The sooner this year ends, the better, Mikhail Sergeyevich."

"What don't you like about it?" Gorbachev responded guardedly.

"That unsatisfied demand has risen sharply. After all, the population's income has grown by 42 billion rubles; this has never happened before. And this means that the country is faced with total financial ruin."

"Well, yes," Gorbachev answered vaguely. One could feel that he, too, was troubled by the evolving situation. His mood was not nearly as cheerful as it had been a year before. But at that moment we could not have foreseen that in 1989 income would rise by another 60 billion rubles, and in 1990, by 90 billion rubles. Altogether, in the three years that followed the decision to "correct" the government's plan, when the reasonable option was voted down and reliance was placed on the ultraradical option, the population's income rose by 190 billion rubles, outstripping the availability of commodities manyfold.

This was a real catastrophe.

What happened? What happened to the economy? Taking a closer look at the processes under way, one might say: The "contractual freedom" that gave enterprises the right to dispose immediately of a considerable part of their products at their own discretion was essentially the spontaneity of market relations. The economy, unprepared for this sudden shock procedure, began to show immediate shortcomings. The flareup of group selfishness led to a situation in which unprofitable goods started being removed from production everywhere; the inexpensive product mix quickly disappeared, and machine-builders refused small-run orders, which put the whole repair base of the country on the brink of disaster. Plants hit on a barter exchange based on the principle "You scratch my back and I'll scratch yours."

Moreover, over many decades strong monopolistic tendencies had arisen in our national economy, in which there are many industrial giants. They were not problems for a planned economy, since cooperative deliveries were strictly regulated. But as soon as industry was let loose to form contractual ties, monopolists choked the consumers with prices. In addition, many plants began to suffocate from a lack of raw materials. Before six months had passed, the industrialists were crying out "Help!" and begging for their state order to be increased, since this would mean guaranteed supplies.

But this was not all. The state order was severely reduced in the machine-building and other manufacturing branches, while in the basic branches, particularly energy fuels, it remained essentially at 100 percent. This placed coal producers, in particular, in a very bad economic position, since they already had to buy many things at contractual prices, while they sold coal at state prices only. This was one of the causes of the powerful miners' strikes that flared up in the summer of 1989. In other words, the radicalization of the plan for 1988 had serious political implications, including not only the miners' strikes but also the developments in the Baltic republics.

Baltic industry, situated at the end of the production chain and oriented basically toward the production of finished goods, continued to receive raw materials punctually at state prices but started selling half its goods at high contractual prices. If the miners were clearly the losers, the Balts were the winners. The possibility of their finding more profitable customers became the impulse for the disruption of long-established ties with consumers in other regions of the country and prompted "republic selfishness" and the idea of regional cost accounting.

Yes, many misfortunes were brought upon our country by the impulsive decision made at the insistence of the radicals at the end of 1987. To this day I cannot forget that stormy Politburo session at which energetic demands were heard to "renounce half measures" and to traverse rapidly, in two years at most, the path to full contractual relations. This was a fateful lack of understanding of economic processes. Today everyone sees what has come of that decision: the disruption of finances, the collapse of the consumer market, and a deep crisis. . . . Radicalism turned out to be a perfect example of political recklessness.

Of course, responsibility for that decision lies with all members of the political leadership, myself included. How many times did I later reproach myself bitterly for not putting the question point-blank, for not going for an open conflict, for not washing the dirty linen in public. Alas, an opportunity missed cannot be brought back.

But we must be clear that the chief blame lies with those who insisted on voting down the sensible government proposal, who demanded and attained a radicalization of the reform.

Three years later, when the economy was already threatened with complete paralysis—since the cooperative ties for 1991 were retained at the level of only 65 percent—the president of the USSR issued a decree requiring temporary retention of former contracts until market mechanisms were worked out. Alas, in doing so Gorbachev did not self-critically tell the nation that it was at his insistence, at his very strong pressuring, that at the end of 1987 the country's economy had been imprudently thrown into a period of shocks.

Paradoxically, this fateful mistake was hidden from the people during the time of proclaimed glasnost. Those primarily responsible for it moved from Old Square to the Kremlin and continued to give advice on running the country.

There is not much point now in berating the people whose thoughtless, politicized, ideologized decisions thrust our country into the clutches of crisis. This is not the time for investigations. But one should, after all, learn a lesson from what has happened!

Leafing through the newspapers for the years 1987–90, one is amazed at the multitude of events in which Gorbachev participated. Under such conditions, it was difficult to think fundamental issues through deeply. Days off were primarily devoted to this aim. One at times gets the impression that Gorbachev's immediate circle intentionally assigned the general secretary an unthinkable work load; events collided and intertwined.

Externally Gorbachev endured the physical and psychological commitments with éclat: he was always collected, charming when necessary, in other instances demanding. Here was a leader with a firm grip on the helm of perestroika. However, I was sometimes reminded of an interesting image suggested by one of the chauffeurs in the old days. When someone drives through the city at a speed of 35 miles per hour, he can easily choose a convenient route. But if you force a driver to dash along unknown streets at 60 miles an hour, he'll only have time to turn the steering wheel to avoid smashing into the nearest impediment. It's hard for him to choose the best route under such conditions, and so he'll heed the prompting of the passenger sitting next to him.

A fitting image . . . It sometimes seemed to me that Gorbachev was being forced to rush at breakneck speed so that all his strength would go to preventing imminent catastrophe. Gorbachev proved himself to be a virtuoso driver of the locomotive of perestroika. But at the speed at which he had to tear along, he could not foresee the future with any degree of sagacity.

And it seems to me that he was rushed with an ulterior motive.

Those who called for circumspection, for a more moderate pace of reforms, were called conservatives. This was particularly manifest at the Politburo session in December 1987, when the initial essence of economic perestroika was essentially distorted.

At that time there was still no talk of a market, privatization, private ownership. These economic categories only appeared in official documents much later—in late 1989, in 1990. At the June 1987 Central Committee plenum, there was not even a hint of a market model of management.

A radical reform of the economy, Gorbachev noted in 1987, absorbed everything that the practical experience of the previous two years, academic thought, and the lessons of building socialism had given us. But only a short time later, the direct opposite was declared; there was no longer any room in it for centralized planning.

Then private ownership made its appearance, and a new course in policy was declared—from a planned economic system to a "free-market system." Again, we saw inconsistency and vacillation.

We know where it led. I recall my meeting with Ryzhkov in August 1990 in his Kremlin office. I no longer held an official position, but I continued to be actively interested in the economic situation, and this was what we discussed.

Ryzhkov was in a state of extreme alarm. The economic situation was terrible, he said, worse than after the Great Patriotic War. The ability to manage had fallen to a low mark. Discipline had collapsed. The government was having difficulty keeping the national economy afloat. In the provinces and republics where Party leadership was stronger—for instance, Saratov Province, which he had recently visited—things were better.

He added:

> After the 28th Party Congress, I don't know what's happening in the Politburo. Before Gorbachev left for the Crimea on vacation, I asked him how he evaluated the situation in the country and what he saw as the way out. Gorbachev answered that the situation was critical, and the way out was in concluding a new Union treaty. . . . The destruction of the Soviet Union is taking place, that's what's tragic. Do you understand, Yegor Kuzmich? Powerful destructive forces have launched an attack on the government and set themselves the goal of bringing us down. Only a sense of responsibility and my alarm over my Motherland are keeping the government, and me personally, from retiring. We understand, after all, that in our stead may come others who will drag the country in a different direction. . . .

I agreed with Ryzhkov's support for a gradual transition to a planned-market economy, and said:

"You know, Nikolai Ivanovich, the people have a completely different opinion of you than what they write in the newspapers. There are many, very many, who support your line."

This was a difficult period for Ryzhkov. The radicals led one attack after another against him, trying to bring down the Ryzhkov government, to clear the way for the reckless new project, the "500-Days" timetable. Ryzhkov was not giving in but was holding his position firmly. If it hadn't been for a sudden heart ailment, I don't think he would have given in this time, either; the lessons of the radical decision made in December 1987 were too dire.

Ryzhkov and I had been brought into the Politburo at the April 1985 Central Committee plenum and officially became Gorbachev's closest comrades in arms in the cause of perestroika. Ryzhkov was appointed chairman of the USSR Council of Ministers; I had been appointed second secretary of the Central Committee. And it was against the two of us that the most vicious campaign was launched in the mass media. They were successful first in removing me, and then, six months later, Ryzhkov.

Alas, Gorbachev did not intervene on behalf of his closest companions in arms, with whom he had initiated perestroika. The issue is not the personal fate of Ryzhkov and Ligachev, but whether this was to the benefit of the cause. What was behind this? A power struggle? A reorientation of the course of perestroika, in which former confederates no longer concurred?

Of course, times had changed. But Gorbachev himself had changed, too.

The history of the sharp turn in Soviet policy made in April 1985 is not yet complete, however. Perestroika spurred a great country to rear up on its hind legs and drove it to the brink of—what? Can catastrophe be averted?

We do not have long to wait for an answer to these questions. And it is these events of the future that will bring in a final historical verdict on Gorbachev.

Afterword

RUSSIA BEFORE THE STORM— LIFE CANNOT GO ON LIKE THIS

Nearly four years have passed since this book was written. April 1995 marked the tenth anniversary of the beginning of perestroika in the Soviet Union, yet even now the debates have not subsided over whether perestroika was necessary or possible. What were the results of the so-called reforms? What has been their impact after all that has happened in the Soviet Union, both inside the country and beyond its borders? Who is to blame for the country's collapse, its devastation? Where does the solution lie to the profound crisis that the states and peoples of the former Soviet Union, having endured the stormy events of the Soviet era, now find themselves in? I will attempt to provide more or less complete answers to these and other questions for you, the thoughtful reader.

I am deeply convinced that perestroika was not only inevitable but also possible. That is my position today, and that was my position when I belonged to the country's political leadership, the Politburo of the Communist Party's Central Committee, in the years 1985–1990.

There is another point of view, though, which says that the Soviet socialist system was not reformable and for this reason could not have been improved. That is a convenient position for some people. The idea of the inherent impossibility of reforming the Soviet system is now being exploited to the utmost by those who betrayed the cause of socialism. It seems to explain their retreat from the Communist Party's policy of renewing socialism and to justify the country's destruction, the restoration of capitalism, and the suffering and anguish of millions of people. It makes sense that if the social system was not amenable to reform, then naturally it had to be broken, eliminated, and replaced. It makes perfect sense. In fact, however, the basic assumption is faulty.

If we put an end to the self-flagellation and self-humiliation at which we are so expert, to a degree unlike any other country in the world, and assess our history objectively, then we are forced to admit that the Soviet Union has to its credit achievements on a global scale: the transformation of backward czarist Russia into a multiethnic world power; the routing of fascism, that twentieth-century plague; the first launching of men into outer space; the first successful operation of nuclear power stations and nuclear submarines; the flowering of science, culture, and education; and the fact that slowly, year by year, life became materially better and spiritually richer.

At the same time, we must bear in mind the fact that the Soviet Union, like no other country in the world, twice suffered serious setbacks and that more than twenty years were spent fighting against aggression and then restoring the nation's economy.

Some political commentators, to diminish the Soviet Union's successes, draw an idyllic picture of prerevolutionary Russia. In point of fact, czarist Russia (until the October 1917 revolution) was marked by low economic, educational, and cultural levels. For example, in Germany, of the 10,000 men called up for the army shortly before World War I, only 4 were illiterate; in England, 100; but in Russia, over 6,000. In the 1930s, twenty years later, illiteracy had been eliminated in the Soviet Union.

Consolidating around the Russian Soviet Federal Socialist Republic and the Russian people, the other republics and ethnic groups formed the Soviet Union and built their relations on the basis of equality, friendship, and mutual assistance. Within the borders of the Soviet Union, 130 nations existed peacefully, developing and enriching one another, a multiplicity of cultures that was a gold mine for world culture.

The Soviet Union, along with its allies in the anti-Hitler coalition, the United States, England, and France, played a decisive role in the rout of fascism (1941–1945) and ensured the most extended peace that Europe has known in centuries. This success was possible thanks to the just Soviet social order, the leading role of the Communist Party, the mass heroism of the Soviet people, and the country's transformation in the 1930s into the second greatest industrial nation in the world.

So much untruth and slander has been splashed on our great victory. Some say we did not fight properly and that the country's leadership panicked. Politicians remind me of a critical fly on the wall of a beautiful building that sees only the unevenness of the wall's brick and so naturally is unable to appreciate the beauty of the building as a whole. Our ill-wishers do not want to recognize the greatness of our victory or the superiority of the Soviet order over Hitler's tyranny; they see rotten twigs and fail to notice the healthy tree. They disown their own people, the victor, their own Fatherland, with all its joys and misfortunes.

Soviet Marshal G. K. Zhukov, a great military leader of modern times, wrote:

> As for the country's leadership, it was never in a state of confusion but decisively led the struggle of the Soviet people. It is perfectly clear that the victory had to be and was the result of a titanic and concerted organizational effort by the Communist Party. Without this fundamental and critical factor, not only the victory over the enemy but the very struggle against the fascist invasion would have been impossible.

It is for good reason that our Communist Party was called a fighting party. Three million Communists perished on the fronts of World War II in the fighting between the Soviet people and the German aggressors. The Communists took the lead both in battle and in labor, in the factories and the fields.

In 1941, in a matter of a mere six months, the country was moved east—to the Urals, to Siberia. More than a thousand enterprises were moved 4,000 kilometers; in early 1942 they started turning out airplanes, tanks, artillery, and ammunition for the front. This was a great achievement for the people and the Party! During the war years I worked at the foremost aviation plant in Siberia, so I know this not just from stories.

The Soviet system demonstrated its vitality in both the defense of the Fatherland and the restoration and development of the nation's economy. Only seven to eight years after the war, thousands of devastated towns and villages had been resurrected from the ashes, and in the postwar period the Soviet Union closed the gap with the United States on basic economic indicators. In short, good gentlemen, it was socialism that brought the country to the summit of history, and it is the Soviet period that is the most significant in its entire history.

In the late 1970s and early 1980s, however, the Soviet form of socialism took a serious downturn, economic growth rates dropped sharply, and the development of socialist democracy lagged. One of the chief problems that the country's leadership faced then was the constantly mounting gap between the Soviet Union and the developed countries of the West in technology and efficiency in civilian output. Industrial labor productivity was half and agriculture a fourth that of the United States. (By the way, in the four years of rule by the pseudodemocrats, the gap in labor productivity grew even bigger: Industry lagged by a factor of six to seven, and agriculture by an even higher factor.)

The slowdown in the country's development and the mounting difficulties in the pre-perestroika period can be attributed to several factors, but above all to the fact that a model of state socialism (not feudal or barracks socialism, as some have said) had been constructed. Too much public property had been put in the hands of the state with respect to the means of production. In particular, the kolkhoz-cooperative form of property was unjustifiably equated to state property in many ways. This imbalance held back the initiative of labor collectives and impeded their participation in production management. I should also mention the state monopoly in production over many types of goods, which necessarily excluded competition.

Besides these factors, huge military expenditures and the mighty military-industrial complex, which swallowed up a significant share of the state's material, technical, and labor resources, inhibiting the development of the economy's civilian sector and the resolution of major social programs, took a disastrous toll. Now that the defense industry has become a much more open economic sector, the world is amazed. In the West, a real hunt is on for Soviet defense technologies. Western specialists say, "This is like the discovery of Atlantis." The military complex ensured the country's proper defense capabilities and allowed it to achieve strategic military parity with the United States and to avert world war, albeit at colossal expense.

By the mid–1980s, quite a few problems had built up in the development of the union-state. Contradictions had arisen between the Center and the republics of the Union, and the resolution of many republic-level issues was unwarrantedly concentrated in all-Union organs in the Center. Often one republic's share of the cost of implementing all-Union tasks was unjustifiably covered by the contributions of other republics, which generated dissatisfaction. Also at times the national and cultural traditions of various ethnic groups were violated.

All this, taken together, hampered the realization of major social programs and the development of the consumer sector of the economy and had a negative effect on the quality of life for working people. In short, it was becoming clear that social transformations were needed, a restructuring, or perestroika, of many spheres of society. There is nothing surprising in this. Sooner or later every society faces the inevitability of reform in the course of its development.

People often ask, "Did perestroika have a theoretical basis, or was it the fruit of its organizers' inspiration?" It cannot be said that perestroika was equipped with an elegant theory, but its basic contours were well defined. Perestroika's fundamental principle was V. I. Lenin's conclusion that the only way to progress was in the direction of socialism. Hence the slogan, "More socialism, more democracy!" Hence also the chain of historical and political events and the efforts to improve society within the context of the Soviet system and on the basis of socialism without the alteration of the economic, political, or social foundations of the system. That meant the predominance of state ownership of the means of production and the diversity of that ownership's form, the expansion of socialist democracy, the strengthening of the soviets and the power of the workers, and the consolidation of the working class, the working peasantry, and the popular intelligentsia.

In elaborating the policy of perestroika, we based ourselves on the theory of the mutual interaction and influence of economics and democracy, the idea that the one could stimulate the other. Hence came the demand to carry out transformations in the economy and the political system simultaneously.

Finally, we assumed the decisive role of the workers under socialism. Hence the activization of labor collectives in resolving production and social issues, in strengthening the role of public opinion, in extending glasnost, and in the nationwide discussion of important legislation. All this participation has been lost. The radical remaking of society is proceeding without consultation with the working people, apart from its will, and, moreover, to its detriment and to the good of an insignificant minority.

True, you do hear it said that the present authorities have no program of transformations and do not know where they are leading the country. In fact, the authorities are attempting to conceal from the people the true goals of their policy by declaring that there is no place in Russia for socialism or capitalism. In actuality, they are following a course to restore the capitalism of a hundred years ago in alliance with foreign powers. In the West, many politicians like present-day Russia and its president. The collapse of the state, the decline of the economy, salaries of seventy dollars and pensions of twenty, crime and vandalism running rampant, the corruption, the hundreds of thousands killed—they like our perishing country.

You often hear that perestroika did not have precise goals or a concrete program and for that reason, they say, it ended in failure. That is not true. That is not true at all.

Perestroika did have precise goals and concrete programs. They were spelled out at the 27th Party Congress in 1986 and at the plenums of the

Communist Party's Central Committee in the years 1985–1987. The goals for revitalizing our socialist society were to create a highly efficient economy, to effect a substantial improvement in the material and spiritual life of the individual, and to expand real participation by the working masses in governing the state.

The following were the principal aims of perestroika:

> In the socioeconomic sphere: modernize the machine-building complex and, on this basis, bring about the planned reconstruction of the nation's economy and its social reorientation; link planning extensively with the development of money-exchange relationships; create the necessary economic conditions for the financial self-sufficiency and self-financing of enterprises without state subsidies; and create major scientific and technical complexes
>
> In the political sphere: democratize the soviets, or councils, at all levels; and expand the rights and authorities of the regions, territories, and republics;
>
> In foreign policy: prevent nuclear war; make the transition from confrontation to real disarmament; and strengthen socialist concord

Perestroika's principal ideas and goals found reflection in the Twelfth Five-Year Plan (1986–1990), for instance, in the program to modernize the machine-building complex (machine tool construction, instrument making, electronics, robotics). Two hundred billion rubles (in 1985 prices) were allocated for this program, twice as much as in the preceding ten years. To satisfy consumer demand, a program was developed to create modern light and food industries, with total allocations of 70 billion rubles, to be spread out between 1988 and 1995 (predicated on the conversion of the defense industry).

We did not get what we had expected, though. Moreover, the positive construction we saw in the Soviet era was replaced by destruction, the collapse of statehood, and the country's loss of its status as a world power. The goals of perestroika—an efficient economy, an improved standard of living, a developed democracy—not only were not achieved but suffered a serious setback. The questions naturally arise, Why did perestroika fail? Why was the country set back decades and made to resemble the scene of a natural disaster?

Along with them another question may be posed: Could the processes begun in 1985 have led the country to results other than those we see today? Yes, without a doubt, the results could have been different. The country could have been even more powerful, and the life of working people more secure, safe, and meaningful.

In order to justify the country's devastation, the "architects of perestroika" and the current rulers are attempting to foist on the public the idea that the Soviet system was not amenable to reform and for that reason had to be broken up and swept away. The truth is that as long as society was being transformed within the framework of the Soviet system, that is, for the purpose of improving it, and not within the framework of dismantling it, the country's affairs were looking up.

Perestroika went through two stages: an upsurge during the first four years, followed by social disintegration and decline in the next. In these memoirs, arguments and facts are cited to prove this thesis. The following should be added: During the period from 1986 to 1989, the Soviet Union achieved its highest volumes ever of industrial and agricultural production. Citizens' real income rose. Yes, people experienced a food shortage, but the per capita consumption of meat and dairy products at that time—note carefully, reader—was 70 and 380 kilos, respectively, or nearly 90 percent of the physiologically essential level of consumption. Now, when there is an "abundance" on the store shelves, that consumption is only 44 and 240 kilos, respectively. This is attributable to high prices and the 40 percent decrease in food output. It takes neither intelligence nor effort for the leaders of any country to create this kind of "abundance."

By the mid–1980s, 80 percent of the country's population were residing in their own apartment. The goal was set to guarantee each family its own apartment or house by the year 2000. During the years of perestroika, the country saw its greatest volume of housing construction, 3 million apartments annually, an increase of 30 percent. Now, the volume of housing construction in the states of the former Soviet Union is 1 million apartments a year, the level of the 1950s. Like locusts, the "democrats" who came to power are gobbling up all the fruits of the people's labor that lie in their path without creating anything worthwhile. Perestroika lost its socialist, genuinely democratic, purpose and ended in 1991 with the state coup and the breakup of the Soviet Union. I wrote about this in 1991, and there is no reason to reconsider this point of view. Moreover, time has confirmed it.

How could this have happened? One must bear in mind the real historical conditions behind the construction of the new society: the backwardness of the productive forces of czarist Russia and the constant threat from the ruling circles of the capitalist world, the inordinately huge expenditures on defense, and the lag behind the West in the consumer sector and the overall economy.

One cannot discount the fact that more than twenty of the seventy-four years of Soviet power were spent repelling aggression and rebuilding the country. Despite that, the country achieved a high level of economic development, although the gap in the standard of living between the peoples of the Soviet Union and of the United States remained quite noticeable. It should be kept in mind, however, that everything we achieved was the result of our own efforts, whereas the developed capitalist countries accumulated much of their wealth by the open plunder of colonial peoples in the past and by ferrying cheap natural resources out of Third World countries today, exploiting their cheap workforce . In this way the capitalist countries have secured a relatively high standard of living for their populations. This is not to deny the talent and highly productive labor of their own peoples.

What happened in our country is primarily the result of the debilitation and eventual elimination of the Communist Party's leading role in society, the ejection of the Party from major policymaking, its ideological and organizational unraveling, the formation in it of factions, careerists' and national separatists' penetration of the leadership of the Party and state as well as the Party and power structures of the republics, and the political conversion of the group headed by Gorbachev and their shift to the position of eliminating the Communist Party and the Soviet state. Gorbachev quit the post of general secretary of his own accord, without convening a plenum of the Central Committee, and offered no resistance to the actions of Yeltsin, who signed both an edict banning the Communist Party and the Belovezhkaya Pushcha agreement on dismembering the Soviet Union. Now, both are heaping the blame on the Communists and the Communist Party. It is a paradox, but a fact.

The burden of the mistakes and crimes committed by the Party's leaders in the 1930s and the massive unwarranted repressions and crude violations of law have had a negative effect. The harmful consequences of Stalin's cult of personality were exposed and surmounted at the initiative of the Communist Party decades ago, but the pseudodemocrats are silent on this point.

Their silence has largely meant that the Communist Party's effort to battle the chief threat—antisocialist, national-separatist forces—has been displaced by the campaign to eliminate the so-called conservative forces, of which I am considered to be the main representative, although I actually came out in favor of improving and reforming society within the framework of the Soviet system. It was these forces that worked to keep the system from being weakened and destroyed.

One other point. In 1990–1991, the gap between the goods and income of workers grew; the consumer goods shortage hit hard, and people's dissatisfaction mounted. In the republics of the former Soviet Union, separatist tendencies gained strength. The Soviet Union's position in the international arena was weakened. There arose in the country political movements that aimed at eliminating the Soviet system and creating a society on the Western model. Relying on active support from foreign powers, the shadow economy, the "elite" of the creative intelligentsia, and a portion of the state apparatus, by means of deceit and demagoguery, especially regarding the nonexistent privileges of the *nomenklatura,* these movements were able to enlist the support of a certain segment of society.

One cannot discuss the reasons for our failure without talking about the fact that final victory in building socialism in the Soviet Union was declared prematurely, and that led to complacency. As we know, Lenin was the first Marxist to propose the idea of building socialism in one country. At the same time, he said, "Final victory is possible only on a world scale and only through the joint efforts of workers in all countries." Lenin's conclusion was not heeded. It was supplanted by another: The victory of socialism in a few countries is sufficient for the ultimate victory of socialism in the Soviet Union. As matter of fact, the victory of socialism in just a few countries offers no guarantee against the restoration of capitalism, especially if capitalism is retained in the principal countries.

Those are a few of the factors that led to the failure of our policy for social renewal and to the profound disarray and eventual collapse of the Soviet Union. The denouement came in the months from August to December 1991. Under the false banner of building "a civil, rule-of-law society," the pseudodemocrats, who were led by Yeltsin and enjoyed the sufferance of Gorbachev, carried out a counterrevolutionary coup: The antipopular ruling regime set about eliminating the soviets, removing workers, peasants, and the working intelligentsia from power and forming an antidemocratic authoritarian regime.

Society's chief contradiction has become the antagonism between labor and capital, between the majority, which is going begging, and a minority that is getting richer and whose interests are served by the government and the corrupt portion of the state. A new bourgeoisie is taking shape in the country; the working class, ousted from power and stripped of its rights of ownership of the basic means of production, is being transformed into a proletariat; and society is entering a period of acute class struggle. The country is moving from profound crisis to utter ruin.

The "democrats" are taking a backseat in major policymaking, leaving behind nothing but a string of disasters and a mountain of lies. They can be credited with nothing constructive, unless one counts the luxurious mansions for the handful of the superrich. The "reforms" serve an insignificant minority, whereas the majority of the people are going begging and are worse and worse off.

By privatizing state property and liberalizing prices (lifting price controls), the "democrats" have picked and torn the country apart. Privatization of property and price liberalization had as their goal increasing production, improving its efficiency, increasing labor productivity, attracting investments, and creating a middle class of property owners as a social bulwark for the present regime. The "reformers" placed their hopes on price liberalization, thinking that increased prices would interest enterprises in increasing production and lead to a decline in consumer prices in the market. Yeltsin declared that we needed a million property owners, not millionaires.

Privatization (popularly known as piratization) and price liberalization (shock therapy) suffered utter defeat without achieving a single one of their stated goals. Moreover, privatization of the nation's property and price liberalization disorganized the economy and led to its decline, with a detrimental effect on most people. First of all, production is falling, labor productivity is declining, and investments in privatized enterprises are being cut. Second, many who did hold vouchers and shares have sold them in order to survive. Major share holdings have been concentrated in the hands of a few, purchased with ill-gotten gains. During mass privatization, the workers agreed to maintain a significant portion of the property in the hands of the enterprise administration so as to save the enterprise itself during the economic crisis, thereby forfeiting all control over administration.

Privatization became the "sale of the century," in which the state property created by and stolen from the people was sold for a song. Not millions of property owners, but a handful of millionaires and billionaires—that was the result of the "democratic reforms." Anyone with any common sense can correctly assess the current situation by comparing what is now to what used to be.

In fact, creation and the steady development of the economy under Soviet power have been replaced by a sharp decline in production in the cities and in the countryside. Compared to 1990 levels, industry has been cut by more than half; machine building, where the achievements of science and technology come to fruition, by 60 percent; clothing and shoe manufacturing by 70–80 percent; and food production by half. Investment in production has been cut by two-thirds, compared to the 1990 level, and for four years virtually no machinery or equipment has been refurbished or replaced, that is, a process of deindustrialization is under way. The science-intensive branches of industry—electronics, instrument making, machine tool construction—are being supplanted. The country is being transformed into a raw materials appendage of the West.

Agriculture is on the brink of total ruin. The output of basic agricultural equipment has come to almost a complete standstill, and the use of mineral fertilizers has decreased by a factor of ten. Domestically made consumer goods are being crowded out of our market, and 40–50 percent of our food is imported. The country is losing its food independence, whereas in 1990, 85 percent of the population's food needs were met by our own production.

Let us take a sphere of human activity such as science, which defines the present and the future. As it was under Soviet power, so is it now under the current rulers. I will cite a famous scholar, Academician B. V. Raushenbakh, from an interview in *For Science,* the newspaper of the Moscow Institute of Physics and Technology (7 April 1995):

> In 1918–1919, V. I. Lenin organized a whole series of scientific institutes, including the Central Institute for Aviation and Hydrodynamics (TsAGI), the Leningrad Institute of Physics and Technology (which produced world-famous scholars Kurchatov, Kapitsa, and Semenov), and the Academy of Agriculture. These huge institutions were created at a time when there seemed to be no hope for the future and the situation in the country was worse than it is now. Now, little Chechnya is burning, but then the entire country was consumed by the flames of civil war.
>
> Under Stalin, a great number of institutes were created. In the mid–1930s, an independent Rockefeller commission, which had organized a philanthropic fund to finance science in poorly developed countries, visited our country. The commission's report was published. Its conclusion: Science was better financed here than in Western Europe. There was no need to help Russia. You have to understand that there was no need, not because it was an ideological opponent, but because science was financed so well that the like was never imagined in the West. For all his cruelty, Stalin was farsighted. Like Lenin, he believed that Russia needed science. Our current rulers don't think we do anymore.

That was the conclusion drawn by Academician Raushenbakh.

I would like to add to that. Soon after World War II, the Siberian Branch of the USSR Academy of Sciences, an entire constellation of major science centers in seven large Siberian cities, was created. It was a world-class feat! I had occasion to take part in the creation in Siberia of the Novosibirsk and Tomsk science cities. At the time, the country was still suffering the harsh aftermath of war, but the government and the Communist Party were generously investing all they could there, equipping science with modern equipment and building comfortable housing for the scientists.

Now, scientists, the best-treated and most-privileged stratum of the population under Soviet power, have been transformed, in the words of Nobel laureate A. M. Prokhorov, into paupers. The anti-Communist pseudodemocrats, although they have pulled down entire scientific collectives and destroyed the careers of many scientists, continue to spout about democracy and Russia's rebirth. And that's the way it is everywhere. It's not a country; it's a natural disaster! Instead of an improvement in material and spiritual life, as we had during the Soviet era, we have the impoverishment of the workers, an annual population drop of a million people, millions unemployed, and moral degeneration.

During the Soviet era, no one went without food, shelter, or work. Now, tens of millions are hungry, homeless, and unemployed. Prices for consumer goods are rising three times faster than wages. More than a third of the population has incomes below the poverty line, and another third comes close to it. The ratio between the incomes of the richest 10 percent and the poorest 10 percent of the population is 1:40, whereas under Soviet rule it was 1:5.

During the years of Soviet power, a person was judged, not by his bag of loot, but by his labor, and lofty moral principles were reinforced: patriotism, internationalism, collectivism, industry, honor, justice. Now, all that is being stamped out of people's consciousness and the historical connection is being broken. The current authorities and the mass media are encouraging the cult of gain, groveling to the rich, contempt for the poor, speculation, hard drinking, prostitution, and savage individualism.

Instead of the peace and quiet of the Soviet era, we are witnessing an unprecedented increase in crime and corruption, hundreds of thousands killed and wounded, and millions of refugees. All measures of development have taken a sharp downturn except mortality and crime—which are rising steeply. This is understandable. The property created by and belonging to the workers is being stolen, society is rife with alcoholism, and the number of unemployed and homeless is growing. The authorities cannot fight the very people they depend upon, that is, the speculators and the corrupt apparatus.

Alcoholism is permeating the country. The annual per capita consumption of pure alcohol is now sixteen liters; the people are being turned into alcoholics because that makes them easier to govern. The only products that have become relatively cheaper than before are alcoholic beverages. Matters have reached the point that expenditures for sports are being covered out of income from the sale of alcoholic beverages and cigarettes, and sports organizations, which derive enormous profit from such sales, are involved in this. You would think that sports, alcohol, and cigarettes were incompatible concepts. But this is the market, after all! No one can be bothered about people's health; money and profit come first.

Young people find themselves in a difficult position, especially those who are inclined to productive activity, science, and culture. Before, young people could study for free, enter any academic institution, receive a stipend, choose the work they liked. Now, many have to pay for their education and it is hard or altogether impossible for them to find a job in their field, which means they cannot start families or get an apartment. In the Soviet land, an advanced system of education was created. All children received a complete and, indeed, mandatory secondary education. Yes, the Communists are "guilty" of that. Now, for the first time in many long years, young men are coming into the army with only an elementary education (through the fourth year). Many children are dropping out of school and taking any job they can find to feed themselves and their family.

As for the freedoms and rights of man, many of them have merely been proclaimed but not backed up by guarantees. Earlier, before the "democrats" seized power, there were two kinds of announcements in the press, radio, and television. First. Wanted, wanted, wanted: workers, engineers, builders, drivers, and so forth. Second. Where you could go to study (for free, of course). Now people are overwhelmed by fear of losing their job and of not being able to feed their family, fear for their children's future and for their personal safety. Under Soviet power, our people never knew anything like it.

How can we talk about human rights if millions of citizens go two or three months without being paid! At the recommendation of foreign advisers, the authorities calculate that an army of unemployed is like a whip compelling people to work better. That's a lie! Praise and moral and material incentives are what people need, not the threat of starvation.

About freedom of movement. In the Soviet Union in the 1930s, a law was passed saying that people could not leave their village and go to the city without permission. After the war of 1941–1945, that law was repealed. Every year hundreds of millions of people moved around the country, paying affordable prices for transport. What happens now? The greater part of the population is unable to buy a ticket on a plane, train, or ship because prices have risen by a factor of tens of thousands, so that now even traveling to attend a relative's funeral is out of the question. The same applies to the means of communication (telephone, telegraph, and post) between points of settlement. Human contact has been restricted to the minimum, and many means of communication have shut down altogether.

That is also true for the information media. Earlier, the average family subscribed to five or six newspapers and magazines; now millions of families are without any newspapers or magazines at all. The prices are fantastic! The inordinate cost of paper and transport has cut the circulation of the central newspapers and magazines by a factor of ten. The pressure is stifling the press economically.

What democracy, by which I mean the power of the people, can we talk about if the working people have been removed from power, the country is ruled by a president endowed with the authorities of a monarch, and the parliament has been stripped of its rights? The only thing the president cannot do, as the saying goes, is turn a man into a woman. According to the constitution, which fewer than one-third of voters ratified, the president, and not the parliament personally, "determines the main directions for domestic and foreign policy." The president likes to repeat, "What I say goes." He stands above any legislative or executive authority.

It is natural to ask, Why didn't the people defend socialism and its accomplishments? Why didn't the counterrevolution meet with resistance on the part of the workers? Is that really the way it was?

The people believed in perestroika because it was accompanied by the slogan, "More socialism, more democracy." Working people were convinced of the need for change within the framework of socialism, but not its destruction. The first years of perestroika did bring improvement in the country. People were enthusiastic. But then a process of decline set in, which led to dissatisfaction among the population and which was exploited by antisocialist forces first to discredit and later to undermine Soviet society.

Bear in mind that perestroika was carried out by the Communist Party, which enjoyed the trust of the working masses. By that time political struggle inside the Party was a thing of the past (at least that was the perception), and it would have been hard to imagine there being people inside the Party leadership who would betray the interests of the country and its people. Or so I, as a member of the country's political leadership, thought. The healthy forces of the Party, including those in the leading echelon, were totally consumed by economic and management problems and had no experience with political struggle. None of the politicians during the years of perestroika or after the state coup of 1991 talked about replacing the social order. The people were deceived.

If the pseudodemocrats had promulgated their plan of action aimed at the collapse of the Soviet Union and the restoration of savage capitalism in advance, the majority would not have supported it. The people would have rejected it. Under the banner of reform the pseudodemocrats are destroying the Soviet social order, although we know that reform means improving the existing order without altering society's economic, political, and social foundations. The pseudodemocrats are dragging the country back toward capitalism, all the while calling themselves reformers. In fact, the current rulers are the restorers of capitalism, political reactionaries.

In order to dupe the people, the so-called reformers, as I already remarked, proclaimed the construction of a civil, rule-of-law state. Clearly, that is a rather vague, absurd definition of a goal. The "democrats" note, practically as a landmark on this path, that now our people worry about unemployment rather than lines for goods. True, there are no more lines in the stores, which is understandable. Prices have risen at a fantastic rate, consumer demand has dropped by a factor of two to three, and in Russia alone the number of unemployed is nearing 10 million.

The mass media, which were handed over to socialism's opponents by the state-Party elite, have unleashed a slanderous campaign and played a destructive role. They have been busy distorting and blackening Soviet history, sowing confusion in people's minds, and planting misinformation in their consciousness. Now, workers are beginning to see through this. People are comparing today with yesterday; they are linking the Soviet Union's achievements, the secure and meaningful life they led during the Soviet era, with the Communists.

Was there any resistance in the Party or society to antisocialist forces, to the policy aimed at destroying the country and shifting it to the bourgeois rails of development? Some are of the opinion that the people are completely disengaged from all that is going on in the country, that the people are keeping silent, offering no resistance to the ruling regime. That is not true.

In late 1989 and early 1990, attempts were made to call an extraordinary plenum of the Communist Party's Central Committee to discuss the unity of the Communist Party and the territorial integrity of the Soviet Union. Demands for convoking such a plenum had come in from many Communists and Party committees in the country.

During those years, measures were taken—I am writing about this subject for the first time—to organize the healthy forces of the Party and society in order to fight off the opportunism and revisionism of Gorbachev and his team and to defend Soviet power. In 1990, the Russian Communist Party was organized (until then the Russian Party organization had been a direct part of the CPSU, the Soviet Communist Party), and in 1989, the Soviet Peasant Union was founded. I took a very active part in this. The creation of the Party and the Peasant Union was a response to numerous demands. Draft resolutions and memoranda to the Politburo justifying the formation of the Russian Communist Party and the Peasant Union were difficult to get through, and a good deal of time was spent on that. At my own initiative, I spoke at the founding convocations of the Russian Communist Party and the Peasant Union.

By the way, during a scholarly conference devoted to the tenth anniversary of the beginning of perestroika, held in May 1995, Gorbachev addressed me from the tribune: "Why, Yegor Kuzmich, why did you need a Russian Communist Party? Wasn't it to oppose me?" I replied from the hall, "It was done to offer resistance to the destructive policy you and your circle were pursuing." With hard work, we got political figures who were well known in the country and who held firmly to the positions of socialism, the defense of Soviet power, and the interests of the working people to join the leadership of the Russian Communist Party and the Peasant Union: I. K. Polozkov, A. G. Melnikov, G. A. Zyuganov, V. A. Starodubtsev, V. V. Chikin, and I. I. Kukhar.

Any talk about the creation of the Russian Communist Party's leading to the collapse of the Soviet Union is pure invention. Those who bear responsibility for the country's destruction have no choice but to say that. The Russian Communist Party and the Peasant Union, along with their leaders, boldly unmasked the "chief architects"—those who liquidated the Party and state—and courageously defended the power of the people and the integrity of the Soviet Union. Even now they are in the front ranks in the battle against the antipopular regime.

In August 1991, a group of state leaders (the State Emergency Committee) courageously attempted to preserve the Soviet Union. If they are to be criticized, it is for their inconsistency and indecision. Although patriots, they were thrown in prison and accused of betraying the homeland. The case against the State Emergency Committee failed and for all intents and purposes turned against the current authorities, who had betrayed the Fatherland and dismembered the Soviet Union.

Furthermore, day after day for five months, a group of Communist politicians (myself among them), prominent jurists, and scholars, not all of them Party members, including V. I. Zorkaltsev, V. A. Kuptsov, G. A. Zyuganov, A. G. Melnikov, I. I. Melnikov, Martemianov, V. I. Mironov, Iu. M. Slobodkin, Iu. I. Ivanov, I. P. Osadchii, and I. M. Bratishchev, defended the honor of the Communist Party in the Russian Constitutional Court, attempting to prove that the edicts of the Russian president (from the period August–November 1991) banning the activities of the Communist Party were illegal and unconstitutional. According to law, the issue of halting the activities of a political party can be decided only in court or at a conference or congress of the party. That is to say nothing of the fact that the Communist Party they had banned had accomplished such a great deed for the Fatherland and all mankind, lifting the country up from the farmer's plow and into space and defending our fellow countrymen from fascist enslavement.

The president accused the Communist Party of attempting to change the existing order by force in August 1991. That accusation ignited ethnic, social, and religious strife. However, the constitutional court, which examined the "Communist Party case," declared it false and implausible. The Communist Party was acting within the framework of the 1977 Soviet Constitution, the draft of which was discussed for many months (unlike the current Yeltsin constitution) and which defined the Party's leading role in society. As soon as the Communist Party was removed from major policymaking (1989–1990) and later banned (1991), the "democrat"-anti-Communists pulled the Soviet Union apart and brought society to the brink of social explosion. The ideology and politics of militant nationalism and anti-Communism, which have led to fratricidal wars, are being sown in the states that have formed as a result. The Communist Party had acted as a guarantor of social stability for society, of friendship among nations, and of tolerance between peoples of diverse religious confessions.

In short, the Communists secured a beachhead in constitutional court for renewed activity by Russian Communists' primary Party organizations. In February 1993, the Communist Party of the Russian Federation was resurrected.

Bitter resistance was offered to the present authorities in September–October 1993. In response to the state coup carried out by the Russian president, the Congress of People's Deputies, as the highest organ of state power, stripped the president of his authority. At the president's instruction, parliament was fired upon, hundreds were killed, and the parliament's leaders imprisoned.

The "democratic army" has tried to present the events of October 1993 as a putsch organized by parliament. In fact, the many demonstrations and meetings outside parliament represented clusters of social fury: citizens' protest against the acute deterioration in their lives and in defense of the constitution and people's power in the form of the soviets. Tens of thousands of Muscovites and people from many cities in Russia and other states took part in the defense of the House of Soviets!

Members of the West's ruling circles, who consider themselves the "fathers of democracy," let the reprisal against the legally elected parliament pass in silence, and some of them openly supported this bloody action. In the Soviet era of the 1970s and 1980s, many Western rulers' chief accusation against the Soviet Union had been the alleged massive human rights violations. That was a time when Soviet people were provided with everything they needed; they were educated, they enjoyed the right to work, to housing, to free education and health care, to a secure old age, and to personal safety. You could walk through any town at night without concern for your life; now murders and robberies are committed in broad daylight. Now, when people are dying of malnutrition, millions are deprived of their civil rights, hundreds of thousands of people are dying in military conflicts (ten thousand in Chechnya alone), there are no protests forthcoming from the West. All that demonstrates the hypocrisy of many Western politicians, their class approach to social phenomena, chief among which are the further weakening of Russia, its economic and political enslavement, and the prevention of a resurrection of a Soviet union-state.

What is more, one should note the powerful factor of the popular patriotic movement, which has the Communists at its core, and which is offering resistance to the ruling regime. In the years 1992–1995 throughout Russia, there were mass workers' demonstrations and meetings, miners' and teachers' strikes, powerful protest actions by the peasantry, a May Day demonstration in Moscow in 1993, when on order from the authorities the people's blood was shed, and, finally, the march by a half million Muscovites on the fiftieth anniversary of the victory in World War II (9 May 1995).

As you see, there has been resistance to antisocialist forces. Why, then, are the pseudodemocrats in power, even though the way of life of the majority of the people gets worse every year? This situation is explained by several factors, including the vital reserves ("the reserves of socialism") that had been stored away by the population. Those reserves are now running out. With the economy's profound decline, many enterprises are continuing to operate three or four days a week so as to provide the smallest wage possible, although they have ceased to finance any development of production, social welfare, or culture. Moreover, enterprises are selling off at rock-bottom prices the clubs, sports facilities, child care institutions, and treatment and rehabilitation centers that serve their workers and specialists, just to come up with the money to pay wages. The government's sops to individual groups of workers are having their effect:

They are dividing the working people and weakening the united front of struggle for common interests.

Finally, and perhaps most important, a powerful political organization capable of leading a movement of leftist forces and popular masses in favor of a genuinely democratic, socialist path of development has yet to come forward. The ruling regime, however, has not exhausted the possibilities for political maneuvering and for deceiving the masses. Although working people are starting to see through the regime, individual groups of people still find themselves under the influence of anti-Communist propaganda. Overall, the Communist Party's influence on the masses is increasing in the states of the former Soviet Union.

*   *   *

That brings us to one of the main problems: What options does the country have for resolving its profound crisis and emerging on the open field of progress?

There are several possibilities. The first is to adopt the Western model and move backward, back to capitalism, to poverty and the denial of civil rights, to mass unemployment and a semicolonial existence. It is perfectly obvious what would come of this. The second is to return to the past, to state socialism, which has exhausted itself and was a brake on forward movement. That too is unacceptable.

The third is to follow our own path. The Communists are opposed to recreating a capitalist society, with its deep stratification into rich and poor; they are in favor of giving power to the working people, in favor of a socialist path of development without distortion or deformation.

In the first stage, as an opposition force, Communist parties will conduct a political struggle against antipopular regimes in order to return the workers to power. They will actively oppose any steps by the current authorities that adversely affect the already difficult situation of the workers. A bloc of popular-patriotic organizations and movements is now being formed with this goal in mind.

At the second, restorational (transitional) stage, after the workers have won power, the Communists will set themselves the following tasks: cleaning up after the governance of the "reformers"; restoring the foundations of socialism; improving the nation's economy; restoring lost social guarantees to working people (the right to work, housing, free education and health care, and so on); and rebuilding a Soviet union-state. At this stage, several intermediate forms are possible, in particular, a mixed economy that is conditioned by the level of productive forces and that restores the role of public property.

After that will come a transition to a higher stage of socialism in which public property predominates and which provides for high economic growth, efficient production, and the well-being of the people. One way out of the impasse into which the present-day authorities have driven the country is to restore a voluntary economic and political union of Soviet-type states on an equal footing.

In March 1991, a nationwide referendum was held on preserving the Soviet Union. Taking part were 147 million people, 112 million, or nearly 76 percent, of whom voted in favor of preserving the Soviet Union. The Supreme Soviet passed a resolution stating that "the decision is final and binding over the entire territory of the USSR." In December of that same year, Yeltsin, Kravchuk, and Shushkevich—the leaders of Russia, Ukraine, and Belarus—ignoring the people's will and the parliamentary resolution, unilaterally, even though they did not possess the authorities of the supreme organs of power, signed the Belovezhkaya Pushcha agreement, dissolving the Soviet Union. The 1922 pact creating the Soviet Union was torn up like a piece of paper. Meanwhile, according to the Soviet Constitution, the only way the republics could decide to secede from the Union was by referendum. Later, much later, votes on independence were held in the republics. Clearly, in no way could such polls take the place of a referendum on seceding from the Union. In short, from any perspective, the decision to liquidate the Soviet Union was criminal, illegal, and anticonstitutional.

To what purpose did the national separatist forces pull the Soviet Union apart, given that dissolution has brought the people so much suffering and anguish? Any assertion that the Union republics scattered of their own accord, any allegation that they did not possess sovereignty, is just what the national democrats need to cover up the crimes they have committed. In reality, the dismemberment of the Soviet Union was needed for the antisocialist forces to wipe out Soviet power and rule despotically over their own people. Naturally, all that is easier to accomplish when the states and the peoples are divided and estranged. A significant role in the disorientation of the national community was played by the declaration of the former leaders of Ukraine and Belarus and the current president of Russia concerning the creation of a Commonwealth of Independent States, which was supposed to retain the former economic space, a unitary monetary system, unitary armed forces, and "transparent" borders. All that proved to be a bluff, a trick to fool the people. Ultimately, those who destroyed the Soviet Union will undoubtedly shoulder full responsibility for what they did.

The national democrats are trying to foist the idea on people that because the Soviet Union was an empire, its collapse was inevitable. For support, they drag in examples of the collapse of empires from the New and Old Worlds, from the British colonial and Austro-Hungarian empires to the empire of Alexander the Great. Meanwhile, they say nothing about the fact that those empires and others like them were created by force and conquest and were based on the oppression of certain nations by others. Slavery, the absence of civil rights, poverty, and illiteracy for the oppressed nations were among their characteristics.

In the Soviet Union there was neither a dominant nor an oppressed nation. What could it have in common with an empire if Soviet power and the Communist Party included all 130 nationalities that inhabited our country? Many of them were granted statehood and their languages were written down for the first time. The peoples and republics that united to form the Soviet Union achieved major gains in the material and spiritual spheres of society and created a new Soviet way of life. In the early 1920s, when the Soviet Union was formed, the republics differed in economic development by as much as a factor of fifty-two; in the 1980s they differed only by a factor of two. In a few short decades, many peoples had made their way from total illiteracy and ignorance to high culture and education on a world standard.

In the Soviet Union, where the traditions of respectful relationships among peoples of different nationalities were reinforced and cultivated, peoples lived peacefully and amicably, and each person, regardless of nationality, felt at home anywhere. Now, interethnic wars are blazing, causing hundreds of thousands of people pain and suffering and leaving millions without a roof.

General P. I. Georgadze had this to say about the situation in "independent" Georgia:

> I am a soldier. I have seen war, I have seen its aftermath, and I have seen natural disasters [earthquakes] in Ashkhabad, Spitak, and Leninakan. All these pale by comparison, though, with what has happened in Georgia as a result of the destruction of the Soviet Union. Georgia has lost all marks of statehood. It has lost its integrity and been chopped up into principalities. There are three independent states on its territory and seven more pretending to that role. For five years, Georgia has waged a war against its own people. More than 100,000 people have perished, and more than a million have fled the country. Industry has come to a standstill, morals are degenerating, and Georgia is threatened with famine.

So it is also in many other states.

On what do we base our conviction that the restoration of a single union is inevitable? The fact of the matter is that powerful factors are at work facilitating unification. They include the centuries-old economic, cultural, and human ties between our peoples, the unitary national economic complex (up to 70 percent of our industrial decline can be attributed to the destruction of cooperation and trade), the high level of development in the republics thanks to their belonging to the Soviet Union, and the peoples' understanding that the only way out of the crisis's quagmire is together, as a single union.

Also at work is the unifying factor of the tens of millions of citizens of the so-called Russian-speaking population: Russians, Ukrainians, and others (approximately 60 million people) who reside outside the borders of their states, many of whom are being subjected to discrimination. Naturally, they feel a great attraction to the idea of reunifying the Soviet peoples in a single union. True, in quite a few instances Russian speakers, because they felt deprived, have left behind the places they called home and have moved to their own states, to Russia, for the most part. Of course, that is a blow to the states they are leaving: Enterprises are shutting down, and entire branches of the economy and science are folding. The public is sounding the alarm.

The problem of separate states that arose as a result of the destruction of the Soviet Union cannot be resolved by resettling millions of peoples. We must restore the single union-state. This would be the highest form of mercy toward those peoples and a real defense of their rights and interests.

*   *   *

Even Russian President Yeltsin, who contributed so much to the collapse of the Soviet Union, stated: "The policy that led to the breakup did not receive the people's support in a single state." The restoration of a single union is the will of the majority of the Soviet people. Sociological research has shown consistently, year after year, that at least 70 percent of the population is in favor of the governmental unification of the Soviet peoples.

Bear in mind that along with the powerful factors encouraging the unification of the states formed out of the former Soviet Union, there are antisocialist, national separatist forces at work dividing the peoples. Those forces include the burgeoning bourgeoisie, the national democrats, and the national chauvinists. Moreover, forces in the West are doing everything in their power to prevent the restoration of a union-state because disunion makes it easier for them to run the world and to establish their so-called new world order.

In December 1994, one Western newspaper wrote, "We must support any event that decreases the likelihood of Russia's rebirth as a superpower." That is understandable. In the past, not a single important world issue was resolved without the Soviet Union's participation. The nations that are trying to defend their political and economic independence against the claims of imperialist states have lost in the demise of the Soviet Union a reliable champion of their freedom and security. The Soviet Union is credited with having given unselfish assistance to many peoples in their struggle for national liberation and in the development of a world civilization. The restoration of a Soviet union-state would pose a barrier to a new redivision of the world and would help extinguish military conflicts and strengthen peace and international security.

Our "reformers" and their allies in the West are attempting to drag Russia and the other countries formed out of the former Soviet Union into a "world community." It is odd to be talking about these countries joining the "world community" and world civilization when they have long been a part of it and have been making their own contribution to the world treasure-house. In reality, the issue lies elsewhere. Examine this idea and it becomes obvious that former Soviet states' joining the "world community" means the final demolition of the Soviet system and the enrichment of the few and the impoverishment of the many. That is democracy according to the principle that gives the donut to one person and the hole to the other.

Communists are not calling on nations to join the old Union, where history knew not only vast accomplishments but also injustices and crimes; the latter were exposed and eliminated by the Communist Party—certainly not by the "democrats," as they frequently make out. You cannot step twice into the same river of history; it is ever-flowing and changing. Even the ancient Greeks knew this. It is important to move on, not retracing the path precisely but extracting from it everything valuable and taking the present into consideration. As they say, the Earth does not spin in reverse.

The Communists' program rings out with a call to restore a renewed Soviet Union. What do we mean by the idea of a "renewed Soviet Union"? By the renewal of a union of peoples and states, we mean, not the mechanical unification of states of various types, but a single union in which the principles of Soviet federation are developed, the deformations and distortions of socialism are overcome, various forms and methods of economic activity take place under the primacy of public property, the role of the soviets—the workers' councils—increases, and the multiparty system is retained. The sovereign states that enter the union would have their broad independence in resolving republic problems and their high responsibility for implementing their obligations to the union-state reinforced.

Economic relations between the republics would proceed under the assumption that expenditures made for joint programs would be carefully recorded and the income accrued would be distributed accordingly; thus any discussion about who is feeding whom would be moot. It should be stated at the outset that until the debts of the past are made public and we find out who has fed and is feeding whom, until that time there can be no future for our peoples or our states. Often this debt calculation is done simply to prevent the governmental unification of peoples.

Ethnic relations would be built on international solidarity, mutual assistance, state support for national cultures and languages, and the eradication of nationalism and anti-Communism. Fratricidal wars have revealed all too clearly the link between nationalism and anti-Communism and the ruinous consequences of the policy of encouraging anti-Communism. Nationalism and anti-Communism are political twins.

For their "services" in the reprisals against the Communists and the dispersal of the elected Soviet power, Russian rulers have actively supported the Chechen nationalists and armed them liberally with weapons. In the final analysis, the anti-Communism and chauvinism of the ruling regimes have meant ruin for tens of thousands of people and the devastation of towns and villages.

As we see, the chauvinism of the ruling regimes, including the Russian one, represents a special danger to the unification of the peoples and states and has nothing to do with the growth of national self-awareness among the Russian people. Any step, even a simple declarative step, toward the restoration of links between the states meets with a hostile reception. Look at how the Russian chauvinists surrounding the president and the Belarussian nationalists turned against the tentative economic rapprochement between Russia and Belarus. They made every effort to push the idea that the elimination of customs would inflict economic damage on our countries, even though we know that Russia and other states have incurred colossal losses, above all, because they no longer participate in a unified economic bloc or market.

In several republics, violations of the rights of the Russian and Russian-speaking population as a whole are provoking a schism in society along ethnic lines, which is impeding the reunification of the peoples into a new union. The confidence of the nations and ethnicities in the Russian people is our common political capital, which has taken centuries to amass. The Soviet Union is inconceivable without Russia, and Russia cannot be a great power without allying with the peoples and states of the former Soviet Union. Right now, Russia stands on a par with France and England in economic might; Russia's total output is less than 15 percent that of the

United States. It is no accident that politicians in the West consider the United States a world power and Russia merely a regional power.

Two types of integration for the states are possible: capitalist and Soviet. Capitalist integration would mean a union of states based on the dominance of private property and the free market; that would work in the interests of the burgeoning bourgeoisie and lead to massive unemployment, a loss of civil rights, poverty for tens of millions of people, and exploitation of weaker countries. Soviet integration would mean a renewed Union of Soviet peoples; it is the path to unity, freedom, independence, and a better life for working people.

The unification movement will strengthen and expand into a Congress of Peoples of the Soviet Union for the restoration of a federative union of Soviet-type states on an equal footing. The unification movement of peoples is by its very nature international, popular, and patriotic; by its content and goals, it is Soviet federalism; by its means and methods for achieving its goal, it is peaceful and democratic. It includes parties of a national patriotic, Communist, and socialist orientation, trade union, veterans, women's, youth, and military organizations, religious figures, the corps of deputies, and the mass media.

The program documents of the unification movement are the "Manifesto to Our Fellow Countrymen" and "For a Renewed Union of Soviet Peoples," which were approved at the First and Second Congress of Peoples of the Soviet Union in 1993 and 1994.

So we are talking not about restoring the Soviet Union, which would imply the exact replication of an existing model, but about rebuilding a renewed Soviet Union. It should be emphasized that the social order's socialist foundations would be retained in the renewed Union.

A necessary and mandatory condition for the restoration of a renewed Union of Soviet peoples is the return to power of the working people. It is important to merge into one common current public movements for the restoration of the people's Soviet sovereignty and the reunification into a single union-state.

The leading force in the struggle to reunify the socialist Fatherland and defend the interests of the working people are the Communist parties. In Russia, Ukraine, Belarus, Georgia, Tajikistan, Kirghizia, and other states of the former Soviet Union, despite periodic bans on the Communist Party and the anti-Communist hysteria, there has been an upsurge in the mass Communist movement, which is substantially changing the political climate.

Of course, with the moral terror and the repeated bans on the activities of the Communist parties and the publication of their newspapers, the

Communists have it rough. We must remember, though, that Communists have been persecuted ever since they first appeared on the political scene in the mid–nineteenth century. Soviet Communists do not have millions of rubles, but they do have millions of people supporting them.

Yeltsin's statement that Communism will not reappear in Russia, made to noisy applause in the U.S. Congress, proved false. Once more the president had misled, this time American senators. Can anyone bury Communism as an idea of social justice, the embodiment of the age-old dream of laboring humanity?

Of course not. Communism can be eliminated only by wiping out the working people, but if that were to happen, humanity would disappear. No, it is as impossible to wipe out Communism as it is unthinkable to extinguish the sun.

Immediately after the ban on the Communist Party (August–November 1991), Communist-oriented parties began to form in the country. The diversity of such parties at that time was historically justified. They carried out a series of powerful political actions in defense of workers and sowed faith in people in the rightness of our common cause. Now, the existence of multiple parties in the Communist movement is dividing Party forces, and Communists everywhere are speaking out in favor of rallying the Party ranks into single-republic Communist parties. That is a difficult process, and much here depends on the kind of people who are leading the parties.

An important stage in rallying the Communist movement was the organization in March 1993, at the 29th Congress of the Communist Party, of the Union of Communist Parties (UCP-CPSU), which temporarily, until the restoration of a single union-state, reorganizes the Communist Party into a Union of Communist Parties. As practice has shown, that was the sole correct solution, given existing realities, the criminal destruction of the Soviet Union, and the formation of independent states. The UCP is a voluntary, international union of Communist parties operating in the former republics of the Soviet Union, which are all treated as equals. The ideological and organizational foundations of the union are a creatively developing Marxism-Leninism, proletarian internationalism, and democratic centralism. The UCP's purpose is to work collectively to solve problems common to the Communist parties, to coordinate political actions, and to share their political experience so as to ensure the unity of Communists' actions.

In the past year or so there have been constant debates about what the UCP-CPSU is, a party or a union of Communist parties. The Party Congress gave an exhaustive answer to this question. The UCP-CPSU is not a party but a union of independent Communist parties. The goal is to move toward a single Communist Party as the Soviet Union is revived.

Such is the dialectic of the development of the modern Communist movement in the former Soviet Union: Communist Party—Union of Communist Parties—one Communist Party. Hence the basic aim: to strengthen the UCP by all possible means.

The UCP has a program, "The Openly Hoisted Banner." Its activities are structured according to its charter. The leading organs of the UCP are the Soviet, elected by the Party Congress, and the Political Executive Committee. The latter has a chairman and deputy chairman; its body is formed by the Soviet. The chairman and his deputies constitute the Secretariat. The main goals of the UCP are the restoration of the people's sovereignty in the form of a Soviet of Workers' Deputies and in other forms of popular self-governance, the country's voluntary return to the socialist path of development, and the restoration of a renewed Union of Soviet peoples.

The Communist parties that belong to the UCP-CPSU count 1.3 million members; more important, the Communist parties' influence on the working masses is growing. Unlike other parties, the Communist parties have a broad, branching network of party organizations in towns and villages, districts and regions, and their numbers are constantly growing. The activities of the parties and the UCP are structured within the framework of the constitutions and laws of the respective states and are aimed at the peaceful struggle to establish the power of the working people; the parties and the UCP, however, are cognizant of the actions of the authorities.

The Communist parties have worked to develop intra-Party democracy, and assemblies, conferences, and congresses of Communists are held regularly. There is an ongoing free exchange of opinions concerning the urgent problems of the Party and society, and hundreds of newspapers are published locally. As for the electronic media, they are almost completely in the hands of the president's administration and the local authorities, and the opposition has been barred access to television and radio. Communists are forced to stir up the masses and disseminate propaganda on the person-to-person principle, primarily through individual group discussions and meetings.

Events of recent years have led to a purging from the Communist parties of political careerists and outsiders, of which there proved to be quite a few. Take just one example. The economist P. Bunich, a deputy in the State Duma, in the past a Communist, recently stated that under socialism the workers were in a semienslaved state (*Trud,* 24 June 1995). Here is what Bunich wrote in his book, *First Appeal to Their Interests* (Glavnoe—zainteresovat', 1986): "The main thing is that capitalism sees its goal in the appropriation of added value and it considers the individual an instrument of production, an inanimate instrument. Under socialism, man works for himself, for his society. The modern worker in the socialist society is educated and competent, has a steady job and stable wages, and feels calm and confident." This speaks for itself. The list of turncoats, of wolves in sheep's clothing, who evoke disgust, contains A. N. Yakovlev, A. A. Sobchak, S. Shakhrai, and others. You have to ask yourself how many times someone can switch allegiances in one life. Indeed, times have been worse, but they have not witnessed more despicable events.

On the whole, the Communist movement is gaining strength. In order for the UCP to achieve its strategic goals, its tactics and the choice of allies are especially important. The social buttress of the Communist parties that belong to the UCP-CPSU is the working class, the peasantry, and the popular intelligentsia.

The UCP program sets forth the positions of the Communist parties with respect to the bourgeoisie, social democracy, and religion. Parties may at various levels undertake joint actions with these elements on individual issues while maintaining their own political and organizational independence.

Let us take the UCP position on the church. The present authorities, while driving millions of people to despair, have been attempting to enlist the church's support. In church sermons one hears calls for "patience and humility," and in the president's speeches, an appeal for "class peace."

In this connection, the pronouncements by Pope John Paul II are of interest. In his 1994 message "To the Third Millennium," the pope, while noting the sins of the church in the past—religious wars, the Inquisition, the schism in Christianity—emphasized that the church has committed one sin not only in the past but also in the present: "tolerance for the manifestations of injustice" and "silence in the face of totalitarianism."

I am not among those who place an equal sign between religion and scientific Communism. They are distinguished by their attitude toward social inequality and their answers to the question of why we should try to overcome the difficulties of life, among other matters. The path to resolving social problems, the Communists believe, is not to be found in a heavenly paradise or in people's suffering deprivations on earth but in fighting to restore the people's power.

Today, however, disagreements between religion and socialism are retreating into the background. The church and the Communists share quite a few similar moral postulates and quite a few points of contact, including the restoration of state unity to the Fatherland, opposition to a way of life and morality alien to us, and the effort to defend the humiliated and aggrieved. We know that whoever betrays the poor betrays Christ.

Coexistence between the church and the Communists is not enough to secure the homeland's salvation and achieve a dignified life for working people. The relationship between them must become a relationship of interaction, as it was during certain periods of Soviet power, especially World War II. In order to win, millions of people must unite!

Very often people ask, What will the Communists do when the workers come to power? Let us take the basic problems: power and property. Among the measures to be taken after the working people come to power, the UCP program lists restoring the sovereignty of the soviets, subordinating the executive organs to them, and restoring the soviets of labor collectives and organs of people's control.

Right now the executive organs of power are superior to the legislative organs, and the workers' organs of self-governance and control over the activities of local administrations have been abolished as useless. The present authorities simply do not need them; they get in the way of their "work"—creating disarray. The swollen state apparatus—the number of workers in the apparatus has grown by a factor of two to three—will be sharply cut and its allocations drastically reduced.

We often hear that parliaments and representative organs of power should include only specialists—jurists, economists, sociologists, and so forth, that there is nothing there for workers and peasants to do. These kinds of discussions attest to a lack of faith in our own people, a dismissive, haughty attitude toward those who labor in the plants and factories, the fields and farms. This kind of discussion has nothing in common with Soviet power.

Those who are supposed to carry out the laws must take part in their elaboration. I know from my own practice (for twenty years I was a deputy in the USSR Supreme Soviet and our regional soviet) that workers, peasants, teachers, doctors, and engineers—people who know life—together with specialists in economics, law, and government, should write the laws we need. Only then will people consider these laws their own and work to implement them.

The top-priority measures after the workers' return to power include stopping the privatization of national property, reviewing the results of privatization, returning illegally acquired property to the labor collectives and the state, and restoring public ownership of the basic means of production. In this process a restorational (transitional) period and a private sector in small goods production and the sale of consumer goods and services would be allowed.

I proposed the idea of allowing a private sector in the economy under the restoration of the national economy in my report to the 30th Congress of the UCP-CPSU, "On a New Edition of Our Program." Passionate debate flared around this idea at the congress. The overwhelming majority of delegates from the Communist parties that belong to the UCP-CPSU accepted this thesis and it went into the program. Individual delegates, however, came out sharply against it because they viewed the proposition as apostasy to Marxism-Leninism. One speaker, recalling my words at the 19th Party Conference in 1988, which I had addressed to Boris Yeltsin ("Boris, you're wrong!"), noted that those words turned out to be correct and prophetic, but this time, as concerned private property, he said, "Yegor, you're wrong!" Responding to this, I said, "I was right then, and I'm right now!"

Yes, at one time I did come out against private property under socialism. "Let us take the issue of private property," I said at a plenum of the Communist Party's Central Committee in early 1990. "I am definitely opposed to the draft platform submitted to the Central Committee for the Congress opening even a crack, of any kind, for the introduction of private property in our socialist society. . . . And if people do insist on it, then we must hold a national referendum."

At present, this issue is being considered with respect to the period of national economic restoration and the foundations of socialism, a period in which private property would be allowed. Why? Conditions have changed markedly. Then, we had the full supremacy of public property and a developing economy; now we have a powerful private sector in the sphere of production and consumption. We have to take into consideration the kind of legacy the "democrats" are leaving us: a collapsing economy, disorganized labor collectives, and a country that can no longer feed itself.

It would take the "democrats" ten to fifteen years to resurrect our half-demolished agriculture through reforms. Moreover, millions of people are now employed in the private sector. A hasty elimination of that sector, which several people are proposing, would lead to mass starvation, even more unemployment, and economic ruin.

By advancing the thesis of preserving the private sector in small goods production and the sale of consumer goods and services, we are neutralizing millions of property owners in the battle for the restoration of workers' power. If we succeed in getting rid of the rackets, and if we introduce sensible taxes, then we will acquire quite a few supporters among those property owners. These are all questions of tactics. Communists cannot stand still in explaining social phenomena, for society is always moving.

The main thing, however, is not just to explain the situation; we have to move it in the right direction.

As for land, here there should be no private property. As a part of the natural complex, the land cannot be an object of purchase and sale. Otherwise we will see the peasants lose land on a massive scale and the formation of a class of large landowners.

The authorities are attempting to choke off the socialist collective farms, the kolkhozes and sovkhozes, by freeing prices for the industrial equipment needed in the countryside while fixing prices for agricultural output. Agriculture has gone into decline because of the discriminatory policy against sovkhozes and kolkhozes even though individual farms produce less than 3 percent of the total agricultural output. Most individual farmers are in a difficult situation and have become a rural quasi-proletariat. Many individual farmers have been forced to cut back on their farming, return to the kolkhozes, or leave town.

The peasants, however, are clinging to the kolkhozes and sovkhozes. They realize that the transition from large-scale collective farms to small individual farms would mean a degradation of the countryside, a step back from free to forced labor. Communists feel that the land should be assigned to those who work it—for family farms, garden plots, and residential housing. And they should have the right to pass it on as inheritance.

After the people's return to power, the Communists envisage a plan to rebuild the economy, above all, the production of food and consumer goods. Their program contains provisions to modernize the machine-building complex and on this basis provide for the technical reequipment of industry and agriculture and an increase in science-intensive, resource-frugal output. The market cannot pull the economy out of its state of collapse. All attempts by the authorities to reduce inflation to a minimum and all their widely proclaimed promises about stabilization have ended in higher prices and lower production, and thus a decrease in real wages. Moreover, economic development must go hand in hand with the preservation and defense of the environment.

Everything that has been taken away from the working people must be returned: power, property, and social rights. We have pledged to provide people with jobs, to bring housing construction up to the level of the years 1986–1989, to provide those in need of shelter with free housing, to abolish paid health care and education, to restore the general availability and volume of all types of transportation and communication, to alleviate people's fear for their personal safety, to put a halt to bribes and corruption, and to eradicate crime. In short, we will strive to give people back the same confidence in the future that they enjoyed in Soviet times.

For this purpose, we will involve workers (now they are kept from this) in restoring legality and social order and in eliminating the causes of crime, such as property redistribution, unemployment, price speculation, and subsidized alcoholism. The new authorities are reducing the "battle" against crime to little more than commissions that discuss security equipment and more laws. They are simply afraid to involve the broader public in turning back the wave of crime, for many representatives of authority at various levels are implicated in all kinds of machinations, bribery, and various "perks" organized at the workers' expense. e By leading such a luxurious life, while condemning so many people to poverty, the current leaders are digging their own graves.

As for foreign policy, the Communists are opposed to confrontation and in favor of real disarmament and strengthening the peace. In the West, voices ring out about how one can deal only with the current leadership in Russia. That is untrue. I take it upon myself to state that the national patriotic forces are in favor of close, mutually beneficial collaboration with foreign countries as well as state and private companies and will guarantee the safety of investments.

What is most important in all this is that we rely on our own forces; foreign capital is just an additional support. If we are really going to argue, as the leaders of the "democrats" do, that Russia cannot find its way out of this crisis without financial resources, then political concessions to the West are inevitable, plain and simple. If you want U.S. dollars and German marks, say foreign politicians, change your social structure and introduce a free market and private property. However, emphasizing our own strengths allows us to conduct a firm policy in defense of the interests of the country and its people, that is, a deeply national, independent policy. Our country and my people have all the intellectual, economic, and natural resources they need to lead Russia out onto the open expanses of progress.

*   *   *

Life cannot go on like this! Everything now is based on the destruction of what was created by Soviet power, on political chicanery, deceit, and violence. With their inherent cynicism, the pseudodemocrats have dubbed this era democratic romanticism.

The present-day authorities are dragging the working people to capitalism by force. Meanwhile, capitalism and the market economy have existed for only a few centuries. Of the 200 states on earth, 15–20 have material sufficiency—frequently by exploiting other countries and peoples. Millions of people are poor and live in slums, 11–12 million children die of hunger every year, and almost a billion people are illiterate. So one has to ask why the Soviet people, who had enjoyed a comfortable and fulfilling life, have to follow the capitalist path for the country, which entails the supremacy of private property and a market economy.

Citizens' political and economic demands are getting louder and louder. A resolution passed by a meeting of the inhabitants of Arzamas-16, Russia's world-famous nuclear center, said, "We have known personally all the charms of capitalism." The nuclear physicists demanded that "the president, who has humiliated Russia more than once and has disgraced himself of his own accord, resign from his post." They came out in favor of holding a Russia-wide referendum on the question, What path for Russia's development do you favor, socialist or capitalist? Those are also the demands of the majority.

Today's rulers are calling on the people to prevent a revolution and frighten them with the prospect of civil war. The rulers say they are in favor of "peace and accord," but they themselves are robbing the working people and growing rich as a result. The "Agreement on Public Accord" that the "democrats" trumpeted so loudly turned out to be nothing but empty promises, and the responsibilities the government undertook have not been met.

Living examples of the dictatorship of personal power, the present-day rulers are attempting to sow fear among people by saying that if the Communists come to power they will establish the dictatorship of the proletariat. The Communists, however, are not raising the issue of a necessary dictatorship of the proletariat. That would depend on the situation and historical conditions.

Lenin said, "Dictatorship is a harsh, difficult, bloody, and tortuous word, and words like that are not to be bandied about lightly." There is a possibility of restoring workers' power by peaceful means, but if those who are getting fat from the labors of working people offer violent resistance, then the workers will be forced to reply adequately and accordingly. That does not necessarily imply a dictatorship of the proletariat.

The problem is that there is a proletarization going on in society, not only of the working class, but also of the impoverished working intelligentsia. The peasantry has linked its fate primarily to collective ownership of the land, so the power of the workers, with their broad social base, may come about in a form other than the dictatorship of the proletariat. Because the workers form the broad majority, their government has the right to quash any resistance—in accordance with the law—offered by those who have capriciously ground the working people into the depths of poverty. Millions of citizens whose life under the rule of the anti-Communist "democrats" has become unbearable and senseless—there is your social base for new political upheavals and massive civil demonstrations against the ruling anti-Communist regime.

I am constantly making trips around the country, and recently I was in the south of Russia and Siberia. Even the "democratic" press has been forced to note that my meetings with the population go "more than favorably with a large confluence of people." People are gaining insight, the masses are shifting to the left, and dissatisfaction with the politics of the "democrats," whose ranks are markedly thinning out and breaking up, is mounting.

Feverishly seeking support, the president is busy forming two blocs in society—a right-centrist "party of power" (comprising bigwigs, officials, and fat bureaucrats) and a left-centrist party (the mass of small parties and organizations, but as the saying goes, Fifty mice will never make a tiger)—in order to create the appearance of conflict between them, trick the working people once again, and prevent the workers from gaining power.

President Yeltsin is losing the confidence of the majority of citizens. It is hard to find a politician who openly comes to the president's defense. Matters have reached the point where Mrs. Yeltsin herself has become involved. Accusing journalists of attacking the president, she demanded they change their attitude toward her spouse. There were no bounds to her indignation. But she did not have a word to say about the hundreds of thousands killed and wounded, the hunger and poverty of so many people, the crime wave, or the moral decay of our young people.

In whose interest does the preservation of the current criminal regime lie? The interest of the criminal bourgeoisie, the corrupt state apparatus, and the privileged elite of the power structures. What is most important for them is to prevent the return of popular rule.

Some politicians assert that there is no common national idea in society that could unite the people. Others feel that the common national idea could be patriotism, or loyalty to the idea of the state. Loyalty to what state, though? What are its foundations? Whom does it serve? Without an answer to these questions, "statehood" is too abstract, and it is scarcely likely to stir and rally the majority of the people.

The Communists have advanced an idea capable of uniting millions of people. That common national idea is the return of what was taken away: power to the people, socialism to society, a single Soviet power to the many peoples.

History does not progress in a straight line. It zigzags, steps back, and turns. The socialist phase of civilization has not managed to avoid those turns, either. Despite the temporary defeat of socialism in the Soviet Union, however, and the sharp narrowing of the Soviet Union's international sphere, the twentieth century will go down in history for the destruction of the colonial system, the defeat fascist tyranny, and the experiment in construction of a socialist society. On the basis of that history, humanity will eventually realize a breakthrough to a socially just society, one in which the individual will come to full fruition.

ABOUT THE BOOK AND AUTHOR

This memoir by the second most powerful Communist Party leader during the early Gorbachev years provides an important alternative view of the USSR's transformation—a view that is gaining ground in Russian politics today. In a substantial new piece for this edition, Mr. Ligachev outlines the political agenda of today's communist coalition—the establishment of a new Soviet Union, with strong economic and political integration of its member-states.

Yegor Ligachev, a seasoned Party boss from Siberia, made a solid career for himself in the capital during the Khrushchev era, but, following Khrushchev's ouster, chose to retreat to the provinces. In 1985, his political patrons brought him back to Moscow to help them build a dynamic new leadership team under Mikhail Gorbachev. The two reform-minded communists launched an effort to inject life and energy into the Party, economy, and society through a series of liberalizing measures. But when Ligachev saw the reforms moving into a revolutionary phase that could result in the Party's loss of control over the helm of state, he found himself increasingly siding with the opposition.

In this gripping book, Ligachev describes the evolving confrontation between opposing forces at high-level Party meetings and sessions of the Politburo as well as in less formal conversations. Along the way, he gives revealing glimpses not only of Gorbachev but also of Yuri Andropov, Andrei Gromyko, Alexander Yakovlev, Eduard Shevardnadze, Boris Yeltsin, and other top leaders. Notorious events such as the 1989 massacre in Tbilisi and the Gdlyan/Ivanov affair—in which, Ligachev argues, he was unjustly implicated—are also highlighted.

Yegor Ligachev, now in his mid-seventies, still resides in Moscow, where he remains an influential figure in the reemerging communist reform movement.

INDEX